THE
SIMONE
WEIL
READER

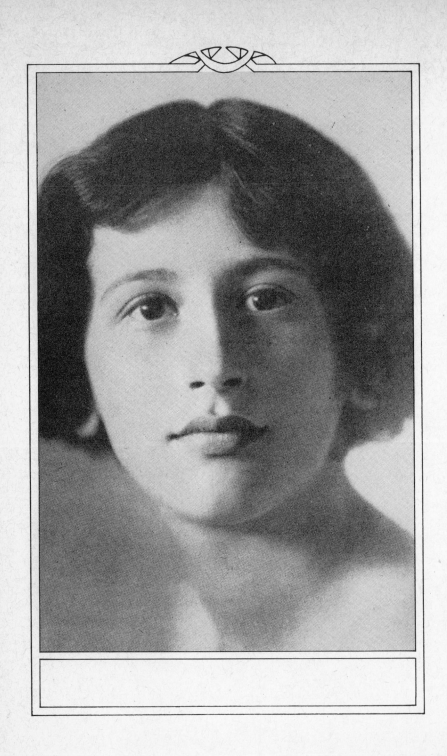

THE
SIMONE
WEIL
READER

Edited by

George A. Panichas

DAVID McKAY COMPANY, INC.

New York

The editor expresses gratitude to the following publishers for permission to reprint from the following works by Simone Weil:

BEACON PRESS. From *Intimations of Christianity Among the Ancient Greeks.* © 1957 by Routledge & Kegan Paul: "The *Iliad*, Poem of Might."

OXFORD UNIVERSITY PRESS. From *Simone Weil: First and Last Notebooks* translated by Richard Rees. © Richard Rees 1970. The "New York Notebook" was first published in French as *La Connaissance surnaturelle* by Editions Gallimard: "The Father's Silence" and "The Things of the World." From *Simone Weil: On Science, Necessity, and the Love of God.* Essays collected, translated, and edited by Richard Rees. © Oxford University Press 1968: "The Love of God and Affliction," "Morality and Literature," "The Responsibility of Writers," and "Scientism—A Review." From *Simone Weil: Selected Essays, 1934-1943* chosen and translated by Richard Rees. © Oxford University Press 1962. First published in French by Editions Gallimard: "Human Personality" and "The Power of Words." From *Simone Weil: Seventy Letters* translated and arranged by Richard Rees. © Oxford University Press 1965. First published by Editions Gallimard: "Letter to Georges Bernanos," "Letter to Joë Bousquet," "Letter to Déodat Roché," and "Letter to Maurice Schumann."

THE PHOENIX. "The Threshold" and "The Stars," translated by William Burford, vol. 3., no. 1 (Winter 1970).

POLITICS. "Factory Work" vol. 3, no. 11 (December 1946) and "What Is a Jew?" vol. 6, no. 11 (Winter 1949).

G. P. PUTNAM'S SONS. From *Gravity and Grace.* Copyright 1952 by G. P. Putnam's Sons: "Beauty," "Decreation," "Evil," "The Great Beast," "Love," "Metaxu." From *The Need for Roots.* Copyright 1952 by G. P. Putnam's Sons: "Equality," and "Freedom of Opinion," and "Uprootedness and Nationhood." From *The Notebooks of Simone Weil.* Copyright 1956 by G. P. Putnam's Sons: "Come With Me" and "Contemplation of the Divine." From *Waiting for God.* Copyright 1951 by G. P. Putnam's Sons. "Concerning the Our Father," "Forms of the Implicit Love of God," "Friendship," "Last Thoughts," "Reflections on the Right Use of School Studies with a View to the Love of God," "Spiritual Autobiography."

UNIVERSITY OF MASSACHUSETTS PRESS. From *Oppression and Liberty.* © 1958 by Routledge & Kegan Paul: "Analysis of Oppression," and "Sketch of Contemporary Social Life."

Library of Congress Cataloging in Publication Data

Weil, Simone, 1909-1943.
The Simone Weil reader.

Bibliography: p.
Includes index.
I. Philosophy—Collected works. I. Panichas, George Andrew. II. Title.
B2430.W472E55 1977   194   77-692
ISBN 0-679-50656-X
ISBN 0-679-50673-X pbk.

10 9 8 7 6 5 4 3 2
Manufactured in the United States of America
Designed by the Ethredges

CONTENTS

PREFATORY
NOTE

The immediate and guiding aim of this book is to introduce the contemporary reader to the work and thought of Simone Weil. In selecting and arranging her writings I have tried to present them in an order and a pattern designed to enable the reader to grasp the essentials of her life-thought. Particularly in arranging the selections I have sought to stress not a progressive development of her thought but rather the dimensions of its meaning. Thematic rather than chronological considerations have informed such an approach. Consequently I have selected and arranged the writings included here with a view to evoking cumulatively the comprehensiveness, the universality, the permanent importance of Simone Weil's achievement in its conjoining spiritual and cultural impact. Inevitably this editorial process must also underline my own judgmental view of Simone Weil as a religious genius and philosopher. Her concern with and delineation of ultimate religious and philosophical questions revolve around an implicit acceptance and affirmation of first principles and first causes. In Simone Weil we have testimony that is the outgrowth of a religious faith constant and consistent in its certitude and elaboration. Her responses, her world-view, are configurations of her spiritual commitments. I have also tried to organize the content in order to dramatize this impelling and unifying religious-philosophical fact. Insofar as she possesses any systematic metaphysical view of life and eternity, it is necessary to acknowledge *this* fact.

"The Spiritual Destiny of a Modern Saint": these words could adequately serve as a subtitle of this book. Simone Weil's own life must be viewed in the very substance of her religious perspective. In a very deep and ascetic sense her life consecrates her thought; is a direct, a prophetic registering of it. The reader will discover the truth of this statement as he listens to and catches the rhythm of her writings, invariably a religious rhythm that defines and places their value and uniqueness. In my general introduction, in my introductions to the five parts, and in my brief prelusive remarks accompanying each selection, I have tried to help the reader not only to participate in Simone Weil's spiritual destiny but also to detect, to appreciate, to evaluate, and, finally, to assimilate the ecumenical significance of her mystic vision. Perhaps more than anything else, then, it has been my purpose in this book to foment a connection between the reader (whatever the state of his belief or unbelief) and a religious visionary. If such connection is made, whether initially or tentatively, and if the sincerity, indeed the purity, of her experience and thought is sympathetically received, found relevant—to quote that overused word of today's parlance— then *The Simone Weil Reader* will have begun to justify its purpose.

Here I want to speak of my personal experience. I have been preparing and working on the manuscript of this book for several years. Increasingly I have found that Simone Weil's writings, when read, reread, contemplated, become a part of one's own spiritual condition; bring about a spiritual cleansing or, at least, understanding; translate into a spiritual experience of improving power and self-illumination. There is nothing that she ever wrote that does not remind me of the heroic greatness and the selflessness of her spiritual vision and destiny. For me her writings ultimately constitute disciplining spiritual lessons in reflection and humility. My understanding of the value of her work is inevitably tied to my perception of her moral teachings. The evolvement, the rhythm, the resonance, the inspiration, the reverence, the beauty, the moral character, criteria, and wisdom of Simone Weil's writings—of her teachings—are, I hope, reflected in the tonal sequence and movement that I have given to this book.

Simone Weil will always demand of us a supernatural transcendence and transfiguration. Recently I have been startlingly reminded of our desperate need of her witness and message by the warning remarks of a well-known historian, Christopher Lasch, concerning the present social behavior and habits of many Americans. We live, he observes, in an increasingly "narcissist society" in which the shaping insistence is on psychic self-improvement and personal survival. Living for the moment, glorifying and gratifying immediate needs, indulging, often indiscriminatingly and at times maddeningly, in any available form of self-attention (now that the Marxist apocalyptic has been found more wanting than ever before): these pronounced tendencies define our present situation and proclaim our new religion of autotherapy in a "new age of faith." It is unnecessary to go on either to describe or to summarize these conditions except to say that the picture that Mr. Lasch provides for us is a depressing portrait of human and spiritual impoverishment. It is also enough to remind us of the strange and frightening absence from the contemporary scene of a religious thinker like Simone Weil, who, in her witness and contribution expresses and communicates the grace that, as she would have it, transfigures gravity: that lifts us from the torments and illusions and diabolisms of our self-made abyss. Transcendence and transfiguration are words that bear repeating: they crystallize the spiritual values that inhere in Simone Weil's achievement. It is to be hoped that *The Simone Weil Reader* recaptures and conveys these values to a reader, Catholic or Protestant, Christian or Jew, believer or unbeliever, who finds himself "thrown" into the modern predicament.

As a book *The Simone Weil Reader* has its own special and autonomous identity, containing the essence of Simone Weil's thought in its representative scope, range, focus. The concentrated form of the book should help the reader to grasp the syncretizing intellectual variety (and vitality), and yet also the internalizing spiritual unity, in outlook and overview, of her writings on religion, politics, sociology, anthropology, philosophy, economics, science, aesthetics, and education. It is now thirty-five years since Simone Weil died. Her life instances a spiritual collision with the demonic. Her testimony stands as a refusal to accede to it. Indeed, there is no other religious thinker who is more pertinent to our time. When one considers the exigencies of the historical era into which she too was "thrown," the barbarity and bru-

tality that it occasioned, the explosive cruelty and ugly hatreds that
it engendered; when one thinks, in short, of the terrible and terrifying
conditions—the collective disadvantages—of life in the secular and pagan world that is ours, Simone Weil remains for us an astonishing
example, as well as a reminding criterion, of the courage of faith.
She provides for us a prophetic wisdom and insight that our civilization
urgently requires. Surely, even if this book does nothing more than
win wider recognition of Simone Weil's spiritual and moral genius, it
will have fulfilled the most ambitious of intentions.

                                                                    —G.A.P.

INTRODUCTION

La mia solitudine l'atrui dolore
*germivo fino all morte.**

I

Simone Weil, according to André Gide, was "the most spiritual writer of this century." She was, Albert Camus asserted, "the only great spirit of our time." T. S. Eliot went so far as to sanctify her life and thought by stating, "We must simply expose ourselves to the personality of a woman of genius, of a kind of genius akin to that of a saint." And Leslie Fiedler, emphasizing Simone Weil's peculiar relevance to the present, has concluded that she "has come to seem more and more a special exemplar of sanctity for our time—the Outsider as Saint in an age of alienation, our kind of saint." She herself was perhaps most aware of her own place and purpose in life, and in history, when she wrote, "Today it is not nearly enough to be a saint, but we must have the saintliness demanded by the present moment, a new saintliness, itself also without precedent." Teacher, classical scholar, intel-

---

* "My solitude held in its grasp the grief of others till my death." These words, written in Italian, appear on a small plaque attached to Simone Weil's gravestone by an anonymous donor.

lectual par excellence, and French-Jewish genius; political and religious nonconformist, Spanish Civil War participant, Free French movement worker; factory and farm laborer; poet, visionary, mystic, suffering "friend of God," religious thinker and philosopher precariously situated at "the intersection of Christianity and everything that is not Christianity" (to quote her own words): Simone Weil combined brilliantly, enigmatically, all of these roles as no other twentieth-century religious thinker has done.

Simone Weil has been increasingly appreciated, if we are to judge by the continuing posthumous publication of her writings covering an astonishingly wide area of knowledge and cultural thought: philosophy, literature, history, art, classics, psychology, politics, mathematics, economics, education. For her the ultimate questions relating to the human condition were existential spiritual questions. She had little faith, and rightly so, in the philosophy of those who believed that, as she well expressed it, "matter [is] a machine for manufacturing good." In her frantic quest for answers, for wisdom, she returned to ancient sources and tradition, particularly to Hellenism and Christianity. Indeed, it can be said that Simone Weil is the great Christian Hellenist of modern times, occupying a place commensurate with that of Christian Hellenists like Justin Martyr, Athenagoras, Clement of Alexandria, and Origen in the early centuries of the Christian era. It is in the line of this great Christian tradition that she should be placed. Not unlike her illustrious predecessors, she too maintained that Christian theology itself was the fruit of Greek genius, that Greek philosophy contained a direct divine revelation, that Christianity is the fulfillment of philosophy, divine wisdom being the first of the gifts of God. "From the flash of genius of Thales until the time when they were crushed by the armed forces of Rome," she writes, the Greeks "searched everywhere—in the regular recurrence of the stars, in sound, in equilibrium, in floating bodies—for proportions in order to love God." "The whole of Greek civilization," she further states, "is a search for bridges to relate human misery with divine perfection."

It is in Plato that Simone Weil sees the crux of "Greek spirituality." His philosophy "is nothing else but an act of love towards God." "Plato's wisdom," she thus stipulates, "is not a philosophy, a research for God by means of human reason. That research was carried out

as well as it can be done by Aristotle. But the wisdom of Plato is nothing other than orientation of the soul towards grace." "This is the
discovery that intoxicated the Greeks," she concludes: "that the reality
of the sensible universe is constituted by a necessity whose laws are
the symbolic expression of the mysteries of faith." Observations like
these typify her view of life and Greek philosophy and return us to
their earliest prototypes in the works of, say, Clement of Alexandria,
who wrote: "And by reflection and direct vision, those among the
Greeks who have philosophized accurately, see God. . . . Now the
Greek philosophy, as it were, purges the soul, and prepares it beforehand for the reception of faith, on which the Truth builds up the
edifice of knowledge." The high place that Simone Weil gives to
Plato, "an authentic mystic . . . the father of Western mysticism,"
accords with that of the fathers of the Eastern church, who not only
admitted to being disciples of Plato but also saw him as a precursor
of Christ—a philosopher who, Clement claimed, was truly noble and
divinely inspired.

Her conception of human destiny is precisely that which emerges
from coalescent Christian and Hellenic elements. She notes that
whereas, for the Greeks, science, art, and the search for God were
united, for us they are separate. Hence the fragmentation of our modern culture. The development of technology, she goes on to claim,
can offer no hope of happiness "until we have learnt how to prevent
men from using technology to dominate their fellows instead of nature." Her relevant modernism, as Fiedler would have it, is one that
undoubtedly makes her fully aware of the world in which she lived,
one in which "moral crisis and a subservience to purely political values" is the predominant condition. Values, she claims, are uprooted
or allowed to decay, their hierarchy disrupted and their meaning corrupted:

> Everything is oriented towards utility, which nobody thinks of de-
> fining; public opinion reigns supreme, in the village of scientists as in
> the great nations. It is as though we had returned to the age of
> Protagoras and the Sophists, the age when the art of persuasion—whose
> modern equivalent is advertising slogans, publicity, propaganda meet-
> ings, the press, the cinema, and radio—took the place of thought and
> controlled the fate of cities and accomplished coups d'état.

Invariably, Simone Weil's criticisms expose those intellectual and scientific aspects of modern culture which betray a moral sense, a "sense of values." The fashion today, she points out, is to progress, to evolve, technically and socially. Metaphysics must consequently surrender to techniques and schemata conducive to progress. "To find a place in the budget for the eternal," she laments, "is not in the spirit of our age." Her strongest criticisms, however, she aims at science, and these breathe the essentially Greek spirit of *sophrosynê*. She begins her premise with an uncompromising statement: "Limitation is the law of the manifested world. Only God . . . is without limits." Deliverance, she goes on to say, "consists in reading limit in all sensible phenomena without exception with the same clarity and immediacy as a meaning in a printed text." A true science, which must have as its essential idea that of equilibrium, which defines limits, should serve as "a preparation for deliverance." Science itself will always depend upon man's intelligence and physique, which are themselves permanently limited. Hence,

> it is absurd to believe that science is capable of unlimited progress. It is limited, like all human things, except that point in man which is assimilated to God; and it is well that it should be limited because it is not an end to which many men ought to devote themselves; it is a means, for every man. What is needed now is not to try to extend it further, but to bring thought to bear upon it.

Whether she is writing about Greek philosophy, art, morality, or the "love of God," Simone Weil's purpose is to show the ultimate truth of the transcendent, the supernatural. Thus, "Greek spirituality" as found in Plato accentuates man's limitations, that is, man's subordination to God. The true religious consciousness, she maintains, must be characterized by the need to achieve "supernatural love," insofar as "the Love of God is the unique source of all certainties." And with Plato as her mainstay, Simone Weil discloses an unmistakable Christian Hellenist orientation when she states: "It is total detachment that is the condition for the love of God, and when once the soul has performed the motion of totally detaching itself from the world so as to turn entirely towards God, it is illumined by the truth which comes down to it from God."

II

Simone Weil's lifework was contemporary with that of Jean-Paul Sartre and of Albert Camus. It is hardly necessary to note that though her writings have been steadily published and acclaimed—acclaimed more than they are read, it would seem—she does not command the sympathy of popular response accorded her two contemporaries. The reasons for this neglect should be clear. She is not, of course, a creative artist, and her outlook is marked by a severe philosophical scrupulosity. More important, unlike Sarte, who affirms man's integrity and commitment in *this* world despite the absurdity of the human situation, and Camus, who affirms the dignity and the (absurd) heroism of man in the face of all his despair and futility, she does not find her solutions in an existential Now. Her final recourse is not to the brutal truth of experience in a world in which Sartre and Camus, who like Simone Weil also addressed themselves to the crises of "corrupt history" in the "terrible twentieth century," found the possibility of "no exit." In this respect her view of life is metaphysical—or, better, eschatological—rather than immediate, or what might be termed (without seeking to oversimplify) the natural and political view of life when viewed purely in time and hence in its incompleteness. For Sartre and Camus life was to constitute a final form of adventure in the guise of "metaphysical revolt" when, as Camus writes in *The Rebel*, one "refuses divinity in order to participate in the common struggles and common destiny"—that consummate adventure in progress and evolution which grips the imagination and makes of man, even as he has the worm in his heart, a "saint without God."

For Simone Weil human life is characterized by its affliction, in short, the absence of God and the condition of anonymity which "deprives its victims of their personality and turns them into things" and places them "at the foot of the Cross, almost at the greatest possible distance from God." Man, according to Simone Weil, can overcome this affliction, but not in ways prescribed by a Sartre or a Camus. And how this is done sums up her metaphysics, her spiritual quest and meaning, which must be seen against a permanent pattern—"the feeling for a permanence above the permanence of one human existence," to borrow Edwin Muir's phraseology. In other words, Simone Weil, as Martin

Buber bitterly complained, sought in the end flight from nature as well as from society. "Reality," writes Buber, "had become intolerable to her, and for her, God was the power which led her away from it." Simone Weil in fact asserted: "We possess nothing in this world other than the power to say I. This is what we should yield up to God, and that is what we should destroy." For her it is the destruction, the disincarnation, the "decreation" of the I that must be attained. This decreation enjoins upon one an uprooting: "It is necessary to uproot oneself. To cut down the tree and make a cross, and then to carry it every day. . . . To exile oneself from every earthly country . . . [for] by uprooting oneself one seeks greater reality."

Buber's complaints against Simone Weil crystallized some of the reasons why her writings have not always aroused sympathy. Man, after all, seems to prefer being an adventurer in this rather than in some other world. In a sense, her answers to the paradox of existence entail a repudiation of that very existence. "All that man vainly desires here below is perfectly realized in God," she declares. "We have all those impossible desires within us as a mark of our destination, and they are good for us provided we no longer hope to fulfill them." Only when man recognizes the state of his affliction, containing "the truth about our condition," "only by looking upon the Cross" for "our country is the Cross," will be he propelled towards the ultimate reality. "They alone will see God who prefer to recognize the truth and die, instead of living a long and happy existence in a state of illusion." Simone Weil sought to find her answers to the meaning of life in her acceptance of "the infinite sweetness of obedience": "For us, this obedience of things in relation to God is what the transparency of a window pane is in relation to light. As soon as we feel this obedience with our whole being, we see God." Her words are finally addressed to those who would be greater than heroes, who would, in a word, accept their affliction, their limit-situation: "Our existence is made up only of his [God's] waiting for our acceptance not to exist. He is perpetually begging from us that existence which he gives. He gives it to us in order to beg it from us."

One must not expect to derive lessons in orthodoxy or in doctrinal sustenance from Simone Weil's writings. Her religious thought, even as it enabled her to reach the apogee of spiritual life, is rife with heterodoxy. Her religious experience is one of intensity and not of systematic coherence. Paradox and contradiction pervade her genuine, and basically Christian, testimony in its uprightness, purity, humility. Read in the special light of Catholic theology, and of the Church's teachings and dogmas as a whole, her faith shows deficiencies, defections, imperfections, as theologians have been wont to point out. She saw, and even looked for, contradictions everywhere, pointing to a disharmony between reason and faith.

> Our life is impossibility, absurdity [she writes in *Gravity and Grace*]. Everything we want contradicts the conditions or the consequences attached to it, every affirmation we put forward involves a contradictory affirmation, all our feelings are mixed up with their opposites.

She rejected all idea of the submission of the intelligence to a divine authority exercised by the Church. She feared and attacked, to the point of blasphemy, the "patriotisms" of historical religions, whether of Judaism or of Christianity, equating these with "social idolatry." She insisted that religious mysteries should be an object of contemplation, not of affirmation or of negotiation. She made matters of faith too personal a mystical experience, lacking apostolic control and guidance. She gave her complete loyalty and attention to an implicit religious faith, neglecting and at times rejecting Christian theology. She focused on the Cross and on the Passion to the exclusion of the Resurrection, the Ascension, the Pentecost, and the Church. Consequently the difficulty of reconciling her spiritual effort and supernatural perspective with her theological deviationism has made her a special case in the eyes of some Catholic thinkers who see in her life and thought too negative an affirmation, as well as a "personal" theology that is too dangerous to be put forward as an example and one that requires careful separation of truth from error.

Towards any religion that considered its cause more just than that of the weak, Simone Weil showed extreme hostility, expressed fearlessly and in language at times etched in asperity. The Church is that "great totalitarian beast," though still the depository of "an incorruptible core of truth." Ancient Rome, both the Republic and the Empire, and Israel are the objects of her most stinging rebukes. Borrowing one of Plato's similes, she writes: "Rome is the Great Beast of atheism and materialism, adoring nothing but itself. Israel is the Great Beast of religion. Neither one nor the other is likable. The Great Beast is always repulsive." Detesting Romanism as being imperialistic and administrative, she believed that ecclesiastical Catholicism continued the Roman tradition of exercising "tyranny over people's souls." These criticisms must be correlated with the high spiritual standards that she demanded of all religions and that forced her to remain "a Christian outside the Church." A religion which in any way subscribes to a false conception of greatness or accepts the dogma of power is not a true religion. Such a religion merely perpetuates "the coarseness of mind and the baseness of heart" that she connected with "the Roman domination." In the Roman subsistence in Catholicism she saw great violence done to the spiritual and mystical content of Christianity. She found especially antipathetic in the Church the incipient Roman habits of chauvinism and exclusivism. For her there was no break in the continuity of the Incarnate Spirit. Her sympathy for the Cathars, it should be noted, was equaled by her sympathy for the Manicheans, the Gnostics, the Taoists, the Buddhists, the Pythagoreans, and the Greek Stoics. "By saying that the Catholic religion is true and other religions false," she declares, "one does an injustice not only to the other religious traditions but to the Catholic faith itself, by placing it on the level of those things which can be affirmed or denied."

In her antipathies, as her views of Rome and of Roman Catholicism disclose, Simone Weil could be violent. The violence of her anti-Judaism is a matter that Jews (and non-Jews) have remarked on. This aspect of her religious thought, considered in the general contexts of her religious eclecticism and syncretism, can be neither dismissed nor ignored, since it also underlies her heterodox Christianity and makes clear the reasons for her heterodoxy. In her hostile rejection of Israel, and particularly in her dismissal of the Old Testament as "a tissue of horrors," with the exception of the Book of Job, most of the Psalms, the Song of Songs, the sapiential books, the second Isaiah and some of the Minor Prophets, and the books of Daniel and Tobias, she categorically opposes some of the central theological essences of Christianity regarding the continuity not only of the Old and the New Testaments but also of the Old and the New Israel: of the Christianity that Saint Paul calls "the Israel of God" and of the new covenant in Christ that he equates with "a new covenant with the house of Israel." Centuries later, in a letter from a Nazi prison, Dietrich Bonhoeffer was to point out that "the only difference between the Two Testaments . . . is that in the Old the blessing included the cross and in the New the cross also includes the blessing." Repeatedly in her writings Simone Weil returns to her anti-Judaism, and hence to its inescapable relationship to her view and indictment of the Church, of which the following quotation from *The Need for Roots* is sufficiently representative:

> But when the Christian religion was officially adopted by the Roman Empire, the impersonal aspect of God and of divine Providence was thrust into the background. God was turned into a counterpart of the Emperor. The operation was rendered easy by the Judaic element in Christianity, of which the latter, owing to its historical origin, had been unable to purge itself. In the texts dating from before the exile, Jehovah's juridical relationship to the Hebrews is that of a master to slaves. They had been Pharaoh's slaves; Jehovah, having taken them out of Pharaoh's hands, has succeeded to Pharaoh's rights. They are his property, and he rules them just as any ordinary man rules his slaves, except that he disposes of a wider range of rewards and punishments. He orders them indifferently to do good and evil, but far more often evil, and in either case they have to obey. It matters little that they should be made to obey from the basest motives, provided the orders are duly executed.

The search of an individual Jew like Simone Weil for a faith has more than a Jewish significance, it has been observed. Nevertheless, theories, often impassioned, concerning her anti-Judaism will always abound. (Anti-Semitism in its genocidal connotation should not be the issue here; her view of sin as the greatest of evils and her profound and obsessive sympathy for even the slightest hurt inflicted on any human life must always be kept in mind.) Yet this is no easy matter to resolve, given her own Judaic heritage and the notable fact that her intemperate denunciations of Judaism were concurrent with the Holocaust. The paradoxes and conundrums of her anti-Judaism will continue to baffle some of her readers and infuriate some of her critics. It is variously suggested that her antagonism to the religion of Israel is best explained by her innate pessimism, her denial of and alienation

hich are incompatible with the Old Testament conception
ion of "blessing"; that the lovelessness of her own exis-
espair and self-hatred, are the germinal causes of her anti-
ans Meyerhoff, addressing himself to this problem in a
vigorously argued essay, "Contra Simone Weil," posits this disquiet-
ing question: "Did she draw up the terrible indictment of the religion
of her people in order to inflict yet deeper wounds upon herself, and
did she believe this new agony would make her more pleasing in the
eyes of the new God?" Fiedler, on the other hand, though taking in
the full force of her anti-Judaism, describes her as being, in the end,
a Jewish rather than a Christian heretic, sharing ultimately with the
people she condemns the same regard for agony and suffering, the
same belief in the experience of alienation as a proof of God's love,
the same unwillingness to yield up terror to consolation. For Fiedler
she is a "prophet out of Israel": "The absurdity, the absolutism, the
incandescence of the prophets survive in Simone Weil, and for all
her blemishes, their terrible purity."

Her interweaving criticisms of Catholicism, or of Romanism, or
of Judaism are those of a religious outsider; whatever the degree of
their exaggeration or aberration, they are of a high spiritual order. In
them we have a heightened religious awareness and concern that speak
of the human condition and of man's relation to the eternal. A daring
heterodoxy and the Church, as Simone Weil would insist, are manifestations of the Spirit. Her own heterodoxy is Christianity in its most
concentrated form and intensity. It is a conception of Christianity,
as well as an overall religious response, that can be overlooked and
misunderstood and yet one that represents the continuation of the
Passion of Christ. Hers is a modern religious heterodoxy that completely contrasts with and opposes those forms of modern secularism
that end in blankness, in indifference (either to the divine or to the
diabolic), in a tortured, twisted nihilism, which all too easily attains
the status of respectability. No matter where its paths led to, her
heterodoxy revolved around an absolute and central standard, that
of acquiring spiritual perfection. "One of the fundamental truths of
Christianity," she postulates, "is that progress toward a lesser perfection is not produced by the desire for a lesser imperfection. Only
the desire for perfection has the virtue of being able to destroy in the

soul some part of the evil that defiles it." Her heart belonged intrinsically to the Church, she emphasized in *Letter to a Priest*, whereas her
religious thought remained outside the theological framework. She
was unwilling to break the integrity of her dialectical principles of
belief or to violate her religious standards. She was unwilling, and
unable, to play "the game of Christianity" that Sören Kierkegaard
refers to when he writes: "Orthodoxy flourishes in the land, no her-
esy, no schism, orthodoxy everywhere, the orthodoxy which consists
in playing the game of Christianity."

III

Simone Weil was always writing down her thoughts—her meditations—in single words, in phrases, sentences, extended paragraphs.
One can find these fragments in her *Notebooks*, containing in two
volumes the notes she made in France during 1940–1942, and in her
First and Last Notebooks. The latter volume consists of notes for the
years 1933–1939 and 1942–1943, when she was in the United States and
in England. As one would expect, these notes are unsystematic, often
repetitious, at times obscure, and at other times imprecise. They are
fragments that should be considered as a whole, however, if their full
import is to be assessed. "Taken all together," Sir Richard Rees writes
in his introduction to *First and Last Notebooks*, "the notebooks provide an unselfconscious and unintentional self-portrait of one of the
most remarkable minds and characters of this century." One should
add that, as fragments, the notes are as noble as they are pious. They
show a religious mind reflecting, struggling with words to crystallize
thought, and then, more important, to render the meaning and the
variety of unified religious experience.

The *Notebooks* in their totality point not only to her remarkable
mind and thought but also to her sustained concern with human problems approached in the light of ultimate religious perception. For her
the "earthly life" is ever in "great need of the super-substantial bread."
"Through our fleshly veils we receive from above presages of eternity
which are enough to efface all doubts on the subject." There is always
present an interaction between secular and eschatological tensions:
between an awareness of matter as "our infallible judge" and the final

certitude that "waiting patiently in expectation is the foundation of the spiritual life." And here, as in all her writings, there are certain "tracks" that cross in and out of her work and thought. The one that is the most manifest is her preoccupation with "waiting" (as opposed, it might be pointed out, to Samuel Beckett's "languishing"). For Simone Weil waiting implies an intense spiritual condition, indeed a final religious state on the edge of redemption: "We cannot take a single step toward heaven. It is not in our power to travel in a vertical direction. If, however, we look heavenward for a long time, God comes and takes us up. He raises us easily."

As such, the experience of waiting—"waiting humbly"—is one by which man is made similar to God. For Simone Weil, waiting is "the Mystical Way." It marks the ultimate perception, the transcendental consciousness, or "the movement of consciousness from lower to higher levels of reality," the awakening of the Self to the consciousness of Divine Reality, of the "deified life," as Evelyn Underhill observes in her great book *Mysticism*. Thus, waiting is identified with humility and expresses in action a certain passivity of thought. "There is no attitude of greater humility than to wait in silence and patience. . . . It is the patience which transmutes time into eternity." Beyond humility, and beyond "the tension accepted in perpetuity," waiting also signifies obedience to time. "Total obedience to time obliges God to bestow eternity." All men, according to Simone Weil's concept, are abandoned in time, which epitomizes the act of abdication by God, who "emptied himself of his divinity and filled us with a false divinity." "Time, which is our one misery, is the very touch of his hand. It is the abdication by which he lets us exist." By his creative will God maintains man in existence that he may renounce it. "God waits like a beggar who stands motionless and silent before someone who will perhaps give him a piece of bread. Time is that waiting. Time is God's waiting as a beggar for our love." The contemplation of time is the key to human life, "the irreducible mystery, upon which no science can get a hold. Humility is inevitable when one knows that one is not sure of oneself for the future. There is no stability unless one abandons the 'I' which is subject to time and modifiable."

It is always as a religious philosopher, not as a theologian, that Simone Weil thinks and writes. That is to say, her vision philosophy, as it can be called, must be appreciated in terms of personal intuition and meditation, rather than in terms of dogma. (In the earlier published *Notebooks* she notes that "the science of religions has not yet begun," and she insists that "to be able to study the supernatural, one must first be capable of discerning it.") As a philosopher who is at once concerned with the problems of history and the religious meaning of life, and who refuses to separate religion from history or history from religion, she adheres to a spiritual criterion. Her adherence to this criterion is uncompromising and nonliberal. "The Gospel," she asserts, "contains a conception of human life, not a theology." Earthly things are the criterion of spiritual things. "The value of a religious or, more generally, a spiritual way of life is appreciated by the amount of illumination thrown upon the things of this world." Yet she is never unaware of the inherent resistance of the secular attitude to such a truth: "This is what we generally don't want to recognize, because we are frightened of a criterion." Iris Murdoch perceives an essential quality in the whole of Simone Weil's thought when she writes: "To read her is to be reminded of a standard."

When she applies her criterion to history, to the world, Simone Weil finds that spiritual poverty is the pervading condition of life. As she puts it succinctly, "We no longer know how to receive grace." Her conclusions regarding both human history and historic reality are profoundly pessimistic. Sadness, a rending spiritual sadness, inevitably describes her own condition as she looks at the world. In *Waiting for God* she explains the threefold nature of this sadness when she admits that fate has permanently stamped it upon her nature; that her own "miserable and conscious sins" are inescapable; that "the miseries of this epoch and all those of all past epochs" make this sadness terrifying. At the same time it is precisely this sadness that makes her social-cultural observations acute and prophetic. Indeed, Simone Weil has a kind of bifurcated vision that in a historical sense is deeply prophetic, particularly as found in works like *The Need for Roots, Oppression and Liberty*, and *Selected Essays, 1934–1943*, and that in a religious sense is mystical, as found in works like *Gravity and Grace* and *Waiting for God* and in her letters and notebooks. In the end her mystic vision is triumphant and leads to her stern rejection of the temporal world and an escape from what Plato, her favorite philosopher, calls the "Cave of Illusion." This bifurcated vision, in all its tensions, helps to explain the violent and aggressive aspect of her prophetic utterances and the pure and saintly aspect of her synthesizing religious search—her final grasp of a transcendent religious faith, which is Christian in the inspirational sense and which she superbly defines as "the submission of those parts which have had no contact with God to the one which has."

Simone Weil's views of the historical situation recur as they are found in her writings relating to cultural and social questions. These views are largely negative, and the note of hopelessness is never far away. What she particularly focuses on, in a way that brings Dostoevsky to mind, is man's arrogance and his self-corruption through the manipulation of power, which contains "the unlimited" and turns man into a thing. Man's love of power distorts his sense of proportion and accounts for what is a base phenomenon, of which physical "gravity" is symbolic. "Humanism," she asserts, "was not wrong in thinking that truth, beauty, equality are of infinite worth, but in thinking that man can obtain them for himself without grace." Such an attitude leads to human breakdown in various forms (in Dostoevsky's novels the "Titans," with Ivan Karamazov as the best example, illustrate this process). It leads to the most dangerous consequence of all: the plight when collectivity dispossesses man and, in effect, debases everything. "Outside the spheres of external observances (bourgeois formality) the whole moral trend of the post-war years (and even before) has been an *apology* for *intemperance* (surrealism) and therefore, ultimately, for madness." Any critical survey of our civilization will "bring to light exactly how it is that man has become the slave of his own creations." Methodical thought and action have surrendered to the quantitative, with man losing control of science and technique and thus building (to borrow Dostoevsky's images) his "Crystal Palace" and becoming part of the "ant-hill." "When humanity fell away from a civilization illumined by faith, probably the first thing it lost was the spirituality of labour." Disequilibrium and alienation are in ascendancy, because

The conditions of modern life destroy the mind-body equilibrium in everything, in thought and in action—in all actions: in work, in fighting

. . . and in love, which is now a luxurious sensation and a game. . . . In its aspect, the civilization we live in overwhelms the human *body*. Mind and body have become strangers to one another. Contact has been lost.

Gustave Thibon, the religious thinker who befriended Simone Weil and, along with the Reverend Father Jean-Marie Perrin, acted as her spiritual legatee, observes that "Simone Weil oscillates between a pessimism which reduces man to nothingness and an optimism which raises him prematurely to divinity." If, then, she sees the social order as essentially evil, she emphasizes that "the world must be regarded as containing something of a void in order that it may have need of God." Her thoughts are always God-oriented, and she insists that "only the unconditioned leads to God," since no resolution can transport one to eternity. The "unconditioned" is contact with God, is the absolute. All sins, she affirms, are attempts to escape from time and to fill the void. At the bottom of each sin there is anger against God. "If we forgive God for his crime against us, which is to have made us finite creatures, he will forgive our crime against him, which is that we are finite creatures." God and humanity she images as "two lovers who have missed their rendezvous. Each is there before the time, but each at a different place, and they wait and wait and wait." Indeed, she concludes, the Crucifixion of Christ "is the image of this fixity of God." The distance that separates God from the created is spanned by compassion, which "should have the same dimension as the act of creation. It cannot exclude a single creature."

No reader will fail to appreciate the aphorisms interspersed throughout Simone Weil's writings. Interest in her philosophic content should not blind one to the qualities of her writing, particularly its simplicity and lucidity. Examples of her aphorisms and the language in which her thinking is expressed are in constant evidence: "Without humility, all the virtues are finite. Only humility makes them infinite." "In another use of the word, justice is the exercise of supernatural love." "The whole of the Freudian doctrine is saturated with the very prejudice which he makes it his mission to combat, namely, that everything that is sexual is base." "The absence of finality is the reign of necessity. Things have causes and not ends. Those who think to discern special designs of Providence are like professors who give themselves up to what they call the explanation of the text, at the expense of a beautiful poem." "Impossibility is what limits possibles; limit is necessity abstracted from time." "Nothing is more difficult than prayer. In all other tasks of the religious life, however exacting, one can sometimes rest; but there is no rest in prayer, up to the end of one's life." "To give a piece of bread is more than preaching a sermon, as Christ's Cross is more than his parables." "Beauty is a providential dispensation by which truth and justice, while still unrecognized, call silently for our attention." "Once we have understood how it develops minute personal failings into public crimes, then nothing is a minute personal failing. One's little faults can only be crimes." "Compassion makes love equal for everybody. Contempt for crime and admiration for greatness are balanced in compassion." "When a soul has attained a love filling the whole universe indiscriminately, this love becomes the bird with golden wings that pierces an opening in the egg of the world."

Eliot has written in his essay "Second Thoughts about Humanism": "Man is man because he can recognise supernatural realities, not because he can invent them. Either everything in man can be traced as a development from below, or something must come from above. There is no avoiding that dilemma: you must either be a naturalist or a supernaturalist." Simone Weil chose to be a supernaturalist. This choice enabled her to see life as being much more than, as one modern novelist has described it, "a strip of pavement over an abyss." Surely she has been one of the few to assert the greater courage, beyond mere tenacity and endurance, by leaping across the abyss from out of "the hands of men" into "the hands of God." In following the various paths of her meditations, one is aware of being, as Eliot said, in "contact with a great soul." But, beyond this, she is the kind of mystic and saint who serves as a guide leading the soul towards God. Admittedly, hers are concerns so unyielding in their spiritual essences —she has been described as suffering from "vertigo of the absolute" —that her conception of what is human is distorted by an excess of love for the superhuman. To insist on such a view, however, is to ignore the peculiar quality of her thought and of her mysticism, which Sir Richard Rees speaks of as "an uncommonly refined common sense." One need only think of her belief in the need "to love men in the same way as the sun would love us if it saw us"; or her insistence that "the most important part of teaching = to teach what it is to *know* (in the scientific sense)"—to know, that is, "with one's whole soul"—to understand why, in spite of her "immoderate affirmations" (to quote Eliot again), she is always looking behind her, beckoning men tormented by the demon of doubt to follow her in the last and greatest quest: "God gives himself to men as powerful or as perfect—it is for them to choose."

Simone Weil's life and thought contain paradigms of spiritual progress won through meditation. As stark and severe as her meditations are, they have much to say about the glory of the inner life; and to meditate on her meditations is to participate in an experience of the inner life that modern man has ignored to his impoverishment. If her achievement reminds us of a standard, it also reminds us of an inner, reverent discipline without which life is incomplete. "Depths of silence," writes Thibon, "have to be traversed in order to grasp the authentic meaning of her words." But when we have grasped it, we are able to communicate with one whose meditations on the life of man and "the needs of the soul" place her among the first philosophers of our civilization.

CHRONOLOGY

Below only the main details of Simone Weil's life are given. No attempt is made to chronicle the writings—essays, reviews, notes, letters —that she published during her lifetime and that are scattered in small and often obscure French periodicals. For a chronological listing of her writings one should consult Michel Thiout's *Jalons sur la route de Simone Weil, 2: Essai de bibliographie des écrits de Simone Weil,* Paris: Minard, Archives des Lettres Modernes, III, 26 (Octobre 1959). In France books containing her various writings have been appearing since 1947; translations of these into English have been coming out since 1951 (see Bibliography).

1909   Simone Adolphine Weil is born in Paris on February 3, the second child and only daughter of Dr. Bernard Weil (1872–1955), a distinguished and well-to-do physician, and his wife, Selma (1879–1965), then living at 19 boulevard de Strasbourg.

      Her brother, André, the only other child of the family, was born on May 6, 1906. He is a famous mathematician, now at the Institute for Advanced Study in Princeton, New Jersey.

1912   The Weil family moves to an apartment at 37 boulevard St. Michel, Paris.

1914   Dr. Weil is almost immediately mobilized into the French army upon the outbreak of World War I.

Mrs. Weil and the two children follow her husband almost everywhere. The school studies of the children are irregular, and they take lessons mostly by correspondence.

1917   Becomes a student at the Laval Lycée.

1919   Spends the holidays with her family at the seaside resort of Penthièvre in Brittany.

Enters the Lycée Fénelon, a public high school and junior college for girls in Paris.

1921   Begins to suffer, at about the age of twelve, from the headaches that are to plague her intermittently for the remainder of her life.

1924   Admitted to the *baccalauréat* on June 22 in the classical section.

Beginning October 1, studies philosophy at the Lycée Victor Duruy.

1925   Takes her *baccalauréat* in philosophy on June 27.

In October enters the Lycée Henri IV, where she spends three years. Studies under Alain (1868–1952), the pen name of the influential French philosopher, teacher, and journalist Emile-Auguste Chartier.

1928   Simone Weil's parents move to an apartment on 3 rue Auguste Comte, facing the Jardin du Luxembourg, Paris, and remain there until 1940.

Passes first in the (entrance) examination of the Ecole Normale Supérieure. (Simone de Beauvoir is second.)

Enters the Ecole Normale at the end of the year. Here she first comes into contact with a syndicalist movement called

La Révolution Prolétarienne and shows her early sympathy for Marxism, pacifism, the trade union movement, and the working classes.

1930   Has her first serious attack of sinusitis, which is to aggravate her health for the rest of her life.

Completes her diploma-monograph, *Science and Perception in Descartes.*

1931   Passes her *agrégation* brilliantly in July.

In August obtains her first position as a teacher of philosophy at the girls' Lycée of Le Puy, seventy miles southwest of Lyons.

1932   In Le Puy actively supports unemployed demonstrators. A public scandal ensues and she is transferred.

Visits Germany in the summer to observe the political situation, just before Hitler's accession to power.

Begins to teach at the girls' lycée in Auxerre, near Paris. Her controversial teaching methods cause problems and her students do poorly in their examinations. The school administrators abolish her position as a teacher of philosophy, and she is released.

1933   Her interest in political sociology begins to take firm shape.

Spends the month of August with her parents at Chambon-sur-Lignon.

Takes a new teaching position at the girls' Lycée in Roanne, a city sixty-five miles to the west of Lyons. Acquires a reputation for being a communist and an atheist.

On December 3, in the city of Saint-Etienne, takes part in the famous "March of the Miners" planned by the National CGT * Miners' Federation to protest against unemployment and wage cuts.

* Conféderation Générale du Travail.

1934   Obtains a year's leave from teaching.

On December 4 begins work as a factory hand at the Alsthom electrical works in Paris, remaining there for four months. This decision marks the beginning of her increasing reverence for physical labor as being the spiritual core of a well-ordered social life.

1935   On April 11 begins work as a packer with Carnaud at the Forges de Basse-Indre in Boulogne-Billancourt. Fails to work fast enough and is dismissed on May 7.

Works June 6–August 22 at the Renault works.

Physically and spiritually exhausted, she leaves the Renault factory; her parents take her for a holiday to Portugal.

Begins to teach at the lycée at Bourges. Her teaching methods here are typically unorthodox but academically successful. Gives away most of her salary.

Religious interests in aspects of Christianity appear.

1936   In March works on the farm of a family in Carron de Gron in Cher in order to learn about problems of farm life.

The Spanish Civil War breaks out in July, and Simone Weil, a pacifist, takes the train for the Republican Front in Barcelona at the beginning of August, posing as a journalist with a certificate from a Paris trade union.

Joins anarchist-syndicalist elements stationed in Aragon, about nine miles from Saragossa.

While remaining in camp to do cooking, she accidentally pours a basin of boiling oil over her left leg. Treated at Terramar Hospital in Sitges. Spends less than two months in Spain.

1937   Her health deteriorates further as a result of her accident in Spain. Her sick leave is extended to the first term of the school year 1937–38.

Continues to think and to write about problems of labor and management, and of peace and war.

Early in the spring visits the winter resort of Montana in Switzerland; then goes to Italy, visiting Milan and Florence. She spends Whitsun in Rome and goes on to Assisi. Alone in the little twelfth-century chapel of Santa Maria degli Angeli, where Saint Francis had often prayed, she kneels down for the first time in her life, drawn by "something stronger than I."

In October she begins to teach again at the Lycée of St. Quentin, some sixty miles north of Paris.

1938 In January is given sick leave until June because of her chronic headaches, their "pain situated around the central point of the nervous system, at the point of junction between soul and body, which goes on even through sleep, never ceasing for a second."

At Easter goes for a ten-day stay to the Benedictine Abbey of Solesmes, famous for its Gregorian plainchant. Experiences a mystical revelation.

A young Englishman introduces her to the English metaphysical poets of the seventeenth century—George Herbert, John Donne, Richard Crashaw. She is particularly responsive to Herbert's "Love."

From this point on her writings show strong religious concerns, with an emphasis on the supernatural, though her interest in social and political problems and organization continues.

Visits Italy in the summer. Spends a month and a half in Asolo and Venice.

1939 On March 19 the German troops enter Prague. Simone Weil's pacifism ends.

Her health is not improved enough for her to resume her teaching duties in 1938–39.

In July leaves for a six-month holiday, during which she spends time with her parents in Geneva.

With war breaking out in September, returns to Paris with her family.

At the end of the year, reads the *Bhagavad-Gita*, then goes on to study Sanskrit.

1940   At the beginning of the year, draws up a "Memorandum on the Formation of a Front-line Nursing Squad," with the hope it will receive governmental support.

With the coming of the armistice in June, crosses the frontier from Nevers into unoccupied France and stays with her family in Vichy for two months.

In October leaves Vichy to live in Marseilles, where she attaches herself to a group of thinkers and writers who express their views through *Les Cahiers du Sud*. Also, in Marseilles, develops an interest in *Les Cahiers d'Etudes Cathares*. Her association with these two journals inspires some of her most important social-religious writings.

Between 1940 and 1942 is engaged in intense mystical contemplation.

Dismissed from the state teaching service under Vichy anti-Jewish laws.

1941   On March 30 attends meetings of the Young Christian Workers' Movement in Marseilles.

At the beginning of June meets the Reverend Father J.-M. Perrin at the Dominican monastery in Marseilles.

Father Perrin helps her to find work on the farm of Gustave Thibon, in Ardèche, about 150 miles north of Marseilles.

Thibon arranges for her to work during the season of the grape harvest on a neighboring farm, from September 22 to October 23.

Continues her studies in Greek and Hindu philosophy and in Sanskrit.

1942   At Easter journeys to Carcassonne. Stops at the Benedictine Abbey of En-Clacat, at Dourgnes.

Thibon sees her for the last time. She leaves with him a dozen thick exercise books containing her day-by-day thoughts, from which he later compiles the text of *Gravity and Grace*.

On May 17 leaves Marseilles for Morocco on the S.S. *Maréchal Lyautey*. On their way to the United States she and her parents remain seventeen days in the refugee camp of Aïn-Seba at Casablanca.

On July 8 their voyage ends when the *Serpa Pinto* docks in New York City. She lives at apartment 6G, 549 Riverside Drive.

In New York becomes friendly with Simone Deitz, whom she had first met in Marseilles. She begins to attend Mass every day in the Catholic Church of Corpus Christi on 121st Street.

Desperate to reach England and take a part in the French Resistance movement, she writes to Maurice Schumann in London for help.

On November 9 leaves her parents in New York City and takes a sixteen-day voyage on the Swedish ship *Valaaren* to Liverpool. Upon her arrival she goes to a wartime detention camp and is detained because of her status as a veteran of the Spanish Republican Army, as well as because of her early pacifist views.

Maurice Schumann obtains her release from the camp on December 14 and she goes to London.

1943   In January takes a room at 31 Portland Road, Holland Park, in the Notting Hill area.

Frequently refuses to eat because the people in German-occupied France are dying of hunger.

Works at the Ministry of the Interior for the Commissariat of Action upon France.

In London continues her close friendship with Simone Deitz and also renews her acquaintance with Maurice Schumann.

Writes *The Need for Roots*, her main political work of her later years, published in 1949. It is the result of reports related to postwar reconstruction of France assigned to her to do for the Free French organization in London.

In mid-April enters Middlesex Hospital but refuses medical treatment and nourishment.

Receives visits of a Catholic priest, who gives her sacerdotal blessing, but adheres to her refusal to be baptized.

On August 17 is admitted to Grosvenor Sanatorium in Ashford, Kent. Continues to take no food and grows steadily weaker.

She dies on Tuesday, August 24, of starvation and pulmonary tuberculosis. Buried in Grave No. 79, Ashford New Cemetery.

THE
SIMONE
WEIL
READER

LOVE

Love bade me welcome; yet my soul drew back,
  Guilty of dust and sin.
But quick-eyed Love, observing me grow slack
  From my first entrance in,
Drew nearer to me, sweetly questioning
  If I lack'd anything.

"A guest," I answer'd, "worthy to be here:"
  Love said, "You shall be he."
"I, the unkind, ungrateful? Ah, my dear,
  I cannot look on Thee."
Love took my hand and smiling did reply,
  "Who made the eyes but I?"

"Truth, Lord; but I have marr'd them: let my shame
  Go where it doth deserve."
"And know you not," says Love, "Who bore the blame?"
  "My dear, then I will serve."
"You must sit down," says Love, "and taste my meat."
  So I did sit and eat.

—GEORGE HERBERT

I

A NEW SAINTLINESS

Of course I knew quite well that my conception of life was Christian. That is why it never occurred to me that I could enter the Christian community.

1909–1943: Simone Weil's life was all too brief. But in its achievement and meaning it was a life of consummate spiritual purity, revealing the need for the "new saintliness" required by modern times. What impresses one most in studying the various fragments of her autobiography is her prophetic awareness of the human condition in the twentieth century. Her reactions, her judgments, are at once spiritual and moral, fearless and devastating. In a sense she saw too much, as an early essay, "Sketch of Contemporary Life," shows, evoking as it does, though it does much more than just this, the destructive and self-destructive energy loosed in a world in which "everything is disequilibrium." Containing her "inventory of modern civilization," this essay also contains her vision of evil: "Our present situation more or less resembles that of a party of absolutely ignorant travellers who find themselves in a motor-car launched at full speed and driverless across broken country." There could be a no more apt image of man's fate in collective, technological, industrial society, of man subordinated to and oppressed by new and vast mechanisms. "Machines do

3

not run in order to enable men to live, but we resign ourselves to feeding men in order that they may serve the machines." Nothing could be more prophetic of the legioned diabolisms of the modern age than this stark and frightening declaration that speaks volumes: "The powerful means are oppressive, the non-powerful means remain inoperative."

Her prophecies were more than divinations. They were also derived from her personal destiny: from her own fervent involvement in the cruel historical process. For however brief her life was, Simone Weil filled it with purposive spiritual action, which in turn nourished and heightened her social, intellectual, and religious sensibility. In quest of the absolute she experienced the inescapability of the world. "This world into which we are cast *does* exist," she writes; "we are truly flesh and blood; we have been thrown out of eternity; and we are indeed obliged to journey painfully through time, minute in, minute out." From the age of five, when she refused to eat sugar because the French soldiers fighting the Germans on the Western Front had none, until her death in England on August 24, 1943, of tuberculosis and malnutrition brought on by having restricted her diet to that made available to her compatriots in German-occupied France, she chose "to journey painfully through time." "Contact with affliction" is invariably at the heart of her experience of the world. It is also a primary condition of her conception of "a new saintliness" even as it permeates her view of the ultimate worth of a "Christianity [that] should contain all vocations without exception since it is Catholic." The truly redemptive function she saw as being found in "knowing the world's affliction and contemplating its reality."

In her life and work, and in her unceasing search for the principle of spiritual unity, Simone Weil sought to conjoin knowledge and contemplation. For her the life of action was a prelude to the life of prayer. She was as much an activist as she was a contemplative. During the 1930s she was a revolutionary idealist who championed the working class and the oppressed. Picketing, refusing to eat more than people on relief, distributing most of her earnings to the poor, writing for radical journals: such actions doubtlessly made her suspect in the eyes of the authorities and led to her being characterized as "a mixture of anarchist and nun." These social-political activities

were synchronous with her teaching career. A remarkable, if enig-
matic, teacher, she served in various French lycées; philosophy and
classical philology were her academic specialties. One need only read
her "Reflections on the Right Use of School Studies with a View to
the Love of God" to grasp the uniqueness of her pedagogical concepts and particularly the special values that she placed on, and demanded of, the educative process as a preparation for a spiritual life.
"Although people seem to be unaware of it today, the development
of the faculty of attention forms the real object and almost the sole
interest of studies," she declares. "Never in any case whatever is a
genuine effort of the attention wasted. It always has its effect on the
spiritual plane and in consequence on the lower one of the intelligence,
for all spiritual light lightens the mind." A kind of suprapragmatism
informs her view of the tasks of learning. One should have as one's
purpose not only that of "increasing the power of attention with a
view to prayer" but also that of acquiring the virtue of humility, "a
far more precious treasure than all academic progress." "When we
force ourselves to fix the gaze, not only of our eyes but of our souls,
upon school exercises in which we have failed through sheer stupidity,
a sense of our mediocrity is borne in upon us with irresistible evidence.
No knowledge is more to be desired." Her educational attitudes can
best be summed up as being those of a spiritual progressivist.

The factory was yet another of Simone Weil's classrooms, as the
essay "Factory Work" makes clear. This essay augments and, more particularly, objectifies "Sketch of Contemporary Life." It underlines another personal "contact with affliction," which is at the same time free
of spiritual pride and of presumption, as she herself conveys in a
confessional letter to Joë Bousquet, a disabled veteran of the Great
War: "I worked for nearly a year [1934–1935] in engineering factories
in the Paris region. The combination of personal experience and
sympathy for the wretched mass of people around me, in which I
formed, even in my own eyes, an undistinguishable item, implanted
so deep in my heart the affliction of social degradation that I have
felt a slave ever since, in the Roman sense of the word." Factory work
marks a solemn and meaningful station in Simone Weil's spiritual
pilgrimage. No mere sociological document or report, it is a spiritual
offshoot of everything that she connotes in the words "concentrated

attention." It is also an excellent example of a sustained attempt at spiritual analysis, a difficult task that Simone Weil saw as condemning oneself to moral loneliness, to lack of understanding, and to the hostility of both the enemies and the servants of an existing order. If her critique of factory work has finally a meditative impact, it also has implicit common sense. Who, today, can find fault with her condemnation of a "productive process" in which "things play the role of men, men the role of things. There lies the root of the evil"? And who can deny the insightfulness of this observation on human misery that brings to mind Dostoevsky: "Humiliation always has for its effect the creation of forbidden zones where thought may not venture and which are shrouded by silence or illusion"? Or, too, this insight that can be placed with the finest diagnostic insights of "brave men" like William Blake and D. H. Lawrence: "It is high time that specialists, engineers, and others concerned, should be exercised not only to make objects, but also not to destroy men." In "Factory Work" one hears the most intimate, certainly the anguished, voice of a saint "proper to the present moment."

Though Simone Weil was a pacifist—"I do not love war; but what has always seemed to me most horrible in war is the position of those in the rear"—she could not prevent herself from participating morally in a great human struggle. ("The effect of a moral symbol," she wrote to Maurice Schumann towards the end of her life, "is independent of statistics.") In the summer of 1936 she joined an anarchist unit fighting in the Spanish Civil War. She spent about two months—her stay was brought to an end by an accident—in the remote Aragonese countryside on the banks of the Ebro, about ten miles from Saragossa. Useless bloodshed, atrocities, and the smell of blood and terror, which she recognized during this brief duration, convinced her of the vile effects of applied, calculated might. "One sets out as a volunteer," she recalled in her letter to Georges Bernanos, "with the idea of sacrifice, and finds oneself in a war which resembles a war of mercenaries, only with much more cruelty and with less human respect for the enemy." This, she realized, was no moral, no authentic and pure struggle, no war of exploited peasants against landed proprietors and their clerical allies, but rather a political war between Russia on the one side and Germany and Italy on the other. Here, too, in this fleeting "contact with affliction," Simone Weil deepened her moral vision and enlarged her spiritual destiny. Above all it enabled her to witness man's "animal nature," "this mechanical necessity [which] holds all men in its grip at every moment." Her experience in Spain was additionally crucial as one of self-recognition that is simultaneously self-cleansing: "I was ten years old at the time of Versailles, and up to then I had been patriotically thrilled as children are in war-time. But the will to humiliate the defeated enemy which revealed itself so loathsomely everywhere at that time (and in the following years) was enough to cure me once for all of that naïve sort of patriotism. I suffer more from the humiliations inflicted by my country than from those inflicted on her."

Yet, even as Simone Weil could not escape the awesomeness of the affliction of the world, she could never escape the one most central spiritual fact, "Faith is the indispensable condition." As her "Spiritual Autobiography," in its integrity, simplicity, and humility, makes abundantly clear, hers was a life of consecration. What we have in this long letter to the Reverend Father J.-M. Perrin, her Dominican friend and adviser, is the testimony of a mystic and saint completing her pilgrimage. No reader can come away from it without making connection with a pure soul. Nor can one disagree with Simone Weil's informing belief that, "as to the spiritual direction of my soul, I think that God himself has taken it in hand from the start and still looks after it." Surely a Divine Presence radiates as the epiphanies of Simone Weil's mystical ascent crystallize here. One of these relates her experience during a visit to Assisi in 1937: "There, alone in the little twelfth-century Romanesque chapel of Santa Maria degli Angeli, an incomparable marvel of purity where Saint Francis often used to pray, something stronger than I compelled me for the first time in my life to go down on my knees." Another relates her experience at Solesmes, where she followed all the liturgical services in 1938, from Palm Sunday to Easter Tuesday: "I was suffering from splitting headaches; each sound hurt me like a blow; by an extreme effort of concentration I was able to rise above this wretched flesh, to leave it to suffer by itself, heaped up in a corner, and to find a pure and perfect joy in the unimaginable beauty of the chanting and the words." Still another relates her experience in the course of reading George

Herbert's poem "Love": "I learned it by heart. Often, at the culminating point of a violent headache, I make myself say it over, concentrating all my attention upon it and clinging with all my soul to the tenderness it enshrines. I used to think I was merely reciting it as a beautiful poem, but without knowing it the recitation had the virtue of a prayer. It was during one of these recitations that . . . Christ himself came down and took possession of me."

These religious experiences were epiphanic and not conversionary. They stamped and reinforced what Simone Weil termed her "implicit faith" in a Christianity that had chosen, even "captured," her. The daughter of freethinking Jewish parents, she was brought up "in complete agnosticism." "I have never been in a synagogue, and have never witnessed a Jewish ceremony," she notes in her interesting letter "What Is a Jew?" From the very beginning hers was the Christian, French, Greek tradition. With special reference to her cultural roots, she recalls: "Since I practically learned to read from Racine, Pascal, and other French writers of the 17th century, since my spirit was thus impregnated at an age when I had not even heard talk of 'Jews,' I would say that if there is a religious tradition which I regard as my patrimony, it is the Catholic tradition." In her "Spiritual Autobiography" she further refers to her instinctive choice of a Christian outlook. "I always adopted the Christian attitude as the only possible one," she says. "I might say that I was born, I grew up, and I always remained within the Christian inspiration." Her Christian attitude was not only implicit but also strict and pure, and helps to explain her admiration for twelfth-century Catharism, which she opposed to the influence of the Old Testament and of the Roman Empire—the tradition of which she saw as being continued by the papacy—and in which she pinpointed the two essential sources of the corruption of Christianity. Since, as she defined it, Christianity is Catholic by right but not in fact, she considered it legitimate on her part to be a member of the Church by right but not in fact. "So many things are outside it, so many things that I love and do not want to give up, so many things that God loves, otherwise they would not be in existence." Christianity could only be Catholic in the sense that she defined it. Until such a definition of Christianity was to be fulfilled, she chose to remain "on the threshold of the Church." An explanation of her refusal to be baptized is thus to be found in her reiteration that "the love of those things that are outside Christianity keeps me outside the Church." A truly Incarnational Christianity must be inclusive, impartial, universal, and thus genuinely Catholic. "The children of God should not have any other country here below but the universe itself," one reads in her "Last Thoughts" (comprising another letter to Father Perrin that complements and refines her "Spiritual Autobiography"), "with the totality of all the reasoning creatures it ever has contained, contains, or ever will contain. That is the native city to which we owe our love."

Only when Christianity is at last free of social trappings and temptations can it arrive at its most authentic and destined point of witness. ("I do not believe that I am outside the Church," she wrote towards the end of her life, "as far as it is the source of sacramental life; only insofar as it is a social body.") Only when a Christian actualizes what the value of his spiritual faith prescribes can he be a Christian by right and in fact. The true measure of our Christianity must comprise the capacity, "in contact with the affliction of other people," to extend ourselves in an act of disincarnation that forces us to come out of ourselves. This act requires the greatest religious courage. It signifies the power of miracle which Simone Weil envisions when she writes: "Those who are unhappy have no need for anything in this world but people capable of giving them their attention. The capacity to give one's attention is a very rare and difficult thing; it is almost a miracle; it *is* a miracle." No statement brings into sharper focus the life-impelling obligation that Simone Weil passionately embraced and that has earned her the right to be called "the saint of the churchless."

SPIRITUAL
AUTOBIOGRAPHY

In this autobiographical letter Simone Weil relates the story of her spiritual progress, of her developing Christian identity, and of her first and permanent influential contacts with Catholicism. It also contains her own forthright and insistent definition of her place as an outsider in the Church. As a spiritual confession this letter is essential to any estimation or understanding of her special religious value to the modern world.

P.S. TO BE READ FIRST

This letter is fearfully long—but as there is no question of an answer —especially as I shall doubtless have gone before it reaches you—you have years ahead of you in which to read it if you care to. Read it all the same, one day or another.

From Marseilles, about May 15.

FATHER,

Before leaving I want to speak to you again, it may be the last time perhaps, for over there I shall probably send you only my news from time to time just so as to have yours.

I told you that I owed you an enormous debt. I want to try to tell you exactly what it consists of. I think that if you could really

10

understand what my spiritual state is you would not be at all sorry that you did not lead me to baptism. But I do not know if it is possible for you to understand this.

You neither brought me the Christian inspiration nor did you bring me to Christ; for when I met you there was no longer any need; it had been done without the intervention of any human being. If it had been otherwise, if I had not already been won, not only implicitly but consciously, you would have given me nothing, because I should have received nothing from you. My friendship for you would have been a reason for me to refuse your message, for I should have been afraid of the possibilities of error and illusion which human influence in the divine order is likely to involve.

I may say that never at any moment in my life have I 'sought for God.' For this reason, which is probably too subjective, I do not like this expression and it strikes me as false. As soon as I reached adolescence, I saw the problem of God as a problem the data of which could not be obtained here below, and I decided that the only way of being sure not to reach a wrong solution, which seemed to me the greatest possible evil, was to leave it alone. So I left it alone. I neither affirmed nor denied anything. It seemed to me useless to solve the problem, for I thought that, being in this world, our business was to adopt the best attitude with regard to the problems of this world, and that such an attitude did not depend upon the solution of the problem of God.

This held good as far as I was concerned at any rate, for I never hesitated in my choice of an attitude; I always adopted the Christian attitude as the only possible one. I might say that I was born, I grew up, and I always remained within the Christian inspiration. While the very name of God had no part in my thoughts, with regard to the problems of this world and this life I shared the Christian conception in an explicit and rigorous manner, with the most specific notions it involves. Some of these notions have been part of my outlook for as far back as I can remember. With others I know the time and manner of their coming and the form under which they imposed themselves upon me.

For instance I never allowed myself to think of a future state, but I always believed that the instant of death is the center and object

of life. I used to think that, for those who live as they should, it
is the instant when, for an infinitesimal fraction of time, pure truth,
naked, certain, and eternal, enters the soul. I may say that I never
desired any other good for myself. I thought that the life leading
to this good is not only defined by a code of morals common to all,
but that for each one it consists of a succession of acts and events
strictly personal to him, and so essential that he who leaves them
on one side never reaches the goal. The notion of vocation was like
this for me. I saw that the carrying out of a vocation differed from the
actions dictated by reason or inclination in that it was due to an
impulse of an essentially and manifestly different order; and not to
follow such an impulse when it made itself felt, even if it demanded
impossibilities, seemed to me the greatest of all ills. Hence my
conception of obedience; and I put this conception to the test when
I entered the factory and stayed on there, even when I was in that
state of intense and uninterrupted misery about which I recently told
you. The most beautiful life possible has always seemed to me to be
one where everything is determined, either by the pressure of circumstances or by impulses such as I have just mentioned and where
there is never any room for choice.

At fourteen I fell into one of those fits of bottomless despair
that come with adolescence, and I seriously thought of dying because
of the mediocrity of my natural faculties. The exceptional gifts of my
brother, who had a childhood and youth comparable to those of Pascal, brought my own inferiority home to me. I did not mind having
no visible successes, but what did grieve me was the idea of being
excluded from that transcendent kingdom to which only the truly
great have access and wherein truth abides. I preferred to die rather
than live without that truth. After months of inward darkness, I
suddenly had the everlasting conviction that any human being, even
though practically devoid of natural faculties, can penetrate to the
kingdom of truth reserved for genius, if only he longs for truth and
perpetually concentrates all his attention upon its attainment. He
thus becomes a genius too, even though for lack of talent his
genius cannot be visible from outside. Later on, when the strain
of headaches caused the feeble faculties I possess to be invaded by a
paralysis, which I was quick to imagine as probably incurable, the

same conviction led me to persevere for ten years in an effort of concentrated attention that was practically unsupported by any hope of results.

Under the name of truth I also included beauty, virtue, and every kind of goodness, so that for me it was a question of a conception of the relationship between grace and desire. The conviction that had come to me was that when one hungers for bread one does not receive stones. But at that time I had not read the Gospel.

Just as I was certain that desire has in itself an efficacy in the realm of spiritual goodness whatever its form, I thought it was also possible that it might not be effective in any other realm.

As for the spirit of poverty, I do not remember any moment when it was not in me, although only to that unhappily small extent compatible with my imperfection. I fell in love with Saint Francis of Assisi as soon as I came to know about him. I always believed and hoped that one day Fate would force upon me the condition of a vagabond and a beggar which he embraced freely. Actually I felt the same way about prison.

From my earliest childhood I always had also the Christian idea of love for one's neighbor, to which I gave the name of justice—a name it bears in many passages of the gospel and which is so beautiful. You know that on this point I have failed seriously several times.

The duty of acceptance in all that concerns the will of God, whatever it may be, was impressed upon my mind as the first and most necessary of all duties from the time when I found it set down in Marcus Aurelius under the form of the *amor fati* of the Stoics. I saw it as a duty we cannot fail in without dishonoring ourselves.

The idea of purity, with all that this word can imply for a Christian, took possession of me at the age of sixteen, after a period of several months during which I had been going through the emotional unrest natural in adolescence. This idea came to me when I was contemplating a mountain landscape and little by little it was imposed upon me in an irresistible manner.

Of course I knew quite well that my conception of life was Christian. That is why it never occurred to me that I could enter the Christian community. I had the idea that I was born inside. But to add dogma to this conception of life, without being forced to do so by

indisputable evidence, would have seemed to me like a lack of honesty.
I should even have thought I was lacking in honesty had I considered
the question of the truth of dogma as a problem for myself or even
had I simply desired to reach a conclusion on this subject. I have an
extremely severe standard for intellectual honesty, so severe that I
never met anyone who did not seem to fall short of it in more than
one respect; and I am always afraid of failing in it myself.

Keeping away from dogma in this way, I was prevented by a sort
of shame from going into churches, though all the same I like being
in them. Nevertheless, I had three contacts with Catholicism that
really counted.

After my year in the factory, before going back to teaching, I
had been taken by my parents to Portugal, and while there I left
them to go alone to a little village. I was, as it were, in pieces, soul and
body. That contact with affliction had killed my youth. Until then
I had not had any experience of affliction, unless we count my own,
which, as it was my own, seemed to me, to have little importance,
and which moreover was only a partial affliction, being biological
and not social. I knew quite well that there was a great deal of affliction
in the world, I was obsessed with the idea, but I had not had prolonged and first-hand experience of it. As I worked in the factory,
indistinguishable to all eyes, including my own, from the anonymous
mass, the affliction of others entered into my flesh and my soul. Nothing separated me from it, for I had really forgotten my past and I
looked forward to no future, finding it difficult to imagine the possibility of surviving all the fatigue. What I went through there marked
me in so lasting a manner that still today when any human being,
whoever he may be and in whatever circumstances, speaks to me
without brutality, I cannot help having the impression that there
must be a mistake and that unfortunately the mistake will in all
probability disappear. There I received forever the mark of a slave,
like the branding of the red-hot iron the Romans put on the fore-
heads of their most despised slaves. Since then I have always regarded
myself as a slave.

In this state of mind then, and in a wretched condition physically,
I entered the little Portuguese village, which, alas, was very wretched
too, on the very day of the festival of its patron saint. I was alone.

It was the evening and there was a full moon over the sea. The wives of the fishermen were, in procession, making a tour of all the ships, carrying candles and singing what must certainly be very ancient hymns of a heart-rending sadness. Nothing can give any idea of it. I have never heard anything so poignant unless it were the song of the boatmen on the Volga. There the conviction was suddenly borne in upon me that Christianity is pre-eminently the religion of slaves, that slaves cannot help belonging to it, and I among others.

In 1937 I had two marvelous days at Assisi. There, alone in the little twelfth-century Romanesque chapel of Santa Maria degli Angeli, an incomparable marvel of purity where Saint Francis often used to pray, something stronger than I was compelled me for the first time in my life to go down on my knees.

In 1938 I spent ten days at Solesmes, from Palm Sunday to Easter Tuesday, following all the liturgical services. I was suffering from splitting headaches; each sound hurt me like a blow; by an extreme effort of concentration I was able to rise above this wretched flesh, to leave it to suffer by itself, heaped up in a corner, and to find a pure and perfect joy in the unimaginable beauty of the chanting and the words. This experience enabled me by analogy to get a better understanding of the possibility of loving divine love in the midst of affliction. It goes without saying that in the course of these services the thought of the Passion of Christ entered into my being once and for all.

There was a young English Catholic there from whom I gained my first idea of the supernatural power of the sacraments because of the truly angelic radiance with which he seemed to be clothed after going to communion. Chance—for I always prefer saying chance rather than Providence—made of him a messenger to me. For he told me of the existence of those English poets of the seventeenth century who are named metaphysical. In reading them later on, I discovered the poem of which I read you what is unfortunately a very inadequate translation. It is called "Love". I learned it by heart. Often, at the culminating point of a violent headache, I make myself say it over, concentrating all my attention upon it and clinging with all my soul to the tenderness it enshrines. I used to think I was merely reciting it as a beautiful poem, but without my knowing it the recitation had the virtue of a prayer. It was during one of these recitations that, as I told you, Christ himself came down and took possession of me.

In my arguments about the insolubility of the problem of God I had never foreseen the possibility of that, of a real contact, person to person, here below, between a human being and God. I had vaguely heard tell of things of this kind, but I had never believed in them. In the *Fioretti* the accounts of apparitions rather put me off if anything, like the miracles in the Gospel. Moreover, in this sudden possession of me by Christ, neither my senses nor my imagination had any part; I only felt in the midst of my suffering the presence of a love, like that which one can read in the smile on a beloved face.

I had never read any mystical works because I had never felt any call to read them. In reading as in other things I have always striven to practice obedience. There is nothing more favorable to intellectual progress, for as far as possible I only read what I am hungry for at the moment when I have an appetite for it, and then I do not read, I *eat*. God in his mercy had prevented me from reading the mystics, so that it should be evident to me that I had not invented this absolutely unexpected contact.

Yet I still half refused, not my love but my intelligence. For it seemed to me certain, and I still think so today, that one can never wrestle enough with God if one does so out of pure regard for the truth. Christ likes us to prefer truth to him because, before being Christ, he is truth. If one turns aside from him to go toward the truth, one will not go far before falling into his arms.

After this I came to feel that Plato was a mystic, that all the *Iliad* is bathed in Christian light, and that Dionysus and Osiris are in a certain sense Christ himself; and my love was thereby redoubled.

I never wondered whether Jesus was or was not the Incarnation of God; but in fact I was incapable of thinking of him without thinking of him as God.

In the spring of 1940 I read the *Bhagavad-Gita*. Strange to say it was in reading those marvelous words, words with such a Christian sound, put into the mouth of an incarnation of God, that I came to feel strongly that we owe an allegiance to religious truth which is quite different from the admiration we accord to a beautiful poem; it is something far more categorical.

Yet I did not believe it to be possible for me to consider the question of baptism. I felt that I could not honestly give up my opinions concerning the non-Christian religions and concerning Israel —and as a matter of fact time and meditation have only served to strengthen them—and I thought that this constituted an absolute obstacle. I did not imagine it as possible that a priest could even dream of granting me baptism. If I had not met you, I should never have considered the problem of baptism as a practical problem.

During all this time of spiritual progress I had never prayed. I was afraid of the power of suggestion that is in prayer—the very power for which Pascal recommends it. Pascal's method seems to me one of the worst for attaining faith.

Contact with you was not able to persuade me to pray. On the contrary I thought the danger was all the greater, since I also had to beware of the power of suggestion in my friendship with you. At the same time I found it very difficult not to pray and not to tell you so. Moreover I knew I could not tell you without completely misleading you about myself. At that time I should not have been able to make you understand.

Until last September I had never once prayed in all my life, at least not in the literal sense of the word. I had never said any words to God, either out loud or mentally. I had never pronounced a liturgical prayer. I had occasionally recited the *Salve Regina*, but only as a beautiful poem.

Last summer, doing Greek with T———, I went through the Our Father word for word in Greek. We promised each other to learn it by heart. I do not think he ever did so, but some weeks later, as I was turning over the pages of the Gospel, I said to myself that since I had promised to do this thing and it was good, I ought to do it. I did it. The infinite sweetness of this Greek text so took hold of me that for several days I could not stop myself from saying it over all the time. A week afterward I began the vine harvest. I recited the Our Father in Greek every day before work, and I repeated it very often in the vineyard.

Since that time I have made a practice of saying it through once each morning with absolute attention. If during the recitation my attention wanders or goes to sleep, in the minutest degree, I begin again until I have once succeeded in going through it with absolutely pure attention. Sometimes it comes about that I say it again out of sheer pleasure, but I only do it if I really feel the impulse.

The effect of this practice is extraordinary and surprises me every time, for, although I experience it each day, it exceeds my expectation at each repetition.

At times the very first words tear my thoughts from my body and transport it to a place outside space where there is neither perspective nor point of view. The infinity of the ordinary expanses of perception is replaced by an infinity to the second or sometimes the third degree. At the same time, filling every part of this infinity of infinity, there is silence, a silence which is not an absence of sound but which is the object of a positive sensation, more positive than that of sound. Noises, if there are any, only reach me after crossing this silence.

Sometimes, also during this recitation or at other moments, Christ is present with me in person, but his presence is infinitely more real, more moving, more clear than on that first occasion when he took possession of me.

I should never have been able to take it upon myself to tell you all this had it not been for the fact that I am going away. And as I am going more or less with the idea of probable death, I do not believe that I have the right to keep it to myself. For after all, the whole of this matter is not a question concerning me myself. It concerns God. I am really nothing in it all. If one could imagine any possibility of error in God, I should think that it had all happened to me by mistake. But perhaps God likes to use castaway objects, waste, rejects. After all, should the bread of the host be moldy, it would become the Body of Christ just the same after the priest had consecrated it. Only it cannot refuse, while we can disobey. It sometimes seems to me that when I am treated in so merciful a way, every sin on my part must be a mortal sin. And I am constantly committing them.

I have told you that you are like a father and brother at the same time to me. But these words only express an analogy. Perhaps at bottom they only correspond to a feeling of affection, of gratitude and admiration. For as to the spiritual direction of my soul, I think that God himself has taken it in hand from the start and still looks after it.

That does not prevent me from owing you the greatest debt of gratitude that I could ever have incurred toward any human being. This is exactly what it consists of.

First you once said to me at the beginning of our relationship some words that went to the bottom of my soul. You said: "Be very careful, because if you should pass over something important through your own fault it would be a pity."

That made me see intellectual honesty in a new light. Till then I had only thought of it as opposed to faith; your words made me think that perhaps, without my knowing it, there were in me obstacles to the faith, impure obstacles, such as prejudices, habits. I felt that after having said to myself for so many years simply: "Perhaps all that is not true," I ought, without ceasing to say it—I still take care to say it very often now—to join it to the opposite formula, namely: "Perhaps all that is true," and to make them alternate.

At the same time, in making the problem of baptism a practical problem for me, you have forced me to face the whole question of the faith, dogma, and the sacraments, obliging me to consider them closely and at length with the fullest possible attention, making me see them as things toward which I have obligations that I have to discern and perform. I should never have done this otherwise and it is indispensable for me to do it.

But the greatest blessing you have brought me is of another order. In gaining my friendship by your charity (which I have never met anything to equal), you have provided me with a source of the most compelling and pure inspiration that is to be found among human things. For nothing among human things has such power to keep our gaze fixed ever more intensely upon God, than friendship for the friends of God.

Nothing better enables me to measure the breadth of your charity than the fact that you bore with me for so long and with such gentleness. I may seem to be joking, but that is not the case. It is true that you have not the same motives as I have myself (those about which I wrote to you the other day), for feeling hatred and repulsion toward me. But all the same I feel that your patience with me can only spring from a supernatural generosity.

I have not been able to avoid causing you the greatest disappointment it was in my power to cause you. But up to now, although I have often asked myself the question during prayer, during Mass, or in the light of the radiancy that remains in the soul after Mass, I have never once had, even for a moment, the feeling that God wants me to be in the Church. I have never even once had a feeling of uncertainty. I think that at the present time we can finally conclude that he does not want me in the Church. Do not have any regrets about it.

He does not want it so far at least. But unless I am mistaken I should say that it is his will that I should stay outside for the future too, except perhaps at the moment of death. Yet I am always ready to obey any order, whatever it may be. I should joyfully obey the order to go to the very center of hell and to remain there eternally. I do not mean, of course, that I have a preference for orders of this nature. I am not perverse like that.

Christianity should contain all vocations without exception since it is catholic. In consequence the Church should also. But in my eyes Christianity is catholic by right but not in fact. So many things are outside it, so many things that I love and do not want to give up, so many things that God loves, otherwise they would not be in existence. All the immense stretches of past centuries, except the last twenty are among them; all the countries inhabited by colored races; all secular life in the white peoples' countries; in the history of these countries, all the traditions banned as heretical, those of the Manicheans and Albigenses for instance; all those things resulting from the Renaissance, too often degraded but not quite without value.

Christianity being catholic by right but not in fact, I regard it as legitimate on my part to be a member of the Church by right but not in fact, not only for a time, but for my whole life if need be.

But it is not merely legitimate. So long as God does not give me the certainty that he is ordering me to do anything else, I think it is my duty.

I think, and so do you, that our obligation for the next two or three years, an obligation so strict that we can scarcely fail in it without treason, is to show the public the possibility of a truly incarnated Christianity. In all the history now known there has never been a period in which souls have been in such peril as they are today in every part of the globe. The bronze serpent must be lifted up again so that whoever raises his eyes to it may be saved.

But everything is so closely bound up together that Christianity cannot be really incarnated unless it is catholic in the sense that I have just defined. How could it circulate through the flesh of all the nations of Europe if it did not contain absolutely everything in itself? Except of course falsehood. But in everything that exists there is most of the time more truth than falsehood.

Having so intense and so painful a sense of this urgency, I should betray the truth, that is to say the aspect of truth that I see, if I left the point, where I have been since my birth, at the intersection of Christianity and everything that is not Christianity.

I have always remained at this exact point, on the threshold of the Church, without moving, quite still, ἐν ὑπομενῇ (it is so much more beautiful a word than *patientia!*); only now my heart has been transported, forever, I hope, into the Blessed Sacrament exposed on the altar.

You see that I am very far from the thoughts that H————, with the best of intentions, attributed to me. I am far also from being worried in any way.

If I am sad, it comes primarily from the permanent sadness that destiny has imprinted forever upon my emotions, where the greatest and purest joys can only be superimposed and that at the price of a great effort of attention. It comes also from my miserable and continual sins; and from all the calamities of our time and of all those of all the past centuries.

I think that you should understand why I have always resisted you, if in spite of being a priest you can admit that a genuine vocation might prevent anyone from entering the Church.

Otherwise a barrier of incomprehension will remain between us, whether the error is on my part or on yours. This would grieve me from the point of view of my friendship for you, because in that case the result of all these efforts and desires, called forth by your charity toward me, would be a disappointment for you. Moreover, although it is not my fault, I should not be able to help feeling guilty of ingratitude. For, I repeat, my debt to you is beyond all measure.

I should like to draw your attention to one point. It is that there is an absolutely insurmountable obstacle to the Incarnation of Christianity. It is the use of the two little words *anathema sit*. It is not their existence, but the way they have been employed up till now. It is that also which prevents me from crossing the threshold of the Church. I remain beside all those things that cannot enter the Church, the universal repository, on account of those two little words. I remain beside them all the more because my own intelligence is numbered among them.

The Incarnation of Christianity implies a harmonious solution of the problem of the relations between the individual and the collective. Harmony in the Pythagorean sense; the just balance of contraries. This solution is precisely what men are thirsting for today.

The position of the intelligence is the key to this harmony, because the intelligence is a specifically and rigorously individual thing. This harmony exists wherever the intelligence, remaining in its place, can be exercised without hindrance and can reach the complete fulfillment of its function. That is what Saint Thomas says admirably of all the parts of the soul of Christ, with reference to his sensitiveness to pain during the crucifixion.

The special function of the intelligence requires total liberty, implying the right to deny everything, and allowing of no domination. Wherever it usurps control there is an excess of individualism. Wherever it is hampered or uneasy there is an oppressive collectivism, or several of them.

The Church and the State should punish it, each one in its own way, when it advocates actions of which they disapprove. When it remains in the region of purely theoretical speculation they still have the duty, should occasion arise, to put the public on their guard, by every effective means, against the danger of the practical influence certain speculations might have upon the conduct of life. But whatever these theoretical speculations may be, the Church and the State have no right either to try to stifle them or to inflict any penalty material or moral upon their authors. Notably, they should not be deprived of the sacraments if they desire them. For, whatever they may have said, even if they have publicly denied the existence of God, they may not have committed any sin. In such a case the Church should declare that they are in error, but it should not demand of them anything whatever in the way of a disavowal of what they have said, nor should it deprive them of the Bread of Life.

A collective body is the guardian of dogma; and dogma is an object of contemplation for love, faith, and intelligence, three strictly individual faculties. Hence, almost since the beginning, the individual has been ill at ease in Christianity, and this uneasiness has been notably one of the intelligence. This cannot be denied.

Christ himself who is Truth itself, when he was speaking before an assembly such as a council, did not address it in the same language as he used in an intimate conversation with his well-beloved friend, and no doubt before the Pharisees he might easily have been accused of contradiction and error. For by one of those laws of nature, which God himself respects, since he has willed them from all eternity, there are two languages that are quite distinct although made up of the same words; there is the collective language and there is the individual one. The Comforter whom Christ sends us, the Spirit of truth, speaks one or other of these languages, whichever circumstances demand, and by a necessity of their nature there is not agreement between them.

When genuine friends of God—such as was Eckhart to my way of thinking—repeat words they have heard in secret amidst the silence of the union of love, and these words are in disagreement with the teaching of the Church, it is simply that the language of the market place is not that of the nuptial chamber.

Everybody knows that really intimate conversation is only possible between two or three. As soon as there are six or seven, collective language begins to dominate. That is why it is a complete misinterpretation to apply to the Church the words "Wheresoever two or three are gathered together in my name, there am I in the midst of them." Christ did not say two hundred, or fifty, or ten. He said two or three. He said precisely that he always forms the third in the intimacy of the tête-à-tête.

Christ made promises to the Church, but none of these promises has the force of the expression "Thy Father who seeth in secret." The word of God is the secret word. He who has not heard this word, even if he adheres to all the dogmas taught by the Church, has no contact with truth.

The function of the Church as the collective keeper of dogma is indispensable. She has the right and the duty to punish those who make a clear attack upon her within the specific range of this function, by depriving them of the sacraments.

Thus, although I know practically nothing of this business, I incline to think provisionally that she was right to punish Luther.

But she is guilty of an abuse of power when she claims to force love and intelligence to model their language upon her own. This abuse of power is not of God. It comes from the natural tendency of every form of collectivism, without exception, to abuse power.

The image of the Mystical Body of Christ is very attractive. But I consider the importance given to this image today as one of the most serious signs of our degeneration. For our true dignity is not to be parts of a body, even though it be a mystical one, even though it be that of Christ. It consists in this, that in the state of perfection, which is the vocation of each one of us, we no longer live in ourselves, but Christ lives in us; so that through our perfection Christ in his integrity and in his indivisible unity, becomes in a sense each one of us, as he is completely in each host. The hosts are not a *part* of his body.

This present-day importance of the image of the Mystical Body shows how wretchedly susceptible Christians are to outside influences. Undoubtedly there is real intoxication in being a member of the Mystical Body of Christ. But today a great many other mystical bodies, which have not Christ for their head, produce an intoxication in their members that to my way of thinking is of the same order.

As long as it is through obedience, I find sweetness in my deprivation of the joy of membership in the Mystical Body of Christ. For if God is willing to help me, I may thus bear witness that without this joy one can nevertheless be faithful to Christ unto death. Social enthusiasms have such power today, they raise people so effectively to the supreme degree of heroism in suffering and death, that I think it is as well that a few sheep should remain outside the fold in order to bear witness that the love of Christ is essentially something different.

The Church today defends the cause of the indefeasible rights of the individual against collective oppression, of liberty of thought against tyranny. But these are causes readily embraced by those who find themselves momentarily to be the least strong. It is their only way of perhaps one day becoming the strongest. That is well known.

You may perhaps be offended by this idea. You are not the Church. During the periods of the most atrocious abuse of power committed by the Church, there must have been some priests like you among the others. Your good faith is not a guarantee, even were it shared by all your Order. You cannot foresee what turn things may take.

In order that the present attitude of the Church should be effective and that she should really penetrate like a wedge into social existence, she would have to say openly that she had changed or wished to change. Otherwise who could take her seriously when they remembered the Inquisition? My friendship for you, which I extend through you to all your Order, makes it very painful for me to bring this up. But it existed. After the fall of the Roman Empire, which had been totalitarian, it was the Church that was the first to establish a rough sort of totalitarianism in Europe in the thirteenth century, after the war with the Albigenses. This tree bore much fruit.

And the motive power of this totalitarianism was the use of those two little words: *anathema sit*.

It was moreover by a judicious transposition of this use that all the parties which in our own day have founded totalitarian régimes were shaped. This is a point of history I have specially studied.

I must give you the impression of a Luciferian pride is speaking thus of a great many matters that are too high for me and about which I have no right to understand anything. It is not my fault. Ideas come and settle in my mind by mistake, then, realizing their mistake, they absolutely insist on coming out. I do not know where they come from, or what they are worth, but, whatever the risk, I do not think I have the right to prevent this operation.

Good-by, I wish you all possible good things except the cross; for I do not love my neighbor as myself, you particularly, as you have noticed. But Christ granted to his well-beloved disciple, and probably to all that disciple's spiritual lineage, to come to him not through degradation, defilement, and distress, but in uninterrupted joy, purity, and sweetness. That is why I can allow myself to wish that even if one day you have the honor of dying a violent death for Our Lord, it may be with joy and without any anguish; also that only three of the beatitudes (*mites, mundo corde, pacifici*) will apply to you. All the others involve more or less of suffering.

This wish is not due only to the frailty of human friendship. For, with any human being taken individually, I always find reasons for concluding that sorrow and misfortune do not suit him, either because he seems too mediocre for anything so great or, on the contrary, too precious to be destroyed. One cannot fail more seriously in the second of the two essential commandments. And as to the first, I fail to observe that, in a still more horrible manner, for every time I think of the crucifixion of Christ I commit the sin of envy.

Believe more than ever and forever in my filial and tenderly grateful friendship.

SIMONE WEIL

SKETCH
OF CONTEMPORARY
SOCIAL LIFE

*"Sketch of Contemporary Social Life," a prophetic indict-
ment of modern civilization, analyzes the most dangerous
tendency of any social organism, the oppression of man.
It forms the concluding section of a long study, written
in 1934, "Reflections Concerning the Causes of Liberty
and Social Oppression," which Camus praised as being un-
equaled, since Marx's writings, in its social, political, and
economic insights. Simone Weil considered it her principal
work.*

*With regard to human affairs, not to laugh, not to cry, not to become
indignant, but to understand.*

—SPINOZA

*The being gifted with reason can make every obstacle serve as material
for his work, and turn it to account.*

—MARCUS AURELIUS

It is impossible to imagine anything more contrary to this ideal than
the form which modern civilization has assumed in our day, at the
end of a development lasting several centuries. Never has the individual been so completely delivered up to a blind collectivity, and never

27

have men been less capable, not only of subordinating their actions
to their thoughts, but even of thinking. Such terms as oppressors and
oppressed, the idea of classes—all that sort of thing is near to losing
all meaning, so obvious are the impotence and distress of all men in
face of the social machine, which has become a machine for breaking
hearts and crushing spirits, a machine for manufacturing irresponsibility, stupidity, corruption, slackness and, above all, dizziness. The
reason for this painful state of affairs is perfectly clear. We are living
in a world in which nothing is made to man's measure; there exists
a monstrous discrepancy between man's body, man's mind and the
things which at the present time constitute the elements of human
existence; everything is disequilibrium. There is not a single category,
group or class of men that is altogether exempt from this destructive
disequilibrium, except perhaps for a few isolated patches of more
primitive life; and the younger generation, who have grown and are
growing up in it, inwardly reflect the chaos surrounding them more
than do their elders. This disequilibrium is essentially a matter of
quantity. Quantity is changed into quality, as Hegel said, and in particular a mere difference in quantity is sufficient to change what is
human into what is inhuman. From the abstract point of view quantities are immaterial, since you can arbitrarily change the unit of
measurement; but from the concrete point of view certain units of
measurement are given and have hitherto remained invariable, such as
the human body, human life, the year, the day, the average quickness
of human thought. Present-day life is not organized on the scale of
all these things; it has been transported into an altogether different
order of magnitude, as though man were trying to raise it to the level
of the forces of outside nature while neglecting to take his own
nature into account. If we add that, to all appearances, the economic
system has exhausted its constructive capacity and is beginning to be
able to function only by undermining little by little its own material
foundations, we shall perceive in all its simplicity the veritable essence
of the bottomless misery that forms the lot of the present generations.

In appearance, nearly everything nowadays is carried out methodically; science is king, machinery invades bit by bit the entire field
of labour, statistics take on a growing importance, and over one-sixth
of the globe the central authority is trying to regulate the whole of

social life according to plans. But in reality methodical thought is progressively disappearing, owing to the fact that the mind finds less and less matter on which to bite. Mathematics by itself forms too vast and too complex a whole to be embraced by one mind; *a fortiori* the whole formed by mathematics and the natural sciences; *a fortiori* the whole formed by science and its applications; and, on the other hand, everything is too intimately connected for the mind to be able really to grasp partial concepts. Now everything that the individual becomes powerless to control is seized upon by the collectivity. Thus science has now been for a long time—and to an ever-increasing extent —a collective enterprise. Actually, new results are always, in fact, the work of specific individuals; but, save perhaps for rare exceptions, the value of any result depends on such a complex set of interrelations with past discoveries and possible future researches that even the mind of the inventor cannot embrace the whole. Consequently, new dis- coveries, as they go on accumulating, take on the appearance of enig- mas, after the style of too thick a glass which ceases to be transparent. *A fortiori* practical life takes on a more and more collective character, and the individual as such a more and more insignificant place in it. Technical progress and mass production reduce manual workers more and more to a passive role; in increasing proportion and to an ever greater extent they arrive at a form of labour that enables them to carry out the necessary movements without understanding their con- nection with the final result. On the other hand, an industrial concern has become something too vast and too complex for any one man to be able to grasp it fully; and furthermore, in all spheres, the men who occupy key posts in social life are in charge of matters which are far beyond the compass of any single human mind. As for the general body of social life, it depends on so many factors, each of which is impenetrably obscure and which are tangled up in inextricable rela- tions with one another, that it would never even occur to anyone to try to understand its mechanism. Thus the social function most essentially connected with the individual, that which consists in co- ordinating, managing, deciding, is beyond any individual's capacity and becomes to a certain extent collective and, as it were, anonymous.

To the very extent to which what is systematic in contemporary life escapes the control of the mind, its regularity is established by

things which constitute the equivalent of what collective thought
would be if the collectivity did think. The cohesiveness of science
is ensured by means of signs; namely, on the one hand, by words or
ready-made phrases whose use is stretched beyond the meanings originally contained in them, on the other hand, by algebraic calculations.
In the sphere of labour, the things which take upon themselves the
essential functions are machines. The thing which relates production
to consumption and governs the exchange of products is money.
Finally, where the function of co-ordination and management is too
heavy for the mind and intelligence of one man, it is entrusted to a
curious machine, whose parts are men, whose gears consist of regula-
tions, reports and statistics, and which is called bureaucratic organization. All these blind things imitate the effort of thought to the life.
Just the mechanism of algebraic calculation has led more than once to
what might be called a new idea, except that the content of such
pseudo-ideas is no more than that of relations between signs; and alge-
bra is often marvellously apt to transform a series of experimental
results into laws, with a disconcerting ease reminding one of the
fantastic transformations one sees in motion-picture cartoons. Automatic machines seem to offer the model for the intelligent, faithful,
docile and conscientious worker. As for money, economists have
long been convinced that it possesses the virtue of establishing harmonious relations between the various economic functions. And bureaucratic machines almost reach the point of taking the place of
leaders. Thus, in all spheres, thought, the prerogative of the individual,
is subordinated to vast mechanisms which crystallize collective life,
and that is so to such an extent that we have almost lost the notion
of what real thought is. The efforts, the labours, the inventions of
beings of flesh and blood whom time introduces in successive waves
to social life only possess social value and effectiveness on condition
that they become in their turn crystallized in these huge mechanisms.
The inversion of the relation between means and ends—an inversion
which is to a certain extent the law of every oppressive society—
here becomes total or nearly so, and extends to nearly everything.
The scientist does not use science in order to manage to see more
clearly into his own thinking, but aims at discovering results that will
go to swell the present volume of scientific knowledge. Machines do

not run in order to enable men to live, but we resign ourselves to feeding men in order that they may serve the machines. Money does not provide a convenient method for exchanging products; it is the sale of goods which is a means for keeping money in circulation. Lastly, organization is not a means for exercising a collective activity, but the activity of a group, whatever it may be, is a means for strengthening organization. Another aspect of the same inversion consists in the fact that signs, words and algebraic formulas in the field of knowledge, money and credit symbols in economic life, play the part of realities of which the actual things themselves constitute only the shadows, exactly as in Hans Andersen's tale in which the scientist and his shadow exchanged roles; this is because signs constitute the material of social relations, whereas the perception of reality is something individual. The dispossession of the individual in favour of the collectivity is not, indeed, absolute, and it cannot become so; but it is hard to imagine how it could go much farther than at present. The power and concentration of armaments place all human lives at the mercy of the central authority. As a result of the vast extension of exchange, the majority of men cannot procure for themselves the greater part of what they consume save through the medium of society and in return for money; the peasants themselves are today to a large extent under this obligation to buy. And as big industry is a system of collective production, a great many men are forced, in order that their hands may come into contact with the material of work, to go through a collectivity which swallows them up and pins them down to a more or less servile task; when it rejects them, the strength and skill of their hands remain useless. The very peasants, who hitherto had managed to escape this wretched condition, have been reduced to it of late over one-sixth of the globe. Such a stifling state of affairs certainly provokes here and there an individualistic reaction; art, and especially literature, bears the marks of it; but since, owing to objective conditions, this reaction cannot impinge on either the sphere of thought or that of action, it remains bottled up in the play of the inner consciousness or in dreams of adventure and gratuitous acts, in other words, it never leaves the realm of shadows; and everything leads one to suppose that even this shadowy reaction is doomed to disappear almost completely.

When man reaches this degree of enslavement, judgments of value can only be based, whatever the particular field may be, on a purely external criterion; language does not possess any term so foreign to thought as properly to express something so devoid of meaning; but we may say that this criterion is constituted by efficiency, provided we thereby understand successes obtained in a vacuum. Even a scientific concept is not valued according to its content, which may be completely unintelligible, but according to the opportunities it provides for co-ordinating, abbreviating, summarizing. In the economic field, an undertaking is judged, not according to the real utility of the social functions it fulfils, but according to its growth so far and the speed with which it is developing; and the same is true of everything. Thus judgment of values is as it were entrusted to material objects instead of to the mind. The efficacy of efforts of whatever kind must always, it is true, be verified by thought, for, generally speaking, all verification proceeds from the mind; but thought has been reduced to such a subordinate role that one may say, by way of simplification, that the function of verification has passed from thought to things. But this excessive complication of all theoretical and practical activities which has thus dethroned thought, finally, when still further aggravated, comes to render the verification exercised by things in its turn imperfect and almost impossible. Everything is then blind. Thus it is that, in the sphere of science, the excessive accumulation of materials of every kind produces such chaos that the time seems to be approaching when any system will appear arbitrary. The chaos existing in economic life is still far more patent. In the actual carrying out of work, the subordination of irresponsible slaves to leaders overwhelmed by the mass of things to attend to, and, incidentally, themselves to a large extent irresponsible, is the cause of faulty workmanship and countless acts of negligence; this evil, which was first of all restricted to the big industrial undertakings, has now spread to the countryside wherever the peasants are enslaved after the manner of the industrial workers, that is to say, in Soviet Russia. The tremendous extension of credit prevents money from playing its regulating role so far as concerns commercial exchanges and the relationships between the various branches of production; and it would be useless to try to remedy this by doses of statistics. The parallel extension of speculation ends up by rendering the prosperity of industries independent, to a large extent, of their good functioning; the reason being that the capital increase brought about by the actual production of each of them counts less and less as compared with the constant supply of fresh capital. In short, in all spheres, success has become something almost arbitrary; it seems more and more to be the work of pure chance; and as it constituted the sole rule in all branches of human activity, our civilization is invaded by an ever-increasing disorder, and ruined by a waste in proportion to that disorder. This transformation is taking place at the very moment when the sources of profit on which the capitalist economy formerly drew for its prodigious development are becoming less and less plentiful, and when the technical conditions of work are themselves imposing a rapidly decreasing tempo on the improvement of industrial equipment.

So many profound changes have been taking place almost unbeknownst to us, and yet we are living in a period when the very axis of the social system is as it were in process of keeling over. Throughout the rise of the industrial system social life found itself oriented in the direction of construction. The industrial equipment of the planet was the supreme battle-ground on which the struggle for power was waged. To increase the size of an undertaking faster than its competitors, and that by means of its own resources—such was, broadly speaking, the aim and object of economic activity. Saving was the rule of economic life; consumption was restricted as much as possible, not only that of the workers, but also that of the capitalists themselves, and, in general, all expenditure connected with other things than industrial equipment. The supreme mission of governments was to preserve peace at home and abroad. The bourgeoisie were under the impression that this state of things would go on indefinitely, for the greater happiness of humanity; but it could not go on indefinitely in this way. Nowadays, the struggle for power, while preserving to a certain extent the same outward appearance, has entirely changed in character. The formidable increase in the part capital plant plays in undertakings, if compared with that of living labour, the rapid decrease in the rate of profit which has resulted, the ever-increasing amount of overhead expenses, waste, leakage, the lack of any regulating device for adjusting the various branches of production to one another—everything prevents social activity from still having as its pivot the development of the undertaking by turning profits into capital. It seems as though the economic struggle has ceased to be a form of competition in order to become a sort of war. It is no longer so much a question of properly organizing the work as of squeezing out the greatest possible amount of available capital scattered about in society by marketing shares, and then of squeezing out the greatest possible amount of money from everywhere by marketing products; everything takes place in the realm of opinion, and almost of fiction, by means of speculation and publicity. Since credit is the key to all economic success, saving is replaced by the maddest forms of expenditure. The term property has almost ceased to have any meaning; the ambitious man no longer thinks of being owner of a business and running it at a profit, but of causing the widest possible sector of economic activity to pass under his control. In a word, if we attempt to characterize, albeit in vague and summary fashion, this almost impenetrably obscure transformation, it is now a question in the struggle for economic power far less of building up than of conquering; and since conquest is destructive, the capitalist system, though remaining outwardly pretty much the same as it was fifty years ago, is wholly turned towards destruction. The means employed in the economic struggle—publicity, lavish display of wealth, corruption, enormous capital investments based almost entirely on credit, marketing of useless products by almost violent methods, speculations with the object of ruining rival concerns—all these tend to undermine the foundations of our economic life far more than to broaden them.

But all that is little enough compared with two related phenomena which are beginning to appear clearly and to cause a tragic threat to weigh upon the life of everyone; namely, on the one hand, the fact that the State tends more and more, and with an extraordinary rapidity, to become the centre of economic and social life, and, on the other hand, the subordination of economic to military interests. If one tries to analyse these phenomena in detail, one is held up by an almost inextricable web of reciprocal causes and effects; but the general trend is clear enough. It is quite natural that the increasingly bureaucratic nature of economic activity should favour the development of the power of the State, which is the bureaucratic organization *par excellence*. The profound change in the economic struggle operates in the same direction; the State is incapable of constructing, but owing to the fact that it concentrates in its hands the most powerful means of coercion, it is brought, as it were, by its very weight gradually to become the central element when it comes to conquering and destroying. Finally, seeing that the extraordinary complication of exchange and credit operations prevents money henceforth from sufficing to co-ordinate economic life, a semblance of bureaucratic co-ordination has to make up for it; and the central bureaucratic organization, which is the State machine, must naturally be led sooner or later to take the main hand in this co-ordination. The pivot around which revolves social life, thus transformed, is none other than preparation for war. Seeing that the struggle for power is carried out by conquest and destruction, in other words by a diffused economic war, it is not surprising that actual war should come to occupy the foreground. And since war is the recognized form of the struggle for power when the competitors are States, every increase in the State's grip on economic life has the effect of orienting industrial life yet a little farther towards preparation for war; while, conversely, the ever-increasing demands occasioned by preparation for war help day by day to bring the all-round economic and social activities of each country more and more into subjection to the authority of the central power. It seems fairly clear that contemporary humanity tends pretty well everywhere towards a totalitarian form of social organization—to use the term which the national-socialists have made fashionable—that is to say, towards a system in which the State power comes to exercise sovereign sway in all spheres, even, indeed above all, in that of thought. Russia presents us with an almost perfect example of such a system, for the greater misfortune of the Russian people; other countries will only be able to approach it, short of upheavals similar to that of October 1917; but it seems inevitable that all of them will approach it more or less in the course of the coming years. This development will only give disorder a bureaucratic form, and still further increase confusion, waste and misery. Wars will bring in their train a frantic consumption of raw materials and capital equipment, a crazy destruction of wealth of all kinds that previous generations have bequeathed us. When chaos and destruction have reached the limit beyond which the very functioning of the economic and social organization becomes materially impossible, our civilization will perish; and humanity, having gone back to a more or less primitive level of existence and to a social life dispersed into much smaller collectivities, will set out again along a new road which it is quite impossible for us to predict.

To imagine that we can switch the course of history along a different track by transforming the system through reforms or revolutions, to hope to find salvation in a defensive or offensive action against tyranny and militarism—all that is just day-dreaming. There is nothing on which to base even attempts. Marx's assertion that the régime would produce its own gravediggers is cruelly contradicted every day; and one wonders, incidentally, how Marx could ever have believed that slavery could produce free men. Never yet in history has a régime of slavery fallen under the blows of the slaves. The truth is that, to quote a famous saying, slavery degrades man to the point of making him love it; that liberty is precious only in the eyes of those who effectively possess it; and that a completely inhuman system, as ours is, far from producing beings capable of building up a human society, models all those subjected to it—oppressed and oppressors alike—according to its own image. Everywhere, in varying degrees, the impossibility of relating what one gives to what one receives has killed the feeling for sound workmanship, the sense of responsibility, and has developed passivity, neglect, the habit of expecting everything from outside, the belief in miracles. Even in the country, the feeling of a deep-seated bond between the land which sustains the man and the man who works the land has to a large extent been obliterated since the taste for speculation, the unpredictable rises and falls in currencies and prices have got countryfolk into the habit of turning their eyes towards the towns. The worker has not the feeling of earning his living as a producer; it is merely that the undertaking keeps him enslaved for long hours every day and allows him each week a sum of money which gives him the magic power of conjuring up at a moment's notice ready-made products, exactly as the rich do. The presence of innumerable unemployed, the cruel necessity of having to beg for a job, make wages appear less as wages than as alms. As for the unemployed themselves, the fact that they are involuntary parasites, and poverty-stricken into the bargain, does not make them any the less parasites. Generally speaking, the relation between work done and money earned is so hard to grasp that it appears as almost accidental, so that labour takes on the aspect of servitude, money that of a favour. The so-called governing classes are affected by the same passivity as all the others, owing to the fact that, snowed under as they are by an avalanche of inextricable problems, they long since gave up governing. One would look in vain, from the highest down to the lowest rungs of the social ladder, for a class of men among whom the idea could one day spring up that they might, in certain circumstances, have to take in hand the destinies of society; the harangues of the fascists could alone give the illusion of this, but they are empty.

As always happens, mental confusion and passivity leave free scope to the imagination. On all hands one is obsessed by a representation of social life which, while differing considerably from one class to another, is always made up of mysteries, occult qualities, myths, idols and monsters; each one thinks that power resides mysteriously in one of the classes to which he has no access, because hardly anybody understands that it resides nowhere, so that the dominant feeling everywhere is that dizzy fear which is always brought about by loss of contact with reality. Each class appears from the outside as a nightmare object. In circles connected with the working-class movement, dreams are haunted by mythological monsters called Finance, Industry, Stock Exchange, Bank, etc.; the bourgeois dream about other monsters which they call ringleaders, agitators, demagogues; the politicians regard the capitalists as supernatural beings who alone possess the key to the situation, and *vice versa*; each nation regards its neighbours as collective monsters inspired by a diabolical perversity. One could go on developing this theme indefinitely. In such a situation, any log whatever can be looked upon as king and take the place of one up to a certain point thanks to that belief alone; and this is true, not merely in the case of men in general, but also in that of the governing classes. Nothing is easier, for that matter, than to spread any myth whatsoever throughout a whole population. We must not be surprised, therefore, at the appearance of "totalitarian" régimes unprecedented in history. It is often said that force is powerless to overcome thought; but for

this to be true, there must be thought. Where irrational opinions hold
the place of ideas, force is all-powerful. It is quite unfair to say, for
example, that fascism annihilates free thought; in reality it is the lack
of free thought which makes it possible to impose by force official
doctrines entirely devoid of meaning. Actually, such a régime even
manages considerably to increase the general stupidity, and there is
little hope for the generations that will have grown up under the conditions which it creates. Nowadays, every attempt to turn men into
brutes finds powerful means at its disposal. On the other hand, one
thing is impossible, even were you to dispose of the best of public
platforms, and that is to diffuse clear ideas, correct reasoning and
sensible views on any wide scale.

It is no good expecting help to come from men; and even were
it otherwise, men would none the less be vanquished in advance by
the natural power of things. The present social system provides no means
of action other than machines for crushing humanity; whatever may
be the intentions of those who use them, these machines crush and will
continue to crush as long as they exist. With the industrial convict prisons constituted by the big factories, one can only produce slaves and
not free workers, still less workers who would form a dominant class.
With guns, aeroplanes, bombs, you can spread death, terror, oppression, but not life and liberty. With gas masks, air-raid shelters and air-
raid warnings, you can create wretched masses of panic-stricken human beings, ready to succumb to the most senseless forms of terror
and to welcome with gratitude the most humiliating forms of tyranny,
but not citizens. With the popular press and the wireless, you can make
a whole people swallow with their breakfast or their supper a series
of ready-made and, by the same token, absurd opinions—for even
sensible views become deformed and falsified in minds which accept
them unthinkingly; but you cannot with the aid of these things arouse
so much as a gleam of thought. And without factories, without arms,
without the popular press you can do nothing against those who
possess all these things. The same applies to everything. The powerful
means are oppressive, the non-powerful means remain inoperative.
Each time that the oppressed have tried to set up groups able to exercise a real influence, such groups, whether they went by the name of
parties or unions, have reproduced in full within themselves all the

vices of the system which they claimed to reform or abolish, namely, bureaucratic organization, reversal of the relationships between means and ends, contempt for the individual, separation between thought and action, the mechanization of thought itself, the exploitation of stupidity and lies as means of propaganda, and so on.

The only possibility of salvation would lie in a methodical co-operation between all, strong and weak, with a view to accomplishing a progressive decentralization of social life; but the absurdity of such an idea strikes one immediately. Such a form of co-operation is impossible to imagine, even in dreams, in a civilization that is based on competition, on struggle, on war. Apart from some such co-operation, there is no means of stopping the blind trend of the social machine towards an increasing centralization, until the machine itself suddenly jams and flies into pieces. What weight can the hopes and desires of those who are not at the control levers carry, when, reduced to the most tragic impotence, they find themselves the mere playthings of blind and brutish forces? As for those who exercise economic or political authority, harried as they are incessantly by rival ambitions and hostile powers, they cannot work to weaken their own authority without condemning themselves almost certainly to being deprived of it. The more they feel themselves to be animated by good intentions, the more they will be brought, even despite themselves, to endeavour to extend their authority in order to increase their ability to do good; which amounts to oppressing people in the hope of liberating them, as Lenin did. It is quite patently impossible for decentralization to be initiated by the central authority; to the very extent to which the central authority is exercised, it brings everything else under its subjection. Generally speaking, the idea of enlightened despotism, which has always had a utopian flavour about it, is in our day completely absurd. Faced with problems whose variety and complexity are infinitely beyond the range of great as of limited minds, no despot in the world can possibly be enlightened. Though a few men may hope, by dint of honest and methodical thinking, to perceive a few gleams in this impenetrable darkness, those whom the cares and responsibilities of authority deprive of both leisure and liberty of mind are certainly not of that number.

In such a situation, what can those do who still persist, against all eventualities, in honouring human dignity both in themselves and in others? Nothing, except endeavour to introduce a little play into the cogs of the machine that is grinding us down; seize every opportunity of awakening a little thought wherever they are able; encourage whatever is capable, in the sphere of politics, economics or technique, of leaving the individual here and there a certain freedom of movement amid the trammels cast around him by the social organization. That is certainly something, but it does not go very far. On the whole, our present situation more or less resembles that of a party of absolutely ignorant travellers who find themselves in a motor-car launched at full speed and driverless across broken country. When will the smash-up occur after which it will be possible to consider trying to construct something new? Perhaps it is a matter of a few decades, perhaps of centuries. There are no data enabling one to fix a probable lapse of time. It seems, however, that the material resources of our civilization are not likely to become exhausted for some considerable time, even allowing for wars; and, on the other hand, as centralization, by abolishing all individual initiative and all local life, destroys by its very existence everything which might serve as a basis for a different form of organization, one may suppose that the present system will go on existing up to the extreme limit of possibility. To sum up, it seems reasonable to suppose that the generations which will have to face the difficulties brought about by the collapse of the present system have yet greater consciousness and ingenuity than the most highly skilled of all those that have followed each other in the course of human history, the ones which will have had to shoulder the maximum of imaginary responsibilities and the minimum of real ones. Once this situation is fully realized, it leaves a marvellous freedom of mind.

What exactly will perish and what subsist of our present civilization? What are the conditions and what is the direction in which history will afterwards unfold itself? These questions are insoluble. What we know in advance is that life will be proportionately less inhuman according as the individual ability to think and act is greater. Our present civilization, of which our descendants will no doubt inherit some fragments, at any rate contains, we feel it only too keenly, the wherewithal to crush man; but it also contains, at least in germ, the wherewithal to liberate him. Our science includes, despite all the obscurities engendered by a sort of new scholasticism, some admirable flashes of genius, some parts that are clear and luminous, some perfectly methodical steps undertaken by the mind. In our technique also the germs of a liberation of labour can be found: probably not, as is commonly thought, in the direction of automatic machines; these certainly appear to be suitable, from the purely technical point of view, for relieving men of the mechanical and unconscious element contained in labour, but, on the other hand, they are indissolubly bound up with an excessively centralized and consequently very oppressive economic organization. But other forms of the machine-tool have produced—above all before the war—perhaps the finest type of conscious worker history has ever seen, namely, the skilled workman. If, in the course of the last twenty years, the machine-tool has become more and more automatic in its functioning, if the work carried out, even on machines of relatively ancient design, has become more and more mechanical, the reason lies in the ever-increasing concentration of the economy. Who knows whether an industry split up into innumerable small undertakings would not bring about an inverse development of the machine-tool, and, at the same time, types of work calling for a yet greater consciousness and ingenuity than the most highly skilled work in modern factories? We are all the more justified in entertaining such hopes in that electricity supplies the form of energy suitable for such a type of industrial organization.

Given that once we have fully realized our almost complete powerlessness in regard to present-day ills we are at any rate relieved of the duty of concerning ourselves with the present state of things, apart from those moments when we feel its direct impact, what nobler task could we assume than that of preparing for such a future in a methodical way by devoting ourselves to drawing up an inventory of modern civilization? It is certainly a task which goes far beyond the narrow possibilities of a single human life; on the other hand, to pursue such a course is to condemn oneself of a certainty to moral loneliness, to lack of understanding, to the hostility of the enemies as well as of the servants of the existing order. As for future generations, nothing entitles us to assume that, across the upheavals which separate us from them, chance may allow the fragmentary ideas that might be elaborated by a few solitary minds in our day even to reach them. But it would be folly to complain of such a situation. No pact with Providence has ever guaranteed the effectiveness of even the most nobly-inspired efforts. And when one has resolved to place confidence, within and around oneself, solely in efforts whose source and origin lie in the mind of the very person who accomplishes them, it would be foolish to wish that some magical operation should enable great results to be obtained with the insignificant forces placed at the disposal of isolated individuals. It is never by such arguments that a staunch mind can allow itself to be deflected, once it has clearly perceived that there is one thing to be done, and one only.

It would thus seem to be a question of separating, in present-day civilization, what belongs of right to man, considered as an individual, and what is of a nature to place weapons in the hands of the collectivity for use against him, whilst at the same time trying to discover the means whereby the former elements may be developed at the expense of the latter. As far as science is concerned, we must no longer seek to add to the already over-great mass which it forms; we must draw up its balance-sheet, so as to enable the mind to place in evidence there what is properly its own, what is made up of clear concepts, and to set aside what is only an automatic procedure for co-ordinating, unifying, summarizing or even discovering; we must try to reduce these procedures themselves to conscious steps on the part of the mind; we must, generally speaking, wherever possible, conceive of and present scientific results as merely a phase in the methodical activity of the mind. For this purpose, a serious study of the history of the sciences is probably indispensable. As for technique, it ought to be studied in a thoroughgoing manner—its history, present state, possibilities of development—and that from an entirely new point of view, which would no longer be that of output, but that of the relation between the worker and his work. Lastly, the analogy between the steps accomplished by the human mind, on the one hand in daily life and particularly in work, on the other hand in the methodical development of science, should be fully brought out. Even if a sequence of mental efforts oriented in this sense were to remain without influence on the future evolution of social organization, it would not lose its value on that account; the future destinies of humanity are not the sole object worthy of consideration. Only fanatics are able to set no value on their own existence save to the extent that it serves a collective cause; to react against the subordination of the individual to the collectivity implies that one begins by refusing to subordinate one's own destiny to the course of history. In order to resolve upon undertaking such an effort of critical analysis, all one needs is to realize that it would enable him who did so to escape the contagion of folly and collective frenzy by reaffirming on his own account, over the head of the social idol, the original pact between the mind and the universe.

REFLECTIONS ON
THE RIGHT USE OF
SCHOOL STUDIES WITH
A VIEW TO
THE LOVE OF GOD

Young people should have read to them "Reflections on
the Right Use of School Studies with a View to the Love
of God." Evoking the contemplative spirit, this beautiful,
provocative essay stresses that school tasks should develop
the power of attention, which not only lightens the mind
but also makes contact with God. Humility, not academic
success, should be a student's highest goal and joy. A
school exercise can be like a sacrament and education a
holy ground. This memorable response by one of the
readers of the essay captures its appeal: "Marvellous
foolishness, of which one believes every word."

The key to a Christian conception of studies is the realization that
prayer consists of attention. It is the orientation of all the attention of
which the soul is capable toward God. The quality of the attention
counts for much in the quality of the prayer. Warmth of heart cannot
make up for it.

The highest part of the attention only makes contact with God,
when prayer is intense and pure enough for such a contact to be established; but the whole attention is turned toward God.

Of course school exercises only develop a lower kind of attention.
Nevertheless, they are extremely effective in increasing the power of

attention that will be available at the time of prayer, on condition that they are carried out with a view to this purpose and this purpose alone.

Although people seem to be unaware of it today, the development of the faculty of attention forms the real object and almost the sole interest of studies. Most school tasks have a certain intrinsic interest as well, but such an interest is secondary. All tasks that really call upon the power of attention are interesting for the same reason and to an almost equal degree.

School children and students who love God should never say: "For my part I like mathematics"; "I like French"; "I like Greek." They should learn to like all these subjects, because all of them develop that faculty of attention which, directed toward God, is the very substance of prayer.

If we have no aptitude or natural taste for geometry, this does not mean that our faculty for attention will not be developed by wrestling with a problem or studying a theorem. On the contrary it is almost an advantage.

It does not even matter much whether we succeed in finding the solution or understanding the proof, although it is important to try really hard to do so. Never in any case whatever is a genuine effort of the attention wasted. It always has its effect on the spiritual plane and in consequence on the lower one of the intelligence, for all spiritual light lightens the mind.

If we concentrate our attention on trying to solve a problem of geometry, and if at the end of an hour we are no nearer to doing so than at the beginning, we have nevertheless been making progress each minute of that hour in another more mysterious dimension. Without our knowing or feeling it, this apparently barren effort has brought more light into the soul. The result will one day be discovered in prayer. Moreover, it may very likely be felt in some department of the intelligence in no way connected with mathematics. Perhaps he who made the unsuccessful effort will one day be able to grasp the beauty of a line of Racine more vividly on account of it. But it is certain that this effort will bear its fruit in prayer. There is no doubt whatever about that.

Certainties of this kind are experimental. But if we do not believe in them before experiencing them, if at least we do not behave as though we believed in them, we shall never have the experience that leads to such certainties. There is a kind of contradiction here. Above a given level this is the case with all useful knowledge concerning spiritual progress. If we do not regulate our conduct by it before having proved it, if we do not hold on to it for a long time by faith alone, a faith at first stormy and without light, we shall never transform it into certainty. Faith is the indispensable condition.

The best support for faith is the guarantee that if we ask our Father for bread, he does not give us a stone. Quite apart from explicit religious belief, every time that a human being succeeds in making an effort of attention with the sole idea of increasing his grasp of truth, he acquires a greater aptitude for grasping it, even if his effort produces no visible fruit. An Eskimo story explains the origin of light as follows: "In the eternal darkness, the crow, unable to find any food, longed for light, and the earth was illumined." If there is a real desire, if the thing desired is really light, the desire for light produces it. There is a real desire when there is an effort of attention. It is really light that is desired if all other incentives are absent. Even if our efforts of attention seem for years to be producing no result, one day a light that is in exact proportion to them will flood the soul. Every effort adds a little gold to a treasure no power on earth can take away. The useless efforts made by the Curé d'Ars, for long and painful years, in his attempt to learn Latin bore fruit in the marvelous discernment that enabled him to see the very soul of his penitents behind their words and even their silences.

Students must therefore work without any wish to gain good marks, to pass examinations, to win school successes; without any reference to their natural abilities and tastes; applying themselves equally to all their tasks, with the idea that each one will help to form in them the habit of that attention which is the substance of prayer. When we set out to do a piece of work, it is necessary to wish to do it correctly, because such a wish is indispensable in any true effort. Underlying this immediate objective, however, our deep purpose should aim solely at increasing the power of attention with a view to prayer; as, when we write, we draw the shape of the letter on paper, not with a view to the shape, but with a view to the idea we want to express. To make this the sole and exclusive purpose of our studies is the first condition to be observed if we are to put them to the right use.

The second condition is to take great pains to examine squarely and to contemplate attentively and slowly each school task in which we have failed, seeing how unpleasing and second rate it is, without seeking any excuse or overlooking any mistake or any of our tutor's corrections, trying to get down to the origin of each fault. There is a great temptation to do the opposite, to give a sideways glance at the corrected exercise if it is bad and to hide it forthwith. Most of us do this nearly always. We have to withstand this temptation. Incidentally, moreover, nothing is more necessary for academic success, because, despite all our efforts, we work without making much progress when we refuse to give our attention to the faults we have made and our tutor's corrections.

Above all it is thus that we can acquire the virtue of humility, and that is a far more precious treasure than all academic progress. From this point of view it is perhaps even more useful to contemplate our stupidity than our sin. Consciousness of sin gives us the feeling that we are evil, and a kind of pride sometimes finds a place in it. When we force ourselves to fix the gaze, not only of our eyes but of our souls, upon a school exercise in which we have failed through sheer stupidity, a sense of our mediocrity is borne in upon us with irresistible evidence. No knowledge is more to be desired. If we can arrive at knowing this truth with all our souls we shall be well established on the right foundation.

If these two conditions are perfectly carried out there is no doubt that school studies are quite as good a road to sanctity as any other.

To carry out the second, it is enough to wish to do so. This is not the case with the first. In order really to pay attention, it is necessary to know how to set about it.

Most often attention is confused with a kind of muscular effort. If one says to one's pupils: "Now you must pay attention," one sees them contracting their brows, holding their breath, stiffening their muscle. If after two minutes they are asked what they have been paying attention to, they cannot reply. They have been concentrating on nothing. They have not been paying attention. They have been contracting their muscles.

We often expend this kind of muscular effort on our studies. As it ends by making us tired, we have the impression that we have been working. That is an illusion. Tiredness has nothing to do with work. Work itself is the useful effort, whether it is tiring or not. This kind of muscular effort in work is entirely barren, even if it is made with the best of intentions. Good intentions in such cases are among those that pave the way to hell. Studies conducted in such a way can sometimes succeed academically from the point of view of gaining marks and passing examinations, but that is in spite of the effort and thanks to natural gifts; moreover such studies are never of any use.

Will power, the kind that, if need be, makes us set our teeth and endure suffering, is the principal weapon of the apprentice engaged in manual work. But, contrary to the usual belief, it has practically no place in study. The intelligence can only be led by desire. For there to be desire, there must be pleasure and joy in the work. The intelligence only grows and bears fruit in joy. The joy of learning is as indispensable in study as breathing is in running. Where it is lacking there are no real students, but only poor caricatures of apprentices who, at the end of their apprenticeship, will not even have a trade.

It is the part played by joy in our studies that makes of them a preparation for spiritual life, for desire directed toward God is the only power capable of raising the soul. Or rather, it is God alone who comes down and possesses the soul, but desire alone draws God down. He only comes to those who ask him to come; and he cannot refuse to come to those who implore him long, often, and ardently.

Attention is an effort, the greatest of all efforts perhaps, but it is a negative effort. Of itself, it does not involve tiredness. When we become tired, attention is scarcely possible any more, unless we have already had a good deal of practice. It is better to stop working altogether, to seek some relaxation, and then a little later to return to the task; we have to press on and loosen up alternately, just as we breathe in and out.

Twenty minutes of concentrated, untired attention is infinitely better than three hours of the kind of frowning application that leads us to say with a sense of duty done: "I have worked well!"

But, in spite of all appearances, it is also far more difficult. Something in our soul has a far more violent repugnance for true attention than the flesh has for bodily fatigue. This something is much more closely connected with evil than is the flesh. That is why every time that we really concentrate our attention, we destroy the evil in ourselves. If we concentrate with this intention, a quarter of an hour of attention is better than a great many good works.

Attention consists of suspending our thought, leaving it detached, empty, and ready to be penetrated by the object; it means holding in our minds, within reach of this thought, but on a lower level and not in contact with it, the diverse knowledge we have acquired which we are forced to make use of. Our thought should be in relation to all particular and already formulated thoughts, as a man on a mountain who, as he looks forward, sees also below him, without actually looking at them, a great many forests and plains. Above all our thought should be empty, waiting, not seeking anything, but ready to receive in its naked truth the object that is to penetrate it.

All wrong translations, all absurdities in geometry problems, all clumsiness of style, and all faulty connection of ideas in compositions and essays, all such things are due to the fact that thought has seized upon some idea too hastily, and being thus prematurely blocked, is not open to the truth. The cause is always that we have wanted to be too active; we have wanted to carry out a search. This can be proved every time, for every fault, if we trace it to its root. There is no better exercise than such a tracing down of our faults, for this truth is one to be believed only when we have experienced it hundreds and thousands of times. This is the way with all essential truths.

We do not obtain the most precious gifts by going in search of them but by waiting for them. Man cannot discover them by his own powers, and if he sets out to seek for them he will find in their place counterfeits of which he will be unable to discern the falsity.

The solution of a geometry problem does not in itself constitute a precious gift, but the same law applies to it because it is the image of something precious. Being a little fragment of particular truth, it is a pure image of the unique, eternal, and living Truth, the very Truth that once in a human voice declared: "I am the Truth."

Every school exercise, thought of in this way, is like a sacrament.

In every school exercise there is a special way of waiting upon truth, setting our hearts upon it, yet not allowing ourselves to go out in search of it. There is a way of giving our attention to the data of a problem in geometry without trying to find the solution or to the words of a Latin or Greek text without trying to arrive at the meaning, a way of waiting, when we are writing, for the right word to come of itself at the end of our pen, while we merely reject all inadequate words.

Our first duty toward school children and students is to make known this method to them, not only in a general way but in the particular form that bears on each exercise. It is not only the duty of those who teach them but also of their spiritual guides. Moreover the latter should bring out in a brilliantly clear light the correspondence between the attitude of the intelligence in each one of these exercises and the position of the soul, which, with its lamp well filled with oil, awaits the Bridegroom's coming with confidence and desire. May each loving adolescent, as he works at his Latin prose, hope through this prose to come a little nearer to the instant when he will really be the slave—faithfully waiting while the master is absent, watching and listening—ready to open the door to him as soon as he knocks. The master will then make his slave sit down and himself serve him with meat.

Only this waiting, this attention, can move the master to treat his slave with such amazing tenderness. When the slave has worn himself out in the fields, his master says on his return, "Prepare my meal, and wait upon me." And he considers the servant who only does what he is told to do to be unprofitable. To be sure in the realm of action we have to do all that is demanded of us, no matter what effort, weariness, and suffering it may cost, for he who disobeys does not love; but after that we are only unprofitable servants. Such service is a condition of love, but it is not enough. What forces the master to make himself the slave of his slave, and to love him, has nothing to do with all that. Still less is it the result of a search the servant might have been bold enough to undertake on his own initiative. It is only watching, waiting, attention.

Happy then are those who pass their adolescence and youth in developing this power of attention. No doubt they are no nearer to goodness than their brothers working in fields and factories. They are near in a different way. Peasants and workmen possess a nearness to God of incomparable savor which is found in the depths of poverty, in the absence of social consideration and in the endurance of long drawn-out sufferings. If, however, we consider the occupations in themselves, studies are nearer to God because of the attention which is their soul. Whoever goes through years of study without developing this attention within himself has lost a great treasure.

Not only does the love of God have attention for its substance; the love of our neighbor, which we know to be the same love, is made of this same substance. Those who are unhappy have no need for anything in this world but people capable of giving them their attention. The capacity to give one's attention to a sufferer is a very rare and difficult thing; it is almost a miracle; it *is* a miracle. Nearly all those who think they have this capacity do not possess it. Warmth of heart, impulsiveness, pity are not enough.

In the first legend of the Grail, it is said that the Grail (the miraculous vessel that satisfies all hunger by virtue of the consecrated Host) belongs to the first comer who asks the guardian of the vessel, a king three-quarters paralyzed by the most painful wound, "What are you going through?"

The love of our neighbor in all its fullness simply means being able to say to him: "What are you going through?" It is a recognition that the sufferer exists, not only as a unit in a collection, or a specimen from the social category labeled "unfortunate," but as a man, exactly like us, who was one day stamped with a special mark by affliction. For this reason it is enough, but it is indispensable, to know how to look at him in a certain way.

This way of looking is first of all attentive. The soul empties itself of all its own contents in order to receive into itself the being it is looking at, just as he is, in all his truth.

Only he who is capable of attention can do this.

So it comes about that, paradoxical as it may seem, a Latin prose or a geometry problem, even though they are done wrong, may be of great service one day, provided we devote the right kind of effort to them. Should the occasion arise, they can one day make us better able to give someone in affliction exactly the help required to save him, at the supreme moment of his need.

For an adolescent, capable of grasping this truth and generous enough to desire this fruit above all others, studies could have their fullest spiritual effect, quite apart from any particular religious belief.

Academic work is one of those fields containing a pearl so precious that it is worth while to sell all our possessions, keeping nothing for ourselves, in order to be able to acquire it.

FACTORY WORK

In 1934–1935 Simone Weil worked as a day laborer in various factories in the Paris suburbs. Disclosing to her the workers' economic slavery, this experience served as a direct contact with unhappiness, which, she said, killed her youth, entered her flesh and soul, and stamped on her the "mark of the slave." Graphically and compassionately, "Factory Work" records both her reactions to and her diagnostic and prescriptive comments on working conditions.

These pages have to do with an experience of factory life dating back to the period before 1936. They may come as something of a surprise to many people whose only direct contact with workingmen was by way of the Popular Front. A workingman's condition is ever-changing, and it may differ from one year to the next. The years before 1936, which were hard and bitter years of economic crisis, better reflect the proletarian condition, somehow, than the trance-like period that followed.

Official declarations will have it that henceforward the French State undertakes to put an end to the proletarian condition, that is, to all that is degrading in the life of a workingman, whether inside the fac-

tory or out. The first obstacle to be overcome in such an undertaking
is ignorance. Of late, it has become more obvious than ever that factory workers are, in a sense, truly uprooted beings, exiles in their own
land. But the real reasons for this are not so generally known. Walks
in the working-class quarters, glimpses of dark, miserable rooms, the
houses, the streets, are no great help in understanding the life that people lead there. An even greater mystery invests the worker's discontent in the factory. Workingmen themselves do not find it easy to
write, speak, or even reflect on such a subject, for the first effect
of suffering is the attempt of thought to *escape*. It refuses to confront
the adversity that wounds it. Thus, when workingmen speak of their
lot, they repeat more often than not the catchwords coined by people
who are not workingmen. The difficulty involved is at least as great for
a veteran worker. He finds it easy to talk of his early past, but very
difficult actually to think about it, for nothing is more swiftly covered over by oblivion than past miseries. A man of talent may,
through fiction and the exercise of imagination, divine and, to some
extent, describe from the outside. There is, for example, Jules
Romains' chapter on factory life in his *Hommes de bonne volonte*. But
that kind of thing does not cut very deep.

How abolish an evil without first having clearly perceived in what
it consisted? What follows may perhaps help to set the terms of the
problem, since they are the fruit of a direct contact with factory life.

Conceivably a plant or factory could fill the soul through a powerful awareness of collective—one might well say, unanimous—life. All
noises have their meaning, they are all rhythmic, they fuse into a kind
of giant respiration of the working collectivity in which it is exhilarating to play one's part. And because the sense of solitude is not
touched, participation becomes even more exhilarating. Pursuing our
hypothetical lead, there are only the metallic noises, the turning
wheels, the bite of metal upon metal; noises that speak neither of
nature nor of life, but of the serious, steady, uninterrupted acting of
men upon things. Though lost in this great hum, one also dominates
it; for over this permanent, yet ever-changing drone bass, what stands
out while yet somehow fused with it, is the sound of one's own
machine. One does not feel insignificant as in a crowd, but indis-

pensable. The transmission belts, supposing them to be present, allow the eye to drink in that unity of rhythm which the whole body feels through the sounds and the barely perceptible vibration of everything. Through the wan hours of winter mornings and evenings when only the electric lights are shining, all the senses are participants in a universe where nothing recalls nature, where nothing is gratuitous, where everything is sheer impact, the painful yet conquering impact of man upon matter. The lamps, the belts, the noise, the hard, cold iron-work, all converge toward the transmutation of man into workman.

If factory life were really this, it would be only too beautiful. But such is, naturally, not the case. The joys here described are the jobs of free men. Those who people the factories do not feel them, except in rare and fleeting moments, for they are not free. They can experience them only when they forget they are not free; but they can rarely forget, for the vise of their servitude grips them through the senses, their bodies, the thousand and one little details that crowd the minutes of which their lives are constituted.

The first detail which, in the work-day, makes their servitude apparent, is the time-clock. The trip from home to plant is dominated by one fact: arrival before a point in time that is arbitrarily determined. Since arrival five or ten minutes ahead of time is of no avail, the flow of time appears as something pitiless, leaving no room for the play of chance. In a man's work-day it is the first onslaught of a regimen whose brutality dominates a life spent among machines: the rule that chance has no place, no "freedom of the city," in a factory. Chance exists there, of course, as it does anywhere else, but it is not *recognized*. What is recognized, often to the great detriment of production, is the barracks formula: "Never mind the reasons!" Contradictory orders are not such according to the logic of the factory. Come what may, the work must go on. It is up to the worker to get on with the job. And he does get on with it.

The big and the little annoyances to which the human organism is constantly subjected—or as Jules Romains puts it: "That assortment of physical pin-pricks that the task does not demand and which are far from advancing it"—contribute no less to an awareness of servitude. We do not refer to the moments of pain bound up with the exigencies of the task at hand—one may even glory in the pride of bearing up under them; but to those that are needless. They wound one's spirit because generally there is no thought of complaining about them. From the very outset the conviction sets in that a snub will be the only answer, that the complaint will be taken in without a word of reply. To speak of such things, then, would be an invitation to humiliation. It often happens that if there is something a workingman cannot stomach, he will pocket the affront and "ask for his time"—i.e., quit the job. It often happens that this type of suffering is in itself very insignificant. If it becomes bitter, it is through steady accumulation of such resentments, which can find no outlet. The fact that he would like to forget, that he cannot feel at home in the plant, that he has no freedom of movement there, that he is an alien given admittance only in his capacity as intermediary between machines and the things to be machined, all this eats into body and soul; and flesh and thought shrink back. It is as though someone were repeating in his ear at every passing moment and with all possibility of reply excluded: "Here, you are nothing. You simply do not count. You are here to obey, to accept everything, to keep your mouth shut." Such reiteration becomes irresistible. One comes to acquiesce down deep that he counts for nothing. All or nearly all factory workers, even the most free in their bearing, have an almost imperceptible something about their movements, their look, and especially in the set of the lips, which reveals that they have been obliged to consider themselves as nothing.

What especially constrains them to this is the way in which they have to take orders. It is often denied that workingmen suffer from the monotony of their work, because it has been noted that they are frequently annoyed by a change of work. Notwithstanding, they are morally surfeited in the course of a long period of monotonous work. A change comes as both a deliverance and an annoyance; at times as a very keen annoyance, in the case of piece work, because of the lowered earnings implied and because it has become second nature, a convention, to attach more importance to money, which is something clear-cut and measurable, than to obscure, impalpable, inexpressible feelings that possess one while at work. But even when work is paid by the hour, there is the feeling of annoyance and irritation, because of the manner in which the change of work is ordered. The new change is suddenly imposed, without advance notice, under the form of a command that must immediately and unquestioningly be obeyed. The one obeying is thus made to feel that his time is incessantly at someone else's beck and call. The modest artisan who possesses a machine shop and who knows that within a fortnight he must have ready so many braces and bits, so many faucets, or so many connecting rods, is not precisely free to do as he pleases with his time either, but at least, once an order is accepted, he may determine in advance the employment he will give his days and hours. If only an employer would say to a workingman a week or two in advance: "For two days you'd better work on these connecting rods, then the braces and bits, and so on," obedience would still be exacted, but at least it would be possible mentally to embrace the immediate future, to outline it beforehand, and in a sense, to possess it. Nothing like that ever happens in a factory. From the moment one is clocked in to the time one is clocked out, one must be ready at any instant to take an order. Like an inert object that anyone may move about at will. If one is at work on a part that is to take another two hours, it is impossible to think ahead to the third hour without thought having to make a detour that constrains it to pass by way of the Boss' unpredictable will . . . without being forcibly reminded that the Boss' orders are all that matter. If ten parts per minute are made, the same thing applies to the five minutes following. This is so even if one expects no new order to supervene; since orders are now the sole factor making for variety, to eliminate them in thought is to condemn oneself to imagining an unbroken succession of ever-identical movements, to visualizing monotonous desert regions of experience that thought has no way of exploring. It is true that a thousand petty incidents may people this desert, but no matter how interesting one may suppose them to be at the moment they occur, they cannot form part of a mental representation of the future. If thought seeks to sidestep that monotony by imagining a change—namely, an unexpected order—it can effect its passage from present time to futurity only by way of a new humiliation. Thus, thought draws back from the future. This perpetual recoil upon the present produces a kind of brutish stupor. The only future that thought can bear to contemplate, and beyond which it is powerless to reach out, is that stretch of futurity that separates the present moment from the conclusion of the work in progress—even here, we are assuming that one is fully and emotionally engaged to begin with, and that he has the good luck of working on a project of some duration. There are moments when work is absorbing enough for thought to occupy itself within the limits just set forth. Then unhappiness, suffering comes to a cessation. But in the evening, once outside the plant, and especially in the morning when one's steps are bent toward the place of work and its time-clock, it is dismal to turn one's thoughts to the day's work looming up just ahead. And Sunday evenings! when the prospect that presents itself to mind is not one day but a whole week of such days, futurity becomes something so terribly bleak, so tremendously overwhelming that thought can only slink back trembling to its lair.

The monotony of a day in a factory, even if unbroken by a change of work, is mingled with a thousand little incidents that stud each working-day and make of it something new, in a sense. But, as in the case of changes of work, such incidents are only too often more wounding than comforting. They seem always to involve some diminution of earnings in the case of piece-work, and are hence distinctly unwelcome. But often they are intrinsically wounding. The pervasive anxiety—the anxiety of not working fast enough—that is diffused through every working moment becomes concentrated at such moments, and when, as is often the case, one has to turn to someone else in order to get on with his work, someone like a foreman, a warehouse keeper, a straw-boss, the feeling of dependency, of impotence, of counting for nothing in the eyes of those upon whom he is dependent, can become painful to the point of making a man cry. The continual possibility of such incidents—a stalled machine, an elusive toolbox, and so on—far from diminishing the weight of the monotony, deprives it of the very remedy that it generally carries within itself, namely the power of hushing and lulling the mind to a point where it may become insensitive to pain. Anxiety thwarts this lulling effect and obliges one to the awareness of monotony, though it is intolerable to be aware of it. Nothing is worse than a mixture of monotony and accident. They are mutually aggravating, at least when accident is bound up with anxiety. In a factory, accident *is* a source of anxiety, for the very reason that accident has no status there; theoretically, though everybody knows that such is not the case, the crates for the finished parts are never missing, the foreman never keeps one in suspense, and every slowing down of production is the worker's fault. Thought is obliged to remain in constant readiness not only to follow the monotonous progress of movements indefinitely repeated, but to find within itself resources to cope with the unexpected. Such an obligation is contradictory, impossible, and exhausting. Body may often be exhausted evenings upon leaving the factory, but mind is more so and invariably so. Whoever has experienced this exhaustion—and remembers it—may read it in the eyes of nearly all the workingmen filing out of a plant. How one would like, alone with his time-card, to check in his soul upon entering the plant, and then check it out intact at quitting time! But the reverse takes place. One takes it into the plant where it undergoes its ordeal; evenings, drained by exhaustion, it can do nothing with its hours of leisure.

It is true that certain incidents in the course of work do cause joy, even when diminishing earnings. To begin with, there are the cases, unfortunately rare, when a treasured testimony of comradeship is received. Then there are those in which one successfully overcomes some difficulty through unaided effort. When wits are exercised, devices tried, obstacles cunningly eliminated, one's mind is occupied with a future that depends only on oneself.

The more the work throws up such difficulties, the more the heart is lifted. But this joy remains incomplete for want of men, whether companions or superiors, to judge and appreciate what has been successfully overcome. One's superiors and the associates working at other operations on the same product are almost always exclusively interested in the products themselves, not in the difficulties overcome. Such indifference is a privation of that human warmth which will always be in some degree necessary. Even the man least desirous of gratifying self-pride feels too much alone in a setting where it is understood that people are interested only in what has been accomplished, never in the ways and means leading up to that accomplishment. Thereby, the joys of work are relegated to the plane of unformulated feelings, impressions, that vanish as swiftly as they come to birth. The comradeship of workingmen, never moving to some positive crystallization, remains but an unshapen, weakened volition, a mere velleity; and the superiors are not men guiding and directing other men, but the organs of an impersonal subordination, cold and brutal as steel. It is true that in this relationship of subordination, the Boss' person may intervene, but always in the form of something capricious. Caprice and impersonal brutality, far from tempering each other, are as reciprocally aggravating as monotony and accident.

In our day it is not only in shops, markets, and exchanges, then, that the products of labor are prized to the exclusion of the labor that created them. To repeat, the same is true of the modern factory, at least at the worker level. Cooperation, understanding, mutual appreciation, bound up with the work, are the monopoly of the higher spheres. At the worker level, the relations established among various jobs and functions are relationships between things, not men. The parts circulate with labels bearing their name, material, and degree of elaboration; one could almost believe that they are the persons, and the workers the interchangeable parts. The parts have their identity card tantamount to a description of civil condition; and when it is necessary, as in certain large factories, to show one's card with the photograph bearing, convict-like, a number on the breast, the symbolic contrast becomes poignant.

Things play the role of men, men the role of things. There lies the root of the evil. There are many different jobs in a factory. The fitter in a machine-shop, who, for instance, makes press matrices, those marvels of ingenuity that are long in the fashioning and ever-varying —he loses nothing working in a factory. But that is a rare instance.

On the other hand, legion are those in the large factories and even in many small ones who execute at high speed, in a specified order, five or six simple movements, indefinitely repeated, each lasting a second or thereabouts, with no other respite than an occasional anxious chase after a crate, an engineer, or whatever—until the exact second when a foreman comes up to move them like so many objects to another machine where they remain until moved again. They are as much things as it is possible for a human creature to be, but things that are not licensed to put their consciousness into abeyance, for they must remain ever alert to confront the unexpected. The succession of

their movements is not designated in factory parlance by the word
'rhythm,' but by 'cadence.' This is only right, for that succession is the
contrary of rhythm. Any series of movements that participates of the
beautiful and is accomplished with no loss of dignity, implies moments
of pause, as short-lived as lightning flashes, but that are the very stuff
of rhythm and give the beholder, even across extremes of rapidity,
the impression of leisureliness. The footracer, at the moment of
beating the world's record, seems to glide home slowly while one
watches his inferior rivals making haste behind him. The better and
the more swiftly a peasant swings his scythe the more the onlookers
have the impression that, as the invariable phrase goes, he is taking his
time. On the other hand, the spectacle presented by men over machines is nearly always one of wretched haste destitute of all grace
and dignity. It comes natural to a man, and it befits him, to pause on
having finished something, if only for an instant, in order to contemplate his handiwork, as God did in Genesis. Those lightning moments
of thought, of immobility and equilibrium, one has to learn to eliminate utterly in a working-day at the factory. Manual operations upon
machines can attain the required cadence only if those second-long
movements follow one another uninterruptedly in something like the
tick-tock succession of a timepiece, with nothing to mark the end of
something concluded and something about to begin. This tick-tock,
the barren monotony of which is scarcely bearable to human ears
over any length of time, workingmen are obliged to reproduce with
their bodies. So uninterrupted a succession tends to plunge one into a
kind of sleep, yet it must be borne without falling asleep. The question here is not merely one of physical travail; if physical distress were
all that resulted, the evil would be a relatively minor one. Every
human enterprise demands a motive to furnish the necessary energy to
bring it to completion; and it is good or bad according as the motive is
high or low. To sink to the exhausting passivity that a factory demands,
the motive has to be found within oneself, for there are no whips and
chains; whips and chains would conceivably make the change-over
easier. The very conditions of the work exclude the intervention of all
motivations except those of the fear of being 'bawled out' or fired, of
the eagerness to fatten one's pay envelope, and, in some cases, an interest in speed records. Everything concurs to recall these motivations

to thought and to transform them into obsessions. Nothing higher is ever appealed to. Moreover they must become obsessive to achieve the necessary efficacy. At the same time that these motives occupy one's spirit, thought withdraws to a fixed point in time in order to avert suffering, and consciousness dims itself as much as the demands of the work will allow. An almost irresistible force, comparable to that of gravity, precludes any feeling for the presence of other human beings laboring away nearby. It is next to impossible not to become as indifferent or brutal as the system in which one is caught; and reciprocally, the brutality of the system is reflected and made obvious by the gestures, looks, words of those about one. After a day thus spent, the workingman has but one plaint, a plaint that cannot reach the ears of men who have never known this condition, and which would not speak to them if it did: *I thought the day would never end.*

Time drags for him and he lives in a perpetual exile. He spends his day in a place where he cannot feel at home. The machines and the parts to be turned and machined are very much at home, and, to repeat, he is given admittance only that he may bring these machines, these parts together. *They* are the objects of solicitude, not he; though, perversely enough, there are occasions when too much attention is directed to him and not enough to them. It is no rarity to see a foreman or straw-boss busy harassing working men and women, watching to see that they do not raise their faces even for the time necessary to exchange a glance, while mounds of iron-work are left to rust away in the corner of some yard. Nothing could be more bitter. But whether the plant is protected or not against waste, the workingman is made to feel that he is an alien. Nothing is more impelling in a man than the need to appropriate, not materially or juridically, but in thought, the places and objects amidst which he passes his life. A cook says, "My kitchen," a gardener, "My lawn," and this is as it should be. Juridical proprietorship is but one of the means to achieve such a feeling. *The perfect social organization would be one which, by that and other means, would give a proprietary feeling to all men.* A workingman, with rare exceptions, cannot, by thought, appropriate anything in a factory. The machines do not belong to him in any sense. He serves one or the other of them according to the latest order received. He serves them, he does not make them serve him.

They are not for him a means of turning a piece of metal to a specified form; he is for them a means whereby they will be fed the parts for an operation whose relationship to the ones preceding and the ones following remains an impenetrable mystery to him.

The parts have their history; they have passed from one stage of development to another. But he counts for nothing in that history, he has not left his mark upon it, he knows nothing of what has gone on. Were he to manifest any curiosity, it would be speedily discouraged; in any case, the same muffled and permanent dread that inhibits his thought from travelling through time also keeps it from wandering through the plant and fixes it to a point in space. The workingman does not know what he produces and consequently, he experiences the sensation, not of having produced, but of having been drained dry. In the plant he expends—occasionally to the uttermost—what is best in him, his capacity to think, feel, be moved. He squanders it all, since he leaves the plant emptied; and yet he has put nothing of himself in his work, neither thought, feelings, nor even, save in a feeble measure, movements determined by him, ordered to some end. His very life slowly ebbs from him without having left a trace behind him. The factory may create useful objects, but they are not for him; and the pay that, sheep-like, he stands in line for every fortnight, that pay impossible to calculate beforehand in the case of piece-work owing to the arbitrary, complicated accounting procedures that it involves, comes to seem more a charitable handout than the price of his hire. The workingman, though indispensable in the productive process, is accounted as practically nothing in it, which is why each physical annoyance needlessly imposed, each show of lack of respect, each brutality, each humiliation, however trivial, appears as a fresh reminder of his alien status. One can actually see women waiting ten minutes outside a plant under a driving rain, across from an open door through which their bosses are passing. They are working women and they will not enter until the whistle has blown. That door is more alien to them than that of any strange house, which they would enter quite naturally if seeking cover. No intimacy binds workingmen to the places and objects amidst which their lives are used up. Wage and other social demands had less to do with the sit-down strikes of '36 than the need to feel at home in the factories at least once in their lives. Society must be corrupted to its very core when workingmen can feel at home in a plant only during a strike, and utter aliens during working hours—when by every dictate of common sense the exact contrary ought to prevail. As long as workingmen are homeless in their own places of work, they will never truly feel at home in their country, never be responsible members of society.

It seems unreasonable to expect credence when one is but setting down impressions. Yet there is no other way of describing a *human* misery. Misery, after all, is made up of impressions. As long as it is possible to live at all, material circumstances of living do not in themselves necessarily account for unhappiness; for the same material circumstances bound up with other feelings could make for happiness. It is the feelings bound up with the circumstances of living then, that make one happy or unhappy; but these feelings are not arbitrarily determined. They are not put over or effaced by suggestion. They can be changed only by a radical transformation of the circumstances themselves. But to change circumstances, they must first be known. Nothing is more difficult to know than the nature of unhappiness; a residue of mystery will always cling to it. For, following the Greek proverb, it is dumb. To seize its exact shadings and causes presupposes an aptitude for inward analysis which is not characteristic of the unhappy. Even if that aptitude existed in this or that individual, unhappiness itself would balk such an activity of thought. Humiliation always has for its effect the creation of forbidden zones where thought may not venture and which are shrouded by silence or illusion. When the unhappy complain, they almost always complain in superficial terms, without voicing the nature of their true discontent; moreover, in cases of profound and permanent unhappiness, a strongly developed sense of shame arrests all lamentation. Thus, every unhappy condition among men creates the silent zone alluded to, in which each is isolated as though on an island. Those who do escape from the island will not look back. The exceptions turn out almost always to be more apparent than real. For instance, the same distance, despite contrary appearances, separates workingmen from the worker turned employer as separates them from the worker become a professional militant.

If someone, come from the outside, penetrates to one of these

islands and subjects himself of his own free will to the unhappiness
in question for a limited time, but still long enough to be penetrated
by it, and if he then relates what he has experienced, the value of his
testimony will be at once called into question. It will be said that
what he experienced was necessarily different from what is felt by
those permanently immured in unhappiness. All this is true enough,
if we suppose that such a person has merely given himself over to
introspection; or if he has merely observed. But if, having lost the
very memory of having come from elsewhere, he yet returns elsewhere, as though on a vacation, and begins to compare what he himself has experienced to what he reads in the faces, eyes, gestures,
postures, words, in trivial and important events, a feeling of certainty
within him is created—difficult to communicate, unfortunately.

The faces drawn with anxiety over the day about to begin, the
dejected looks in the morning subway-trains; the profound weariness,
spiritual rather than physical, reflected in the general bearing, the
expression, the set of the mouth, at quitting-time; the looks and attitudes of caged beasts, after the ten-day closing when a factory re-
opens its doors as the signal for the beginning of another interminable
year; the pervasive brutality; the importance almost every one attaches to details trivial in themselves but distressing as symbols, such
as the matter of identification cards; the pitiful boasts bandied about
by the crowds at the entrances to hiring halls, boasts which express
so many real humiliations; the incredibly poignant words that sometimes escape, inadvertently, the lips of men and women who had
seemed to be just like all the rest; the hatred and loathing of the
factory, of the place of work, often evidenced in words and acts,
a loathing that casts its shadow over any possible comradeship and
impels working men and women, once they have cleared the factory
exit, to hasten separately to their respective homes, with scarcely a
greeting exchanged; the joy during the sit-down strikes, of possessing
the factory in thought, of exploring its several parts, the completely
new pride in showing it to their loved ones and of pointing out their
work stations—a fleeting joy and pride that expressed, by contrast,
in so poignant a manner the permanent suffering of minds nailed
down to a point in time; all the emotional tides of workfolk, so mysterious to onlookers, in reality so easy to seize; how not trust to

these signs, when at the very moment he reads them about him, he experiences within him the feelings corresponding to those signs?

The factory ought to be a place where, for all the inevitability of physical and spiritual travail, working people can taste joy and nourish themselves on it. But for this to happen, things would have to be changed, considerably in some respects, only moderately in others. All systems of social reform or transformation seem to miss the point. Were they to be realized, the evil would be left intact. They look to changes that are either too sweeping or too superficial. They would change too little what underlies the evil, too much the circumstances that are not its cause. Some promise a ridiculously exaggerated reduction of the work-day. But the conversion of a people into a swarm of idlers, who for two hours a day would be slaves, is neither desirable nor morally possible, if materially so. No one would accept two daily hours of slavery. To be accepted, slavery must be of such a daily duration as to break something in a man. If there is a possible remedy, it is of a different order, less easily conceivable. It is one requiring an inventive effort. It is necessary to transform incentives, to reduce or abolish what makes for disgust with one's work, to transform the relation of worker to factory, of worker to machine, and to make possible a radically changed awareness of the passing of time while working.

It is desirable neither that the prospect of unemployment should be a nightmare without issue nor that work should mean a flood of cheap pseudo-luxuries that excite desires without satisfying needs. These are scarcely contestable points. But the conclusion to be drawn is that both acquisitiveness and the fear of dismissal must cease to be the main incentives ever in the foreground of a workingman's mind and be relegated to their natural status as secondary incentives. Their place in the foreground must be taken by other incentives.

In all work one of the most powerful incentives is the feeling of an end to be accomplished and a job to be done. In a factory, especially in the operation of machines, this incentive is often completely absent. When, for the thousandth time, a worker brings a part into contact with a machine tool, he finds himself—aside from the fatigue of it—in the position of a child who has been put to stringing pearls in order to keep him out of mischief. The child obeys because he dreads punishment and looks forward to a piece of candy, but the only meaning he can find in his activity is conformity to an order given by someone who has authority over him. The case would be otherwise if a workingman knew clearly, from day to day, moment to moment, just what part he was playing in every step of the productive process and what place the factory occupied in society. If a workingman's job is to drop a die punch on a piece of brass destined for some device in a subway, he ought to know it. Moreover he ought to have a clear-cut image of the place and function of that piece of brass on the subway line, what operations it has already undergone and which ones are to follow before being put into place. The plea here is not, of course, for a lecture to each worker at the beginning of each piece of work. What is possible is such things as having each work group occasionally explore the plant by turns for several hours, at the usual wages, all to the accompaniment of appropriate explanations. Even better would be to allow each worker to bring his family along. And why not? Is it natural that a woman should never be allowed a glimpse of the establishment where her husband daily expends his best energies? A workingman truly wedded to his job would be proud and happy to show his place of work to his wife and children. It would also be fitting to let every workingman see from time to time the finished article in whose manufacture he has had a part, however modest, and that he should grasp exactly what his part in it was. The problem is naturally varying for each factory, each process, but it is possible to find, according to particular circumstances, an infinite variety of methods to stimulate and satisfy a workingman's curiosity concerning his work. The demands on imagination are not too exacting, once the end is clearly conceived, which is that of rending the veil that money interposes between a workingman and his work. Workingmen believe with that kind of belief not precisely expressible in words—and which thus expressed would seem absurd—that their labor is converted into money of which a small part comes back to them and the lion's share goes to the Boss. They should find it possible to understand not with that superficial layer of intelligence that we apply to self-evident truths—they already have that kind of understanding—but with all their body and soul, so to speak, that through all their travail they are creating objects called up by the needs of society, and that they have a real if finite right to be proud of them.

It is true that as long as they are limited over long periods of time to repeating identical sequences of five or six simple movements, they cannot be said really to be manufacturing objects. As long as this is true, there will always be an abased and malevolent proletariat at the heart of society, whatever else is done. True that certain mentally arrested human types are naturally apt for this kind of work. But it is not true that their number equals the number of men who now work that way—far from it. After all, out of one hundred children born into middle-class families the proportion of these, once they have become adults, that are engaged in purely routine tasks is far lower than in the case of one hundred children born into working families; yet the distribution of aptitudes is on an average probably the same. The remedy is not hard to come upon, at least in periods when metal is normally available. Whenever an operation calls for these repeated sequences of a small number of simple movements, an automatic machine should perform them—this without exception. Men are preferably used now because they are machines that can obey a voice, and it suffices to receive an order for them swiftly to substitute a certain combination of movements for another. But there are automatic multiple function machines that can also be shifted from one process to another by substituting one cam for another. This kind of machine is still a novelty and hence incompletely developed. But no one can foresee to what point of perfection it may be brought, if the trouble is taken to develop it. Things still called machines might then make their appearance, but which, from the point of view of the man who works, would be the diametric opposite of most machines now in use. It often happens that the same word may conceal opposite realities. A specialized machine worker now has for his share in a manufacturing process only the automatic repetition of certain movements, whereas to the machine that he serves goes the whole share, stamped and crystallized in its metal, of synthesis and intelligence that an assembly-line process may imply. Such a reversal is unnatural, criminal. But if a person had for his task the regulation of an automatic machine and the contriving of the cams appropriate to the varying parts to be turned or machined, he would assume, on the one hand, his share of the synthetic and intellective efforts required, and on the other, a manual effort involving, like that of the artisan, real skill. Such a relationship between man and machine would be entirely satisfactory.

Time and rhythm constitute the most important factor of the whole problem of work. Certainly it is not the work itself that is at issue. It is at once inevitable and fitting that work should involve monotony and tedium; indeed, what considerable earthly undertakings in whatever domain have ever been free of tedium and monotony? There is more monotony in a Gregorian Chant or a Bach Concerto than in an operetta. This world into which we are cast *does* exist; we are truly flesh and blood; we have been thrown out of eternity; and we are indeed obliged to journey painfully through time, minute in and minute out. This travail is our lot, and the monotony of work is but one of the forms that it assumes. But it remains not the less true that our thought was intended to master time, and this vocation, for such it is, must be kept inviolate in every man. The absolutely uniform and at the same time varied and continually surprising succession of our days and seasons are exactly conformable to our misery and our grandeur. Everything that is in some degree beautiful and good reproduces in some way this mixture of uniformity and variety; everything that does not is bad and degrading. The peasant's toil is necessarily obedient to the world's rhythm. The workingman's labor is, by its very nature, relatively independent of it, but it could approximate it. What actually happens in a factory is that uniformity and variety are mingled all right, but the mixture is scarcely that achieved by the sun and the stars, to pursue our cosmic instance. For the sun and the stars, time is filled beforehand with a framework of ordered and limited variety having regular recurrences. This framework may lodge an infinite variety of events that are absolutely unforeseeable and partially innocent of order. The futurity of one working in a factory, on the other hand, is empty because of its absolute unforeseeableness, and deader than the past because of the identity of the moments, which succeed one another like the ticking of the clock. A uniformity that imitates the movements of a clock, not that of the constellations, a variety that recognizes no rule and consequently excludes all possibility of foreknowledge, make for a time that is uninhabitable and irrespirable to man.

The transformation of the machine can alone keep work time from aping clock time. But even this is not enough. The future must be opened up for the workingman through removal of the blinders that keep him from exercising his sense of foresight. Only then may he experience the feeling of advancing on the plane of time, of moving with each effort toward a specific end. As things stand, the effort he is called upon to make, at the moment, leads him nowhere, unless to the hour of quitting-time; and since one working day gives rise to another, no more than that, the achieved end in question is nothing less than a form of death. He has no way of visualizing achievement except under the form of wages, especially in the case of piece-work, which bends him to an obsession with money. Throwing the future open to workingmen in the sense of making it possible for them to envisage it, is a problem the formulation of which must vary from case to case. Seen generally, the solution of the problem implies not only a certain knowledge on the part of each worker of the functioning of the factory as a whole, but an organization of the factory that makes for some kind of autonomy of each shop unit in relation to the whole establishment, of each worker in relation to his shop. As for immediate perspectives, each workingman ought to know more or less what will be expected of him a week or a fortnight in advance, and even have some say-so in the order of performance of various tasks. As for remoter perspectives, he ought to be in a position to stake them out, certainly not as far ahead or as accurately as those directing the plant, yet in a manner somehow analogous. Even though nothing might accrue to his actual rights, he would experience that feeling of proprietorship for which a man's heart thirsts and which, without eliminating the fact of pain, abolishes disgust with his lot.

Such reforms are difficult and some circumstances peculiar to the present time do not diminish the difficulty. On the other hand, it may turn out that suffering was the indispensable condition for a feeling that something had to be changed. The main obstacles remain the moral ones. It is difficult to vanquish fear and contempt. Workingmen, certainly many of them, have become well-nigh incurably bitter after so many thousands of wounding pin-pricks and affronts, so much so that they instinctively view as a snare everything proposed from above, especially by their employers. This morbid distrust, which could render hopeless any effort at amelioration, cannot be overcome without patience and perseverance. Many employers fear that any effort at reform, however mild, would be but a new weapon in the hands of militant leaders to whom they attribute all social evils without exception and whom they picture in some way as mythological monsters. It goes against their grain to admit that workingmen may have certain moral qualities, now given no outlet, that could work toward social stability, if only the proper incentives were allowed to take their course. Even if they were convinced of the utility of social reforms, they would hang back through an exaggerated feeling of solicitude for trade secrets. Yet experience should have taught them by now that the mute bitterness and hostility deeply rooted in a workingman's heart must be far more dangerous than a competitor's inquisitiveness. For the rest, the effort to be made concerns not only employers and workingmen, but society at large. The school, notably. It must be conceived in an entirely new way, that it may shape men capable of understanding the total aspects of the work in which they will be taking part. Not that the level of theoretic studies must be lowered; rather, the contrary. More should be done to excite intelligence to wakefulness, but at the same time teaching must itself become more concrete.

The evil whose cure is here proposed concerns all society. No society can be stable in which a whole stratum of the population labors daily with a heart-felt loathing. This loathing for their work colors their whole view of life all their life. The humiliation that accompanies each of their efforts seeks its compensation in a kind of spirit of working-class imperialism, nurtured by the propagandas issuing from Marxism. Were a bolt-maker to experience a legitimate and limited pride in the making of bolts, there could be no question of infusing him with a factitious, unlimited pride by holding before him the thought that his class is destined to make and dominate history. Similar considerations are applicable to private life, notably family life and relations between the sexes. The dreary exhaustion from factory work leaves a gaping void that clamors to be filled. It can be filled only by rapid, violent gratifications the resulting corruption of which is contagious for all classes of society. The correlation is not immediately obvious, but it does exist. The family can expect no consideration among the people of this country as long as a part of that people continue to work in loathing and disgust.

Our factories have become festering-grounds of evil, and the evil of the factories must be corrected. It is difficult, but perhaps not impossible. It is high time that specialists, engineers, and others concerned, should be exercised not only to make objects, but also not to destroy men. Not to render them docile, nor even to make them happy, but quite simply not to force them to abase themselves.

LETTER TO
GEORGES BERNANOS

Little is in print concerning Simone Weil's brief experience in the Spanish Civil War. In supplying details of that experience, her letter of reminiscence to Georges Bernanos, the novelist and philosopher, is especially valuable. Her role in the struggle was brought to an end when, while cooking at the front, she spilled boiling oil over her left leg. Initially sympathetic to the anarchist movement, she seemed bound, not unlike George Orwell, to undergo disillusion and disaffection.

[*1938*]

MONSIEUR,

However silly it may be to write to an author, since his profession must always involve him in a flood of correspondence, I cannot refrain from doing so after having read *Les Grands cimetières sous la lune*. Not that it is the first book of yours to touch me. The *Journal d'un curé de campagne* is in my opinion the best of them, at least of those I have read, and really a great book. But the fact that I have liked other books of yours gave me no reason for intruding upon you to say so. This last one, however, is a different matter. I have had an experience which corresponds to yours, although it was

73

much shorter and was less profound; and although it was apparently
—but only apparently—embraced in a different spirit.

I am not a Catholic, although—and this must no doubt appear
presumptuous to any Catholic, coming from a non-Catholic—nothing
that is Catholic, nothing that is Christian, has ever seemed alien to
me. I have sometimes told myself that if only there were a notice
on church doors forbidding entry to anyone with an income above
a certain figure, and a low one, I would be converted at once. From
my childhood onwards I sympathized with those organizations which
spring from the lowest and least regarded social strata, until the time
when I realized that such organizations are of a kind to discourage
all sympathy. The last one in which I felt some confidence was the
Spanish C.N.T. I had travelled a little in Spain before the civil war;
only a little, but enough to feel the affection which it is hard not
to feel for the Spanish people. I had seen the anarchist movement as
the natural expression of that people's greatness and of its flaws, of
its worthiest aspirations and of its unworthiest. The C.N.T. and F.A.I.
were an extraordinary mixture, to which anybody at all was admitted
and in which, consequently, one found immorality, cynicism, fanaticism and cruelty, but also love and fraternal spirit and, above all, that
concern for honour which is so beautiful in the humiliated. It seemed
to me that the idealists preponderated over the elements of violence
and disorder. In July, 1936, I was in Paris. I do not love war; but
what has always seemed to me most horrible in war is the position of
those in the rear. When I realized that, try as I would, I could not
prevent myself from participating morally in that war—in other words,
from hoping all day and every day for the victory of one side and the
defeat of the other—I decided that, for me, Paris was the rear and I
took the train to Barcelona, with the intention of enlisting. This was at
the beginning of August 1936.

My stay in Spain was brought to a compulsory end by an accident. I was a few days in Barcelona, and then in the remote Aragonese
countryside on the banks of the Ebro, about ten miles from Saragossa,
at the very place where the river was recently crossed by Yagüe's
troops; then I was at Sitges, in the palace converted into a hospital,
and then again in Barcelona. A stay of about two months in all.
I left Spain against my will and with the intention of returning; but

later I decided voluntarily not to do so. I no longer felt any inner compulsion to participate in a war which, instead of being what it had appeared when it began—a war of famished peasants against landed proprietors and their clerical supporters—had become a war between Russia on the one hand and Germany and Italy on the other.

I recognize the smell of civil war, the smell of blood and terror, which exhales from your book; I have breathed it too. I must admit that I neither saw nor heard of anything which quite equalled the ignominy of certain facts you relate, such as the murders of elderly peasants or the *Ballillas* chasing old people and beating them with truncheons. But for all that, I heard quite enough. I was very nearly present at the execution of a priest. In the minutes of suspense I was asking myself whether I should simply look on or whether I should try to intervene and get myself shot as well. I still don't know which I would have done if a lucky chance had not prevented the execution.

So many incidents come crowding . . . but they would take too long to tell; and to what purpose? Let one suffice. I was at Sitges when the militiamen returned, defeated, from the expedition to Majorca. They had been decimated. Out of forty young boys from Sitges nine were dead, as was learnt when the remaining thirty-one came back. The very next night there were nine revenge operations. In that little town, in which nothing at all had happened in July, they killed nine so-called fascists. Among the nine was a baker, aged about thirty, whose crime, so I was told, was that he had not joined the 'Somaten' militia. His old father, whose only child and only support he was, went mad. One more incident: In a light engagement a small international party of militiamen from various countries captured a boy of fifteen who was a member of the Falange. As soon as he was captured, and still trembling from the sight of his comrades being killed alongside him, he said he had been enrolled compulsorily. He was searched and a medal of the Virgin and a Falange card were found on him. Then he was sent to Durruti, the leader of the column, who lectured him for an hour on the beauties of the anarchist ideal and gave him the choice between death and enrolling immediately in the ranks of his captors, against his comrades of yesterday. Durruti gave this child twenty-four hours to think it over, and when the time was up he said no and was shot. Yet Durruti was in some ways an admirable man. Although I only heard of it afterwards, the death of this little hero has never ceased to weigh on my conscience. Another incident: A village was finally captured by the red militia after having been taken and re-taken over and over again. In the cellars there were found a handful of haggard, terrified, famished creatures and among them three or four young men. The militiamen reasoned as follows: If these young men stayed behind and waited for the fascists the last time we retired from here, it means that they must be fascists too. They therefore shot them immediately, but gave some food to the others and thought themselves very humane. Finally, here is an incident from the rear: Two anarchists once told me how they and some comrades captured two priests. They killed one of them on the spot with a revolver, in front of the other, and then told the survivor that he could go. When he was twenty yards away they shot him down. The man who told me this story was much surprised when I didn't laugh.

At Barcelona an average of fifty people were killed every night in punitive raids. This is proportionately much less than in Majorca because Barcelona is a town of nearly a million inhabitants; moreover, it had been the scene of a three-day battle of sanguinary street-fighting. But statistics are probably not to the point in such a matter. The point is the attitude towards murder. Never once, either among Spaniards or even among the French who were in Spain as combatants or as visitors—the latter being usually dim and harmless intellectuals—never once did I hear anyone express, even in private intimacy, any repulsion or disgust or even disapproval of useless bloodshed. You speak about fear. Yes, it is true that fear played some part in all this butchery; but where I was it did not appear to play the large part that you assign to it. Men who seemed to be brave—there was one at least whose courage I personally witnessed —would retail with cheery fraternal chuckles at convivial meal-times how many priests they had murdered, or how many 'fascists', the latter being a very elastic term. My own feeling was that when once a certain class of people has been placed by the temporal and spiritual authorities outside the ranks of those whose life has value, then nothing comes more naturally to men than murder. As soon as men know that they can kill without fear of punishment or blame, they kill; or at least they encourage killers with approving smiles. If anyone happens to feel a slight distaste to begin with, he keeps quiet and he soon begins to suppress it for fear of seeming unmanly. People get carried away by a sort of intoxication which is irresistible without a fortitude of soul which I am bound to consider exceptional since I have met with it nowhere. On the other hand I met peaceable Frenchmen, for whom I had never before felt contempt and who would never have dreamed of doing any killing themselves, but who savoured that blood-polluted atmosphere with visible pleasure. For them I shall never again be able to feel any esteem.

The very purpose of the whole struggle is soon lost in an atmosphere of this sort. For the purpose can only be defined in terms of the public good, of the welfare of men—and men have become valueless. In a country where the great majority of the poor are peasants the essential aim of every extreme-left party should be an improvement of the peasants' conditions; and perhaps the main issue of this war, at the beginning, was the redistribution of land. But those peasants of Aragon, so poor and so splendid in the pride they have cherished through all their humiliations—one cannot say that they were even an object of curiosity to the militiamen. Although there was no insolence, no injury, no brutality—at least I saw none and I know that theft and rape were capital crimes in the anarchist militias —nevertheless, between the armed forces and the civilian population there was an abyss, exactly like the abyss between the rich and the poor. One felt it in the attitude of the two groups, the one always rather humble, submissive and timid, the other confident, off-hand and condescending.

One sets out as a volunteer, with the idea of sacrifice, and finds oneself in a war which resembles a war of mercenaries, only with much more cruelty and with less human respect for the enemy.

I could say much more on the same lines, but I must limit myself. Having been in Spain, I now continually listen to and read all sorts of observations about Spain, but I could not point to a single person, except you alone, who has been exposed to the atmosphere of the civil war and has resisted it. What do I care that you are a royalist, a disciple of Drumont? You are incomparably nearer to me than my comrades of the Aragon militias—and yet I loved them.

What you say about nationalism, war, and French foreign policy after the war is equally sympathetic to me. I was ten years old at the time of Versailles, and up to then I had been patriotically thrilled as children are in war-time. But the will to humiliate the defeated enemy which revealed itself so loathsomely everywhere at that time (and in the following years) was enough to cure me once for all of that naïve sort of patriotism. I suffer more from the humiliations inflicted by my country than from those inflicted on her.

I am afraid I have bothered you with a very long letter. I will only add an expression of my keen admiration.

s. WEIL

Mlle Simone Weil, 3 rue Auguste-Comte, Paris (VIe)

P.S. I wrote my address automatically. I expect, for one thing, that you have better to do than to answer letters. And in any case I am going to Italy for a month or two and if a letter from you should be forwarded it might be held up somewhere.

WHAT IS A JEW?
A Letter to
a Minister of Education

This letter was written in November 1940. Earlier she had unsuccessfully requested a teaching position. A racist statute instituted by the Vichy government denied the rights of Jews and persons of Jewish descent like Simone Weil. (She was careful not to condemn all those working with Vichy. Since the armistice was "a collective act of cowardice," she believed that the words "traitor," "coward," and "collaborator" should be used guardedly.) The letter provides information on her family background and her own separation from Judaism.

MONSIEUR LE MINISTRE,

In January, 1938, I took a sick leave, which I renewed in July, 1938, for one year, and again for another year in 1939. When my leave expired last July, I asked for a teaching post, preferably in Algeria. My request was not answered. I very much want to know why.

It occurs to me that the new Statute on Jews, which I have read in the press, is perhaps connected with your failure to reply. So I want to know to whom this Statute applies, so that I may be enlightened as to my own standing. I do not know the definition of the word, "Jew"; that subject was not included in my education.

The Statute, it is true, defines a Jew as: "a person who has three or more Jewish grandparents." But this simply carries the difficulty two generations farther back.

Does this word designate a religion? I have never been in a synagogue, and have never witnessed a Jewish religious ceremony. As for my grandparents—I remember that my paternal grandmother used to go to the synagogue, and I think I have heard that my paternal grandfather did so likewise. On the other hand, I know definitely that both my maternal grandparents were free-thinkers. Thus if it is a matter of religion, it would appear that I have only two Jewish grandparents, and so am not a Jew according to the Statute.

But perhaps the word designates a race? In that case, I have no reason to believe that I have any link, maternal or paternal, to the people who inhabited Palestine two thousand years ago. When one reads in Josephus how thoroughly Titus exterminated this race, it seems unlikely that they left many descendants. . . . My father's family, as far back as our memory went, lived in Alsace; no family tradition, so far as I know, said anything about coming there from any other place. My mother's family comes from Slavic lands, and, so far as I know, was composed only of Slavs. But perhaps the Statute must be applied to my grandparents themselves, perhaps we must now investigate whether each of them had less than three Jewish grandparents? I think it may be quite difficult to get reliable information on this point.

Finally, the concept of heredity may be applied to a race, but it is difficult to apply it to a religion. I myself, who professes no religion and never have, have certainly inherited nothing from the Jewish religion. Since I practically learned to read from Racine, Pascal, and other French writers of the 17th century, since my spirit was thus impregnated at an age when I had not even heard talk of "Jews," I would say that if there is a religious tradition which I regard as my patrimony, it is the Catholic tradition.

In short: mine is the Christian, French, Greek tradition. The Hebraic tradition is alien to me, and no Statute can make it otherwise. If, nevertheless, the law insists that I consider the term, "Jew," whose meaning I don't know, as applying to me, I am inclined to submit, as I would to any other law. But I should like to be officially enlightened on this point, since I myself have no criterion by which I may resolve the question.

If the Statute does not apply to me, then I should like to enjoy those rights which I am given by the contract implied in my title of "professor" ("agregée").

SIMONE WEIL

LETTER TO
DÉODAT ROCHÉ

The vanquished twelfth-century civilization of the pays
d'oc, *Catharism (or Albigensianism), greatly appealed to
Simone Weil for its detestation of power and for its spiritual austerity and purity. Its moral doctrine recommended
a form of suicide by starvation, which Simone Weil herself chose to follow. In Catharism, which the Church
designated as heretical, she saw the embodiment of Christian Platonism—"the last living expression in Europe of
pre-Roman antiquity," as she phrases it in the following
letter.*

23 January 1940 [sic, *for 1941*]

I have read at Ballard's your article for the Oc number, 'The Cathars
and Spiritual Love'. Thanks to Ballard I had previously read your
paper on Catharism. These two pieces have made a strong impression
on me.

I have long been greatly attracted to the Cathars, although knowing little about them. One of the chief reasons for this attraction is
their opinion about the Old Testament, which you express so well
in your article when you say so truly that the worship of power

caused the Hebrews to lose the idea of good and evil. I have always been kept away from Christianity by its ranking these stories, so full of pitiless cruelty, as sacred texts; and the more so because for twenty centuries these stories have never ceased to influence all the currents of Christian thought—at least if one means by Christianity the churches so denominated today. St. Francis of Assisi himself, who was as clear of this taint as it is possible to be, founded an Order which quickly began to participate in murder and massacre almost immediately after it was formed. I have never been able to understand how it is possible for a reasonable mind to regard the Jehovah of the Bible and the Father who is invoked in the Gospel as one and the same being. The influence of the Old Testament and of the Roman Empire, whose tradition was continued by the Papacy, are to my mind the two essential sources of the corruption of Christianity.

Your studies have confirmed a thought of mine which I already had before reading them. It is that Catharism was the last living expression in Europe of pre-Roman antiquity. I believe that before the conquests of Rome the countries of the Mediterranean and the Near East formed a civilization, which was not homogeneous because it varied greatly from one country to another, but was continuous; and I believe that one and the same thought inhabited all its best minds and was expressed in various forms in the mysteries and the initiatory sects of Egypt, Thrace, Greece, and Persia, and that the works of Plato are the most perfect written expression which we possess of that thought. The scarcity of texts makes it, of course, impossible to prove this opinion. But one indication among others is the fact that Plato himself always presents his doctrine as issuing from an ancient tradition, but without ever stating its country of origin. The simplest explanation, in my opinion, is that the philosophical and religious traditions of the countries he knew were merged in one single stream of thought. It is from this thought that Christianity issued; but only the Gnostics, Manichaeans, and Cathars seem to have kept really faithful to it. They alone really escaped the coarseness of mind and baseness of heart which were disseminated over vast territories by the Roman domination and which still, today, compose the atmosphere of Europe.

There is something more in the Manichaeans than in antiquity, or at least than in antiquity as known to us; there are some magnificent conceptions, such as the descent of divinity among men and the rending of the spirit and its dispersal throughout matter. But what above all makes the fact of Catharism a sort of miracle is that it was a religion and not simply a philosophy. I mean that around Toulouse in the 12th century the highest thought dwelt within a whole human environment and not only in the minds of a certain number of individuals. That, it seems to me, is the sole difference between philosophy and religion, so long as religion is something not dogmatic.

No thought attains to its fullest existence unless it is incarnated in a human environment, and by environment I mean something open to the world around, something which is steeped in the surrounding society and is in contact with the whole of it, and not simply a closed circle of disciples around a master. For the lack of such an environment in which to breathe, a superior mind makes a philosophy for itself; but that is a second best and it produces thought of a lesser degree of reality. Probably there was an environment for the Pythagoreans, but this is a subject about which we have practically no knowledge. In Plato's time there was no longer anything of the sort; and one feels continually in his work his regret for the absence of such an environment, a nostalgic regret.

Excuse these rambling reflections; I only wanted you to see that my interest in the Cathars is not a matter of simple historical curiosity, or even of simple intellectual curiosity. It gave me joy to read in your article that Catharism may be regarded as a Christian Pythagoreanism or Platonism; for in my eyes there is nothing above Plato. Simple intellectual curiosity cannot give one contact with the thought of Pythagoras and Plato, because in regard to thought of that kind knowledge and adhesion are one single act of the mind. I believe it is the same as regards the Cathars.

Never has the revival of this kind of thought been so necessary as today. We are living at a time when most people feel, confusedly but keenly, that what was called enlightenment in the 18th century, including the sciences, provides an insufficient spiritual diet; but this feeling is now leading humanity into the darkest paths. There is an urgent need to refer back to those great epochs which favoured the kind of spiritual life of which all that is most precious in science and art is no more than a somewhat imperfect reflection.

That is why I so anxiously hope that your studies of Catharism will arouse the widespread public attention they deserve. But studies of such a theme, however good, cannot suffice. If only you could find a publisher, a collection of original texts, presented intelligibly to the public, would be infinitely desirable. . . .

LETTER TO
JOË BOUSQUET

Written in a period of intense spiritual contemplation, this letter gives a short personal history of Simone Weil's religious thought. In it she talks about her central ideas of affliction, of love, of the effort of attention; what she says about the mystical dimension of her religious experiences is highly revealing. The consummateness, the sincerity, and the courage of her faith radiate in what she writes here.

[*Marseille*] *12 May 1942*

CHER AMI,

First of all, thank you for what you have just done for me. If your letter is effective, as I hope, you will have done it, not for me but for others through me, for your younger brothers who should be infinitely dear to you since the same fate has struck them. Perhaps some of them will owe to you, just before the moment of death, the solace of an exchange of sympathy.

You are specially privileged in that the present state of the world is a reality for you. Perhaps even more so than for those who at this moment are killing and dying, wounding and being wounded, because they are taken unawares, without knowing where they are or what is happening to them; and, like you in your time, they are unable to think thoughts appropriate to their situation. As for the others, the people here for example, what is happening is a confused nightmare for some of them, though very few, and for the majority it is a vague background like a theatrical drop-scene. In either case it is unreal.

But you, on the other hand, for twenty years you have been repeating in thought that destiny which seized and then released so many men, but which seized you permanently; and which now returns again to seize millions of men. You, I repeat, are now really equipped to think it. Or if you are still not quite ready—as I think you are not—you have at least only a thin shell to break before emerging from the darkness inside the egg into the light of truth. It is a very ancient image. The egg is this world we see. The bird in it is Love, the Love which is God himself and which lives in the depths of every man, though at first as an invisible seed. When the shell is broken and the being is released, it still has this same world before it. But it is no longer inside. Space is opened and torn apart. The spirit, leaving the miserable body in some corner, is transported to a point outside space, which is not a point of view, which has no perspective, but from which this world is seen as it is, unconfused by perspective. Compared to what it is inside the egg, space has become an infinity to the second or rather the third power. The moment stands still. The whole of space is filled, even though sounds can be heard, with a dense silence which is not an absence of sound but is a positive object of sensation; it is the secret word, the word of Love who holds us in his arms from the beginning.

You, when once you have emerged from the shell, will know the reality of war, which is the most precious reality to know because war is unreality itself. To know the reality of war is the Pythagorean harmony, the unity of opposites; it is the plenitude of knowledge of the real. That is why you are infinitely privileged, because you have war permanently lodged in your body, waiting for years in patient fidelity until you are ripe to know it. Those who fell beside you did not have time to collect their thought from its frivolous wandering and focus it upon their destiny. And those who came back un-wounded have all killed their past by oblivion, even if they have seemed to remember it, because war is affliction and it is as easy to direct one's thought voluntarily towards affliction as it would be to persuade an untrained dog to walk into a fire and let itself be burnt. To think affliction, it is necessary to bear it in one's flesh, driven very far in like a nail, and for a long time, so that thought may have time to grow strong enough to regard it. To regard it from outside, having succeeded in leaving the body and even, in a sense, the soul as well. Body and soul remain not only pierced through but nailed down at a fixed point. Whether or not affliction imposes literal immobility, there is always enforced immobility in this sense that a part of the soul is always steeped, monotonously, incessantly, and inextricably, in pain. Thanks to this immobility the infinitesimal seed of divine love placed in the soul can slowly grow and bear fruit in patience—ἐν ὑπομενῇ is the divinely beautiful Gospel expression. Translators say *in patientia,* but ὑπομένειν is quite another thing. It means to remain where one is, motionless, in expectation, unshaken and unmoved by any external shock.

Fortunate are those in whom the affliction which enters their flesh is the same one that afflicts the world itself in their time. They have the opportunity and the function of knowing the truth of the world's affliction and contemplating its reality. And that is the redemptive function itself. Twenty centuries ago, in the Roman Empire, slavery was the affliction of the age, and crucifixion was its extreme expression.

But alas for those who have this function and do not fulfill it.

When you say that you do not feel the difference between good and evil, your words are not serious if taken literally because you are speaking of another man in you who is clearly the evil in you; you are well aware—or when there is any doubt a careful scrutiny can nearly always dispel it—which of your thoughts, words and deeds strengthen that other man in you at your expense and which ones strengthen you at his. What you mean is that you have not yet consented to recognize this difference as the distinction between good and evil.

It is not an easy consent to give, because it commits one irrevocably. There is a kind of virginity in the soul as regards good, which is lost for ever once the soul has given this consent—just as a woman's virginity is lost after she has yielded to a man. The woman may become unfaithful, adulterous, but she will never again be a virgin. So she is frightened when she is about to yield. Love triumphs over this fear.

For every human being there is a point in time, a limit, unknown to anyone and above all to himself, but absolutely fixed, beyond which the soul cannot keep this virginity. If, before this precise moment, fixed from all eternity, it has not consented to be possessed by the good, it will immediately afterwards be possessed in spite of itself by the bad.

A man may yield to the bad at any moment of his life, because he yields to it unconsciously and unaware that he is admitting an external authority into his soul; and before surrendering her virginity to it the soul drugs herself with an opiate. To be possessed by the bad, it is not necessary to have consented to it; but the good never possesses the soul until she has said yes. And such is the fear of consummating the union that no soul has the power to say yes to the good unless she is urgently constrained by the almost immediate approach of the time-limit which will decide her eternal fate. For one man this time-limit may occur at the age of five, for another at the age of sixty. In any case, neither before nor after it has been reached is it possible to locate it temporally; in the sphere of duration this instantaneous and eternal choice can only be seen refracted. For those who have yielded to the bad a long time before the limiting moment is reached, this moment is no longer real. The most a human being can do is to guard intact his faculty for saying yes to the good, until the time when the limiting moment has almost been reached.

It appears to me certain that for you the limiting moment has not yet arrived. I lack the power to read men's hearts, but it seems to me that there are signs that it is not far distant. Your faculty for consent is certainly intact.

I think that when you have consented to the good you will break the shell, after an interval perhaps, but doubtless a short one; and the moment you are outside it there will be pardon for that bullet which once pierced the centre of your body, and thus also for the whole universe which drove it there.

The intelligence has a part in preparing the nuptial consent to God. It consists in looking at the evil in oneself and hating it. Not trying to get rid of it, but simply descrying it and keeping one's eyes fixed upon it until one feels repulsion—even before one has said yes to its opposite.

I believe that the root of evil, in everybody perhaps, but certainly in those whom affliction has touched and above all if the affliction is biological, is day-dreaming. It is the sole consolation, the unique resource of the afflicted; the one solace to help them bear the fearful burden of time; and a very innocent one, besides being indispensable. So how could it be possible to renounce it? It has only one disadvantage, which is that it is unreal. To renounce it for the love of truth is really to abandon all one's possessions in a mad excess of love and to follow him who is the personification of Truth. And it is really to bear the cross; because time is the cross.

While the limiting moment is still remote, it is not necessary to do this; but it is necessary to recognize day-dreaming for what it is. And even while one is sustained by it one must never forget for a moment that in all its forms—those that seem most inoffensive by their childishness, those that seem most respectable by their seriousness and their connexion with art or love or friendship—in all its forms without exception, it is falsehood. It excludes love. Love is real.

I would never dare to speak to you like this if all these thoughts were the product of my own mind. But although I am unwilling to place any reliance on such impressions, I do really have the feeling, in spite of myself, that God is addressing all this to you, for love of you, through me. In the same way, it does not matter if the consecrated host is made of the poorest quality flour, not even if it is three parts rotten.

You say that I pay for my moral qualities by distrust of myself. But my attitude towards myself, which is not distrust but a mixture of contempt and hatred and repulsion, is to be explained on a lower level—on the level of biological mechanisms. For twelve years I have suffered from pain around the central point of the nervous system, the meeting-place of soul and body; this pain persists during sleep and has never stopped for a second. For a period of ten years it was so great, and was accompanied by such exhaustion, that the effort of attention and intellectual work was usually almost as despairing as that of a condemned man the day before his execution; and often much more so, for my efforts seemed completely sterile and without even any temporary result. I was sustained by the faith, which I acquired at the age of fourteen, that no true effort of attention is ever wasted, even though it may never have any visible result, either direct or indirect. Nevertheless, a time came when I thought my soul menaced, through exhaustion and an aggravation of the pain, by such a hideous and total breakdown that I spent several weeks of anguished uncertainty whether death was not my imperative duty—although it seemed to me appalling that my life should end in horror. As I told you, I was only able to calm myself by deciding to live conditionally, for a trial period.

A little earlier, when I had already been for years in this physical state, I worked for nearly a year in engineering factories in the Paris region. The combination of personal experience and sympathy for the wretched mass of people around me, in which I formed, even in my own eyes, an undistinguishable item, implanted so deep in my heart the affliction of social degradation that I have felt a slave ever since, in the Roman sense of the word.

During all this time, the word God had no place at all in my thoughts. It never had, until the day—about three and a half years ago—when I could no longer keep it out. At a moment of intense physical pain, while I was making the effort to love, although believing I had no right to give any name to the love, I felt, while completely unprepared for it (I had never read the mystics), a presence more personal, more certain, and more real than that of a human being; it was inaccessible both to sense and to imagination, and it resembled the love that irradiates the tenderest smile of somebody one loves. Since that moment, the name of God and the name of Christ have been more and more irresistibly mingled with my thoughts.

Until then my only faith had been the Stoic *amor fati* as Marcus Aurelius understood it, and I had always faithfully practised it—to love the universe as one's city, one's native country, the beloved fatherland of every soul; to cherish it for its beauty, in the total integrity of the order and necessity which are its substance, and all the events that occur in it.

The result was that the irreducible quantity of hatred and repulsion which goes with suffering and affliction recoiled entirely upon myself. And the quantity is very great, because the suffering in question is located at the very root of my every single thought, without exception.

This is so much the case that I absolutely cannot imagine the possibility that any human being could feel friendship for me. If I believe in yours it is only because I have confidence in you and you have assured me of it, so that my reason tells me to believe it. But this does not make it seem any the less impossible to my imagination.

Because of this propensity of my imagination I am all the more tenderly grateful to those who accomplish this impossibility. Because friendship is an incomparable, immeasurable boon to me, and a source of life—not metaphorically but literally. Since it is not only my body but my soul itself that is poisoned all through by suffering, it is impossible for my thought to dwell there and it is obliged to travel elsewhere. It can only dwell for brief moments in God; it dwells often among things; but it would be against nature for human thought never to dwell in anything human. Thus it is literally true that friendship gives to my thought all the life it has, apart from what comes to it from God or from the beauty of the world.

So you can see what you have done for me by giving me yours.

I say these things to you because you can understand them; for your last book contains a sentence, in which I recognize myself, about the mistake your friends make in thinking that you exist. That shows a type of sensibility which is only intelligible to those who experience existence directly and continuously as an evil. For them it is certainly very easy to do as Christ asks and deny themselves. Perhaps it is too easy. Perhaps it is without merit. And yet I believe that to have it made so easy is an immense privilege.

I am convinced that affliction on the one hand, and on the other hand joy, when it is a complete and pure commitment to perfect beauty, are the only two keys which give entry to the realm of purity, where one can breathe: the home of the real.

But each of them must be unmixed: the joy without a shadow of incompleteness, the affliction completely unconsoled.

You understand me, of course. That divine love which one touches in the depth of affliction, like Christ's resurrection through crucifixion, that love which is the central core and intangible essence of joy, is not a consolation. It leaves pain completely intact.

I am going to say something which is painful to think, more painful to say, and almost unbearably painful to say to those one loves. For anyone in affliction, evil can perhaps be defined as being everything that gives any consolation.

A pure joy, which in some cases may replace pain or in others may be superimposed on it, is not a consolation. On the other hand, there is often a consolation in morbidly aggravating one's pain. I don't know if I am expressing this properly; it is all quite clear to me.

The refuge of laziness and inertia, a temptation to which I succumb very often, almost every day, or I might say every hour, is a particularly despicable form of consolation. It compels me to despise myself.

I perceive that I have not answered your letter, and yet I have a lot to say about it. I must do it another time. Today I'll confine myself to thanking you for it.

Yours most truly,

S. WEIL

I enclose the English poem, *Love*, which I recited to you. It has played a big role in my life, because I was repeating it to myself at the moment when Christ came to take possession of me for the first time. I thought I was only reciting a beautiful poem but, unknown to me, it was a prayer.

LETTER TO
MAURICE SCHUMANN

Hoping to play a part in the war against Nazism, Simone Weil formulated a plan that would enable her to serve in a mission as a member of a corps of front-line nurses. In the following letter she asks the help of a former class-mate, Maurice Schumann, then serving as a spokesman for the Free French in London. The plan never materialized, although, as her biographer, Jacques Cabaud, observes, it does illustrate Simone Weil's idealism—"a sort of moral need never to shelter herself from any struggle; a restless will to act, immediately, upon any idea that seemed to her to be good; a tendency to meet and to out-do violence and suffering by total sacrifice."

New York, 30 July 1942

CHER AMI,

I very often listened to your praises in France. You are very popular there. Every time I heard you spoken of in this way I was delighted, and I remembered Henri IV and the lecture-room where we listened to Chartier.

I embarked for New York from Marseille, where I had been for a year and a half, on 14 May. Although urged by my parents, who

94

wanted to escape from anti-semitism without being separated from me, I would never have left if I had known how difficult it is to get from New York to London.

I had considerable responsibility for distributing one of the most important clandestine publications in the free zone, *Les Cahiers du Témoignage Chrétien.* I had the consolation, amid all the surrounding sadness, of sharing in the country's suffering; and I knew enough about my own particular type of imagination to be aware that France's misfortune would hurt me much more from a distance than when I was there. And so it does; and the passing of time only makes the pain more and more unbearable. Moreover, I have the feeling that by leaving France I committed an act of desertion. This thought is intolerable.

To leave was like tearing up my roots, and I forced myself to it solely in the hope that it would enable me to take a bigger and more effective part in the efforts and dangers and sufferings of this great struggle.

I had and still have two ideas, one or the other of which I would like to realize.

One of them is set forth in the enclosed paper. I believe it might save the lives of many soldiers, considering the number of deaths in battle due to lack of *immediate* care (cases of 'shock', 'exposure', loss of blood).

In the spring of '40 I tried to get it adopted in France, and was well on the way to success, but events moved too rapidly. I was in Paris, where I remained, in the belief that there would be fighting, until 13 June. On that day I left, having seen on the walls the placards proclaiming Paris an open city. Since the armistice my one desire has been to get to England. I made several attempts to do so, legally or illegally, but they all failed. A year and a half ago I let my parents begin negotiations, on my behalf as well as their own, to emigrate to America—in the belief that New York could be simply a stepping-stone to London. Everybody here tells me it was a mistake.

My second thought was that I could work more effectively in secret operations if I left France and returned with precise instructions and a mission—preferably dangerous.

I will not go into details about this because I have done so in another letter to you, which I have entrusted to a friend of my family's who is soon leaving for England.

It seems to me that the first condition for carrying out either of these ideas is to move from New York to London.

I imagine you are in a position to help me, and I urgently beg for your support. I really believe I can be useful; and I appeal to you as a comrade to get me out of the too painful moral situation in which I find myself.

A lot of people don't understand why it is a painful moral situation; but you certainly do. We used to have a great deal in common once, when we were students together. It gave me real joy when I learnt, in France, that you have an important position in London.

I confidently rely on you.

With all good wishes,
SIMONE WEIL

(*Enclosure*)

PLAN FOR AN ORGANIZATION OF FRONT-LINE NURSES

The following project was favourably reported on in France, by the Army Commission of the Senate at the War Ministry, in May 1940. Owing to the rapid evolution of events, no attempt at putting it into practice was possible.

Attached hereto is a letter about the project from Joë Bousquet, a disabled veteran of the first world war. Wounded in the spine in 1918, he has been immobilized in bed ever since then by the resultant paraplegia. The experience of war has remained much closer to him than to those who resumed a normal life after 1918; on the other hand, his judgement is that of a mature man. Therefore his opinion is valuable.

The project is concerned with the formation of a special body of front-line nurses. It would be a very mobile organization and should in principle be always at the points of greatest danger, to give 'first aid' during battles. It could start as an experiment with a small nucleus of ten, or even less; and it could come into operation at the shortest possible notice, because hardly any preparation is required. An elementary knowledge of nursing would suffice, because nothing can be done under fire except dressings, tourniquets, and perhaps injections.

The indispensable moral qualities for the work are not of a kind which can be taught, and it would be no problem to eliminate any women who volunteered without possessing them. The horrors of war are so distinct today in everyone's imagination that one can regard any woman who is capable of volunteering for such work as being very probably capable of performing it.

This project may appear impracticable at first sight, because of its novelty. But a little reflection will show that it is not only practicable but very easy to carry out. The consequences of its failure would be almost negligible, whereas its success would be of really considerable value.

It is easy to try out because it could be started with a very small number of volunteers; and just because the initial number would be so small, no organization would be required. If the first experiment succeeded, the original nucleus would be gradually enlarged and the organization would be developed *pari passu* with its requirements. In any case, the nature of its work would prevent the organization from ever becoming very large; nor is it necessary that it should be.

Nothing could prevent the experiment from succeeding, except the incapacity of the women engaged in it to fulfil their task.

There are only two risks. First, that the women's courage might fail under fire; and second, that their presence among the soldiers might have undesirable moral effects.

Neither could arise if the women who volunteer are of a quality which corresponds to their resolution. Soldiers would never show disrespect to a woman who was brave under fire. The sole necessary precaution would be to ensure that the women were only with the soldiers during battles and not during rest periods.

Clearly, these women would need to have a good deal of courage. They would need to offer their lives as a sacrifice. They should be ready to be always at the most dangerous places and to face as much if not more danger than the soldiers who are facing the most; and this without being sustained by the offensive spirit but, on the contrary, devoting themselves to the wounded and dying.

But if the experiment succeeded, its advantages would be proportional to the difficulty.

This difficulty is more apparent than real, in view of the small number of volunteers and particularly of the first nucleus which, once again, could be fewer than ten. It is probable, and almost certain, that one could easily find ten women of sufficient courage.

For those who were added later to the original nucleus there would be the strong spur of emulation.

If, at the first experiment, the women should fail under fire, or behave unsuitably in their relations with the soldiers, it would be simple to disband the organization, return the women to the rear, and drop the whole scheme.

The experiment having been conducted on a minute scale and without publicity, the consequences would be nil, except for any resulting losses of life.

But these losses would be infinitesimal, in number, on the scale of the war. One can say negligible; because the death of two or three human beings is, in fact, hardly considered as a loss at all in an operation of war.

In a general way, there is no reason to regard the life of a woman, especially if she has passed her first youth without marrying or having children, as more valuable than a man's life; and all the less so if she has accepted the risk of death. It would be simple to make mothers, wives, and girls below a certain age ineligible.

The question of physical stamina is less important than it appears at first sight, even if the group had to work in very severe climates, because the nature of the work would make it easy to ensure long and frequent periods of rest. The women would not be called upon for long-sustained endurance like soldiers. It would be easy to proportion their efforts to their capacities.

At first, the fact that modern war is motorized may appear an obstacle; but on reflection it appears that this probably rather facilitates the scheme.

When infantry is moved up to the line in lorries there seems very little objection to arranging that in one of every so many lorries there shall be a place reserved for a woman. It would mean one rifle less, but the presence of this woman would have a material and moral effect which would certainly make that disadvantage negligible.

It may be thought that even if the experiment succeeded with a small nucleus it would be impossible to recruit larger numbers because of the difficulty of the work.

But even if the membership of the group never exceeded a few dozen, though this is unlikely, its value would still be very considerable.

Equally, if after a certain time the losses were considered too heavy to justify continuing the experiment, its achievements up to that time would remain and would far outweigh the losses.

Thus the objections which immediately arise on first consideration of this project are reduced to very little, one could almost say to nothing, on closer examination. Its advantages, on the other hand, become more obvious and appear all the greater the more clearly one considers them. The first and most obvious is the actual work which these women would regularly have to do. Being present at the most dangerous places and accompanying the soldiers under fire, which ordinary stretcher-bearers, first aid men, and nurses do not do, they would often be able to save lives by giving summary but immediate aid.

The moral support they would bring to all those they assisted would also be inestimable. They would comfort men's last moments by receiving messages for their families; they would mitigate by their presence and their words the agony of waiting, sometimes so long and so painfully, for the arrival of stretcher-bearers.

If that were all, it would be already a sufficient reason for organizing such a group of women. The considerable advantage it represents is offset by almost no disadvantages. But there are other considerations involved with this project which may perhaps be of capital importance in the general conduct of the war.

In order to estimate them, one must remember the essential role played in the present war by moral factors. They count for very much more than in past wars; and it is one of the main reasons for Hitler's successes that he was the first to see this.

Hitler has never lost sight of the essential need to strike everybody's imagination; his own people's, his enemies', and the innumerable spectators'. His own people's, in order to drive them incessantly forward; the enemy's, in order to provoke the maximum of psychological disarray; the spectators, in order to astonish and impress.

For this purpose, one of his most effective instruments has been such special bodies as the S.S., and the groups of parachutists who were the first to land in Crete, and others as well.

These groups consist of men selected for special tasks, who are prepared not only for risking their lives but for death. That is the essential point. They have a different inspiration from the rest of the army, an inspiration resembling a faith or a religious spirit.

Not that Hitlerism deserves to be called a religion. But it is quite undoubtedly a religion-substitute, and that is one of the principal causes of its power.

These men are unmoved by suffering and death, either for themselves or for all the rest of humanity. Their heroism originates from an extreme brutality. The groups they compose correspond perfectly to the spirit of the régime and the designs of their leader.

We cannot copy these methods of Hitler's. First, because we fight in a different spirit and with different motives; and also because, when it is a question of striking the imagination, copies never succeed. Only the new is striking.

But if we neither can nor ought to copy these methods, we do need to have their equivalents. This need is perhaps a vital one.

If the Russians have so far stood up to the Germans better than other people, one of the reasons may be that they dispose of psychological methods equivalent to Hitler's.

We ought not to copy the Russians either. We ought to create something new. This gift of creation is in itself a sign of moral vitality which will encourage the hopes of those who count upon us, while discouraging the enemy's hopes.

The value of special formations in which every member is ready to die can hardly be disputed. Not only can they be entrusted with tasks for which other troops are less suitable, but their mere existence is a powerful stimulant and source of inspiration for an army. For this, all that is necessary is that the spirit of sacrifice be expressed in acts and not words.

In our age, propaganda is an essential factor for success. It was the making of Hitler; nor has it been neglected by his enemies.

But although we give a lot of thought to propaganda for the rear, we think less about it for the front. Yet it is just as important there; only it requires different methods. At the rear, propaganda is carried on by words. At the front, verbal propaganda must be replaced by the propaganda of action.

The existence of special formations inspired by the spirit of total sacrifice is a continual propaganda of action. Such formations are necessarily the product of a religious inspiration; not in the sense of adherence to any definite church, but in a much less easily definable sense, for which nevertheless only the word religious is appropriate. There are circumstances in which this inspiration is an even more important factor for victory than the purely military ones. This can be verified by studying how Joan of Arc or Cromwell won their victories. It may well be that our own circumstances are of this kind. Our enemies are driven on by an idolatry, a substitute for religious faith. It may be that our victory depends upon the presence among us of a corresponding inspiration, but authentic and pure. And not only the presence of such an inspiration, but its expression in appropriate symbols. An inspiration is only active when it is expressed, and not in words but in deeds.

The S.S. are a perfect expression of the Hitlerian inspiration. If one may believe neutral reports, they exhibit at the front the heroism of brutality, and carry it to the extreme possible limits of courage. To demonstrate to the world that we are worth more than our enemies, we cannot claim to have more courage, because it would be quantitatively impossible. But we can and ought to demonstrate that our courage is qualitatively different, is courage of a more difficult and rarer kind. Theirs is a debased and brutal courage; it springs from the will to power and destruction. Just as our aims are different from theirs, so our courage too springs from a wholly different inspiration.

There could be no better symbol of our inspiration than the corps of women suggested here. The mere persistence of a few humane services in the very centre of the battle, the climax of inhumanity, would be a signal defiance of the inhumanity which the enemy has chosen for himself and which he compels us also to practise. The challenge would be all the more conspicuous because the services would be performed by women and with a maternal solicitude. These women would in fact be only a handful and the number of soldiers they could help would be proportionately small; but the effect of a moral symbol is independent of statistics.

A courage not inflamed by the impulse to kill, but capable of supporting, at the point of greatest danger, the prolonged spectacle of wounds and agony, is certainly of a rarer quality than that of the young S.S. fanatics.

A small group of women exerting day after day a courage of this kind would be a spectacle so new, so significant, and charged with such obvious meaning, that it would strike the imagination more than any of Hitler's conceptions have done. What is now necessary is to strike harder than he. This corps of women would undoubtedly offer one way of doing so.

Although composed of unarmed women, it would certainly impress the enemy soldiers, in the sense that their presence and their behaviour would be a new and unexpected revelation of the depth of the moral resources and resolution on our side.

The existence of this corps would equally impress the general public, both in the countries involved in the war and in the neutrals. Its symbolic force would be appreciated everywhere. The contrast between this force and the S.S. would make a more telling argument than any propaganda slogan. It would illustrate with supreme clarity the two roads between which humanity today is forced to choose.

And the impression upon our own soldiers would certainly be greater still.

The enemy's soldiers have an advantage over ours, from the purely military point of view, in having been separated from their families for ten years while they were being drilled for war. The war atmosphere seems natural to them, because they have scarcely known any other. Having breathed only the air of violence, destruction, and conquest, they have no conception of the value of home life. So, whatever its hardships, this war is not an upheaval for them, but simply the continuation and fruition of what went before.

But French and English and American youths have felt and still feel uprooted by it. Their previous experience was of quiet family life, and all they want is to return to it after a victory whose purpose is to safeguard it.

An aggressor country always enjoys a considerable initial advantage in morale, provided the aggression was prepared and premeditated. The German aggression has uprooted our young men from their natural life and set them in an atmosphere which is alien to them, but natural to their enemies. In order to defend their homes they have to begin by leaving them, and indeed almost forgetting them, because they must live in surroundings where there is nothing to recall them. Thus the atmosphere of the war prevents them from remembering the war's purpose. On the side of the aggressor the exact opposite happens. So it is not surprising that the aggressor holds the initiative.

And that is why the impetus of aggression is never opposed with equal impetus unless the defenders are fighting on their own ground, near their homes, and almost desperate with the fear of losing them.

To transform our soldiers into brutal young fanatics like Hitler's youth is neither possible nor desirable. But their fire can be kindled to the full by keeping as clearly alive as possible the thought of the homes they are defending.

How could this be done better than by sending with them into the firing-line and wherever there is the most brutal carnage something which evokes the homes they have been obliged to leave, and which evokes them not sentimentally but inspiringly? In this way they would be spared a single moment of the depressing sense of a complete break between themselves and all that they love.

This corps of women could be precisely such a concrete and inspiring evocation of far distant homes.

The ancient Germans, those semi-nomadic tribes whom the Romans could never subjugate, were aware of the inspirational value of a feminine presence in the thick of battle. They used to place in the vanguard of their lines a young girl surrounded by the élite of their youthful warriors.

And the Russians today, it is said, find it an advantage to let women serve in the firing-line.

Besides caring for the wounded, the members of this feminine corps would be able to perform all sorts of other services. At critical moments, when there is too much to be done, it would be natural for officers and N.C.O.'s to make use of them for any task except the handling of weapons: for liaison, rallying-points, transmission of orders. At such times, assuming that they retained their sang-froid, their sex would be a positive asset for these tasks.

Clearly, they would need to have been carefully selected. The presence of women can be an embarrassment if they do not possess a certain amount of that cool and virile resolution which prevents them from setting any store by themselves in any circumstances whatever. This cool resolution is a quality not often found allied in the same person with the tenderness required for comforting pain and agony. But although the combination is rare, it can be found.

No woman would think of volunteering for the service outlined here unless she possessed both the tenderness and the cool resolution, or unless she was unbalanced. But those in the second category could easily be weeded out before the moment of coming under fire.

It would suffice, to begin with, to find about ten women genuinely fitted for such a task. These women certainly exist. It would be easy to find them.

It seems to me impossible to conceive any other way in which these few women could be so effectively used as in the work I have suggested. And in a struggle so severe and so vital we ought so far as possible to use every human being with the maximum of effectiveness.

ADDENDUM.—Herewith an extract from the *Bulletin of the American College of Surgeons*, of April 1942 (p. 104):
'The early application of simple prophylactic or therapeutic measures can frequently prevent shock or overcome mild shock, whereas employment of all presently available methods may prove futile if shock has persisted and become increasingly severe upon the field.'

According to the American Red Cross, by far the greatest proportion of deaths in battle are the result of 'shock', 'exposure', and loss of blood, *which can only be prevented by immediate treatment.*

The American Red Cross has developed a system of plasma injections which can be operated *on the battle-field* in cases of shock, burns, and haemorrhage (ibid., p. 137).

LAST THOUGHTS

Simone Weil wrote her last letter to Father Perrin from
a refugee camp in Casablanca. Again she emphasizes a
main theme: that in affliction "the splendour of God's
mercy shines." And again she focuses on a main con-
stituent of her heterodoxy: the love and acceptance of
those things outside a visible Christianity.

May 26, 1942
From Casablanca

FATHER,

It was a very kind act on your part to write to me all the same.

I valued having a few affectionate words from you at the moment
of leaving.

You quoted some glorious words of Saint Paul. I hope though
that in owning my wretchedness to you I did not give you the impression of misunderstanding God's mercy. I hope I have never fallen, and
never shall fall, to such a depth of cowardice and ingratitude. I do not
need any hope or any promise in order to believe that God is rich in
mercy. I know this wealth of his with the certainty of experience; I
have touched it. What I know of it through actual contact is so far beyond my capacity of understanding and gratitude that even the prom-

106

ise of future bliss could add nothing to it for me; since for human intelligence the addition of two infinites is not an addition.

God's mercy is manifest in affliction as in joy, by the same right, more perhaps, because under this form it has no human analogy. Man's mercy is only shown in giving joy, or maybe in inflicting pain with a view to outward results, bodily healing or education. But it is not the outward results of affliction that bear witness to divine mercy. The outward results of true affliction are nearly always bad. We lie when we try to disguise this. It is in affliction itself that the splendor of God's mercy shines, from its very depths, in the heart of its inconsolable bitterness. If still persevering in our love, we fall to the point where the soul cannot keep back the cry "My God, why hast thou forsaken me?" if we remain at this point without ceasing to love, we end by touching something that is not affliction, not joy, something that is the central essence, necessary and pure, something not of the senses, common to joy and sorrow: the very love of God.

We know then that joy is the sweetness of contact with the love of God, that affliction is the wound of this same contact when it is painful, and that only the contact matters, not the manner of it.

It is the same as when we see someone very dear to us after a long absence; the words we exchange with him do not matter, but only the sound of his voice, which assures us of his presence.

The knowledge of this presence of God does not afford consolation; it takes nothing from the fearful bitterness of affliction; nor does it heal the mutilation of the soul. But we know quite certainly that God's love for us is the very substance of this bitterness and this mutilation.

I should like out of gratitude to be capable of bearing witness to this.

The poet of the *Iliad* loved God enough to have this capacity. This indeed is the implicit signification of the poem and the one source of its beauty. But it has scarcely been understood.

Even if there were nothing more for us than life on earth, even if the instant of death were to bring us nothing new, the infinite superabundance of the divine mercy is already secretly present here below in its entirety.

If, by an absurd hypothesis, I were to die without ever having committed any serious faults and yet all the same I were to fall to the bottom of hell, I should nevertheless owe God an infinite debt of gratitude for his infinite mercy, on account of my earthly life, and that notwithstanding the fact that I am such a poor unsatisfactory creature. Even in this hypothesis I should think all the same that I had received all my share of the riches of divine mercy. For already here below we receive the capacity for loving God and for representing him to ourselves with complete certainty as having the substance of real, eternal, perfect, and infinite joy. Through our fleshly veils we receive from above presages of eternity which are enough to efface all doubts on this subject.

What more can we ask or desire? A mother or a lover who knew for certain that her son, or her beloved, was full of joy would have no thought in her heart capable of asking or desiring anything else. We have much more. What we love is perfect joy itself. When we know this, even hope becomes superfluous; it no longer has any meaning. The only thing left to hope for is the grace not to be disobedient here below. The rest is the affair of God alone and does not concern us.

That is why I lack nothing, although my imagination, mutilated as it is by overlong and uninterrupted suffering, cannot conceive of salvation as of something possible for me. What you say can have no effect except to persuade me that you really have some friendship for me. From that point of view I treasure your letter greatly. It has not been able to affect me in any other way. But that was not necessary.

I know enough of my miserable weakness to suppose that a little adverse fortune would perhaps suffice to fill my soul with suffering to such a point that for a long time no room would be left for the thoughts I have just described to you. But even that does not matter very much. Certitude does not depend upon states of soul. Certitude is always in perfect security.

There is only one time when I really know nothing of this certitude any longer. It is when I am in contact with the affliction of other people, those who are indifferent or unknown to me as much as the others, perhaps even more, including those of the most remote ages of antiquity. This contact causes me such atrocious pain and so utterly rends my soul that as a result the love of God becomes almost impossible for me for a while. It would take very little more to make me say impossible. So much so that I am uneasy about myself. I reassure myself a little by remembering that Christ wept on foreseeing the horrors of the destruction of Jerusalem. I hope he will forgive me my compassion.

You give me pain by writing that the day of my baptism would be a great joy for you. After having received so much from you, it is in my power to cause you joy; and yet it does not enter my head for a second to do so. I cannot help it. I really believe that only God has the power to prevent me from causing you joy.

Even if we only consider the plane of purely human relations, the gratitude I owe you is infinite. I think that, except you, all those human beings for whom I have made it easy to hurt me through my friendship have amused themselves by doing so, frequently or occasionally, consciously or unconsciously, but all of them at some time or another. Where I recognized it to be conscious, I took a knife and cut out the friendship, without however warning the person in question.

They did not behave like this from malice, but as a result of the well-known phenomenon that makes hens rush upon one of their number if it is wounded, attacking and pecking it.

All men bear this animal nature within them. It determines their attitude toward their fellows, with or without their knowledge and consent. Thus it sometimes happens that without the mind realizing anything, the animal nature in a man senses the mutilation of the animal nature in another and reacts accordingly. It is the same for all possible situations and the corresponding animal reactions. This mechanical necessity holds all men in its grip at every moment. They only escape from it in proportion to the place held in their souls by the authentically supernatural.

Even partial discernment is very difficult in this matter. If, however, it really were completely possible, we should have there a criterion of the part played by the supernatural in the life of a soul, a sure criterion, exact as a balance and quite independent of any religious beliefs. It is that among many other things that Christ indicated when he said: "These two commandments are one."

It is only with you that I have never felt the backlash of this mechanism. My situation with regard to you is like that of a beggar, reduced by extreme poverty to a state of constant hunger, who for the space of a year had been going at intervals to a prosperous house where he was given bread, and who, for the first time in his life had not suffered humiliation. Such a beggar, if he had a whole life to give in exchange for each morsel of bread, and if he gave them all, would think that his debt was in no way diminished.

But the fact that with you human relations perpetually enshrine the light of God should raise gratitude to a still higher degree in my case.

Yet I am not going to give you any signs of gratitude unless it be to say things concerning you that might give you every reason to be irritated with me. For it is no way fitting that I should say them, nor even think them. I have no right to do this, and I am well aware of it.

As, however, it is a fact that I have thought them, I dare not keep them from you. If they are not true they will do no harm. It is not impossible that they contain some truth. In that case there would be good reason to think that God was sending you this truth through the pen I am holding. It is more suitable for some thoughts to come by direct inspiration; it is more suitable for others to be transmitted through some creature. God uses either way with his friends. It is well known that no matter what thing, a donkey for instance, can be used as agent without making any difference. It pleases God perhaps to choose the most worthless objects for this purpose. I am obliged to tell myself these things so as not to be afraid of my own thoughts.

When I let you have a written sketch of my spiritual autobiography, I had a reason. I wanted to make it possible for you to see for yourself a concrete and certain example of implicit faith. Certain, for I knew that you know that I am not lying.

Wrongly or rightly you think that I have a right to the name of Christian. I assure you that when in speaking of my childhood and youth I use the words vocation, obedience, spirit of poverty, purity, acceptance, love of one's neighbor, and other expressions of the same kind, I am giving them the exact signification they have for me now. Yet I was brought up by my parents and my brother in a complete agnosticism, and I never made the slightest effort to depart from it; I never had the slightest desire to do so, quite rightly, I think. In spite of that, ever since my birth, so to speak, not one of my faults, not one of my imperfections really had the excuse of ignorance. I shall have to answer for everything on that day when the Lamb shall come in anger.

You can take my word for it too that Greece, Egypt, ancient India, and ancient China, the beauty of the world, the pure and authentic reflections of this beauty in art and science, what I have seen of the inner recesses of human hearts where religious belief is unknown, all these things have done as much as the visibly Christian ones to deliver me into Christ's hands as his captive. I think I might even say more. The love of those things that are outside visible Christianity keeps me outside the Church.

Such a spiritual destiny must seem unintelligible to you. But for this very reason it provides useful matter for reflection. It is good to reflect about whatever forces us to come out of ourselves. I have difficulty in imagining how it can be that you really have some friendship for me; but as you apparently have, it may be for this purpose.

In theory you fully admit the possibility of implicit faith. In practice also you have a breadth of mind and an intellectual honesty that are very exceptional. Yet they still seem to me very insufficient. Only perfection is sufficient.

Wrongly or rightly I have often thought I could detect a bias in some of your attitudes. Notably a certain unwillingness when it comes to real facts to admit the possibility of implicit faith in particular cases. At least I had that impression in talking to you about B_____. And above all about a Spanish peasant whom I regard as being not very far from sanctity. It is true that it was probably my own fault more than anything else; my awkwardness is so great than I always do harm to those I love when I speak of them; I have often experienced this. But it also seems to me that when one speaks to you of unbelievers who are in affliction and accept their affliction as a part of the order of the world, it does not impress you in the same way as if it were a question of Christians and of submission to the will of God. Yet it is the same thing. At any rate if I really have the right to be called a Christian, I know from experience that the virtue of the Stoics and that of the Christians are one and the same virtue. I mean true Stoical virtue of course, which is before anything else love, not the caricature which a few Roman brutes made of it. In theory I do not think that you would be able to deny it either. But, when it comes to facts and to concrete examples from the contemporary world, you dislike recognizing the possibility of Stoical virtue having supernatural efficacity.

You also hurt me very much one day by using the word false when you meant nonorthodox. You corrected yourself immediately. To my mind there is a confusion of terms there which is incompatible with perfect intellectual honesty. It is impossible that such a thing should be pleasing to Christ, who is the Truth.

It seems to me certain that this constitutes a serious imperfection in you. And why should there be any imperfection in you? It does not suit you in the least to be imperfect. It is like a wrong note in a beautiful song.

I believe this imperfection comes from attaching yourself to the Church as to an earthly country. As a matter of fact, as well as being your bond with the heavenly country, it is a terrestrial country for you. You live there in an atmosphere of human warmth. That makes a little attachment almost inevitable.

Such an attachment is perhaps for you that infinitely fine thread, of which Saint John of the Cross speaks, which so long as it is not broken holds the bird down on the ground as effectively as a great metal chain. I imagine that the last thread, although very fine, must be the most difficult to cut, for when it is cut we have to fly and that is frightening. But all the same the obligation is imperative.

The children of God should not have any other country here below but the universe itself, with the totality of all the reasoning creatures it ever has contained, contains, or ever will contain. That is the native city to which we owe our love.

Less vast things than the universe, among them the Church, impose obligations which can be extremely far-reaching. They do not, however, include the obligation to love. At least that is what I believe. I am moreover convinced that no obligation relating to the intelligence is to be found among them either.

Our love should stretch as widely across all space, and should be as equally distributed in every portion of it, as is the very light of the sun. Christ has bidden us to attain to the perfection of our heavenly Father by imitating his indiscriminate bestowal of light. Our intelligence too should have the same complete impartiality.

Every existing thing is equally upheld in its existence by God's creative love. The friends of God should love him to the point of merging their love into his with regard to all things here below.

When a soul has attained a love filling the whole universe indiscriminately, this love becomes the bird with golden wings that pierces an opening in the egg of the world. After that, such a soul loves the universe, not from within but from without; from the dwelling place of the Wisdom of God, our first-born brother. Such a love does not love beings and things in God, but from the abode of God. Being close to God it views all beings and things from there, and its gaze is merged in the gaze of God.

We have to be catholic, that is to say, not bound by so much as a thread to any created thing, unless it be to creation in its totality. Formerly, in the case of the saints, it was possible for this universality to be implicit, even in their own consciousness. They were able implicitly to give the rightful place in their soul, on the one hand to the love due only to God and to all his creation, on the other to their obligations to all that is smaller than the universe. I think that Saint Francis and Saint John of the Cross were like this. That was why they were both poets.

It is true that we have to love our neighbor, but, in the example that Christ gave as an illustration of this commandment, the neighbor is a being of whom nothing is known, lying naked, bleeding, and unconscious on the road. It is a question of completely anonymous, and for that reason, completely universal love.

It is also true that Christ said to his disciples: "Love one another." But I think that there is a question of friendship, a personal friendship between two beings, by which God's friends should be bound each to each. Friendship is the one legitimate exception to the duty of only loving universally. Moreover, to my way of thinking, it is not really pure unless it is so to speak surrounded on all sides by a compact envelope of indifference which preserves a distance.

We are living in times that have no precedent, and in our present situation universality, which could formerly be implicit, has to be fully explicit. It has to permeate our language and the whole of our way of life.

Today it is not nearly enough merely to be a saint, but we must have the saintliness demanded by the present moment, a new saintliness, itself also without precedent.

Maritain said this, but he only enumerated the aspects of saintliness of former days, which, for the time being at least, have become out of date. He did not feel all the miraculous newness the saintliness of today must contain in compensation.

A new type of sanctity is indeed a fresh spring, an invention. If all is kept in proportion and if the order of each thing is preserved, it is almost equivalent to a new revelation of the universe and of human destiny. It is the exposure of a large portion of truth and beauty hitherto concealed under a thick layer of dust. More genius is needed than was needed by Archimedes to invent mechanics and physics. A new saintliness is a still more marvelous invention.

Only a kind of perversity can oblige God's friends to deprive themselves of having genius, since to receive it in superabundance they only need to ask their Father for it in Christ's name.

Such a petition is legitimate, today at any rate, because it is necessary. I think that under this or any equivalent form it is the first thing we have to ask for now; we have to ask for it daily, hourly, as a famished child constantly asks for bread. The world needs saints who have genius, just as a plague-stricken town needs doctors. Where there is a need there is also an obligation.

I cannot make any use of these thoughts, nor of all those that go with them in my mind. In the first place the considerable imperfection I am cowardly enough to leave within myself keeps me at far too great a distance from the point at which they can be put into practice. That is unpardonable on my part. So great a distance, in the best of cases, can only be crossed with the help of time.

But even if I had already crossed it, I am an instrument already rotten. I am too worn out. And even if I believed in the possibility of God's consenting to repair the mutilations of my nature, I could not bring myself to ask it of him. Even if I were sure of his consenting, I could not. Such a request would seem to me an offense against the infinitely tender Love which has made me the gift of affliction.

If no one consents to take any notice of the thoughts that, though I cannot explain why, have settled in so inadequate a being as myself, they will be buried with me. If, as I believe, they contain some truth, it will be a pity. I am prejudicial to them. The fact that they happen to be in me prevents people from paying any attention to them.

I see no one but you whom I can implore to give them your attention. I should like you to transfer the charity you have so generously bestowed from me to that which I bear within me, and which I like to think is of far more value than I am myself.

It is a great sorrow for me to fear that the thoughts that have descended into me should be condemned to death through the contagion of my inadequacy and wretchedness. I never read the story of the barren fig tree without trembling. I think that it is a portrait of me. In it also, nature was powerless, and yet it was not excused. Christ cursed it.

That is why although there are perhaps not any particular, truly serious faults in my life, except those I have owned to you, I think when I consider things in the cold light of reason that I have more just cause to fear God's anger than many a great criminal.

It is not that I actually do fear it. By a strange twist, the thought of God's anger only arouses love in me. It is the thought of the possible favor of God and of his mercy that makes me tremble with a sort of fear.

On the other hand the sense of being like a barren fig tree for Christ tears my heart.

Happily God can quite easily send not only the same thoughts, supposing they are good, but a great many much better ones to somebody who is unblemished and capable of serving him.

But who knows if those I bear in me are not sent, partly at any rate, so that you should make some use of them? They can only be destined for someone who has a little friendship for me, a friendship that is true. Indeed, for other people, in a sense I do not exist. I am the color of dead leaves, like certain unnoticed insects.

Forgive me if in all I have just written to you anything from my pen should strike you as erroneous or out of place. Do not be angry with me.

I do not know whether I shall be able to send you my news or to receive yours in the course of the weeks and months that are to come. But it is only for me that this separation is a misfortune, and therefore, it is not important.

I can only assure you yet again of my filial gratitude and my boundless friendship.

SIMONE WEIL

II

PRELUDE
TO POLITICS

Analysis of Oppression
The Iliad, *Poem of Might*
Uprootedness and Nationhood

*The world is the closed door. It is a barrier. And at the same time it
is the way through.*

Simone Weil believed that "the social order, though necessary, is
essentially evil, whatever it may be." Yet, however bleak her conclusions regarding the social organization, and matter, may have been, she
devoted deep thought to its manifestations. No less than her spiritual
meditations, her social-political reflections are fraught with prophetic meaning and are the result of a rigorous critical process in
which vision and wisdom prevail. Her political awareness is exceptional
for its sensitive and comprehensive response to the mechanisms of
social power. Her insights are relevant, indeed incontrovertible, when
one studies in particular her two main contributions to political theory
and thought, *Oppression and Liberty* and *The Need for Roots*. (This
latter, undertaken in exile at the invitation of the Free French authorities in London, is the only full-scale book that she wrote, the remainder of her works being compilations of essays, letters, notes, *pensées*.)
It should be noted that her social-political reflections are not limited
to these two works; that they occupy her most constant attention.
Richly blending high intelligence and spiritual strength, she ex-
plores the depths of modern social-political systems, theory, prob-

lems, issues, and ideologies. The conditions of contemporary culture and politics distressed her terribly, but she insisted on confronting them directly and honestly, fully and responsibly. Though hard, her assessment of these conditions discloses intrinsic compassion and sympathy. "If, as is only too possible," she asserts, "we are to perish, let us see to it that we do not perish without having existed." Her vision of hell is never without her vision of heaven. More than anything else it is the oppression and the debasement of the human spirit that arouse her greatest protest, as well as her Christlike anguish for "the lame, the halt, the blind." Certainly there is considerable truth in describing Simone Weil as "a prophet of grace."

Her critique of the social-political structure of contemporary society, and of modern theories of evolutionism, progressivism, and (secular) humanism, is at once antiempirical and antimaterialistic. It is a critique that is informed and impelled by a faith in spiritual creativity. In this respect her indictment both of capitalism and of Marxism is equally damning, insofar as she sees in both political systems the deification of social matter, or as she was to state in one of her most piercing observations: "And the materialist is a man. That is why he cannot prevent himself from ultimately regarding matter as a machine for manufacturing good." Faith in matter, especially as it has been embraced and espoused by modern-day liberals, heralds the brutal uniformity that leaves little room for thought and thus in the end for either justice or prudence, which she saw as required conditions of the spiritual life. "We are only geometricians in regard to matter," she writes; "the Greeks were first of all geometricians in the apprenticeship of virtue." In the materialistic view of life she saw the fundamental causes of the kind of uprootedness that appears in an age and in a society in which money and the state replace all other bonds of attachment and in which religion ceases to play any part: "Workers need poetry more than bread. They need that their life should be a poem. They need some light from eternity. Religion alone can be the source of such poetry. It is not religion but revolution which is the opium of the people."

Oppression, Simone Weil concluded, is the reigning monarch of all social organization. Hence the true emperor is the empire: the modern centralized state as the final, the absolute and despotic authority and as the real object of worship. "Human history is simply the history of the servitude which makes men—oppressors and oppressed alike—the plaything of the instruments of domination they themselves have manufactured, and thus reduces living humanity to being the chattel of inanimate chattels." In ancient times Rome personified the prototypal imperialistic spirit. Spiritual life in Rome was hardly more than an expression of the will to power, she maintained. Even the Christian sect emerged as the struggle of the Greek spirit against the Rome of "an unlimited and shameless brutality," of "the shrewd employment of cruelty." In modern times Hitlerism became Rome's royal successor. "Everything that disgusts and also everything that shocks us in his [Hitler's] methods is what he has in common with Rome," she observes. Her analysis of oppression is relentless in its tone. She eyes facts and delineates social-political conditions with an uncompromising argumentative ferocity, that same ferocity, in fact, that even some of her friends detected (and feared) in discussions with her. Her social-political writings reveal Simone Weil as a critic of considerable power, vigorously and rigorously applying and demanding high standards of discrimination and arriving at judgments of a stern moral character. She is as tough, it could be said, as a modern saint should be. The power of Satan lies at the heart of all forms of human oppression, she maintains. Against the prince of this world one has to fight with all of one's might.

The religion of power, she insists, is inseparable from the conditions of servitude, of oppression. It is something that is inevitable and common with all totalitarianism—with Romanism, Marxism, Hitlerism; with the "collective values" promulgated and enforced by all principalities of oppression from ancient through modern times. Oppression is the substance of power; power is the form of oppression. But it is also its own fatality, "the most fatal of all vicious circles," insofar as power always cuts both ways: against the one who commands as much as against the one who obeys. It is an ongoing process that enslaves everybody, strong and weak alike. Yet no oppressive social system ever escapes or defeats the internal contradiction, "like the seed of death," contained within itself: "It is made up of the opposition between the necessarily unlimited character of the material bases of power and the necessarily unlimited character of the race for power considered as relationship between men." Simone Weil, it should be noted, respected Marx's deep concern for human misery and his concomitant belief that weakness also can be a social mechanism for "producing paradise." Yet she saw the absurdity of his position, as she was to emphasize in perhaps the last words she ever wrote, in the spring of 1943: "Marx accepted this contradiction of strength in weakness, without accepting the supernatural which alone renders the contradiction valid." In the religion of power she saw the willful, the unceasing destruction of the quintessential elements of spirituality; the violation of all reverence for the integrity of mind and for man created in the image of God. In her appraisal and condemnation of the uses of power Simone Weil spoke on the basis of spiritual, and Christian, standards. Failure to satisfy such standards, whether on the Left or the Right, aroused her unrelenting ire. To the politicians who, as Shakespeare once said, would circumvent God himself, and to political theorists and thinkers who bow down to the dictates of the so-called realpolitik, Simone Weil is perhaps something of an *enfant terrible*. That soldier-politician extraordinaire, General Charles de Gaulle, one even hears, pronounced her crazy!

Perhaps at no other point in her social-political commentaries does Simone Weil reveal the most memorable triumph of Spirit than in her classic essay, "The *Iliad,* Poem of Might," which was the first of her writings to reach the English-speaking world. Its opening sentences bring to mind the poetic power and insights of Leo Tolstoy: "The true hero, the real subject, the core of the *Iliad,* is might. That might which is wielded by men rules over them, and before it man's flesh cringes. The human soul never ceases to be modified by its encounter with might, swept on, blinded by that which it believes itself able to handle, bowed beneath the power of that which it suffers." In its communicated truths and humanity, it catches the horror of war not only in its immediate historical situation but also in its universal contexts. Containing her apex-thought, as it were, it is an essay that repays frequentation, such is its truth of meaning and relevance. Bringing together ancient and modern experience, it probes the lessons of history in the clear light of the wisdom of the ages. The battle being fought on the plains of Troy is not a local war but a universal, a total war that has no end in human repercussions—and costs. War is diabolism that oppresses victor and vanquished. War becomes the objective correlative of the "empire of might," as she terms it. "Such is the empire of might; it extends as far as the empire of nature." Its savage, rending effects are not to be counted only in terms of human casualties. In war, as in the heart of man, God and Satan are locked in combat. The spiritual dimension of such ultimate struggle is as immeasurable and portentous as the physical dimension is measurable and concrete.

The nature of might is such, Simone Weil shows, that it transforms man into a thing and violates, differently but equally, the soul of the victim and of the victimizer, "brothers in the same misfortune." "Might suffered at the hands of another is as much a tyranny over the soul as extreme hunger at the moment when food means life or death." It first denies and then kills life, for, "when exercised to the full, it makes a thing of man in the most literal sense, for it makes him a corpse. There where someone stood a moment ago, stands no one. This is the spectacle which the *Iliad* never tires of presenting." If might crushes the soul of the weak, it also does irreparable damage to the strong: "And so pitilessly as might crushes, so pitilessly it maddens whoever possesses, or believes he possesses it." "The strong man is never absolutely strong, nor the weak man absolutely weak, but each one is ignorant of this." More prodigious than the power to kill outright is the power of might to reify life. This is always a greater condemnation since it is the greatest humiliation of the life of the soul. In war the human soul is subordinated to might, that is to say, to matter. There can be no human heroes; might is the only hero. Yet, too, there always exists the possibility for another kind of hero, that spiritual hero whom Simone Weil must surely have in mind when she states: "Only he who knows the empire of might and knows how not to respect it is capable of love and justice."

The necessity that belongs to war is both onerous and terrifying. No one can for long escape the fact of defeat or of death. "The day comes when fear, defeat or the death of beloved companions crushes the warrior's soul beneath the necessity of war. Then war ceases to be a play or a dream; the warrior understands at last that it really exists. This is a hard reality, infinitely too hard to be borne, for it comprises death." What Simone Weil goes on to say about the ever-present spec-

ter of death in and the insensibility induced by the experience of war
discloses the same high degree of lucidity, of purity, and of simplicity
that she worshiped in Hellenism. "The thought of death cannot be sustained, or only in flashes from the moment when one understands
death as a possible eventuality." What survivor of a great war dares to
deny the truth of a statement like this: "That men should have death
for their future is a denial of nature. As soon as the practice of war
has revealed the fact that each moment holds the possibility of death,
the mind becomes incapable of moving from one day to the next
without passing through the spectre of death"? In these circumstances,
the tragedy of soul ensues, which for Simone Weil is the greatest of all
tragedies: "That soul daily suffers violence which every morning must
mutilate its aspirations because the mind cannot move about in a time
without passing through death." A sense of doom for the soul that is
dominated by death prevails with a double intensity: "The despair
which thrusts toward death is the same one that impels toward killing." Hector's plea to Achilles for deliverance—"I am at thy knees,
Achilles; have pity, have regard for me; / Here as a suppliant, O Son of
Zeus, I am worthy of respect"—holds a truth that rings far beyond the
Scaean gates: "And how should he who has destroyed in himself the
very thought that there may be joy in the light, how should he respect
such humble and vain pleadings from the vanquished?"

T. S. Eliot places Simone Weil's social-political writings "in that
category of prolegomena to politics which politicians seldom read,
and which most of them would be unlikely to understand or to know
how to apply." Never much of an optimist, he is nonetheless quite
right in his conclusion. Politicians are forever thinking of or scheming
for technic victory, in war or in peace. Not unpredictably they forget
that, as she expresses it, "The winning of battles is not determined
between men who plan and deliberate, who make resolution and
carry it out, but between men drained of these faculties, transformed,
fallen to the level either of inert matter, which is all passivity, or to
the level of blind forces, which are all momentum." Intent on social-
political transformations at any price, they generally forget the state
of man's soul and man's relation to spiritual principle. "Geometricians
in regard to matter," the practitioners of politics are blind to that
indefinable existence which is our soul and God. In this respect,

whether or not they know or admit it, most people are politicians: their name is legion. They continue to erect the "wall of partition" between life and soul, endlessly, but needlessly, constructing barriers and bolting doors. But in the end they forget a central spiritual fact, containing as it surely must the greatest revelation and the infinite possibility that inhere in these words of Simone Weil, words that modern man should ponder even unto his peril: "The world is the closed door. It is a barrier. And at the same time it is the way through."

ANALYSIS
OF OPPRESSION

All power is unstable, Simone Weil believes. Ultimately the uses and consequences of power are both constructive and destructive. Below, in analyzing some of the reasons why, despite material and technical progress, man finds himself in a servile condition, she points to a great social paradox: As man increasingly exploits his power over the universe, and thus escapes from the caprices of blind nature, he also surrenders to the no less blind caprices of the struggle for power.

The problem is, in short, to know what it is that links oppression in general and each form of oppression in particular to the system of production: in other words, to succeed in grasping the mechanism of oppression, in understanding by what means it arises, subsists, transforms itself, by what means, perhaps, it might theoretically disappear. This is, to all intents and purposes, a novel question. For centuries past, noble minds have regarded the power of oppressors as constituting a usurpation pure and simple, which one had to try to oppose either by simply expressing a radical disapproval of it, or else by armed force placed at the service of justice. In either case, failure has always been complete; and never was it more strikingly so than when it took on momentarily the appearance of victory, as happened with the French Revolution, when, after having effectively succeeded in bringing about the disappearance of a certain form of oppression, people stood by, helpless, watching a new oppression immediately being set up in its place.

In his ponderings over this resounding failure, which had come to crown all previous ones, Marx finally came to understand that you cannot abolish oppression so long as the causes which make it inevitable remain, and that these causes reside in the objective—that is to say material—conditions of the social system. He consequently elaborated a completely new conception of oppression, no longer considered as the usurpation of a privilege, but as the organ of a social function. This function is that very one which consists in developing the productive forces, in so far as this development calls for severe efforts and serious hardships; and Marx and Engels perceived a reciprocal relationship between this development and social oppression.

In the first place, according to them, oppression becomes established only when improvements in production have brought about a division of labour sufficiently advanced for exchange, military command and government to constitute distinct functions; on the other hand, oppression, once established, stimulates the further development of the productive forces, and changes in form as and when this development so demands, until the day when, having become a hindrance to it instead of a help, it disappears purely and simply.

However brilliant the concrete analyses may be by which Marxists have illustrated this thesis, and although it constitutes an improvement on the naïve expressions of indignation which it replaced, one cannot say that it throws light on the mechanism of oppression. It only partially describes its origins; for why should the division of labour necessarily turn into oppression? It by no means entitles us to a reasonable expectation of its ending; for if Marx believed himself to have shown how the capitalist system finally hinders production, he did not even attempt to prove that, in our day, any other oppressive system would hinder it in like manner. Furthermore, one fails to understand why oppression should not manage to continue, even after it has become a factor of economic regression. Above all, Marx omits to explain why oppression is invincible as long as it is useful, why the oppressed in revolt have never succeeded in founding a non-oppressive society, whether on the basis of the productive forces of their time, or even at the cost of an economic regression which could hardly increase their misery; and, lastly, he leaves completely in the dark the general principles of the mechanism by which a given form of oppression is replaced by another.

What is more, not only have Marxists not solved a single one of these problems, but they have not even thought it their duty to formulate them. It has seemed to them that they had sufficiently accounted for social oppression by assuming that it corresponds to a function in the struggle against nature. Even then, they have only really brought out this correspondence in the case of the capitalist system; but, in any case, to suppose that such a correspondence constitutes an explanation of the phenomenon is to apply unconsciously to social organisms Lamarck's famous principle, as unintelligible as it is convenient, "the function creates the organ". Biology only started to be a science on the day when Darwin replaced this principle by the notion of conditions of existence. The improvement lies in the fact that the function is no longer considered as the cause, but as the result of the organ—the only intelligible order; the part played by cause is henceforth attributed only to a blind mechanism, that of heredity combined with accidental variations. Actually, by itself, all this blind mechanism can do is to produce haphazardly anything whatsoever; the adaptation of the organ to the function here enters into play in such a manner as to limit chance by eliminating the non-viable structures, no longer as a mysterious tendency, but as a condition of existence; and this condition is defined by the relationship of the organism under consideration to its partly inert, partly living environment, and more especially to similar rival organisms. Adaptation is henceforth conceived in regard to living beings as an exterior and no longer an interior necessity.

It is clear that this luminous method is not only valid in biology, but wherever one is confronted by organized structures which have not been organized by anybody. In order to be able to appeal to science in social matters, we ought to have effected with respect to

Marxism an improvement similar to that which Darwin effected with respect to Lamarck. The causes of social evolution must no longer be sought elsewhere than in the daily efforts of men considered as individuals. These efforts are certainly not directed haphazardly; they depend, in each individual case, on temperament, education, routine, customs, prejudices, natural or acquired needs, environment, and above all, broadly speaking, human nature, a term which, although difficult to define, is probably not devoid of meaning. But given the almost infinite diversity of individuals, and especially the fact that human nature includes among other things the ability to innovate, to create, to rise above oneself, this warp and woof of incoherent efforts would produce anything whatever in the way of social organization, were it not that chance found itself restricted in this field by the conditions of existence to which every society has to conform on pain of being either subdued or destroyed. The men who submit to these conditions of existence are more often than not unaware of them, for they act not by imposing a definite direction on the efforts of each one, but by rendering ineffective all efforts made in directions disallowed by them.

These conditions of existence are determined in the first place, as in the case of living beings, on the one hand by the natural environment and on the other hand by the existence, activity and especially competition of other organisms of the same species, that is to say here of other social groups. But still a third factor enters into play, namely, the organization of the natural environment, capital equipment, armaments, methods of work and of warfare; and this factor occupies a special position owing to the fact that, though it acts upon the form of social organization, it in turn undergoes the latter's reaction upon it. Furthermore, this factor is the only one over which the members of a society can perhaps exercise some control.

This outline is too abstract to serve as a guide; but if on the basis of this summary view we could arrive at some concrete analyses, it would at last become possible to formulate the social problem. The enlightened goodwill of men acting in an individual capacity is the only possible principle of social progress; if social necessities, once clearly perceived, were found to lie outside the range of this goodwill in the same way as those which govern the stars, each man would have nothing more to do but to watch history unfolding as one watches the seasons go by, while doing his best to spare himself and his loved ones the misfortune of being either an instrument or a victim of social oppression. If this is not so, it would be necessary first of all to define by way of an ideal limit the objective conditions that would permit of a social organization absolutely free from oppression; then seek out by what means and to what extent the conditions actually given can be transformed so as to bring them nearer to this ideal; find out what is the least oppressive form of social organization for a body of specific objective conditions; and lastly, define in this field the power of action and responsibilities of individuals as such. Only on this condition could political action become something analogous to a form of work, instead of being, as has been the case hitherto, either a game or a branch of magic.

Unfortunately, in order to reach this stage, what is required is not only searching, rigorous thinking, subjected, so as to avoid all possibility of error, to the most exacting checking, but also historical, technical and scientific investigations of an unparalleled range and precision, and conducted from an entirely new point of view. However, events do not wait; time will not stop in order to afford us leisure; the present forces itself urgently on our attention and threatens us with calamities which would bring in their train, amongst many other harrowing misfortunes, the material impossibility of studying or writing otherwise than in the service of the oppressors. What are we to do? There would be no point in letting oneself be swept along in the *mêlée* by an ill-considered enthusiasm. No one has the faintest idea of either the objectives or the means of what is still from force of habit called revolutionary action. As for reformism, the principle of the lesser evil on which it is based is certainly eminently reasonable, however discredited it may be through the fault of those who have hitherto made use of it; though remember, if it has so far served only as a pretext for capitulation, this is due not to the cowardice of a few leaders, but to an ignorance unfortunately common to all; for as long as the worst and the best have not been defined in terms of a clearly and concretely conceived ideal, and then the precise margin of possibilities determined, we do not know which is the lesser evil, and consequently we are compelled to accept under this name anything effectively imposed by those who dispose of force, since any existing evil whatever is always less than the possible evils which uncalculating action invariably runs the risk of bringing about. Broadly speaking, blind men such as we are in these days have only the choice between surrender and adventure. And yet we cannot avoid the duty of determining here and now the attitude to adopt with regard to the present situation. That is why, until we have—if, indeed, such a thing is possible—taken to pieces the social mechanism, it is permissible perhaps to try to outline its principles; provided it be clearly understood that such a rough sketch rules out any kind of categorical assertion, and aims solely at submitting a few ideas, by way of hypotheses, to the critical examination of honest people. Besides, we are far from being without a guide on the subject. If Marx's system, in its broad outlines, is of little assistance, it is a different matter when it comes to the analyses he was led to make by the concrete study of capitalism, and in which, while believing that he was limiting himself to describing a system, he probably more than once seized upon the hidden nature of oppression itself.

Among all the forms of social organization which history has to show, there are very few which appear to be really free from oppression; and these few are not very well known. All of them correspond to an extremely low level of production, so low that the division of labour is pretty well unknown, except between the sexes, and each family produces little more than its own requirements. It is sufficiently obvious, moreover, that such material conditions necessarily rule out oppression, since each man, compelled to sustain himself personally, is continually at grips with outside nature; war itself, at this stage, is war of pillage and extermination, not of conquest, because the means of consolidating a conquest and especially of turning it to account are lacking. What is surprising is not that oppression should make its appearance only after higher forms of economy have been reached, but that it should always accompany them. This means, therefore, that as between a completely primitive economy and more highly developed forms of economy there is a difference not only of degree, but also of kind. And, in fact, although from the point of view of consumption there is but a change-over to slightly better conditions, production, which is the decisive factor, is itself transformed in its very essence. This transformation consists at first sight in a progressive emancipation with respect to nature. In completely primitive forms of production—hunting, fishing, gathering—human effort appears as a simple reaction to the inexorable pressure continually exercised on man by nature, and that in two ways. To start with, it takes place, to all intents and purposes, under immediate compulsion, under the ever-present spur of natural needs; and, by an indirect consequence, the action seems to receive its form from nature herself, owing to the important part played therein by an intuition comparable to animal instinct and a patient observation of the most frequent natural phenomena, also owing to the indefinite repetition of methods that have often succeeded without men's knowing why, and which are doubtless regarded as being welcomed by nature with special favour. At this stage, each man is necessarily free with respect to other men, because he is in direct contact with the conditions of his own existence, and because nothing human interposes itself between them and him; but, on the other hand, and to the same extent, he is narrowly subjected to nature's dominion, and he shows this clearly enough by deifying her. At higher stages of production, nature's compulsion continues certainly to be exercised, and still pitilessly, but in an apparently less immediate fashion; it seems to become more and more liberalized and to leave an increasing margin to man's freedom of choice, to his faculty of initiative and decision. Action is no longer tied moment by moment to nature's exigencies; men learn how to store up reserves on a long-term basis for meeting needs not yet actually felt; efforts which can be only of indirect usefulness become more and more numerous; at the same time a systematic co-ordination in time and in space becomes possible and necessary, and its importance increases continually. In short, man seems to pass by stages, with respect to nature, from servitude to dominion. At the same time nature gradually loses her divine character, and divinity more and more takes on human shape. Unfortunately, this emancipation is only a flattering semblance. In reality, at these higher stages, human action continues, as a whole, to be nothing but pure obedience to the brutal spur of an immediate necessity; only, instead of being harried by nature, man is henceforth harried by man. However, it is still the same pressure exerted by nature that continues to make itself felt, although indirectly; for oppression is exercised by force, and in the long run all force originates in nature.

The notion of force is far from simple, and yet it is the first that has to be elucidated in order to formulate the problems of society. Force and oppression—that makes two; but what needs to be understood above all is that it is not the manner in which use is made of some particular force, but its very nature, which determines whether it is oppressive or not. Marx clearly perceived this in connection with the State; he understood that this machine for grinding men down, cannot stop grinding as long as it goes on functioning, no matter in whose hands it may be. But this insight has a far more general application. Oppression proceeds exclusively from objective conditions. The first of these is the existence of privileges; and it is not men's laws or decrees which determine privileges, nor yet titles to property; it is the very nature of things. Certain circumstances, which correspond to stages, no doubt inevitable, in human development, give rise to forces which come between the ordinary man and his own conditions of existence, between the effort and the fruit of the effort, and which are, inherently, the monopoly of a few, owing to the fact that they cannot be shared among all; thenceforward these privileged beings, although they depend, in order to live, on the work of others, hold in their hands the fate of the very people on whom they depend, and equality is destroyed. This is what happens to begin with when the religious rites by which man thinks to win nature over to his side, having become too numerous and complicated to be known by all, finally become the secret and consequently the monopoly of a few priests; the priest then disposes, albeit only through a fiction, of all of nature's powers, and it is in their name that he exercises authority. Nothing essential is changed when this monopoly is no longer made up of rites but of scientific processes, and when those in possession of it are called scientists and technicians instead of priests.

Arms, too, give rise to a privilege from the day when, on the one hand, they are sufficiently powerful to render any defence by un-armed against armed men impossible, and, on the other, the handling of them has become sufficiently advanced, and consequently difficult, to require a long apprenticeship and continuous practice. For hence-forth the workers are powerless to defend themselves, whereas the warriors, albeit incapable of production, can always take forcible pos-session of the fruits of other people's labour; the workers are thus at the mercy of the warriors, and not the other way about. The same thing applies to gold, and more generally to money, as soon as the divi-sion of labour is so far developed that no worker can live off his own products without having exchanged at any rate some of them for those of others; the organization of exchange then becomes necessarily the monopoly of a few specialists who, having money under their control, can both obtain for themselves, in order to live, the products of others' labour, and at the same time deprive the producers of the indispen-sably necessary.

In short, wherever, in the struggle against men or against nature, efforts need to be multiplied and co-ordinated to be effective, co-ordi-nation becomes the monopoly of a few leaders as soon as it reaches a certain degree of complexity, and execution's primary law is then obedience; this is true both for the management of public affairs and for that of private undertakings. There may be other sources of privilege, but these are the chief ones; furthermore, except in the case of money, which appears at a given moment of history, all these fac-tors enter into play under all systems of oppression; what changes is the way in which they are distributed and combined, the degree of concentration of power, and also that more or less closed and conse-quently more or less mysterious character of each monopoly. Never-theless, privileges, of themselves, are not sufficient to cause oppression. Inequality could be easily mitigated by the resistance of the weak and the feeling of justice of the strong; it would not lead to a still harsher form of necessity than that of natural needs themselves, were it not for the intervention of a further factor, namely, the struggle for power.

As Marx clearly understood in the case of capitalism, and as a few moralists have perceived in a more general way, power contains a sort of fatality which weighs as pitilessly on those who command as on those who obey; nay more, it is in so far as it enslaves the former that, through their agency, it presses down upon the latter. The struggle against nature entails certain inescapable necessities which nothing can turn aside, but these necessities contain within themselves their own limits; nature resists, but she does not defend herself, and where she alone is involved, each situation presents certain well-defined obstacles which arouse the best in human effort. It is altogether different as soon as relations between man and man take the place of direct contact between man and nature. The preservation of power is a vital necessity for the powerful, since it is their power which provides their sustenance; but they have to preserve it both against their rivals and against their inferiors, and these latter cannot do otherwise than try to rid themselves of dangerous masters; for, through a vicious circle, the master produces fear in the slave by the very fact that he is afraid of him, and vice versa; and the same is true as between rival powers.

What is more, the two struggles that every man of power has to wage—first against those over whom he rules, secondly against his rivals—are inextricably bound up together and each is all the time rekindling the other. A power, whatever it may be, must always tend towards strengthening itself at home by means of successes gained abroad, for such successes provide it with more powerful means of coercion; besides, the struggle against its rivals rallies behind it its own slaves, who are under the illusion they have a personal interest in the result of the battle. But, in order to obtain from the slaves the obedience and sacrifices indispensable to victory, that power has to make itself more oppressive; to be in a position to exercise this oppression, it is still more imperatively compelled to turn outwards; and so on. We can follow out the same chain of events by starting from another link; show how a given social group, in order to be in a position to defend itself against the outside powers threatening to lay hands on it, must itself submit to an oppressive form of authority; how the power thus set up, in order to maintain its position, must stir up conflicts with rival powers; and so on, once again. Thus it is that the most fatal of vicious circles drags the whole society in the wake of its masters in a mad merry-go-round.

There are only two ways of breaking the circle, either by abolishing inequality, or else by setting up a stable power, a power such that there exists a balance between those who command and those who obey. It is this second solution that has been sought by all whom we call upholders of order, or at any rate all those among them who have been moved neither by servility nor by ambition; it was doubtless so with the Latin writers who praised "the immense majesty of the Roman peace", with Dante, with the reactionary school at the beginning of the nineteenth century, with Balzac, and is so today with sincere and thoughtful men of the Right. But this stability of power—objective of those who call themselves realists—shows itself to be a chimera, if one examines it closely, on the same grounds as the anarchists' utopia.

Between man and matter, each action, whether successful or not, establishes a balance that can only be upset from outside; for matter is inert. A displaced stone accepts its new position; the wind consents to guide to her destination the same ship which it would have sent off her course if sails and rudder had not been properly adjusted. But men are essentially active beings and have a faculty of self-determination which they can never renounce, even should they so desire, except on the day when, through death, they drop back into the state of inert matter; so that every victory won over men contains within itself the germ of a possible defeat, unless it goes as far as extermination. But extermination abolishes power by abolishing its object. Thus there is, in the very essence of power, a fundamental contradiction that prevents it from ever existing in the true sense of the word; those who are called the masters, ceaselessly compelled to reinforce their power for fear of seeing it snatched away from them, are for ever seeking a dominion essentially impossible to attain; beautiful illustrations of this search are offered by the infernal torments in Greek mythology. It would be otherwise if one man could possess in himself a force superior to that of many other men put together; but such is never the case; the instruments of power—arms, gold, machines, magical or technical secrets—always exist independently of him who disposes of them, and can be taken up by others. Consequently all power is unstable.

Generally speaking, among human beings, since the relationships between rulers and ruled are never fully acceptable, they always constitute an irremediable disequilibrium which is continually aggravating itself; the same is true even in the sphere of private life, where love, for example, destroys all balance in the soul as soon as it seeks to dominate or to be dominated by its object. But here at any rate there is nothing external to prevent reason from returning and putting everything to rights by establishing liberty and equality; whereas social relationships, in so far as the very methods of labour and of warfare rule out equality, seem to cause madness to weigh down on mankind in the manner of an external fatality. For, owing to the fact that there is never power, but only a race for power, and that there is no term, no limit, no proportion set to this race, neither is there any limit or proportion set to the efforts that it exacts; those who give themselves up to it, compelled to do always better than their rivals, who in their turn strive to do better than they, must sacrifice not only the existence of the slaves, but their own also and that of their nearest and dearest; so it is that Agamemnon sacrificing his daughter lives again in the capitalists who, to maintain their privileges, acquiesce lightheartedly in wars that may rob them of their sons.

Thus the race for power enslaves everybody, strong and weak alike. Marx saw this clearly with reference to the capitalist system. Rosa Luxemburg used to inveigh against the aspect of "aimless merry-go-round" presented by the Marxist picture of capitalist accumulation, that picture in which consumption appears as a "necessary evil" to be reduced to the minimum, a mere means for keeping alive those who devote themselves, whether as leaders or as workers, to the supreme object, which is none other than the manufacture of capital equipment, that is to say of the means of production. And yet it is the profound absurdity of this picture which gives it its profound truth; a truth which extends singularly beyond the framework of the capitalist system. The only characteristic peculiar to this system is that the instruments of industrial production are at the same time the chief weapons in the race for power; but always the methods pursued in the race for power, whatever they may be, bring men under their subjection through the same frenzy and impose themselves on them as absolute ends. It is the reflection of this frenzy that lends an epic grandeur to works such as the *Comédie Humaine*, Shakespeare's *Histories*, the *chansons de geste*, or the *Iliad*. The real subject of the *Iliad* is the sway exercised by war over the warriors, and, through them, over humanity in general; none of them knows why each sacrifices himself and all his family to a bloody and aimless war, and that is why, all through the poem, it is the gods who are credited with the mysterious influence which nullifies peace negotiations, continually revives hostilities, and brings together again the contending forces urged by a flash of good sense to abandon the struggle.

Thus in this ancient and wonderful poem there already appears the essential evil besetting humanity, the substitution of means for ends. At times war occupies the forefront, at other times the search for wealth, at other times production; but the evil remains the same. The common run of moralists complain that man is moved by his private interest: would to heaven it were so! Private interest is a self-centred principle of action, but at the same time restricted, reasonable and incapable of giving rise to unlimited evils. Whereas, on the other hand, the law of all activities governing social life, except in the case of primitive communities, is that here each one sacrifices human life—in himself and in others—to things which are only means to a better way of living. This sacrifice takes on various forms, but it all comes back to the question of power. Power, by definition, is only a means; or to put it better, to possess a power is simply to possess means of action which exceed the very limited force that a single individual has at his disposal. But power-seeking, owing to its essential incapacity to seize hold of its object, rules out all consideration of an end, and finally comes, through an inevitable reversal, to take the place of all ends. It is this reversal of the relationship between means and end, it is this fundamental folly that accounts for all that is senseless and bloody right through history. Human history is simply the history of the servitude which makes men—oppressors and oppressed alike—the plaything of the instruments of domination they themselves have manufactured, and thus reduces living humanity to being the chattel of inanimate chattels.

Thus it is things, not men, that prescribe the limits and laws governing this giddy race for power. Men's desires are powerless to control it. The masters may well dream of moderation, but they are prohibited from practising this virtue, on pain of defeat, except to a very slight extent; so that, apart from a few almost miraculous exceptions, such as Marcus Aurelius, they quickly become incapable even of conceiving it. As for the oppressed, their permanent revolt, which is always simmering, though it only breaks out now and then, can operate in such a way as to aggravate the evil as well as to restrict it; and on the whole it rather constitutes an aggravating factor in that it forces the masters to make their power weigh ever more heavily for fear of losing it.

From time to time the oppressed manage to drive out one team of oppressors and to replace it by another, and sometimes even to change the form of oppression; but as for abolishing oppression itself, that would first mean abolishing the sources of it, abolishing all the monopolies, the magical and technical secrets that give a hold over nature, armaments, money, co-ordination of labour. Even if the oppressed were sufficiently conscious to make up their minds to do so, they could not succeed. It would be condemning themselves to immediate enslavement by the social groupings that had not carried out the same change; and even were this danger to be miraculously averted, it would be condemning themselves to death, for, once men have forgotten the methods of primitive production and have transformed the natural environment into which these fitted, they cannot recover immediate contact with nature.

It follows that, in spite of so many vague desires to put an end to madness and oppression, the concentration of power and the aggravation of its tyrannical character would know no bounds were these not by good fortune found in the nature of things. It behoves us to determine roughly what these bounds can be; and for this purpose we must keep in mind the fact that if oppression is a necessity of social life, this necessity has nothing providential about it. It is not because it becomes detrimental to production that oppression can come to an end; the "revolt of the productive forces", so naïvely invoked by Trotsky as a factor in history, is a pure fiction. We should be mistaken likewise in assuming that oppression ceases to be ineluctable as soon as the productive forces have been sufficiently developed to ensure welfare and leisure for all. Aristotle admitted that there would no longer be anything to stand in the way of the abolition of slavery if it were possible to have the indispensable jobs done by "mechanical slaves", and when Marx attempted to forecast the future of the human species, all he did was to take up this idea and develop it. It would be true if men were guided by considerations of welfare; but from the days of the *Iliad* to our own times, the senseless demands made by the struggle for power have taken away even the leisure for thinking about welfare. The raising of the output of human effort will remain powerless to lighten the load of this effort as long as the social structure implies the reversal of the relationship between means and ends, in other words, as long as the methods of labour and of warfare give to a few men a discretionary power over the masses; for the fatigues and privations that have become unnecessary in the struggle against nature will be absorbed by the war carried on between men for the defense or acquisition of privileges. Once society is divided up into men who command and men who execute, the whole of social life is governed by the struggle for power, and the struggle for subsistence only enters in as one factor, indispensable to be sure, of the former.

The Marxist view, according to which social existence is determined by the relations between man and nature established by production, certainly remains the only sound basis for any historical investigation; only these relations must be considered first of all in terms of the problem of power, the means of subsistence forming simply one of the data of this problem. This order seems absurd, but it merely reflects the essential absurdity lying at the very heart of social life. A scientific study of history would thus be a study of the actions and reactions which are perpetually arising between the organization of power and the methods of production; for although power depends on the material conditions of life, it never ceases to transform these conditions themselves. Such a study goes very far beyond our possibilities at the moment; but before grappling with the infinite complexity of the facts, it is useful to make an abstract diagram of this interplay of actions and reactions, rather in the same way as astronomers have had to invent an imaginary celestial sphere so as to find their way about among the movements and positions of the stars.

We must try first of all to draw up a list of the inevitable necessities which limit all species of power. In the first place, any sort of power relies upon instruments which have in each situation a given scope. Thus you do not command in the same way, by means of soldiers armed with bows and arrows, spears and swords as you do by means of aeroplanes and incendiary bombs; the power of gold depends on the role played by exchanges in economic life; that of technical secrets is measured by the difference between what you can accomplish with their aid and what you can accomplish without them; and so on. As a matter of fact, one must always include in this balance-sheet the subterfuges by which the powerful obtain through persuasion what they are totally unable to obtain by force, either by placing the oppressed in a situation such that they have or think they have an immediate interest in doing what is asked of them, or by inspiring them with a fanaticism calculated to make them accept any and every sacrifice. Secondly, since the power that a human being really exercises extends only to what is effectively under his control, power is always running up against the actual limits of the controlling faculty, and these are extremely narrow. For no single mind can encompass a whole mass of ideas at once; no man can be in several places at once; and for master and slave alike there are never more than twenty-four hours in a day. Collaboration apparently constitutes a remedy for this drawback; but as it is never absolutely free from rivalry, it gives rise to infinite complications. The faculties of examining, comparing, weighing, deciding, combining are essentially individual, and consequently the same thing applies also to power, whose exercise is inseparable from these faculties; collective power is a fiction, at any rate in final analysis. As for the number of interests that can come under the control of one single man, that depends to a very large extent on individual factors such as breadth and quickness of intelligence, capacity for work, firmness of character; but it also depends on the objective conditions of the control exercised, more or less rapid methods of transport and communication, simplicity or otherwise of the machinery of power. Lastly, the exercise of any form of power is subject to the existence of a surplus in the production of commodities, and a sufficiently large surplus so that all those engaged, whether as masters or as slaves, in the struggle for power, may be able to live. Obviously, the extent of such surplus depends on the methods of production, and consequently also on the social organization. Here, therefore, are three factors that enable one to conceive political and social power as constituting at each moment something analogous to a measurable force. However, in order to complete the picture, one must bear in mind that the men who find themselves in relationship, whether as masters or as slaves, with the phenomenon of power are unconscious of this analogy. The powerful, be they priests, military leaders, kings or capitalists, always believe that they command by divine right; and those who are under them feel themselves crushed by a power which seems to them either divine or diabolical, but in any case supernatural. Every oppressive society is cemented by this religion of power, which falsifies all social relations by enabling the powerful to command over and above what they are able to impose; it is only otherwise in times of popular agitation, times when, on the contrary, all—rebellious slaves and threatened masters alike—forget how heavy and how solid the chains of oppression are.

Thus a scientific study of history ought to begin by analysing the reactions brought to bear at each moment by power on the conditions which assign to it objectively its limits; and a hypothetical sketch of the play of these reactions is indispensable in order to conduct such an analysis, far too difficult incidentally, considering our present possibilities. Some of these reactions are conscious and willed. Every power consciously strives, in proportion to the means at its disposal —a proportion determined by the social organization—to improve production and official control within its own sphere; history offers many an example of this, from the Pharaohs down to the present day, and it is on this that the notion of enlightened despotism is founded. On the other hand, every power strives also, and again consciously, to destroy among its competitors the means whereby to produce and govern, and is the object on their part of a similar attempt. Thus the struggle for power is at the same time constructive and destructive, and brings about economic progress or decadence, depending on whichever aspect wins the day; and it is clear that in a given civilization destruction will take place to an extent all the greater the more difficult it is for a power to expand without coming up against rival powers approximately as strong as itself. But the indirect consequences of the exercise of power are far more important than the conscious efforts of the wielders of power.

Every power, from the mere fact that it is exercised, extends to the farthest possible limit the social relations on which it is based; thus military power multiplies wars, commercial capital multiplies exchanges. Now it sometimes happens, through a sort of providential accident, that this extension gives rise, by some mechanism or other, to new resources that make a new extension possible, and so on, more or less in the same way as food strengthens living beings in full process of growth and enables them thus to win still more food so as to acquire still greater strength. All régimes provide examples of such providential accidents; for without them no form of power could endure, and consequently those powers that benefit from them are the only ones to subsist. Thus war enabled the Romans to carry off slaves, that is to say workers in the prime of life, whom others had had to provide for during childhood; the profit derived from slave labour made it possible to reinforce the army, and the stronger army undertook more important wars which brought in new and bigger consignments of slaves as booty. Similarly, the roads which the Romans built for military purposes later facilitated the government and exploitation of the conquered provinces, and thus contributed towards storing up resources for future wars.

If we turn now to modern times, we see, for example, that the extension of exchanges has brought about a greater division of labour, which in its turn has made a wider circulation of commodities indispensable; furthermore, the increased productivity which has resulted from this has furnished new resources that have been able to transform themselves into commercial and industrial capital. As far as big industry is concerned, it is clear that each important advance in mechanization has created at the same time resources, instruments and a stimulus towards a further advance. Similarly, it was the technique of big industry which came to provide the means of control and information indispensable to the centralized economy that is the inevitable outcome of big industry, such as the telegraph, the telephone, the daily press. The same may be said with regard to the means of transport.

One could find all through history an immense number of similar examples, bearing on the widest and the narrowest aspects of social life. One may define the growth of a system by the fact that all it needs to do is to function in order to create new resources enabling it to function on a larger scale.

This phenomenon of automatic development is so striking that one would be tempted to imagine that a happily constituted system, if one may so express it, would go on enduring and progressing endlessly. That is exactly what the nineteenth century, socialists included, imagined with regard to the system of big industry. But if it is easy to imagine in a vague way an oppressive system that would never fall into decadence, it is no longer the same if one wants to conceive clearly and concretely the indefinite extension of a specific power. If it could extend endlessly its means of control, it would tend indefinitely towards a limit which would be something like ubiquity; if it could extend its resources endlessly, everything would be as though surrounding nature were evolving gradually towards that unqualified abundance from which Adam and Eve benefited in the earthly paradise; and, finally, if it could extend indefinitely the range of its own instruments—whether it be a question of arms, gold, technical secrets, machines or anything else—it would tend towards abolishing that correlation which, by indissolubly linking together the notions of master and of slave, establishes between master and slave a relationship of mutual dependence.

One cannot prove that all this is impossible; but one must assume that it is impossible, or else decide to think of human history as a fairy-tale. In general, one can only regard the world in which we live as subject to laws if one admits that every phenomenon in it is limited; and it is the same for the phenomenon of power, as Plato had understood. If we want to consider power as a conceivable phenomenon, we must think that it can extend the foundations on which it rests up to a certain point only, after which it comes up, as it were, against an impassable wall. But even so it is not in a position to stop; the spur of competition forces it to go ever farther and farther, that is to say to go beyond the limits within which it can be effectively exercised. It extends beyond what it is able to control; it commands over and above what it can impose; it spends in excess of its own resources. Such is the internal contradiction which every oppressive system carries within itself like a seed of death; it is made up of the opposition between the necessarily limited character of the material bases of power and the necessarily unlimited character of the race for power considered as relationship between men.

For as soon as a power goes beyond the limits assigned to it by the nature of things, it narrows down the bases on which it rests, renders these limits themselves narrower and narrower. By spreading beyond what it is able to control, it breeds a parasitism, a waste, a confusion which, once they have appeared, increase automatically. By attempting to command where actually it is not in a position to compel obedience, it provokes reactions which it can neither foresee nor deal with. Finally, by wishing to spread the exploitation of the oppressed beyond what the objective resources make possible, it exhausts these resources themselves; this is doubtless what is meant by the ancient and popular tale of the goose with the golden eggs. Whatever may be the sources from whence the exploiters draw the material goods which they appropriate, a day arrives when such and such a method of development, which was at first, as it went on spreading, more and more productive, finally becomes, on the other hand, increasingly costly. That is how the Roman army, which had first of all brought wealth to Rome, ended by ruining it; that is how the knights of the Middle Ages, whose battles had first of all brought a relative security to the peasants, who found themselves to a certain extent protected against acts of brigandage, ended in the course of their interminable wars by laying waste the countryside which fed them; and it certainly seems as though capitalism is passing through a phase of this kind. Once more, it cannot be proved that it must always be so; but it has to be assumed, unless the possibility of inexhaustible resources is also assumed. Thus it is the nature itself of things which constitutes that justice-dealing divinity the Greeks worshipped under the name of Nemesis, and which punishes excess.

When a specific form of domination finds itself thus arrested in its development and faced with decadence, it does not follow that it begins to disappear progressively; sometimes it is then, on the contrary, that it becomes most harshly oppressive, that it crushes human beings under its weight, that it grinds down body, heart and spirit without mercy. However, since everyone begins little by little to feel the lack of the resources required by some to maintain their supremacy, by others to live, a time comes when, on every hand, there is a feverish search for expedients. There is no reason why such a search should not remain fruitless; and in that case the régime can only end by collapsing for want of the means of subsistence and being replaced, not by another and better organized régime, but by a disorder, a poverty, a primitive condition of existence which continue until some new factor or other gives rise to new relationships of force. If it happens otherwise, if the search for new material resources is successful, new patterns of social life arise and a change of régime begins to form slowly and, as it were, subterraneously. Subterraneously, because these new forms can only develop in so far as they are compatible with the established order and do not represent, in appearance at any rate, any danger for the powers that be; otherwise nothing could prevent these powers from destroying them, as long as they remain the stronger. For the new social patterns to triumph over the old, this continued development must already have brought them to play effectively a more important role in the functioning of the social organism; in other words, they must have given rise to more powerful forces than those at the disposal of the official authorities. Thus there is never really any break in continuity, not even when the change of régime seems to be the result of a bloody struggle; for all that victory then does is to sanction forces that, even before the struggle, were the decisive factor in the life of the community, social patterns that had long since begun gradually to replace those on which the declining régime rested. So it was that, under the Roman Empire, the barbarians had begun to occupy the most important posts, the army was disintegrating little by little into armed bands led by adventurers, and the system of military colonies gradually replaced slavery by serfdom—all this long before the great invasions. Similarly, the French bourgeoisie did not by any means wait until 1789 to get the better of the nobility. The Russian Revolution, thanks to a singular conjunction of circumstances, certainly seemed to give rise to something entirely new; but the truth is that the privileges it abolished had not for a long time rested on any social foundation other than tradition; that the institutions arising out of the insurrection did not perhaps effectively function for as long as a single morning; and that the real forces, namely big industry, the police, the army, the bureaucracy, far from being smashed by the Revolution, attained, thanks to it, a power unknown in other countries.

Generally speaking, the sudden reversal of the relationship between forces which is what we usually understand by the term "revolution" is not only a phenomenon unknown in history, but furthermore, if we examine it closely, something literally inconceivable, for it would be a victory of weakness over force, the equivalent of a balance whose lighter scale were to go down. What history offers us is slow transformations of régimes, in which the bloody events to which we give the name "revolutions" play a very secondary role, and from which they may even be absent; such is the case when the social class which ruled in the name of the old relationships of force manages to keep a part of the power under cover of the new relationships, and the history of England supplies an example. But whatever may be the patterns taken by social transformations, all one finds, if one tries to lay bare the mechanism, is a dreary play of blind forces that unite together or clash, that progress or decline, that replace each other, without ever ceasing to grind beneath them the unfortunate race of human beings. At first sight there seems to be no weak spot in this sinister mesh of circumstances through which an attempt at deliverance might find its way. But it is not from such a vague, abstract and miserably hasty sketch as this that one can claim to draw any conclusion.

We must pose once again the fundamental problem, namely, what constitutes the bond which seems hitherto to have united social oppression and progress in the relations between man and nature? If one considers human development as a whole up to our own time, if, above all, one contrasts primitive tribes, organized practically without inequality, with our present-day civilization, it seems as if man cannot manage to lighten the yoke imposed by natural necessities without an equal increase in the weight of that imposed by social oppression, as though by the play of a mysterious equilibrium. And even, what is stranger still, it would seem that if, in fact, the human collectivity has to a large extent freed itself from the crushing burden which the gigantic forces of nature place on frail humanity, it has, on the other hand, taken in some sort nature's place to the point of crushing the individual in a similar manner.

What makes primitive man a slave? The fact that he hardly orders his own activity at all; he is the plaything of need, which dictates each of his movements or very nearly, and harries him with its relentless spur; and his actions are regulated not by his own intelligence, but by the customs and caprices—both equally incomprehensible—of a nature that he can but worship with blind submission. If we consider simply the collectivity, men seem nowadays to have raised themselves to a condition that is diametrically the opposite of that servile state. Hardly a single one of their tasks constitutes a mere response to the imperative impulsion of need; work is accomplished in such a way as to take charge of nature and to organize her so that needs can be satisfied. Humanity no longer believes itself to be in the presence of capricious divinities whose good graces must be won over; it knows that it has merely to handle inert matter, and acquits itself of this task by methodically following out clearly conceived laws. At last we seem to have reached that epoch predicted by Descartes when men would use "the force and actions of fire, water, air, the stars and all the other bodies" in the same way as they do the artisans' tools, and would thus make themselves masters of nature. But, by a strange inversion, this collective dominion transforms itself into servitude as soon as one descends to the scale of the individual, and into a servitude fairly closely resembling that associated with primitive conditions of existence.

The efforts of the modern worker are imposed on him by a constraint as brutal, as pitiless and which holds him in as tight a grip as hunger does the primitive hunter. From the time of that primitive hunter up to that of the worker in our large factories, passing by way of the Egyptian workers driven by the lash, the slaves of antiquity, the serfs of the Middle Ages constantly threatened by the seignorial sword, men have never ceased to be goaded to work by some outside force and on pain of almost immediate death. And as for the sequence of movements in work, that, too, is often imposed from outside on our workers, exactly as in the case of primitive men, and is as mysterious for the ones as it was for the others; what is more, in this respect, the constraint is in certain cases incomparably more brutal today than it has ever been. However tied and bound a primitive man was to routine and blind gropings, he could at least try to think things out, to combine and innovate at his own risk, a liberty which is absolutely denied to a worker engaged in a production line. Lastly, if humanity appears to have reached the stage of controlling those forces of nature which, however, in Spinoza's words, "infinitely surpass those of mankind"—and that in almost as sovereign a fashion as a rider controls his horse—that victory does not belong to men taken individually; only the largest collectivities are in a position to handle "the force and actions of fire, water, air . . . and all the other bodies that surround us"; as for the members of these collectivities, both oppressors and oppressed are alike subjected to the implacable demands of the struggle for power.

Thus, in spite of progress, man has not emerged from the servile condition in which he found himself when he was handed over weak and naked to all the blind forces that make up the universe; it is merely that the power which keeps him on his knees has been as it were transferred from inert matter to the human society of which he is a member. That is why it is this society which is imposed on his worship through all the various forms that religious feeling takes in turn. Hence the social question poses itself in a fairly clear manner; the mechanism of this transfer must be examined; we must try to find out why man has had to pay this price for his power over nature; form an idea of what would constitute the least unhappy position for him to be in, that is to say the one in which he would be the least enslaved to the twin domination of nature and society; and lastly, discern what roads can lead towards such a position, and what instruments present-day civilization could place in men's hands if they aspired to transform their lives in this way.

We accept material progress too easily as a gift of the gods, as something which goes without saying; we must look fairly and

squarely at the conditions at the cost of which it takes place. Primitive
life is something easy to understand; man is spurred on by hunger, or
at any rate by the anguished thought that he will soon go hungry,
and he sets off in search of food; he shivers in the cold, or at any rate
at the thought that he will soon feel cold, and he goes in search of
heat-creating or heat-preserving materials; and so on. As for the way
in which to set about the matter, this is given him in the first place
by the habit acquired in childhood of imitating his seniors, and also
as a result of the habits which he has given himself in the course
of innumerable tentative efforts, by repeating those methods which
have succeeded; when caught off his guard, he continues to proceed
by trial and error, spurred on as he is to act by a sharp urge which
never leaves him a moment's peace. In all this process, man has
only to yield to his own nature, not master it.

On the other hand, as soon as we pass to a more advanced stage
of civilization, everything becomes miraculous. Men are then found
laying by things that are good to consume, desirable things, which
they nevertheless go without. They are found giving up to a large
extent the search for food, warmth, etc., and spending the best part
of their energy on apparently unprofitable labours. As a matter of
fact, most of these labours, far from being unprofitable, are infinitely
more profitable than the efforts of primitive man, for they result in an
organization of outside nature in a manner favourable to human existence; but this efficacy is indirect and often separated from the actual
effort by so many intermediaries that the mind has difficulty in covering them; it is a long-term efficacy, often so long-term that it is
only future generations which will benefit from it; while, on the other
hand, the utter fatigue, physical pains and dangers connected with
these labours are felt immediately, and all the time. Now, everybody
knows from his own experience how unusual it is for an abstract idea
having a long-term utility to triumph over present pains, needs and
desires. It must, however, do so in the matter of social existence, on
pain of a regression to a primitive form of life.

But what is more miraculous still is the co-ordination of labour.
Any reasonably high level of production presupposes a more or less
extensive co-operation; and co-operation shows itself in the fact that

the efforts of each one have meaning and efficacy only through their relationship to and exact correspondence with the efforts of all the rest, in such a way that all the efforts together form one single collective piece of work. In other words, the movements of several men must be combined according to the manner in which the movements of a single man are combined. But how can this be done? A combination can only take place if it is intellectually conceived; while a relationship is never formed except within one mind. The number 2 thought of by one man cannot be added to the number 2 thought of by another man so as to make up the number 4; similarly, the idea that one of the co-operators has of the partial work he is carrying out cannot be combined with the idea that each of the others has of his respective task so as to form a coherent piece of work. Several human minds cannot become united in one collective mind, and the expressions "collective soul", "collective thought", so commonly employed nowadays, are altogether devoid of meaning. Consequently, for the efforts of several to be combined, they all need to be directed by one and the same mind, as the famous line in *Faust* expresses it: "One mind is enough for a thousand hands."

In the egalitarian organization of primitive tribes, it is not possible to solve a single one of these problems, neither that of privation, nor that of incentive to effort, nor that of co-ordination of labour; on the other hand, social oppression provides an immediate solution, by creating, to put it broadly, two categories of men—those who command and those who obey. The leader co-ordinates without difficulty the efforts of those who are under his orders; he has no temptation to overcome in order to reduce them to what is strictly necessary; and as for the stimulus to effort, an oppressive organization is admirably equipped for driving men beyond the limit of their strength, some being whipped by ambition, others, in Homer's words, "under the goad of a harsh necessity".

The results are often extraordinary when the division between social categories is deep enough for those who decide what work shall be done never to be exposed to feeling or even knowing about the exhausting fatigue, the pains and the dangers of it, while those who do it and suffer have no choice, being continually under the

sway of a more or less disguised menace of death. Thus it is that
man escapes to a certain extent from the caprices of blind nature
only by handing himself over to the no less blind caprices of the
struggle for power. This is never truer than when man reaches—
as in our case—a technical development sufficiently advanced to give
him the mastery over the forces of nature; for, in order that this may
be so, co-operation has to take place on such a vast scale that the
leaders find they have to deal with a mass of affairs which lie utterly
beyond their capacity to control. As a result, humanity finds itself
as much the plaything of the forces of nature, in the new form
that technical progress has given them, as it ever was in primitive
times; we have had, are having, and will continue to have bitter
experience of this. As for attempts to preserve technique while shak-
ing off oppression, they at once provoke such laziness and such confusion that those who have engaged in them are more often than
not obliged to place themselves again almost immediately under the
yoke; the experiment was tried out on a small scale in the producers'
co-operatives, on a vast scale at the time of the Russian Revolution.
It would seem that man is born a slave, and that servitude is his
natural condition.

THE *ILIAD,*
POEM OF MIGHT

"The ILIAD, *Poem of Might," Simone Weil's most famous essay, is an astonishing contemplation of the historical crisis situation brought on by Hitler. She had first started to write it in 1939; it was published in Marseilles, in the* CAHIERS DU SUD, *in December 1940 and January 1941. As a permanent and universal "mirror of reality," the* ILIAD *teaches us, above all, she emphasizes, "how to accept the fact that nothing is sheltered from fate, how never to admire might, or hate the enemy, or to despise sufferers."*

The true hero, the real subject, the core of the *Iliad,* is might. That might which is wielded by men rules over them, and before it man's flesh cringes. The human soul never ceases to be modified by its encounter with might, swept on, blinded by that which it believes itself able to handle, bowed beneath the power of that which it suffers. Those who dreamt that might, thanks to progress, belonged henceforth to the past, have been able to see its living witness in this poem: those who know how to discern might throughout the ages, there at the heart of every human testament, find here its most beautiful, most pure of mirrors.

Might is that which makes a thing of anybody who comes under its sway. When exercised to the full, it makes a thing of man in the most literal sense, for it makes him a corpse. There where someone stood a moment ago, stands no one. This is the spectacle which the *Iliad* never tires of presenting.

> . . . *the horses*
> *Thundered the empty chariots over the battle-lanes*
> *Mourning their noble masters. But those upon earth*
> *Now stretched, are dearer to the vultures than to*
> *their wives.*

The hero is become a thing dragged in the dust behind a chariot.

> *All about the dark hair*
> *Was strewn; and the whole head lay in dust,*
> *That head but lately so beloved. Now Zeus had*
> *permitted*
> *His enemies to defile it upon its native soil.*

The bitterness of this scene, we savour it whole, alleviated by no comforting fiction, no consoling immortality, no faint halo of patriotic glory.

> *His soul from his body took flight and sped towards*
> *Hades*
> *Weeping over its destiny, leaving its vigour and*
> *its youth.*

More poignant still for its pain of contrast is the sudden evocation, as quickly effaced, of another world, the far-off world, precarious and touching of peace, of the family, that world wherein each man is, for those who surround him, all that counts most.

> *Her voice rang through the house calling her*
> *bright-haired maids*
> *To draw a great tripod to the fire that there might be*
> *A hot bath for Hector upon his return from combat.*
> *Foolish one! She knew not that far away from hot baths*
> *The arm of Achilles had felled him because of green-*
> *eyed Athena.*

Indeed he was far from hot baths, this sufferer. He was not the only one. Nearly all the *Iliad* takes place far from hot baths. Nearly all of human life has always passed far from hot baths.

The might which kills outright is an elementary and coarse form of might. How much more varied in its devices; how much more astonishing in its effects is that other which does not kill; or which delays killing. It must surely kill, or it will perhaps kill, or else it is only suspended above him whom it may at any moment destroy. This of all procedures turns a man to stone. From the power to transform him into a thing by killing him there proceeds another power, and much more prodigious, that which makes a thing of him while he still lives. He is living, he has a soul, yet he is a thing. A strange being is that thing which has a soul, and strange the state of that soul. Who knows how often during each instant it must torture and destroy itself in order to conform? The soul was not made to dwell in a thing; and when forced to it, there is no part of that soul but suffers violence.

A man naked and disarmed upon whom a weapon is directed becomes a corpse before he is touched. Only for one moment still he deliberates, he strives, he hopes.

> *Motionless Achilles considered. The other drew near,*
>   *seized*
> *By desire to touch his knees. He wished in his heart*
> *To escape evil death, and black destiny....*
> *With one arm he encircled those knees to implore him,*
> *With the other he kept hold of his bright lance.*

But soon he has understood that the weapon will not turn from him, and though he still breathes, he is only matter, still thinking, he can think of nothing.

> *Thus spake the brilliant son of Priam*
> *With suppliant words. He hears an inflexible reply ...*
> *He spoke; and the other's knees and heart failed him,*
> *He dropped his lance and sank to the ground with*
>   *open hands,*
> *With both hands outstretched. Achilles unsheathes*
>   *his sharp sword,*

Struck to the breastbone, along the throat, and then
    the two-edged sword
Plunges home its full length. The other, face down upon
    the ground,
Lay inert, his dark blood flowed drenching the earth.

When, a stranger, completely disabled, weak and disarmed, appeals to a warrior, he is not by this act condemned to death; but only an instant of impatience on the part of the warrior suffices to deprive him of life. This is enough to make his flesh lose that principal property of all living tissue. A morsel of living flesh gives evidence of life first of all by reflex, as a frog's leg under electric shock jumps, as the approaching menace or the contact with a horrible thing, or terrifying event, provokes a shudder in no matter what bundle of flesh, nerves and muscles. Alone, the hopeless suppliant does not shudder, does not cringe; he no longer has such licence; his lips are about to touch that one of all objects which is for him the most charged with horror.

None saw the entrance of great Priam. He paused,
Encircled Achilles' knees, kissed those hands,
Terrible slayers of men, that had cost him so many sons.

The spectacle of a man reduced to such a degree of misery freezes almost as does the sight of a corpse.

As when dire misfortune strikes a man, if in his own
    country
He has killed, and he arrives at another's door,
That of some wealthy man; a chill seizes those who
    see him;
So Achilles shivered at the sight of divine Priam,
So those with him trembled, looking from one to the other.

But this only for a moment, soon the very presence of the sufferer is forgotten:

He speaks. Achilles, reminded of his own father, longed to
    weep for him.

Taking the old man by the arm, he thrusts him
  gently away.
Both were lost in remembrance; the one of Hector,
  slayer of men,
And in tears he faints to the ground at Achilles' feet.
But Achilles wept for his father and then also
For Patroclus. And the sound of their sobbing rocked
  the halls.

It is not for want of sensibility that Achilles had, by a sudden gesture, pushed the old man glued against his knees to the ground. Priam's words, evoking his old father, had moved him to tears. Quite simply he had found himself to be as free in his attitudes, in his movements, as if in place of a suppliant an inert object were there touching his knees. The human beings around us exert just by their presence a power which belongs uniquely to themselves to stop, to diminish, or modify, each movement which our bodies design. A person who crosses our path does not turn aside our steps in the same manner as a street sign, no one stands up, or moves about, or sits down again in quite the same fashion when he is alone in a room as when he has a visitor. But this undefinable influence of the human presence is not exercised by those men whom a movement of impatience could deprive of their lives even before a thought had had the time to condemn them. Before these men others behave as if they were not there; and they, in turn, finding themselves in danger of being in an instant reduced to nothing, imitate nothingness. Pushed, they fall; fallen, they remain on the ground, so long as no one happens to think of lifting them up. But even if at last lifted up, honoured by cordial words, they still cannot bring themselves to take this resurrection seriously enough to dare to express a desire; an irritated tone of voice would immediately reduce them again to silence.

He spoke and the old man trembled and obeyed.

At least some suppliants, once exonerated, become again as other men. But there are others, more miserable beings, who without dying have become things for the rest of their lives. In their days is no give and take, no open field, no free road over which anything can pass to

or from them. These are not men living harder lives than others, not
placed lower socially than others, these are another species, a compromise between a man and a corpse. That a human being should be
a thing is, from the point of view of logic, a contradiction; but when
the impossible has become a reality, that contradiction is as a rent in
the soul. That thing aspires every moment to become a man, a woman,
and never at any moment succeeds. This is a death drawn out the length
of a life, a life that death has frozen long before extinguishing it.

A virgin, the daughter of a priest, suffers this fate:

> *I will not release her. Before that old age shall*
> *   have taken her,*
> *In our dwelling, in Argos, far from her native land*
> *Tending the loom, and sharing my bed.*

The young wife, the young mother, the wife of a prince suffers
it:

> *And perhaps one day in Argos you will weave cloth*
> *   for another*
> *And you shall fetch Messeian or Hyperian*
> *   water*
> *In spite of yourself, under stress of dire necessity.*

The child heir to a royal sceptre suffers it:

> *These doubtless shall depart in the depths of*
> *   hollow ships*
> *I among them; you, my child, will either go with me*
> *To a land where humiliating tasks await you*
> *And you will labour beneath the eyes of a pitiless master. . . .*

Such a fate for her child is more frightful to the mother than
death itself, the husband wishes to perish before seeing his wife
reduced to it. A father calls down all the scourges of heaven upon
the army that would subject his daughter to it. But for those upon
whom it has fallen, so brutal a destiny wipes out damnations, revolts,
comparisons, meditations upon the future and the past, almost mem-

ory itself. It does not belong to the slave to be faithful to his city or to his dead.

It is when one of those who made him lose all, who sacked his city, massacred his own under his very eyes, when one of those suffers, then the slave weeps. And why not? Only then are tears permitted him. They are even imposed. But during his servitude are not those tears always ready to flow as soon as, with impunity, they may?

> *She speaks in weeping, and the women moan*
> *Taking Patroclus as pretext for each one's private*
> *   anguish.*

On no occasion has the slave a right to express anything if not that which may please the master. This is why, if in so barren a life, a capacity to love should be born, this love could only be for the master. Every other way is barred to the gift of loving, just as for a horse hitched to a wagon, the reins and the bridle bar all directions but one. And if by miracle there should appear the hope of becoming again someone, to what pitch would not that gratitude and that love soar for those very men who must still, because of the recent past, inspire horror?

> *My husband, to whom my father and my revered mother gave me,*
> *I saw before the city, transfixed by the sharp bronze.*
> *My three brothers, born of our one mother,*
> *So beloved! have met their fatal day.*
> *But you, when swift Achilles killed my husband*
> *And laid waste the city of divine Mynes,*
> *Did not allow me to weep. You promised me that the divine*
> *   Achilles*
> *Would take me for his legitimate wife and carry*
> *   me off in his vessels*
> *To Phthia to celebrate our marriage among the*
> *   Myrmidons.*
> *Therefore without ceasing I weep for you who have*
> *   always been so gentle.*

One cannot lose more than the slave loses, he loses all inner life. He only retrieves a little if there should arise an opportunity to change his destiny. Such is the empire of might; it extends as far as the empire of nature. Nature also, where vital needs are in play, wipes out all interior life, even to a mother's sorrow.

> *For even Niobe of the beautiful hair, had thought*
>   *of eating,*
> *She who saw twelve children of her house perish,*
> *Six daughters and six sons in the flower of youth.*
> *The sons Apollo killed with his silver bow*
> *In his anger against Niobe, the daughters, Artemis,*
>   *lover of arrows, slew.*
> *It was because Niobe made herself equal to Leto saying:*
> *'She has two children, I have given birth to many.'*
> *And those two, although only two, brought death to all.*
> *Nine days they lay dead; and none came to bury them.*
> *The neighbours had become stones by the will of Zeus.*
> *On the tenth day they were interred by the Gods of*
>   *the sky,*
> *But Niobe had thought of eating, when she was weary*
>   *of tears.*

None ever expressed with so much bitterness the misery of man, which renders him incapable of feeling his misery.

Might suffered at the hands of another is as much a tyranny over the soul as extreme hunger at the moment when food means life or death. And its empire is as cold, and as hard as though exercised by lifeless matter. The man who finds himself everywhere the most feeble of his fellows is as lonely in the heart of a city, or more lonely, than anyone can be who is lost in the midst of a desert.

> *Two cauldrons stand at the doorsill of Zeus*
> *Wherein are the gifts he bestows, the evil in one,*
>   *the good in the other. . . .*
> *The man to whom he makes evil gifts he exposes to outrage;*
> *A dreadful need pursues him across divine earth;*
> *He wanders respected neither by men nor by Gods.*

And as pitilessly as might crushes, so pitilessly it maddens whoever possesses, or believes he possesses it. None can ever truly possess it. The human race is not divided, in the *Iliad*, between the vanquished,

the slaves, the suppliants on the one hand, and conquerors and masters
on the other. No single man is to be found in it who is not, at
some time, forced to bow beneath might. The soldiers, although free
and well-armed, suffer no less outrage.

> *Every man of the people whom he saw he shouted at*
> *And struck with his sceptre and reprimanded thus:*
> *'Miserable one, be still, listen while others speak,*
> *Your superiors. You have neither courage nor strength,*
> *You count for nothing in battle, for nothing in the*
> *   assembly.'*

Thersites pays dear for these words, though perfectly reasonable
and not unlike those pronounced by Achilles:

> *He strikes him so that he collapses with tears fast flowing,*
> *A bloody welt rises upon his back*
> *Beneath the golden sceptre; he sits down, frightened.*
> *In a stupor of pain he wipes his tears.*
> *The others, though troubled, found pleasure and*
> *   laughed.*

But even Achilles, that proud unvanquished hero, is shown to
us at the beginning of the poem weeping for humiliation and frus-
trating pain after the woman he had wanted for his wife was carried
away under his very eyes and without his having dared to offer any
opposition.

> *...But Achilles,*
> *Weeping, sat down at a distance far from his companions,*
> *Beside the whitening waves, his eyes fixed upon*
> *   the boundless sea.*

Agamemnon humiliates Achilles deliberately to show that he
is the master.

> *...Thus you will realize*
> *That I have more power than you, and all others shall tremble*
> *To treat me as an equal and to contradict me.*

But a few days later even the supreme leader weeps in his turn, is forced to humble himself, to plead and to know the sorrow of doing so in vain.

Neither is the shame of fear spared to a single one of the combatants. The heroes tremble with the others. A challenge from Hector suffices to throw into consternation all the Greeks without the least exception, except Achilles and his men, who are absent.

> *He speaks and all were silent and held their peace;*
> *They were ashamed to refuse, frightened to accept.*

But from the moment that Ajax advances, fear changes sides:

> *The Trojans felt a shiver of terror through their limbs,*
> *Even Hector's heart bounded in his breast,*
> *But he no longer had license to tremble or*
> *   seek refuge.*

Two days later, it is Ajax's turn to feel terror:

> *Zeus, the father, from above causes fear to mount*
> *   in Ajax;*
> *He stands, distraught, putting his seven-skinned*
> *   shield behind him,*
> *Trembling before the crowd like a beast at bay.*

It happens once, even to Achilles: he trembles and groans with fright, not, it is true, before a man but before a great river. Himself excepted, absolutely all are at some moment shown vanquished. Valour contributes less in determining victory than blind destiny, which is represented by the golden scales of Zeus:

> *At this moment Zeus the father makes use of his*
> *   golden scales.*
> *Placing therein the two fates of death that reaps all,*
> *One for the Trojans, breakers of horses, one for the*
> *   bronze-clad Greeks.*
> *He seized the scales in the middle; it was the fatal day of the*
> *   Greeks that sank.*

Because it is blind, destiny establishes a sort of justice, blind also, which punishes men of arms with death by the sword; the *Iliad* formulated the justice of retaliation long before the Gospels, and almost in the same terms:

Ares is equitable, he kills those who kill.

If all men, by the act of being born, are destined to suffer violence, that is a truth to which the empire of circumstances closes their minds. The strong man is never absolutely strong, nor the weak man absolutely weak, but each one is ignorant of this. They do not believe that they are of the same species. The weak man no more regards himself as like the strong man than he is regarded as such. He who possesses strength moves in an atmosphere which offers him no resistance. Nothing in the human element surrounding him is of a nature to induce, between the intention and the act, that brief interval where thought may lodge. Where there is no room for thought, there is no room either for justice or prudence. This is the reason why men of arms behave with such harshness and folly. Their weapon sinks into an enemy disarmed at their knees; they triumph over a dying man, describing to him the outrages that his body will suffer; Achilles beheads twelve Trojan adolescents on Patroclus' funeral pyre as naturally as we cut flowers for a tomb. They never guess as they exercise their power, that the consequences of their acts will turn back upon themselves. When with a word one can make an old man be silent, obey, tremble, does one reflect upon the importance in the eyes of the gods of the curses of the old man, who is also a priest? Does one abstain from carrying off the woman Achilles loves when one knows she and he cannot do otherwise than obey? While Achilles enjoys the sight of the unhappy Greeks in flight, can he think that this flight, which will last as long and finish when he wills, may cost the life of his friend and even his own life? Thus it is that those to whom destiny lends might, perish for having relied too much upon it.

It is impossible that they should not perish. For they never think of their own strength as a limited quantity, nor of their relations with others as an equilibrium of unequal powers. Other men do not impose upon their acts that moment for pausing from which alone our consideration for our fellows proceeds: they conclude from this that destiny has given all licence to them and none to their inferiors. Henceforth they go beyond the measure of their strength, inevitably so, because they do not know its limit. Thus they are delivered up helpless before chance, and things no longer obey them. Sometimes chance serves them, at other times it hinders, and here they are, exposed, naked before misfortune without that armour of might which protected their souls, without anything any more to separate them from tears.

This retribution, of a geometric strictness, which punishes automatically the abuse of strength, became the principal subject of meditation for the Greeks. It constitutes the soul of the Greek epic; under the name of Nemesis it is the mainspring of Aeschylus' tragedies. The Pythagoreans, Socrates, Plato, take this as the point of departure for their thoughts about man and the universe. The notion has become familiar wherever Hellenism has penetrated. It is perhaps this Greek idea which subsists, under the name of Kharma, in Oriental countries impregnated by Buddhism; but the Occident has lost it and has not even in any one of its languages a word to express it; the ideas of limit, of measure, of equilibrium, which should determine the conduct of life, have no more than a servile usage in its technique. We are only geometricians in regard to matter; the Greeks were first of all geometricians in the apprenticeship of virtue.

The progress of the war in the *Iliad* is no more than this play of the scales. The victor of the moment feels himself invincible, even when only a few hours earlier he had experienced defeat; he forgets to partake of victory as of a thing which must pass. At the end of the first day of combat recounted in the *Iliad*, the victorious Greeks could doubtless have obtained the object of their efforts, that is, Helen and her wealth; at least if one supposes, as Homer does, that the Greek army was right to believe that Helen was in Troy. The Egyptian priests, however, who ought to have known, affirmed later to Herodotus that she was in Egypt. In any case, on that particular evening, the Greeks did not want her.

'Let us at present accept neither the wealth of Paris
Nor of Helen; each one sees, even the most ignorant,
That Troy now stands at the edge of doom.'
He spoke and all among the Achaeans acclaimed.

What they want is no less than all. All the riches of Troy as booty, all the palaces, the temples and the houses as ashes, all the women and all the children as slaves, all the men as corpses. They forget one detail; this is that all is not in their power; for they are not in Troy. Perhaps they may be there tomorrow, perhaps never.

Hector, that very day, succumbs to the same fault of memory:

For this I know well in my entrails and in my heart;
That day will come when holy Ilion shall perish
And Priam of the mighty sword and Priam's nation.
But I think less of the sorrow prepared for the Trojans,
Less of Hecuba herself, and of King Priam,
And my brothers, so many and so brave,
Who will fall to the dust beneath the enemy's lash,
Than of you, when one of the Greeks in bronze
*   armour*
Shall drag you away weeping, and rob you of your liberty.
For myself: may I be dead and may the earth cover me
Before I hear your cries or see you dragged away.

What would he not give at this moment to avoid such horrors which he believes inevitable? All that he can offer must be in vain. Yet only two days later the Greeks fled miserably, and Agamemnon himself wanted to take to the sea again. Hector, who by giving way a little might easily have obtained the enemy's departure, was no longer willing to allow them to leave with empty hands:

Let us build fires everywhere that their brilliance
*   may enflame the sky*
For fear lest into the darkness the long-haired Greeks
May flee away and throw themselves upon the broad
*   back of the seas. . . .*
Let more than one carry a wound to digest even at
*   home,*

And thus may all the world be afraid
To bring to the Trojans, tamers of horses, the
    misery of war.

His desire is carried out, the Greeks remain, and the next day, at noon, they make a pitiable object of Hector and his forces.

They, fleeing across the plain, were like cattle
Which a lion coming in the night drives before him. . . .
Thus the mighty Agamemnon, son of Athens, pursued them,
Killing without pause the hindmost; thus they fled.

In the course of the afternoon, Hector regains advantage, withdraws again, then puts the Greeks to rout, is set back in his turn by Patroclus' fresh forces. Patroclus, pushing his advantage beyond its strength, ends by finding himself exposed, unarmed, and wounded by Hector's javelin, and that evening the victorious Hector receives with severe reprimand Polydamas' prudent advice:

'*Now that I have received from the crafty son*
    of Kronos
A glorious victory near the ships, forcing the Greeks into
    the sea,
Fool! Never voice such counsel before the
    people.
No Trojan will listen to you; as for me, I
    forbid it.'
Thus spoke Hector, and the Trojans acclaimed him.

The next day Hector is lost. Achilles has pushed him back across the whole plain and will kill him. Of the two, he has always been the stronger in combat; how much more so now after several weeks of rest and spurred on by vengeance to victory against a spent enemy! Here is Hector alone before the walls of Troy, completely alone awaiting death and trying to gather his soul to face it.

Alas! if I should retreat behind the gate and the
    rampart
Polydamas would be first to shame me. . . .
Now that by my folly I have destroyed my people,

I fear the Trojans, and the long-robed
      Trojan women.
And I fear to hear it said by those less brave
      than I:
'Hector, too confident of his strength, has lost
      our land.'
But what if I put away my arched shield,
My stout helmet, and leaning my lance against
      the rampart
I went forth to meet the illustrious Achilles?
But why now should my heart give me such counsel?
I will not approach him; he would have no pity,
No regard; he would kill me if I were thus naked,
Like a woman.

Hector escapes none of the grief and ignominy that belong to
the ruined. Alone, stripped of all the prestige of might, the courage
that upheld him outside the walls cannot preserve him from flight:

Hector, at the sight of him was seized with
      trembling. He could not resolve
To remain. . . .
It is not for a ewe nor for an ox-hide,
Nor for the ordinary compensations of the hunt that
      they strive.
It is for a life that they run, that of Hector,
      tamer of horses.

Fatally wounded, he augments the triumph of the victor by his
vain entreaties.

I implore thee by thy life, by thy knees, by thy
      parents.

But those who are familiar with the *Iliad* know the death of
Hector was to give but short-lived joy to Achilles and the death
of Achilles brief joy to the Trojans, and the annihilation of Troy but
brief joy to the Achaians.

For violence so crushes whomever it touches that it appears at
last external no less to him who dispenses it than to him who endures it. So the idea was born of a destiny beneath which the

aggressors and their victims are equally innocent, the victors and the vanquished brothers in the same misfortune. The vanquished is a cause of misfortune for the victor as much as the victor is for the vanquished.

> *An only son is born to him, for a short life; moreover*
> *He grows old abandoned by me, since far from home*
> *I linger before Troy, doing harm to you and to your sons.*

A moderate use of might, by which alone man may escape being caught in the machinery of its vicious circle, would demand a more than human virtue, one no less rare than a constant dignity in weakness. Further, moderation itself is not always without peril; for the prestige which constitutes three-fourths of might is first of all made up of that superb indifference which the powerful have for the weak, an indifference so contagious that it is communicated even to those who are its object. But ordinarily it is not a political idea which counsels excess. Rather is the temptation to it nearly irresistible, despite all counsels. Reasonable words are now and then pronounced in the *Iliad*; those of Thersites are reasonable in the highest degree. So are Achilles' words when he is angry:

> *Nothing is worth life to me, not all the rumoured*
> *wealth of Ilium, that so prosperous city. . . .*
> *For one may capture oxen and fat sheep*
> *But a human life, once lost, is not to be recaptured.*

Reasonable words fall into the void. If an inferior pronounced them he is punished and turns silent. If a leader, he does not put them into action. If need be he is always able to find a god to counsel him the opposite of reason. At last the very idea that one might wish to escape from the occupation bestowed by fate, that to kill and to be killed, disappears from the consciousness.

> *. . . we, to whom Zeus*
> *From our youth to old age, has assigned the struggle*
> *In painful wars, until we perish even to the last one. . . .*

Already these combatants, as so much later Craonne's, felt themselves 'wholly condemned'.

They are caught in this situation by the simplest of traps. At the
outset their hearts are light, as hearts always are when one feels
power within one and against one only the void. Their weapons are
in their hands; the enemy is absent. Unless one's soul is stricken by the
enemy's reputation, one is always stronger than he during his absence.
An absent enemy does not impose the yoke of necessity. As yet no
necessity appears in the consciousness of those who thus set forth,
and this is why they go off as if to a game, as if for a holiday freed
from the daily grind.

> *Where have our braggings gone, our vaunted bravery,*
> *Which we shouted so proudly at Lemnos*
> *While gorging upon the flesh of horned bullocks,*
> *And drinking from cups overflowing with wine?*
> *Saying: against an hundred or two hundred Trojans*
> *Each one would hold combat; and here only one is*
>   *too much for us!*

Even when war is experienced, it does not immediately cease
to appear as a game. The necessity that belongs to war is terrible,
wholly different from that belonging to peaceful works; the soul
only submits to the necessity of war when escape from it is impossible; and so long as the soul does escape, it lives irresponsible
days, empty of necessity, days of frivolity, of dream, arbitrary and
unreal. Danger is then an abstraction, the lives which one takes seem
like toys broken by a child, and no more important; heroism is a
theatrical pose soiled by artificial braggings. If, added to this, an influx
of vitality comes to multiply and inflate the power of action, the man
believes that, thanks to divine intervention, he is irresistible, providen-
tially preserved from defeat and from death. War is easy then, and
ignobly loved.

But for the majority of soldiers this state of soul does not last.
The day comes when fear, defeat or the death of beloved companions
crushes the warrior's soul beneath the necessity of war. Then war
ceases to be a play or a dream; the warrior understands at last that

it really exists. This is a hard reality, infinitely too hard to be borne, for it comprises death. The thought of death cannot be sustained, or only in flashes from the moment when one understands death as a possible eventuality. It is true that every man is destined to die and that a soldier may grow old among his comrades, yet for those whose souls are subservient to the yoke of war, the relationship between death and the future is different than for other men. For those others death is the acknowledged limit pre-imposed upon their future; for these warriors, death itself is their future, the future assigned to them by their profession. That men should have death for their future is a denial of nature. As soon as the practice of war has revealed the fact that each moment holds the possibility of death, the mind becomes incapable of moving from one day to the next without passing through the spectre of death. Then the consciousness is under tension such as it can only endure for short intervals. But each new dawn ushers in the same necessity. Such days added to each other make up years. That soul daily suffers violence which every morning must mutilate its aspirations because the mind cannot move about in a time without passing through death. In this way war wipes out every conception of a goal, even all thoughts concerning the goals of war. The possibility of so violent a situation is inconceivable when one is outside it, its ends are inconceivable when one is involved in it. Therefore no one does anything to bring about its end. The man who is faced by an armed enemy cannot lay down his arms. The mind should be able to contrive an issue; but it has lost all capacity for contriving anything in that direction. It is completely occupied with doing itself violence. Always among men, the intolerable afflictions either of servitude or war endure by force of their own weight, and therefore, from the outside, they seem easy to bear; they last because they rob the resources required to throw them off.

Nevertheless, the soul that is dominated by war cries out for deliverance; but deliverance itself appears in tragic guise, in the form of extreme destruction. A moderate and reasonable end to all its suffering would leave naked, and exposed to consciousness, memories of such violent affliction as it could not endure. The terror, the pain, the exhaustion, the massacres, the deaths of comrades, we cannot believe that these would only cease to ravage the soul if they were drowned in the intoxication of force. The thought that such vast efforts should have brought only a negative, or limited profit, hurts too much.

What? Shall we allow Priam and the Trojans, to glory
In Argive Helen, she for whom so many Greeks
Have perished before Troy, far from their native
    land?
What? Would you abandon Troy, the city of wide streets,
For which we have suffered so many afflictions?

What does Helen matter to Ulysses? Or even Troy with all its wealth, since it can never compensate for the ruin of Ithaca? Troy and Helen matter to the Greeks only as the causes of their shedding so much blood and tears; it is in making oneself master that one finds one is the master of horrible memories. The Soul, which is forced by the existence of an enemy, to destroy the part of itself implanted by nature, believes it can only cure itself by the destruction of the enemy, and at the same time the death of beloved companions stimulates the desire to emulate them, to follow their dark example:

Ah, to die at once, since without my help
My friends had to die. How far from home
He perished, and I was not there to defend him.
Now I depart to find the murderer of one so beloved:
Hector. I will receive death at whatever moment
Zeus and all the other gods shall accomplish it.

So it is that the despair which thrusts toward death is the same one that impels toward killing.

I know well that my fate is to perish here,
Far from my loved father and mother; but still
I will not stop till the Trojans have had their
    glut of war.

The man torn by this double need for death belongs, so long as he has not become something different, to another race than the living race. When the vanquished pleads that he may be allowed to see the

light of day, what echo may his timid aspiration to life find in a
heart driven by such desperation? The mere fact that the victor is
armed, the other disarmed, already deprives the life that is threatened
of the least vestige of importance. And how should he who has
destroyed in himself the very thought that there may be joy in the
light, how should he respect such humble and vain pleadings from
the vanquished?

> *I am at thy knees, Achilles; have pity, have regard*
> *　　for me;*
> *Here as a suppliant, O Son of Zeus, I am worthy of*
> *　　respect:*
> *It was first at your house that I ate the bread of*
> *　　Demeter,*
> *When from my well-tended vineyard you captured me.*
> *And selling me, you sent me far from my father and*
> *　　my own,*
> *To holy Lemnos; a sacrifice of one hundred oxen were*
> *　　paid for me.*
> *I was redeemed for three hundred more; Dawn breaks*
> *　　for me*
> *Today the twelfth time since I returned to Ilium*
> *After so many sorrows. Again at the mercy of your*
> *　　hands*
> *A cruel fate has placed me. How Zeus the father*
> *　　must hate me*
> *To have delivered me to you again; for how small*
> *　　a part in life*
> *Did my mother, Laothoe, daughter of the ancient*
> *　　Altos, bear me.*

See what response this feeble hope gets!

> *Come friend, you must die too! Who are you to*
> *　　complain?*
> *Patroclus was worth much more than you, yet he*
> *　　is dead.*
> *And I, handsome and strong as you see me,*
> *I who am of noble race, my mother was a goddess;*
> *Even over me hangs death and a dark destiny.*
> *Whether at dawn, in the evening, or at noon*
> *My life too shall be taken by force of arms. . . .*

Whoever has had to mortify, to mutilate in himself all aspiration to live, of him an effort of heart-breaking generosity is required before he can respect the life of another. We have no reason to suppose any of Homer's warriors capable of such an effort, unless perhaps Patroclus. In a certain way Patroclus occupies the central position in the *Iliad*, where it is said that: 'he knew how to be tender toward all', and wherein nothing of a cruel or brutal nature is ever mentioned concerning him. But how many men do we know in several thousand years of history who have given proof of such divine generosity? It is doubtful whether we could name two or three. In default of such generosity the vanquished soldier is the scourge of nature; possessed by war, he, as much as the slave, although in quite a different way, is become a thing, and words have no more power over him than over inert matter. In contact with might, both the soldier and the slave suffer the inevitable effect, which is to become either deaf or mute.

Such is the nature of might. Its power to transform man into a thing is double and it cuts both ways; it petrifies differently but equally the souls of those who suffer it, and of those who wield it. This property of might reaches its highest degree in the midst of combat, at that moment when the tide of battle feels its way toward a decision. The winning of battles is not determined between men who plan and deliberate, who make a resolution and carry it out, but between men drained of these faculties, transformed, fallen to the level either of inert matter, which is all passivity, or to the level of blind forces, which are all momentum. This is the final secret of war. This secret the *Iliad* expresses by its similes, by making warriors apparitions of great natural phenomenon: a conflagration, a flood, the wind, ferocious beasts, any and every blind cause of disaster. Or else by likening them to frightened animals, trees, water, sand, to all that is moved by the violence of external forces. Greeks and Trojans alike, from one day to the next, sometimes from one hour to the next, are made to suffer in turn these contrary transmutations.

Like cattle which a murderous lion assaults
While they stand grazing in a vast and marshy meadow
By thousands . . . ; all tremble. So then the Achaians

*In panic were put to rout by Hector and by Zeus the
    father.
All of them. . . .
As when destructive fire runs through the depths
    of a wood;
Everywhere whirling, swept by the wind, when the trees
Uprooted are felled by pressure of the violent fire;
Even so did Agamemnon son of Athens bring down the heads
Of the fleeing Trojans.*

The art of war is nothing but the art of provoking such transformations. The material, the procedures, even the inflicting of death
upon the enemy, are only the means to this end; the veritable object
of the art of war is no less than the souls of the combatants. But
these transformations are always a mystery, and the gods are the authors of them because it is they who excite men's imaginations. However this comes about, this double ability of turning men to stone
is essential to might, and a soul placed in contact with it only escapes
by a sort of miracle. Miracles of this sort are rare and brief.

The frivolity, the capriciousness of those who disrespectfully
manipulate the men or the things which they have, or believe they
have at their mercy, the despair which drives the soldier to destroy,
the crushing of the slave and of the vanquished, the massacres, all
these contribute to make a picture of utter, uniform horror. Might
is the only hero in this picture. The resulting whole would be a
dismal monotony were there not, sprinkled here and there, luminous
moments, brief and divine moments in the souls of men. In such
moments the soul which awakes, only to lose itself again to the
empire of might, awakes pure and intact; realizes itself whole. In
that soul there is no room for ambiguous, troubled or conflicting
emotions; courage and love fill it all. Sometimes a man is able to find
his soul in deliberating with himself when he tries, as Hector did before Troy, without the help of gods or of men, all alone to face his
destiny. Other moments wherein men find their souls are the moments
when they love; almost no type of pure love between men is lacking
from the *Iliad*.

The tradition of hospitality, carried through several generations,
has ascendancy over the blindness of combat:

Thus I am for you a beloved guest in the heart of
    Argos....
Let us avoid one another's lances, even in
    the fray.

The love of a son for his parents, of a father, or of a mother, for the son, is constantly expressed in a manner as moving as it is brief:

Thetis replied, shedding tears:
You were born to me for a short life my child,
    as you say....

Likewise fraternal love:

My three brothers born of our same mother
So cherished....

Married love, condemned to misfortune, is of a surprising purity. The husband, in evoking the humiliations of slavery which await his beloved wife, omits to mention that one of which only to think would be to forecast memories that would soil their tenderness. Nothing could be more simple than the words spoken by his wife to the husband who goes to his death:

    ... It were better for me
If I lose you, to be under the ground, I shall have
No other refuge, when you have met your fate,
Nothing but griefs.

No less moving are the words addressed to the dead husband:

You are dead before your time, my husband; so
    young, and I your widow
Am left alone in the house; with our child still
    very little,
Whom we bore, you and I, the ill-fated. And I
    doubt
He will ever grow up....
For you did not die in bed stretching
    your hands to me,

Nor spoke one wise word that for always
I might think on, while shedding tears day
*   and night.*

The most beautiful friendship, that between companions in combat, is the final theme of the epic.

*   ... But Achilles*
Wept, dreaming of his much-loved companion;
*   and sleep*
That overcomes all, would not take him; as he
*   turned himself from side to side.*

But the triumph, the purest love of all, the supreme grace of all
wars, is that friendship which mounts up to brim the hearts of mortal
enemies. This quells the hunger to avenge the death of a son, of
a friend. It spans, by an even greater miracle, the breach that lies
between the benefactor and the suppliant, between the victor and the
vanquished.

But when the desire to drink and to eat was appeased,
Then Dardanian Priam began to admire Achilles;
How mighty and handsome he was; he had the look
*   of a god.*
And Dardanian Priam, in turn, was admired by
*   Achilles,*
Who gazed at his beautiful visage and drank in
*   his words.*
And when both were assuaged by their contemplation
*   of each other. . . .*

Such moments of grace are rare in the *Iliad*, but they suffice
to make what violence kills, and shall kill, felt with extremest regret.

And yet such an accumulation of violences would be cold without that accent of incurable bitterness which continually makes itself
felt, although often indicated only by a single word, sometimes only
by a play of verse, by a run over line. It is this which makes the
Iliad a unique poem, this bitterness, issuing from its tenderness, and
which extends, as the light of the sun, equally over all men. Never

does the tone of the poem cease to be impregnated by this bitterness, nor does it ever descend to the level of a complaint. Justice and love, for which there can hardly be a place in this picture of extremes and unjust violence, yet shed their light over the whole without ever being discerned otherwise than by the accent. Nothing precious is despised, whether or not destined to perish. The destitution and misery of all men is shown without dissimulation or disdain, no man is held either above or below the common level of all men, and whatever is destroyed is regretted. The victors and the vanquished are shown equally near to us, in an equal perspective, and seem, by that token, to be the fellows as well of the poet as of the auditors. If there is a difference it is the affliction of the enemy which is perhaps the more keenly felt.

> *Thus he fell there, overcome by a sleep of bronze,*
> *The ill-fated, far from his wife, while defending*
>   *his people. . . .*

What a tone to use in evoking the fate of the adolescent whom Achilles sold at Lemnos!

> *Eleven days his heart rejoiced among those he loved*
> *Returning from Lemnos; on the twelfth once again*
> *God delivered him into the hands of Achilles,*
>   *who would*
> *Send him to Hades, although against his will.*

And the fate of Euphorbus, he who saw but a single day of war:

> *Blood drenches his hair, hair like that of the Graces.*

When Hector is mourned:

> *. . . the guardian of chaste wives and of little*
>   *children.*

These words are enough to conjure up a picture of chastity ruined by violence and of little children taken by force of arms. The fountain at the gates of Troy becomes an object of piercing nostalgia when the condemned Hector passes it running to save his life.

> *There were the wide wash basins, quite near,*
> *Beautiful, all of stone, where splendid vestments*
> *Were washed by the wives of Troy and by its most*
> *   beautiful daughters,*
> *Formerly, during the peace, before the advent of*
> *   the Achaeans.*
> *It was this way that they ran, fleeing, and the*
> *   other following behind.*

The whole *Iliad* is overshadowed by the greatest of griefs that can come among men; the destruction of a city. This affliction could not appear more rending if the poet had been born in Troy. Nor is there a difference in tone in those passages which tell of the Achaeans dying far from home.

The brief evocations of the world of peace are painful just because that life, the life of the living, appears so full and calm:

> *As soon as it was dawn and the sun rose,*
> *From both sides blows were exchanged and men fell.*
> *But at the very hour when the woodsman goes home to*
> *   prepare his meal*
> *From the valleys and hills, when his arms are wearied*
> *From cutting down great trees,*
> *   and a great longing floods his heart,*
> *And a hunger for sweet food gnaws at his entrails,*
> *At that hour, by their valour, the Danaans broke*
> *   the front.*

All that has no part in war, all that war destroys or threatens, the *Iliad* envelops in poetry; this it never does for the facts of war. The passage from life to death is veiled by not the least reticence.

> *Then his teeth were knocked out; from both sides*
> *Blood came to his eyes; blood that from his lips*
> *   and nostrils*

> *He vomited, open-mouthed; death wrapped him in*
> *its black cloud.*

The cold brutality of the facts of war is in no way disguised just because neither victors nor vanquished are either admired, despised or hated. Destiny and the gods almost always decide the changing fate of the combatants. Within the limits assigned by fate, the gods have sovereign power to mete out victory and defeat; it is always they who provoke the madness, the treachery, by which, each time, peace is inhibited. War is their particular province and their only motives are caprice and malice. As for the warriors themselves, the similes which make them appear, victors or vanquished, as beasts or things, they cannot make us feel either admiration or disdain, but only sorrow that men could be thus transformed.

The extraordinary equity which inspires the *Iliad* may have had other examples unknown to us; it has had no imitators. One is hardly made to feel that the poet is a Greek and not a Trojan. The tone of the poem seems to carry direct proof of the origin of the most ancient passages; although history may never give us light thereon. If one believes with Thucydides that eighty years after the destruction of Troy the Achaeans in turn were conquered, one may wonder whether these songs, in which iron is so rarely mentioned, may not be the chants of a conquered people of whom perhaps some were exiled. Obliged to live and to die 'very far from the homeland' like the Greeks before Troy, having, like the Trojans, lost their cities, they saw their likeness in the victors, who were their fathers, and also in the vanquished, whose sufferings resembled their own. Thus the truth of this war, though still recent, could appear to them as in the perspective of years, unveiled either by the intoxication of pride or of humiliation. They could picture it to themselves at once as the fallen and as the conquerors, and thus understand what never the defeated nor the victorious have ever understood, being blinded by one or the other state. This is only a dream; one can hardly do more than dream about a time so far distant.

By whatever means, this poem is a miraculous object. The bitterness of it is spent upon the only true cause of bitterness: the subordi-

nation of the human soul to might, which is, be it finally said,
to matter. That subordination is the same for all mortals, although
there is a difference according to the soul's degree of virtue, according to the way in which each soul endures it. No one in the *Iliad*
is spared, just as no one on earth escapes it. None of those who
succumb to it is for that reason despised. Whatever, in the secret soul
and in human relations, can escape the empire of might, is loved, but
painfully loved because of the danger of destruction that continually
hangs over it. Such is the spirit of the only veritable epic of the western world. The *Odyssey* seems to be no more than an excellent
imitation, now of the *Iliad*, then of some oriental poem. The *Aeneid*
is an imitation which, for all its brilliance is marred by coldness,
pomposity and bad taste. The *chansons de geste* were not able to
attain grandeur for want of a sense of equity. In the *Chanson de
Roland* the death of an enemy is not felt by the author and the
reader in the same way as the death of Roland.

Attic tragedy, at least that of Aeschylus and of Sophocles, is the
true continuation of the epic. Over this the idea of justice sheds
its light without ever intervening; might appears here in all its rigidity
and coldness, always accompanied by its fatal results from which
neither he who uses it, nor he who suffers it, can escape. Here the
humiliation of a soul that is subject to constraint is neither disguised, nor veiled by a facile piety; neither is it an object of disdain.
More than one being, wounded by the degradation of affliction, is
here held up to be admired. The Gospels are the last and most
marvellous expression of Greek genius, as the *Iliad* is its first expression. The spirit of Greece makes itself felt here not only by the fact
of commanding us to seek to the exclusion of every other good 'the
kingdom of God and his righteousness' but also by its revelation of
human misery, and by revealing that misery in the person of a divine
being who is at the same time human. The accounts of the Passion
show that a divine spirit united to the flesh is altered by affliction,
trembles before suffering and death, feels himself, at the moment
of deepest agony, separated from men and from God. The sense of
human misery gives these accounts of the Passion that accent of
simplicity which is the stamp of Greek genius. And it is this same

sense which constitutes the great worth of Attic tragedy and of the *Iliad*. Certain expressions in the Gospels have a strangely familiar ring, reminiscent of the epic. The adolescent Trojan, sent against his will to Hades, reminds one of Christ when he told St. Peter: 'Another shall gird thee and carry thee where thou wouldst not.' This accent is inseparable from the idea which inspired the Gospels; for the understanding of human suffering is dependent upon justice, and love is its condition. Whoever does not know just how far necessity and a fickle fortune hold the human soul under their domination cannot treat as his equals, nor love as himself, those whom chance has separated from him by an abyss. The diversity of the limitations to which men are subject creates the illusion that there are different species among them which cannot communicate with one another. Only he who knows the empire of might and knows how not to respect it is capable of love and justice.

The relations between the human soul and destiny; to what extent each soul may mould its own fate; what part in any and every soul is transformed by a pitiless necessity, by the caprice of variable fortune; what part of the soul, by means of virtue and grace, may remain whole—all these are a subject in which deception is easy and tempting. Pride, humiliation, hate, disdain, indifference, the wish to forget or to ignore—all these contribute toward that temptation. Particularly rare is a true expression of misfortune: in painting it one almost always affects to believe, first, that degradation is the innate vocation of the unfortunate; second, that a soul may suffer affliction without being marked by it, without changing all consciousness in a particular manner which belongs to itself alone. For the most part the Greeks had such strength of soul as preserved them from self-deception. For this they were recompensed by knowing in all things how to attain the highest degree of lucidity, of purity and of simplicity. But the spirit which is transmitted from the *Iliad* to the Gospels, passed on by the philosophers and tragic poets, has hardly gone beyond the limits of Greek civilization. Of that civilization, since the destruction of Greece, only reflections are left.

The Romans and the Hebrews both believed themselves exempt from the common misery of man, the Romans by being chosen by destiny to be the rulers of the world, the Hebrews by the favour of their God, and to the exact extent in which they obeyed Him. The Romans despised foreigners, enemies, the vanquished, their subjects, their slaves; neither have they any epics or tragedies. The Hebrews saw a trace of sin in all affliction and therefore a legitimate motive for despising it. They saw their vanquished as an abomination in God's sight and therefore condemned to expiate their crimes. Thus cruelty was sanctioned and even inevitable. Nor does any text of the Old Testament sound a note comparable to that of the Greek epic, unless perhaps certain parts of the poem of Job. The Romans and Hebrews have been admired, read, imitated in actions and in words, cited every time there was need to justify a crime, throughout twenty centuries of Christianity.

Furthermore, the spirit of the Gospels was not transmitted in all its purity to successive generations of Christians. From the earliest times it was believed to be a sign of grace when the martyrs joyfully endured suffering and death; as if the effects of grace could be realized more fully among men than in the Christ. Those who remember that even the incarnate God Himself could not look on the rigours of destiny without anguish, should understand that men can only appear to elevate themselves above human misery by disguising the rigours of destiny in their own eyes, by the help of illusion, of intoxication, or of fanaticism. Unless protected by an armour of lies, man cannot endure might without suffering a blow in the depth of his soul. Grace can prevent this blow from corrupting the soul, but cannot prevent its wound. For having too long forgotten this the Christian tradition has been able only very rarely to find that simplicity which makes each phrase of the accounts of the Passion so poignant.

Despite the brief intoxication caused, during the Renaissance, by the discovery of Greek letters, the Greek genius has not been revived in the course of twenty centuries. Something of it appears in Villon, Shakespeare, Cervantes, Molière, and once in Racine. In the École des Femmes, in Phèdre, human misery is revealed in its nakedness in connection with love. That was a strange century in which, contrary to what happened in the epic age, man's misery could only be revealed in love. The effects of might in war and in politics had always to be enveloped in glory. Doubtless one could add still other names. But nothing of all that the peoples of Europe have produced is worth the first known poem to have appeared among them. Perhaps they will rediscover that epic genius when they learn how to accept the fact that nothing is sheltered from fate, how never to admire might, or hate the enemy, or to despise sufferers. It is doubtful if this will happen soon.

UPROOTEDNESS AND NATIONHOOD

Simone Weil completed THE NEED FOR ROOTS *shortly before her death in 1943. This book is, to quote one critic, a "lengthy programmatic essay . . . [that] stands by itself as her only sustained and comprehensive effort toward systematic statement." The tragedy not only of modern France but also of Western society is etched in these pages. Man's physical and spiritual uprootedness, his severance of ties with the cultural and historical past, his rejection of the "other Reality," and the moral consequences of all of these negations: these are central concerns, as the second and longest part of* THE NEED FOR ROOTS, *from which "Uprootedness and Nationhood" is excerpted below, shows. Here, at her most polemical point in trying to link personal morality and public affairs, Simone Weil challenges all shopworn values of the Right and the Left.*

There is still another kind of uprootedness to be considered so as to be able to have a rough idea of our principal disease. It is the kind one might call geographical, that is to say, concerned with human collectivities occupying clearly defined territorial limits. The actual significance of these collectivities has well-nigh disappeared, except in one case only—that of the nation. But there are, and have been, very many other examples; some on a smaller, sometimes quite a small, scale, in the shape of a town, collection of villages, province, or region; others comprising many different nations; and yet others comprising bits of many different nations.

The nation, single and separate, has taken the place of all that— the nation, or in other words, the State; for there is no other way of defining the word nation than as a territorial aggregate whose various parts recognize the authority of the same State. One may say that, in our age, money and the State have come to replace all other bonds of attachment.

For a long time now, the single nation has played the part which constitutes the supreme mission of society toward the individual human being, namely, maintaining throughout the present the links with the past and the future. In this sense, one may say that it is the only form of collectivity existing in the world at the present time. The family doesn't exist. What nowadays goes by that name is a minute collection of human beings grouped around each of us: father and mother, husband or wife, and children; brothers and sisters being already a little remote. Latterly, in the midst of the general distress, this little nucleus has developed an almost irresistible force of attraction, to the extent sometimes of making people cast aside every kind of duty; but that is because there alone people could find a little living warmth against the icy cold, which all of a sudden had descended on them. It was an almost animal reaction.

But no one thinks nowadays about his ancestors who died fifty or even only twenty or ten years before his birth; nor about his descendants who will be born fifty or even only twenty or ten years after his death. Consequently, from the point of view of the collectivity and its particular function, the family no longer counts.

Looked at from this point of view, a profession doesn't count either. A corporation or guild was a link between the dead, the living and those yet unborn, within the framework of a certain specified occupation. There is nothing today which can be said to exist, however remotely, for the purpose of carrying out such a function. French trade-unionism, around 1900, may possibly have shown a certain tendency in this direction, but it never came to anything.

Finally, the village, district, province, or region—all the geographical units smaller than the nation—have almost ceased to count; as have all geographical units composed of many nations or bits of many nations, too. When one used to say, for example, a few centuries ago, "Christendom," the word had quite a different affective implication from that of the present-day "Europe."

To sum up, Man has placed his most valuable possession in the world of temporal affairs, namely, his continuity in time, beyond the limits set by human existence in either direction, entirely in the hands of the State. And yet, it is just in this very period when the nation stands alone and supreme that we have witnessed its sudden and extraordinarily rapid decomposition. This has left us stunned, so that we find it extremely difficult to think clearly on the subject.

The French people, in June and July, 1940, were not a people waylaid by a band of ruffians, whose country was suddenly snatched from them. They are a people who opened their hands and allowed their country to fall to the ground. Later on—but after a long interval— they spent themselves in ever more and more desperate efforts to pick it up again; but some one had placed his foot on it.

Now a national sense has returned. The words "to die for France" have again taken on a meaning they hadn't possessed since 1918. But in the movement of opposition which has seized hold of the French people, hunger, cold, the always hateful presence of foreign soldiers exercising complete authority, the breaking-up of families, for some exile, captivity—all these sufferings have at least played a very large part, most likely a decisive one. The best proof of this lies in the difference in spirit distinguishing the occupied from the unoccupied zone. Nature has not dispensed any greater amount of patriotic fervor to those living north than to those living south of the Loire. Different situations have simply produced different states of mind. The example set by England, hopes of a German defeat, have also been important contributory factors.

France's only reality today consists in memories and hopes. The Republic never seemed so beautiful as under the Empire: one's native land never seems so beautiful as when under the heel of a conqueror, if there is hope of seeing it again intact. That is why one shouldn't take the present intensity of national feeling for a guide as to its actual efficacy, once liberation has been effected, for ensuring the stability of public life.

The memory of the sudden dissolution of this feeling in June, 1940, is one so charged with shame, that one prefers not to think about it, to rule it out altogether and only to think about how to set things to rights again for the future. In private life also, each of us is always tempted to set his own failings to a certain extent, on one side, relegate them to some attic, invent some method of calculation whereby they turn out to be of no real consequence. To give way to this temptation is to ruin the soul; it is the one above all, that has to be conquered.

We have all succumbed to this temptation, on account of the public shame, which has been so deep that each one of us has felt wounded to the quick in his own feelings of personal honor. Without this temptation, reflections concerning so extraordinary an event would already have given rise to some new patriotic doctrine, some new patriotic conception.

From the social point of view, more especially, it will be impossible to avoid considering the notion of patriotism. Not considering it afresh, but considering it for the first time; for, unless I am mistaken, it never has been considered. Strange indeed, for a notion which has played and still plays so important a role, isn't it? That just shows what sort of a place we really accord to thought.

The idea of patriotism had lost all credit among French workmen during the last quarter of a century. The Communists put it into circulation again after 1934, to the accompaniment of plentiful tricolor flags and singing of the Marseillaise. But they hadn't the least compunction in withdrawing it and placing it on the shelf again a little before the war. It is not in the name of patriotism that they started setting up a resistance. They only began adopting it again about nine months after the defeat. Little by little they have adopted it entirely. But only simpletons would take that to mean a veritable reconciliation between the working class and the country. Workmen are dying for their country—that is only too true. But we live in an age so impregnated with lies that even the virtue of blood voluntarily sacrificed is insufficient to put us back on the path of truth.

For very many years, workmen were taught that internationalism was the most sacred of all duties, and patriotism the most shameful of all bourgeois prejudices. Then more years were spent teaching them that patriotism was a sacred duty, and anything that wasn't patriotism a betrayal. How, at the end of all that, could they be expected to react otherwise than crudely and in obedience to propaganda?

A healthy working-class movement is out of the question, unless it be given a doctrine assigning a place to the idea of patriotism, and a clearly defined, that is, a limited, place. Moreover, this need is only more evident in working-class circles than elsewhere because the problem of patriotism has been so much discussed in them for so long. But it is a need common to the whole country. It is unpardonable that a word, which nowadays is almost always to be found coupled with the word duty, should hardly ever have been made the subject of any investigation. As a rule, all people can find to quote in connection with it is a mediocre page of Renan's.

The nation is a recent innovation. In the Middle Ages, allegiance was owed to the lord, or the city, or both, and by extension to territorial areas not very clearly defined. The sentiment we call patriotism certainly existed, often to a very intense degree; only its object was not set within territorial limits. The sentiment covered variable extensions of land, according to circumstances.

Actually, patriotism has always existed, as far back as we can go in history. Vercingetorix really died for Gaul; the Spanish tribes, which resisted conquest by the Romans, sometimes to the point of extermination, died for Spain, knowing they were doing so, and declaring it; those who died at Marathon and Salamis died for Greece; at a time when Greece, not having yet been reduced to a province, was in relation to Rome in the same position as Vichy France is to Germany, children in the Greek towns used openly to pelt collaborators with stones and call them traitors, with the same indignation we feel today.

What had never existed right up to recent times was some definite, circumscribed thing, permanently installed as an object of patriotic devotion. Patriotism was something diffuse, nomadic, which expanded or contracted according to degrees of similarity and common danger. It was mixed up with different kinds of loyalty—loyalty to other men, a lord, a king, or a city. The whole formed something very complicated, but also very human. To express the sense of obligation everyone feels toward his country, people would usually talk about "the public" or "the public good," an expression which can serve equally well to indicate a village, town, province, France, Christendom, or Mankind.

People also talked about the kingdom of France. In the latter expression, the sense of obligation toward the country was mingled with that of fidelity to the king. But two obstacles have prevented this sentiment from ever being a pure one, not even in the time of Joan of Arc. It must be remembered that the population of Paris was against Joan of Arc.

The first obstacle was that, on the death of Charles V, France, to use Montesquieu's words, ceased to be a monarchy and fell into the state of despotism from which she only emerged in the eighteenth century. Nowadays, we find it so natural to pay taxes to the State, that we have difficulty in imagining the moral upheaval in the midst of which this custom was first introduced. In the fourteenth century, to pay any taxes other than exceptional levies acquiesced in for war purposes was looked upon as dishonorable, a disgrace reserved for conquered countries, and the manifest sign of slavery. The same feeling is found expressed in the Spanish *Romancero*, and also in Shakespeare, "That England . . . hath made a shameful conquest of itself."

Charles VI, during his minority, aided and abetted by his uncles, by using corruption and the vilest cruelty, brutally compelled the people of France to accept a perfectly arbitrary tax, renewable at will, which literally reduced the poor to starvation, while the noblemen frittered away the proceeds. It is for this reason that the English of Henry V's day were first of all welcomed as liberators, at a time when the Armagnacs represented the side of the rich and the Burgundians that of the poor.

The French people, brutally and at one fell swoop made to submit to the yoke, thereafter, right up to the eighteenth century, gave
only spasmodic signs of independence. Throughout the whole of this
period they were looked upon by other Europeans as the perfect
example of an enslaved people, a people who could be treated like
cattle by their sovereign.

But meanwhile, there arose deep down in the heart of this people
a suppressed hatred of the king—all the more bitter for remaining un-
expressed—a traditional hatred never to be extinguished. One senses it
already in a heart-rending complaint by the peasants under Charles
VI. It must have played a part in the mysterious popularity of the
League in Paris. After Henry IV's assassination, a child of twelve
was put to death for having publicly declared that he would do as
much to the little Louis XIII. Richelieu began his career by a speech
in which he called upon the clergy to proclaim that all regicides
would be damned, giving as his reason the fact that those nursing such
a design were filled with far too fanatical an enthusiasm to be restrained by any temporal penalty.

This hatred reached its climax at the end of the reign of Louis
XIV. Having been repressed by a terror of like intensity, it exploded,
in accordance with the disconcerting time lags of history, eighty years
later; and it was the unfortunate Louis XVI who received the full
blast. This same hatred made it impossible for a monarchical restora-
tion really to take place in 1815. Even today, it makes it absolutely impossible for the Comte de Paris to be freely accepted by the French
people, in spite of the example set by a man like Bernanos. In some
respects, this is a pity: a number of problems could be solved in this
way; but so it is.

Another source which has poisoned the love of Frenchmen for
the kingdom of France lies in the fact that at all times among the
lands owing obedience to the king of France, there were some that
regarded themselves as conquered territory and were treated as such.
It must be admitted that the forty kings who in a thousand years made
France did so often with a brutality worthy of our own age. If a
natural correspondence exists between the tree and its fruit, we
mustn't be surprised if the fruit is, in fact, very far from being perfect.

For example, history can show us deeds of an atrocity equal to, but not greater than—save perhaps a few rare exceptions—that of the conquest by the French of the lands situated to the south of the Loire, at the beginning of the thirteenth century. These lands, where a high level of culture, tolerance, liberty, and spiritual life prevailed, were filled with an intensely patriotic feeling for what they termed their "language"—a word that, for them, was synonymous with native land. To them, the French were as much foreigners and barbarians as the Germans are to us. In order to drive terror immediately into every heart, the French began by destroying the town of Béziers *in toto*, and obtained the results sought. Once the country had been conquered, they installed the Inquisition there. A muffled spirit of unrest went on smoldering among these people, and later on induced them to embrace with fervor the Protestant religion, which, according to D'Aubigné, in spite of very great divergencies in doctrine, is directly traceable to the Albigenses. We can judge how strong the hatred of the central power was in these parts, by the religious devotion manifested in Toulouse in connection with the remains of the Duke of Montmorency, beheaded for plotting against Richelieu. The same latent sense of protest caused them to throw themselves enthusiastically into the French Revolution. Later on, they became Radical-Socialists, anticlericals. Under the Third Republic, they no longer hated the central power; they had largely acquired control of it and were exploiting it.

We may note that on each occasion their protest has been characterized by a more intense uprootedness and by a lower spiritual and intellectual level. We may also note that since they were conquered, these lands have made a rather feeble contribution toward French culture, whereas before they were so brilliantly alive culturally. French thought has been more enriched by the Albigenses and troubadours of the twelfth century, who were not Frenchmen, than by the entire output from this part of France in the course of succeeding centuries.

The dukedom of Burgundy was the home of an original and extremely brilliant culture, which didn't survive the dukedom's disappearance. The Flemish cities were secretly, at the end of the fourteenth century, on the friendliest terms with Paris and Rouen; nevertheless, wounded Flemings preferred to die rather than be looked after by the soldiers of Charles VI. Some of the latter went on a pillaging expedition into Holland, and brought back some rich burghers whom they decided to kill. In a sudden access of pity, they offered them their lives if they would only become subjects of the French king. They replied that, once dead, their very bones would protest, if they were able, at being subjected to the authority of the king of France. A Catalan historian of the same period, in telling the story of the Sicilian Vespers, writes, "The French, who, wherever they exercise power, are as cruel as it is possible to be . . ."

The Bretons were in despair when their sovereign Anne was forced to marry the king of France. If these same Bretons could return today, or better, have returned some years ago, would they find or have found very strong reasons for thinking they had been mistaken? However discredited the Breton autonomist movement may be by the type of people manipulating it and the sinister ends they pursue, there is no doubt that this propaganda stands for something real both in fact and in the minds of the population concerned. There are hidden treasures in these people which have never managed to see the light of day. French culture doesn't suit them; their own is unable to put forth shoots; hence they find themselves, as a people, relegated to the very bottom of the lower social strata. A large proportion of illiterate soldiers are Breton men, and, so it is said, a large proportion of Parisian prostitutes are Breton women. Autonomy would not be a remedy, but this doesn't mean that the disease doesn't exist.

Franche-Comté, which lived freely and happily under the very distant suzerainty of the Spanish, fought in the seventeenth century in order not to become French. The people of Strasbourg wept when they saw the troops of Louis XIV entering their city in time of peace, without a previous declaration of any kind, through a violation of a solemn undertaking worthy of Hitler.

Paoli, the last Corsican hero, battled heroically to prevent his country from coming under French rule. There is a monument to his honor in a church in Florence; in France he is hardly remembered. Corsica is an example of the danger of infection involved in uprootedness. After having conquered, colonized, corrupted, and debased the people of that island, we have now had to put up with them in the shape of prefects of police, police narks, sergeant majors, *pions* and other functions of a like nature, in pursuit of which they, in their turn, have treated the French like a more or less conquered people. They have also contributed toward giving France in the minds of numerous natives belonging to the colonies a reputation for cruelty and brutality.

Although the kings of France are praised for having assimilated the countries they conquered, the truth is that they to a large extent uprooted them. This is an easy method of assimilation, within the reach of anybody. People who have their culture taken away from them either carry on without any at all, or else accept the odds and ends of the culture one condescends to give them. In either event, they don't stand out individually, so they appear to be assimilated. The real marvel is to assimilate populations so that they preserve their culture, though necessarily modified, as a living thing. It is a marvel which very seldom takes place.

It is true that, under the *Ancien Régime*, the French showed themselves to be intensely conscious of their Frenchness in all periods of particular splendor for France: in the thirteenth century, when the whole of Europe flocked to the University of Paris; in the sixteenth century, when the Renaissance, already extinguished or not yet lighted elsewhere, had its seat in France; in the early part of Louis XIV's reign, when arms and letters enjoyed a dual prestige. It is none the less certain that it was not the kings who welded together these disparate territories. It was solely the Revolution.

Already during the eighteenth century there existed in France, in very different ranks of society, alongside the grossest forms of corruption, a bright, pure flame of patriotism. Take for example, the brilliantly gifted young peasant, brother of Restif de la Bretonne, who was hardly more than a child when he became a soldier out of pure love for the public weal, and was killed at the age of seventeen. But that was already the Revolution at work. People felt a presentiment of it, waited for it, longed for it, right throughout the century.

The Revolution melted all the peoples subject to the French

Crown into one single mass, and that by their enthusiasm for national sovereignty. Those who had been Frenchmen by force, became so by free consent; many of those who were not French wanted to become so. For to be French, thenceforward, meant belonging to the sovereign nation. If all the peoples, everywhere, had become sovereigns—as was hoped—none could take away from France the honor of having been the first to begin. Besides, frontiers no longer counted. Foreigners were only people who went on being the slaves of tyrants. Foreigners of a genuinely republican spirit were willingly accepted as honorary Frenchmen.

Thus, in France, there has been this paradox of a patriotism founded, not on love of the past, but on the most violent break with the country's past. And yet, the Revolution had a past in the more or less underground part of French history: everything connected with the freeing of the serfs, liberties of the towns, social struggles; the revolts in the fourteenth century, the beginnings of the Burgundian movement, the Fronde; and then writers like D'Aubigné, Théophile de Viau, Retz. Under François I, a project for creating a people's militia was set aside, because the noblemen objected that if it was put into operation the militiamen's grandsons would find themselves noblemen and their own grandsons serfs. So great was the dynamic force thrusting beneath the surface of this people.

But the influence of the *Encyclopédistes*, all of them uprooted intellectuals, all obsessed with the idea of progress, killed any chance of inspiration being sought in a revolutionary tradition. Besides, the prolonged terror under Louis XIV had left a gap difficult to bridge. It is because of this that, in spite of Montesquieu's efforts in a contrary sense, the liberating current of the eighteenth century found itself without historical roots: 1789 really was an open break.

The sentiment which then went by the name of patriotism was solely concerned with the present and the future. It was the love of the sovereign nation, based to a large extent on pride in belonging to it. The quality of being French seemed to be not so much a natural fact as a choice on the part of the will, like joining a party or church in our own day.

As for those who remained attached to the past history of

France, their attachment took the form of a personal and dynastic fidelity to the king. They saw nothing wrong in looking to foreign kings to send them armed help. They were not traitors. They remained faithful to what they thought they owed faithfulness, exactly like the men who brought about the death of Louis XVI.

The only people at the time who were patriots, in the sense that word took on later, were those who appeared in the eyes of their contemporaries—and have since appeared in those of posterity—as archtraitors; men like Talleyrand, who served, not, as has been said, every regime, but France behind every regime. But for such men France was neither the sovereign nation nor the king; it was the French State. Subsequent events have shown how right they were.

For, when the illusion of national sovereignty showed itself to be manifestly an illusion, it could no longer serve as an object of patriotism; on the other hand, kingship was like one of those severed plants one doesn't replant again. Patriotism had to change its meaning and turn itself toward the State. But thereby it straightway ceased to be popular. For the State was not something brought into being in 1789; it dated from the beginning of the seventeenth century, and shared some of the hatred nursed by the people against the monarchy. Thus it happened that, by a historical paradox, which at first sight seems surprising, patriotism changed to a different social class and political camp. It had been on the Left; it went over to the Right.

The change-over was completed following upon the Commune and the inauguration of the Third Republic. The May massacre of 1871 was a blow from which, morally, French workmen have perhaps never recovered. And it is not so long ago as all that. A workman of fifty at the present time can well have listened to horrified accounts of it from the lips of his father, then a child. The nineteenth-century French Army was a specific creation of the Revolution. Even soldiers in the service of the Bourbons, Louis Philippe, or Napoleon III must certainly have fired on the people very much against their own inclination. In 1871, for the first time since the Revolution, leaving out the brief interlude of 1848, France possessed a republican army. This same army, composed of decent young fellows from the French countryside, set about massacring workmen with an extraordinary display of sadistic pleasure. It was enough to produce a considerable shock.

The principal cause of this was doubtless the need of compensation for the disgrace of the defeat, that same need that led us a little later on to conquer the unfortunate Annamites. Everything points to the fact that, unless supernatural grace intervenes, there is no form of cruelty or depravity of which ordinary, decent people are not capable, once the corresponding psychological mechanisms have been set in motion.

The Third Republic was another shock. It is easy to believe in national sovereignty so long as wicked kings or emperors hold the nation in thrall; people think: if only they weren't there! . . . But when they *are* no longer there, when democracy has been installed and nevertheless the people are indubitably not sovereign, bewilderment is inevitable.

The year 1871 was the last year of that particular sort of French patriotism born in 1789. Frederick, the German Prince Imperial—afterward Frederick II—a humane, reasonable, and intelligent man, was very much surprised by the intensity of this patriotism, which he encountered everywhere throughout the course of the campaign. He couldn't understand why the Alsatians, hardly knowing a word of French, speaking a dialect closely allied to German, brutally conquered at a relatively recent date, refused to have anything to do with Germany. He discovered that the motive for this was the pride felt in belonging to the country that had produced the French Revolution, to the sovereign nation. Their annexation, by separating them from France, doubtless helped them to preserve this state of mind, at any rate partially, right up to 1918.

The Paris Commune was not, to begin with, a social movement at all, but an outburst of patriotism and even of extreme chauvinism. All through the nineteenth century, moreover, the aggressive turn taken by French patriotism had alarmed the rest of Europe. The war of 1870 was the direct outcome of this; for though France had not made preparations for war, she had none the less declared it without any plausible reason. Dreams of imperial conquest had remained alive among the people right throughout the century. At the same time, toasts were drunk to world independence. Conquering the world and liberating the world are, in fact, two incompatible forms of glory, but which can be easily reconciled with one another in reverie.

All this bubbling-up of popular feeling died away after 1871. Two things, nevertheless, caused an appearance of patriotic continuity to be maintained. One was the resentment at being defeated. There was not yet at that time any real reason for bearing the Germans a grudge. They had not been the aggressors; they had pretty well refrained from committing atrocities; and it was not our place to reproach them with violating the rights of peoples in connection with Alsace-Lorraine, whose population is largely Germanic, from the moment we began sending our first expeditions into Annam. But we bore them a grudge for having beaten us, just as though they had violated some divine, eternal, imprescriptible right to victory on the part of France.

In our present hatred of them, for which, unfortunately, there exist only too many legitimate reasons, this curious sentiment also plays its part. It was also one of the motives behind the action of certain collaborationists right at the beginning. If France found herself on the side of the vanquished, they thought, it could only be because of some faulty deal, some mistake, some misunderstanding; her natural place was on the side of the victors; therefore, the easiest, the least arduous, least painful method of bringing about the indispensable rectification was to change sides. This state of mind was very prevalent in certain circles at Vichy in July, 1940.

But what above all prevented French patriotism from disappearing altogether under the Third Republic, after losing nearly all its vital sap, was the fact that there was nothing else. The French had nothing except France to which to remain faithful; and when they abandoned her for a while, in June, 1940, one saw how hideous and pitiful could be the spectacle of a people no longer attached by bonds of fidelity to anything whatever. That is why, later on, they once again clung on exclusively to France. But if the French people recover their sovereignty—at least, what nowadays goes by that name—the same difficulty as before 1940 will reappear, namely, that the reality designated by the word France will be above all a State.

The State is a cold concern, which cannot inspire love, but itself kills, suppresses everything that might be loved; so one is forced to love it, because there is nothing else. That is the moral torment to which all of us today are exposed.

Here lies perhaps the true cause of that phenomenon of the leader, which has sprung up everywhere nowadays and surprises so many people. Just now, there is in all countries, in all movements, a man who is the personal magnet for all loyalties. Being compelled to embrace the cold, metallic surface of the State has made people, by contrast, hunger for something to love which is made of flesh and blood. This phenomenon shows no signs of disappearing, and, however disastrous the consequences have been so far, it may still have some very unpleasant surprises in store for us; for the art, so well known in Hollywood, of manufacturing stars out of any sort of human material, gives any sort of person the opportunity of presenting himself for the adoration of the masses.

Unless I am mistaken, the idea of making the State an object of loyalty appeared for the first time in France and in Europe with Richelieu. Before his time, people used to talk in religious-like tones about the public weal, the country, the king, or the local lord. It was he who first adopted the principle that whoever exercises a public function owes his entire loyalty, in the exercise of that function, not to the public, or to the king, but to the State and nothing else. It would be difficult to give an exact definition of the State. But it is, unfortunately, only too obvious that the word stands for something very real.

Richelieu, who possessed the intellectual clarity so common at that time, defined in luminous terms the difference between politics and morals, over which there has subsequently arisen so much confused thinking. Here is more or less what he said: We should beware of applying the same rules to the welfare of the State as to that of the soul; for the welfare of souls is attended to in the world above, whereas that of States is only attended to in this world.

That is cruelly exact. A Christian ought to be able to draw therefrom but one conclusion: That whereas to the welfare of the soul, or in other words to God, a total, absolute, and unconditional loyalty is owed; the welfare of the State is a cause to which only a limited and conditional loyalty is owed.

But although Richelieu believed himself to be a Christian, and no doubt sincerely, his conclusion was a totally different one, namely, that a man responsible for the welfare of the State and the men under him must employ to this end all useful means, without any exception, and, if necessary, sacrifice thereto their own lives, their sovereign, their people, foreign countries, and any and every species of obligation.

It represents—but in a much nobler form—Maurras' doctrine, "*Politique d'abord*." But Maurras, with perfect logic, is an atheist. The Cardinal, in postulating something whose whole reality is confined to this world as an absolute value, committed the sin of idolatry. Nor, in this connection, is it metal, stone, or wood which is really dangerous. The real sin of idolatry is always committed on behalf of something similar to the State. It was this sin that the devil wanted Christ to commit when he offered him the kingdoms of this world. Christ refused. Richelieu accepted. He had his reward. But he always believed himself to be acting solely out of devotion, and in a sense it was true.

His devotion to the State uprooted France. His policy was to kill systematically all spontaneous life in the country, so as to prevent anything whatsoever being able to oppose the State. If certain limits seem to have been set to his action in this sense, that is only because he was beginning and was astute enough to proceed gradually. All one needs to do is to read Corneille's dedicatory prefaces to realize to what vile depths of servility he had managed to reduce people's minds. Later on, to shield our national glory from shame, some people hit on the idea of saying that all this was merely the polite language of the time. But it's a lie. To convince oneself of the fact, all one has to do is to read what Théophile de Viau has written. Only Théophile died prematurely as a result of an arbitrary imprisonment, whereas Corneille lived to a grand old age.

Literature is only useful to us here as a sign; but it is a sure sign. Corneille's servile language shows that Richelieu wanted to enslave people's very minds; not for his own benefit, for in his self-abnegation he was probably sincere, but for that of the State he represented. His conception of the State was already totalitarian. He applied it as much as he was able to by subjecting the country, to the full extent by means of the time allowed, to a police regime. He thus destroyed a considerable part of the moral life of the country. If France submitted herself to be gagged in this way, it is because the nobility had so laid her waste by nonsensical and atrociously cruel civil wars that she consented to buy civil peace at that price.

After the Fronde outburst, which in its beginnings, from many points of view, was a forerunner of 1789, Louis XIV set himself up in power far more in the spirit of a dictator than in that of a legitimate sovereign. That is what his phrase, *"L'Etat, c'est moi,"* indicates. It is not a kingly conception. Montesquieu has explained all this very clearly, in roundabout terms. But what he couldn't yet perceive in his time was that there have been two stages in the decline of the French monarchy. After Charles V, the monarchy degenerated into a personal despotism. But from Richelieu onward, it was replaced by a State machine with totalitarian tendencies, which, as Marx points out, has not only outlasted all changes of regime, but has been strengthened and perfected by each succeeding change.

During the Fronde and under Mazarin, France, in spite of the general distress, was morally able to breathe. Louis XIV found her full of brilliant men of genius whom he recognized and encouraged. But at the same time he carried on, to a much higher degree of intensity, the policy of Richelieu. In this way he reduced France in a very short time to a desert from the moral point of view, not to mention one of fearful material poverty.

If one reads Saint-Simon, not as a literary and historical curiosity, but as a document dealing with the lives of human beings who actually lived, one is overcome with horror and disgust at such a turgid atmosphere of mortal ennui, such widespread spiritual, moral, and intellectual baseness. La Bruyère, the letters of Liselotte—all the documents of the time, read in the same spirit, leave the same impression. Going back even a little further, one should certainly realize, for example, that Molière didn't write his *Misanthrope* just for fun.

Louis XIV's regime was really already totalitarian. The country was ravaged by terrorism and denunciation. The idolizing of the State in the person of the sovereign was organized with an impudence which was an outrage to all Christian consciences. The art of propaganda was already thoroughly understood, as is shown by that ingenuous admission by the chief of police to Liselotte regarding the orders received not to allow any book on any subject to appear which didn't contain an extravagant eulogy of the king.

Under this regime, uprootedness in the French provinces, the suppression of all local life, reached a far higher degree of intensity. The eighteenth century provided a lull. The operation whereby national sovereignty was substituted for royal sovereignty under the Revolution had only this drawback, the nonexistence of national sovereignty. As in the case of Orlando's mare, that was the only defect to be found. In point of fact, there existed no known means of creating something concrete corresponding to these words. Thenceforward, there remained only the State, which naturally reaped the benefit of the strong desire for unity—"unity or death"—which had developed around the belief in national sovereignty. Whence, further destruction in the sphere of local life. With the aid of war—war having been from the very start the mainspring of all this business—the State, under the Convention and the Empire, became ever more and more totalitarian.

Louis XIV had debased the Gallic Church by associating it with the cult of his own person and by imposing obedience on it even in matters of religion. This servile attitude of the Church toward the sovereign was very largely responsible for the anti-clericalism of the following century.

But when the Church committed the irreparable mistake of making common cause with the monarchy, it thereby cut itself off from the general life of the nation. Nothing was better able to serve the totalitarian designs of the State. The only result could be the laical system, prelude to that open adoration of the State as such which is now so much in favor.

Christians are defenseless against the laical spirit. For either they must throw themselves entirely into political action, party politics, to put temporal power back again into the hands of the clergy, or the supporters of the clergy; or else they must resign themselves to being irreligious, in their turn, in all that appertains to the secular side of their own lives, which is what usually happens today, to a far greater extent than those concerned realize themselves. In either case, they set aside the proper function of religion, which is to suffuse with its light all secular life, public or private, without ever in any way dominating it.

During the nineteenth century, the railways caused frightful havoc from the point of view of uprootedness. George Sand was still able to see in her native Berry customs, which maybe went back for several thousand years, the very memory of which would have been entirely lost but for the hasty notes she took down concerning them.

Loss of the past, whether it be collectively or individually, is the supreme human tragedy, and we have thrown ours away just like a child picking off the petals of a rose. It is above all to avoid this loss that peoples will put up a desperate resistance to being conquered.

Now the totalitarian phenomenon of the State arises through a conquest carried out by the public authorities of the people under their care, without being able to spare them the evils necessarily accompanying all conquest, in order to possess a better instrument for carrying out foreign conquest. This is what happened formerly in France and has happened more recently in Germany, not to mention Russia.

But the development of the State exhausts a country. The State eats away its moral substance, lives on it, fattens on it, until the day comes when no more nourishment can be drawn from it, and famine reduces it to a condition of lethargy. That was the condition France had reached. In Germany, on the other hand, the centralization of the State is quite a recent development, consequently there the State possesses all the aggressiveness supplied by a superabundance of food of high energizing content. As for Russia, popular life is so intensely strong there, that one wonders whether, in the end, it isn't the people that will devour the State, or rather reabsorb it.

The Third Republic in France, was a very curious affair; one of its most curious features being that its entire structure, outside the actual arena of parliamentary life, was derived from the Empire. The love Frenchmen have for abstract logic makes it very easy for them to be deceived by labels. The English have a kingdom with a republican content; we had a republic with an imperial content. Moreover, the Empire itself was linked, over and beyond the revolution, back in an unbroken chain to the monarchy; not the ancient French monarchy, but the totalitarian, police-ridden one of the seventeenth century.

The personality of Fouché is a symbol of this continuity. The repressive apparatus of the French State continued on throughout all changes without being troubled or interrupted, with an ever-increasing power of action. That is why the State, in France, remained a target for people's resentment, hatred and aversion, which, in the past, had been aroused by royal government turned tyrannical. We have actually lived through this strange paradox, so strange that one couldn't even be aware of it at the time: a democracy in which all public institutions, and all things connected with them, were openly hated and despised by the entire population.

No Frenchman had the slightest qualms about robbing or cheating the State in the matter of customs, taxes, subsidies, or anything else. We must except certain ranks of civil servants; but they formed part of the State machine. If the middle classes went much further than anybody else in the country in dealings of this sort, it was solely because far more opportunities came their way. The police, in France, are held in such profound contempt that many Frenchmen regard this attitude as one necessarily built into the everlasting moral structure of the respectable citizen. Guignol forms part of genuine French folklore, which goes back to the *Ancien Régime* and has never grown out of date. The epithet *"policier"* constitutes in French one of the most scathing insults, and it would be interesting to know if exact equivalents exist in other languages. But, of course, the police are really nothing other than the active instrument at the service of the authorities. The feelings of the French people with regard to this instrument have remained the same as they were in the days when peasants were obliged, as Rousseau noted, to conceal the fact that they had a piece of ham in the house.

Similarly, the whole series of political institutions were the object of disgust, derision, and disdain. The very word politics had taken on a profoundly pejorative meaning incredible in a democracy. "Oh, he's a politician," "All that, that's just politics"—such phrases expressed final and complete condemnation. In the eyes of a number of French people, even the parliamentary profession itself—for it was a profession—had something ignominious about it. Some Frenchmen prided themselves on keeping away from all contact with what they termed "*la politique*," except on the day of the elections, or even on that day, too; others looked upon their local deputy as a sort of servant, a being created and put into the world specially to serve their own private interests. The only feeling which tempered the contempt for public affairs was the party spirit, at any rate among such as had caught this disease.

One would seek in vain to find a single aspect of public life that was able to arouse in the French the remotest feelings of loyalty, gratitude, or affection. In the heyday of laical enthusiasm, there had been public education; but for a long time now education has ceased to be anything, both in the eyes of parents and children alike, except a machine for producing diplomas, in other words, jobs. As to items of social legislation, never had the French people, to the extent to which their appetite in that direction was satisfied, regarded them as other than concessions extorted from niggardly authorities as a direct result of bringing violent pressure to bear.

No other interest replaced the one lacking for public affairs. Each successive regime having destroyed at an ever increasing rate local and regional life, it had finally ceased to exist. France was like a dying man whose members are already cold, and whose heart alone goes on beating. Hardly anywhere was there any real throb of life except in Paris; but even there, as soon as you reached the suburbs, an atmosphere of moral decay began to make itself felt.

In those outwardly peaceful days before the war, the ennui of the little French provincial towns constituted perhaps as real a form of cruelty as that of more visible atrocities. Isn't it as cruel to condemn human beings to spend those unique, irreplaceable years between the cradle and the grave in a dismal atmosphere of ennui, as to have them starved or massacred? It was Richelieu who started throwing this pall of ennui over France, and since his time the atmosphere has only grown stuffier and stuffier. When war broke out, a state of asphyxiation had been reached.

If the State has morally killed everything, territorially speaking, smaller than itself, it has also turned territorial frontiers into prison walls to lock up people's thoughts. As soon as one examines history a little closely, and outside of the ordinary manuals, one is amazed to see to what extent certain periods almost without material means of communication surpassed ours in the wealth, variety, fertility, and vitality of their exchanges of thought over the very widest expanses. That is the case with the Middle Ages, pre-Roman antiquity, the period immediately preceding historical times. In our day, with our radios, airplanes, latest developments in transport of all kinds, printing and the press, the modern phenomenon of the nation keeps shut up in separate little compartments even so naturally universal a thing as science. Frontiers, of course, are not impassable; but just as they subject the traveler to an unending series of irritating and laborious formalities, so in the same way all contact with foreign ways of thinking, in no matter what sphere, demands a mental effort in order to get across the frontier. The effort required is considerable, and quite a number of people are not prepared to make it. Even in the case of those who do, the fact that such an effort *has* to be made prevents the formation of organic links across the frontiers.

It is true that there are international churches and parties. But as for the churches, they offer us the supreme scandal of clergy and faithful asking God at the same time, with the same rites, the same words, and it must be supposed, an equal amount of faith and purity of heart, to grant a military victory to one or other of two warring camps. This shocking spectacle has been going on for a long time; but in our century religious life has been subordinated to that of the nation as never before. And as for parties, their internationalism is either a pure fiction, or else it takes the form of a total subserviency to one particular nation. Lastly, the State has also broken all the bonds that could, outside the sphere of public life, provide a goal for the exercise of loyalty. Much as the French Revolution did, by suppressing the trades corporations, to encourage technical progress, morally speaking it created a corresponding amount of evil, or at any rate finally sealed an evil already partly accomplished. It cannot be too often repeated that nowadays, whenever people refer to such organizations, in no matter what circles, the last thing they have in mind is anything resembling the old trades corporations.

Once the trades corporations had disappeared, labor became, in the individual lives of men, a means whose corresponding end was money. There is somewhere in the charter of the League of Nations a sentence declaring that henceforth labor shall no longer be regarded as a commodity. It was a joke in the worst possible taste. We live in an age when a host of worthy people, who judge themselves to be very far removed from what Lévy-Bruhl called the prelogical mentality, have believed in the magical efficacy of words far more than any savage from the depths of Australia ever did. When you take some indispensable commercial product off the market, you have to arrange for it to be distributed in some other way. Nothing of the kind was attempted in connection with labor, which, naturally, has continued being a commodity.

Hence, professional loyalty becomes merely a form of commercial honesty. In a society founded on exchange, the heaviest form of social reprobation falls on robbery and swindling, and especially swindling by a dealer who sells poor quality goods guaranteeing them all the time to be first class. Accordingly, when one sells one's labor, honesty demands that one should furnish goods of a quality corresponding to the price paid. But honesty is not the same as loyalty. A wide distance separates these two virtues.

A strong current of loyalty flows through working-class association, which was for a long time the dominant impulse behind trade-union activity. But several obstacles have prevented this loyalty from forming a solid buttress to moral life. On the one hand, the commercial side of social life has penetrated into the working-class movement, by wage questions being given first place; and the more questions of money dominate, the quicker the spirit of loyalty disappears. On the other hand, to the extent to which the working-class movement is a revolutionary one, it has escaped from this drawback, but has acquired the weaknesses inherent in all forms of rebellion.

Richelieu, some of whose observations are so extraordinarily lucid, declares having learned from experience that, all other things being equal, rebels are always half as strong as the defenders of official power. Even if people think they are upholding a good cause, the feeling that they are in rebellion weakens them. Without some psychological mechanism of this sort, there could be no stability about human societies. This mechanism explains the firm hold obtained by the Communist party. Revolutionary workmen are only too thankful to have a State at the back of them—a State which gives an official character, legitimacy, and reality to their actions, that only a State can confer, and which at the same time is situated too far away from them, geographically, to be able to disgust them. In just the same way, the *Encyclopédistes*, feeling deeply uncomfortable at finding themselves in conflict with their own ruler, showed desperate anxiety to obtain the favor of the rulers of Prussia and Russia. One can also understand, making use of this analogy, why more or less revolutionary workmen who had resisted the attraction of Russian prestige were not able to prevent themselves succumbing to the German variety.

Apart from those who have given themselves entirely to the Communist party, workmen cannot find in loyalty toward their own class a sufficiently concrete, sufficiently clearly defined aim to satisfy their need of inner stability. Few notions are so vague as that of social class. Marx, who built up the whole of his system upon it, never attempted to define it, nor even simply to investigate it. The only information to be extracted from his works on the subject of social classes is that they are things which engage in strife. That is not enough. Besides, it is not one of those notions which, without being able to be defined in words, are clear to the mind. It is even harder to conceive it or feel it without some definition than it is to define it.

The loyalty implicit in adherence to some religious form also counts little enough—strange though this may be—in modern life. In spite of great and obvious differences, a result which is in a sense analogous is produced by the English system of a national Church and the French system of the separation of Church and State. Only the latter seems the more destructive.

Religion has been proclaimed a private affair. According to present-day habits of mind, this doesn't mean that it resides in the secret places of the soul, in that inner sanctuary where even the individual conscience doesn't penetrate. It means that it is a matter of choice, opinion, taste, almost of caprice, something like the choice of a political party, or even that of a tie; or else that it is a matter to do with one's family, education, personal surroundings. Having become a private concern, it has lost the obligatory character associated with public manifestations, and consequently can no longer lay claim to loyalty unchallenged.

A number of revealing remarks show that this is so. How often, for instance, we hear the following commonplace repeated, "Whether Catholics, Protestants, Jews, or free thinkers, we're all Frenchmen," exactly as though it were a question of small territorial fragments of the country, as who should say, "Whether from Marseilles, Lyons, or Paris, we're all Frenchmen." In a document promulgated by the Pope, one may read, "Not only from the Christian point of view; but, more generally, from the human point of view . . ." as though the Christian point of view—which either has no meaning at all, or else it claims to encompass everything in this world and the next—possessed a minor degree of generality than the human point of view. It is impossible to conceive a more terrible admission of religious bankruptcy. That is how the *anathema sit* have to be paid for. To sum up, religion, degraded to the rank of a private matter, reduces itself to the choice of a place in which to spend an hour or two every Sunday morning.

What is comical about the situation is that religion, that is to say, Man's relationship to God, is not nowadays regarded as too sacred a matter to be interfered with by any outside authority, but is placed among the things which the State leaves to each one's own particular fancy, as being of small importance from the point of view of public affairs. At least, that has been the case in the recent past, and that is the contemporary meaning attached to the word "tolerance."

Thus there exists nothing, apart from the State, to which loyalty can cling; which is why up to 1940 loyalty had not been withdrawn from it. For men feel that there is something hideous about a human existence devoid of loyalty. Amidst the general debasement of all words in the French vocabulary, which have anything to do with moral concepts, the words *traître* and *trahison* have lost none of their forcefulness. Men feel also that they are born for sacrifice; and the only form of sacrifice remaining in the public imagination was military sacrifice, that is, a sacrifice offered to the State.

Indeed, all that was left was the State. The ideal of the Nation, in the sense in which the men of 1789 or 1792 understood the word, which then used to bring tears of joy to people's eyes—all that belonged irremediably to the past. Even the word nation had changed its meaning. In our day, it no longer denotes the sovereign people, but the sum total of peoples recognizing the authority of the same State; it is the political structure created by a State and the country under its control. When one talks about national sovereignty nowadays, all it really means is the sovereignty of the State. A conversation between a contemporary of ours and a man of 1792 would lead to some highly comic misunderstandings. For not only is the State in question not the sovereign people, but it is the very self-same inhuman, brutal, bureaucratic, police-ridden State bequeathed by Richelieu to Louis XIV, by Louis XIV to the Convention, by the Convention to the Empire, and by the Empire to the Third Republic. And what is more, it is instinctively recognized and hated as such.

Thus we have witnessed this strange spectacle—a State, the object of hatred, repugnance, derision, disdain, and fear, which, under the name of *patrie*, demanded absolute loyalty, total self-abnegation, the supreme sacrifice, and obtained them, from 1914 to 1918, to an extent which surpassed all expectations. It set itself up as an absolute value in this world, that is, as an object of idolatry; and it was accepted and served as such, honored with the sacrifice of an appalling number of human lives. A loveless idolatry—what could be more monstrous, more heart-rending?

When anybody goes much further in his devotion than his heart prompts him to do, a violent reaction, a sort of revulsion of feeling inevitably sets in later on. This is frequently observable in families where an invalid requires things to be done for him which exceed the affection he inspires. His relatives harbor a resentment, which is suppressed as too unworthy to admit, but which is ever-present, like some secret poison.

That is exactly what happened between Frenchmen and France, after 1918. They had given too much to France, more than they had it in them to give to her.

All the flow of antipatriotic, pacifist, and internationalist ideas after 1918 claimed to be in the name of those killed in the war and the veterans; and in the case of the latter, a good deal of it really had its source among themselves. There were also, it is true, extremely patriotic veterans' associations. But the expression of their patriotism had a hollow ring, and was lacking altogether in persuasive force. It reminded one of the language of people who, having suffered too much, continually feel the need to remind themselves that they haven't suffered in vain. For too high a degree of suffering in relation to what the heart prompts can produce one or other of two attitudes: either the violent rejection of the object to which too much has been sacrificed, or else the clinging to it in a sort of despair.

Nothing did more harm to patriotism than the reminder, repeated *ad nauseam*, of the part played by the police behind the battle front. Nothing was more calculated to wound the susceptibilities of Frenchmen, by pointing out to them, standing behind their country, that police-ridden State, the traditional object of their hatred. At the same time, extracts from the sensational press during the war years, read over again later on quite calmly and with appropriate feelings of disgust, and connected up with the role of the police, left them with the impression that they had been hoaxed. There is nothing that a Frenchman is less able to forgive. Since the very words which expressed patriotic feeling had become discredited, the feeling itself became relegated, in a sense, to the category of feelings one is ashamed to talk about. There was a time, not so long ago either, when to have expressed patriotic sentiments in working-class circles—at least, in some of them—would have seemed to those present like a breach of propriety.

All the evidence points to the fact that the most courageous soldiers in 1940 were veterans of the previous war. One can only conclude that their post-1918 reactions had a deeper influence over the minds of their children than over their own. This is a very frequent phenomenon and quite easy to understand. Those who were eighteen in 1914 had had their characters formed in the years preceding the war.

It has been said that the schools at the beginning of the century had formed a generation for victory, and that those after 1918 turned out a beaten one. There is undoubtedly a lot of truth in this. Still, the schoolmasters from 1918 onward were mostly veterans, and very many children who reached the age of ten between 1920 and 1930 must have had such men as teachers.

If the effect of this reaction was felt in France more than in other countries, this was because of a far more acute form of uprootedness there, resulting from a far older and more intense form of State centralization, the demoralizing effects of victory, and the complete license allowed in the field of propaganda.

The balance was also upset in regard to the notion of patriotism, but compensated in an inverse sense, this compensation taking place in the realm of pure speculation. Owing to the fact that the State had remained, in the midst of a total void, the only reality entitled to demand of Man his loyalty and sacrifice, the notion of patriotism presented itself to the mind as an absolute value. The country was beyond good and evil. It is what is expressed in the English saying, "Right or wrong, my country." But people often go further. They refuse to admit that their country can ever be wrong.

However small the inclination of men of all classes may be for making an effort of critical examination, a patent absurdity, even if they refuse it conscious recognition, throws them into a state of uneasiness, which weakens the spirit. In reality, nothing is more mixed up with ordinary, daily human affairs than philosophy, but it is an implied philosophy.

To posit one's country as an absolute value that cannot be defiled by evil is manifestly absurd. Country is merely another name for nation; and the nation is a self-contained unit composed of various territorial areas and peoples assembled together as a result of historical events in which chance has played a great part, so far as human intelligence is able to judge, and where good and evil are always mingled with one another. The nation is a fact, and a fact is not an absolute value. It is just one fact among other similar facts. More than one nation exists on the earth's surface. Ours is certainly unique. But each of the others, considered by itself and with affection, is unique in the same degree.

It was the fashion before 1940 to talk about "eternal France."

Such words are a sort of blasphemy. One is compelled to say the same about the moving pages which have been written by great French Catholic writers on the vocation of France, the eternal salvation of France, and other similar themes. Richelieu showed a much clearer perception when he said that the salvation of States was only brought about in this world. France is something which is temporal, terrestrial. Unless I am mistaken, it has never been suggested that Christ died to save nations. The idea of a nation being chosen by God for itself simply belongs to the old Mosaic law.

So-called pagan antiquity would never have blundered into so gross a confusion. The Romans regarded themselves as specially chosen, but solely for world dominion. They were not concerned with the next world. Nowhere does it appear that any city or people should have thought itself chosen for a supernatural destiny. The mysteries, which represented, to a certain extent, the official road to salvation, as the Churches do today, were local institutions, but recognized as being on an equal footing among themselves. Plato describes how Man, assisted by the power of grace, passes out of the cavern of this world; but he doesn't say that a whole city can pass out of it. On the contrary, he depicts the collectivity as something animal, which hinders the soul's salvation.

Antiquity is often accused of having only been able to recognize collective values. In fact, this mistake was only made by the Romans, who were atheists, and by the Hebrews; and in the latter case, only up to the time of the Babylonian exile. But if it is wrong to attribute this mistake to pre-Christian antiquity, it is also wrong not to recognize that we are continually committing ourselves, corrupted as we are by the dual Roman-Hebrew tradition, which all too often carries the day with us as against pure Christian inspiration.

Christians today find it awkward to have to recognize that, if the word patriotism is used in its strongest possible sense, its complete sense, a Christian has only one country that can be the object of such patriotism, and which is situated outside this world. For he has but one *Patros*, who lives outside this world. "Lay up for yourselves treasures in heaven . . . for where your treasure is, there will your heart be also." It is therefore forbidden to have one's heart on this earth.

Christians today don't like raising the question of the respective rights over their heart enjoyed by God and their country. The German bishops ended one of their most courageous protests by saying that they refused ever to have to make a choice between God and Germany. And why did they refuse to do this? Circumstances can always arise which make it necessary to choose between God and no matter what earthly object, and the choice must never be in doubt. But the French bishops would not have expressed themselves any differently. Joan of Arc's popularity during the past quarter of a century was not an altogether healthy business; it was a convenient way of forgetting that there is a difference between France and God. Yet this lack of inward courage to challenge the accepted notion of patriotism didn't make for greater energy in patriotic performance. Joan of Arc's statue was occupying a prominent place in every church throughout the country, all through those terrible days when Frenchmen abandoned France to her fate.

"If any man come to me, and hate not his father and mother, and wife, and children, and brethren, and sisters, yea, and his own life also, he cannot be my disciple." If it is commanded to hate all that, using the word "hate" in a certain sense, it is certainly forbidden also to love one's country, using the word "love" in a certain sense. For the proper object of love is goodness, and "God alone is good."

Such facts are self-evident, but, by some magic spell or other, go altogether unrecognized in our age. Otherwise it would have been impossible for a man like Father de Foucauld—who, out of charity, had chosen to bear witness to Christ among non-Christian populations—to consider that he had the right at the same time to supply the *Deuxième Bureau* with information on the subject of these same populations.

It would be salutary for us to ponder the devil's terrible words with reference to the kingdoms of this world, as he showed them all to Christ, "All this power . . . is delivered unto me. . . ." Not a single kingdom is excepted.

What didn't shock the Christians shocked the workmen. A tradition still sufficiently recent so as not to be quite dead, makes the love of justice the central inspiration behind the French working-class movement. During the first half of the nineteenth century, it was a passionate love, which took the side of the oppressed all over the world.

As long as the people constituted as a sovereign nation were synonymous with the country, no problem arose concerning their relationship to justice. For it was agreed—quite arbitrarily, and on the flimsiest interpretation of the *Contrat Social*—that a sovereign nation doesn't commit acts of injustice toward either its members or its neighbors; it being supposed that the causes making for injustice were all bound up with the nonexistence of the sovereign nation.

But as soon as, behind the country, there stands the old State, justice is far away. In the modern form of patriotism, justice hasn't much of a part to play, and above all nothing is said which might encourage any relationship between patriotism and justice to be drawn. One dare not assert that there is an equivalence between the two conceptions; one wouldn't dare, in particular, make such an assertion before a gathering of workmen, who, beneath their social oppression, feel the State's cold, metallic touch, and realize in a confused sort of way that the same cold touch must prevail in international relations. When a lot is talked about patriotism, little is heard about justice; and the sense of justice is so strong among workmen, even if they are materialists, owing to the fact that they are always under the impression they are being deprived of it, that any form of moral education in which justice hardly figures cannot possibly exercise any hold over them. When they die for France, they always need to feel that at the same time they are dying for something very much greater, taking part in the universal struggle against injustice. For them, to use a now famous expression, patriotism is not enough.

The same thing applies wherever a flame, a spark, however indistinct, of truly spiritual life burns. By its light, patriotism is not enough. And for those in whom this light is absent, patriotism, in its highest aspects, is far too exalted; it can then only constitute a sufficiently strong incentive in the form of the blindest national fanaticism.

It is true that men are capable of dividing their minds into compartments, in each of which an idea lives a sort of life of its own, undisturbed by other ideas. They don't care for either critical or synthetic effort, and won't submit to making either unless obliged.

But in situations of fear, anguish, when the flesh draws back before the prospect of death, or too great a degree of suffering or danger, in the mind of every man, even if he is completely uneducated, a manufacturer of arguments suddenly stands forth, who elaborates proofs to demonstrate why it is legitimate and right to avoid that particular death, suffering, or danger. Such proofs can be either good or bad, depending on the particular case. At all events, at the time, the body's disturbed condition gives them an intensity of persuasive force that no orator has ever succeeded in acquiring.

There are people to whom things do not happen in this way. That is either because their natures protect them from fear, that their flesh, blood, and bowels remain unaffected by the presence of death or suffering; or else because their minds have attained such a degree of unity that this manufacturer of arguments has no opportunity of getting to work in them. With others, again, he is able to get to work, and makes his arguments felt, but they are scorned nevertheless. That in itself presupposes either an already high degree of inward unity, or else powerful outward incentives.

Hitler's profound remark on the subject of propaganda, namely that brute force is unable to prevail over ideas if it is alone, but that it easily manages to do so by taking unto itself a few ideas of no matter how base a nature, provides also the key to the inner life. The tumults of the flesh, however violent they may be, cannot prevail over a thought in the mind, if they act alone. But their victory is an easy one if they communicate their persuasive force to some other thought, however inferior it may be. That is the important point. No thought is of too inferior a quality for this role of ally of the flesh. But the flesh needs thought of some kind as an ally.

That is why, whereas in normal times people—even cultured ones —live, without the slightest inconvenience, with the most colossal inward contradictions, in times of supreme crisis the least flaw in the realm of consciousness acquires the same importance as if the most lucid of philosophers were at hand, maliciously ready to take advantage of the fact; and this happens to everybody, however ignorant he or she may be.

In times of greatest stress, which are not necessarily those of the greatest danger, but those when Man finds himself, in face of the tumult raging in his flesh and blood and bowels, alone and bereft of all outward support, those whose inward lives depend entirely on one idea are the only ones capable of resisting. Which is why totalitarian systems form men able to withstand anything.

Patriotism can only become a single idea of this sort in a regime of the Hitlerian type. This could easily be proved, in detail, but it isn't worth while since the evidence is so overwhelming. If patriotism is not such an idea, and yet, all the same, has a part to play, then either there must exist disorder in the inward consciousness, and some hidden weakness of the spirit, or else there must be some other idea, dominating all the rest, and in relation to which patriotism has a perfectly clearly recognized role, but a limited and subordinate one.

This latter was not the case under the Third Republic—not in any class of society. What there was everywhere was moral incoherence; which is why a pet argument manufacturer was busy in everybody's mind between 1914 and 1918. Most people resisted by making a supreme effort, thanks to that sort of reaction which often encourages men to rush blindly, through fear of bringing dishonor upon themselves, to the opposite extreme to that to which fear urges them. But when the mind is exposed to danger and suffering as a result of obeying this impulse alone, it quickly becomes worn out. The agonized arguments, which were unable to bring their influence to bear on personal conduct, go gnawing away all the more surely in the very depths of the mind, and make their influence felt retrospectively. That is what happened after 1918. And those who had not made any sacrifice and were ashamed of it were very quick, for other reasons, to catch the infection. In such an atmosphere were children brought up who, a little later on, were to be asked to go out and die.

One can realize how far this inward disintegration had proceeded with the French, when one reflects that even today the idea of collaboration with the enemy is not entirely out of favor. On the other hand, if encouragement is sought in the spectacle of the Resistance, if one tells oneself that the resisters find no difficulty at all in deriving inspiration from patriotism and from a host of other motives, one must at the same time go on reminding oneself that France, as a nation, finds herself at the moment on the side of justice, the general good, and things of that kind, that is to say, among the beautiful things which don't exist. The allied victory will take her out of this category, and put her back into the realm of facts; many difficulties, which seemed to be disposed of, will reappear. In a sense, misfortune simplifies everything. The fact that France entered along the path of resistance more slowly, later than most of the other occupied countries, shows that it would be a mistake to be without apprehensions as to the future.

One can see clearly to what a point of moral incoherence our regime has attained if one considers the schools. Moral philosophy forms part of the curriculum, and even those teachers who didn't care to make it the subject of dogmatic teaching, taught it inevitably in a diffuse sort of way. And the central conception of morals is justice and the obligations it imposes toward one's neighbor.

But when it is a question of history, morals cease to play any part. The question is never raised as to France's obligations abroad. Sometimes she is referred to as being just and generous, as though that were something superogatory, a feather in her cap, a crown to her glory. The conquests she has made and then allowed to slip from her grasp can, perhaps, be regarded with a certain doubt, like those of Napoleon; but never the ones she has managed to hold on to. The past is nothing else but the story of France's growth, and it is considered that this growth must necessarily be a good thing from every point of view. No one ever asked himself whether in the course of her growth she hasn't brought about destruction. To look into the possibility of her having at some time or another destroyed things which were worth as much as she, would seem the most appalling blasphemy. Bernanos says that the people of *Action Française* look upon France as a prime baby who has only to grow and put on flesh to satisfy his parents' every wish. But there are others besides them. It is the general opinion which, without ever being expressed, is always implied in the way in which the country's past history is regarded. And, besides, the comparison with a baby is too flattering. The living things that are only asked to put on flesh are rabbits, pigs, and chickens. Plato found the right expression when he compared the collectivity to an animal. And those who are blinded by its prestige, which means every one except for a few predestined individuals, "call just and beautiful the things that are necessary, being incapable of discerning and teaching what a distance separates the essence of what is necessary from the essence of what is good."

Everything is done to make children feel—not that they don't feel it naturally—that things concerning the country, the nation, the nation's growth have a degree of importance, which sets them apart from other things. And it is precisely in regard to those things that justice, consideration for others, strict obligations assigning limits to ambitions and appetites—all that moral teaching one is trying to instill into the lives of little boys—never get mentioned.

What conclusion is there to be drawn other than that morals are among the number of less important things, which, like religion, a trade, the choice of a doctor or a grocer, belong to the lower plane of private life?

But with morals, properly speaking, thus relegated to a lower plane, no other system is advanced as a substitute. For the superior prestige of the nation is bound up with the exaltation of war. It furnishes no motives for action in peacetime, except in a regime which constitutes a permanent preparation for war, like the Nazi regime. Save in such a regime as the latter, it would be dangerous to remind people too much that this country of theirs, which asks its children to lay down their lives, has a reverse side—the State, with its taxes, customs, police. This is carefully avoided, and so it never occurs to anybody that to hate the police or defraud the customs and income-tax authorities is to display a lack of patriotism. A country like England forms to a certain extent an exception, on account of a centuries-old tradition of liberty guaranteed by the authorities. Thus, this dual system of morals, in time of peace, weakens the power of the unchanging moral law, without putting anything in its place.

This duality is present at all times, everywhere, and not only in the schools. For nearly every day, in normal times, when a Frenchman reads the paper, discusses things at home or in the local *bistro*, he is moved to think for France, in the name of France. From that moment, and until he enters again into his own private self, he loses even all recollection of the virtues which, in a more or less vague and abstract way, he recognizes it is his personal duty to practice. When it is a question of oneself, and even of one's family, it is a more or less recognized thing that one mustn't be too boastful; that one must beware of one's judgments when one is at the same time judge and prosecutor; that one must ask oneself whether opposition on the part of others may not be at least partly justified; that one mustn't try to occupy the whole stage, or think solely of oneself; in short, that limits must be set to egoism and pride. But when it comes to national egoism, national pride, not only is a field unlimited, but the highest possible degree of it seems to be imposed by something closely resembling an obligation. Regard for others, recognition of one's own faults, modesty, the voluntary limitation of one's desires—all are now turned into so many crimes, so many sacrileges. Among several sublime sentiments which the Egyptian *Book of the Dead* puts into the mouth of the just man after death, perhaps the most moving is the following, "I have never turned a deaf ear to just and true words." But in international affairs, every one regards it as a sacred duty to turn a deaf ear to just and true words, if they go contrary to the interests of France. Or else, do we admit that words contrary to the interests of France can never be just and true ones? That would come to exactly the same thing.

There are certain errors of taste which good breeding, in the absence of morality, prevents people from falling into in private life, and which seem perfectly natural on a national scale. Even the most odious of patronesses would hesitate to assemble together all their protégés to remind them of the huge benefits they had received and of the corresponding gratitude they owed in return. But a French Governor of Indo-China doesn't hesitate, in the name of France, to talk in that fashion, even immediately after the most atrocious acts of repression or the most scandalous famines; and he expects to hear himself echoed, and, indeed, insists upon it.

This is a custom inherited from the Romans. They never committed any acts of cruelty, never granted any favors, without boasting in each case of their generosity and clemency. No one was ever received in audience, no matter what the subject might be, even a simple alleviation of some terrible form of oppression, without first beginning by the familiar catalogue of praise. In this way they brought dishonor upon entreaty, which before then had been an honorable act, by burdening it with lies and flattery. In the *Iliad,* you never find a Trojan, on his knees before a Greek and imploring for his life, putting the remotest trace of flattery in his words.

Our patriotism comes straight from the Romans. That is why French children are encouraged to seek inspiration for it in Corneille. It is a pagan virtue, if these two words are compatible. The word pagan, when applied to Rome, early possesses the significance charged with horror which the early Christian controversialists gave it. The Romans really were an atheistic and idolatrous people; not idolatrous with regard to images made of stone or bronze, but idolatrous with regard to themselves. It is this idolatry of self which they have bequeathed to us in the form of patriotism.

This duality in the moral sphere is a far more appalling scandal if, instead of lay morality, one thinks of the Christian virtues, of which lay morality is in any case simply an edition for general public use, a diluted solution. The essential fact about the Christian virtues, what lends them a special savor of their own, is humility—the freely accepted movement toward the bottom. It is through this that the saints resemble Christ. "Who, being in the form of God, thought it not robbery to be equal with God. . . . He humbled himself. . . . Though he were a Son, yet learned he obedience by the things which he suffered."

But when a Frenchman thinks about France, pride, for him, is a duty, according to present notions; humility would be a betrayal. It is this betrayal which is perhaps what the Vichy Government is most bitterly reproached with. People are right in that, for its humility is of a debased kind; it is that of the slave who cringes and lies to avoid receiving blows. But in matters of this sort, a humility of a really high order is something unknown to us. We cannot even conceive such a thing possible. In order merely to be able to conceive it, we should have to make a special effort of the imagination.

In the soul of a Christian, the presence of the pagan virtue of patriotism acts as a dissolvent. We received it from the hands of Rome without giving it baptism. It is strange to reflect that the barbarians, or those who were so named, were baptized almost without any difficulty at the time of the invasions; but the heritage of ancient Rome never was, no doubt because it was impossible for it to be, and that in spite of the fact that the Roman Empire turned Christianity into a State religion.

It would be difficult, moreover, to imagine a more cruel injury. As for the barbarians, it is not surprising that the Goths accepted Christianity without difficulty, if, as their contemporaries thought, they were of the same blood as those Getae, the noblest of the Thracians, whom Herodotus calls immortalizers because of their intense faith in eternal life. The barbarian heritage became mingled with the Christian spirit to form that unique, inimitable, perfectly homogeneous product known as chivalry. But between the spirit of Rome and that of Christ there has never been any fusion. If fusion had been possible, the Apocalypse would have lied in representing Rome as the woman seated on the beast, the woman full of the names of blasphemy.

The Renaissance was first of all a resurrection of the Greek spirit and then of the Roman spirit. It is only in this second stage that it acted as a dissolvent of Christianity. It is in the course of this second stage that there came into being the modern form of nationality, the modern form of patriotism. Corneille was right to dedicate his *Horace* to Richelieu, and to do so in terms which baseness provides suitable accompaniment to the almost delirious pride which permeates this tragedy. Such baseness and such pride are inseparable: we see that well enough in Germany today. Corneille himself is an excellent example of the sort of asphyxia which seizes Christian morality when it comes into contact with the Roman spirit. His *Polyeucte* would seem to us comical if habit had not blinded us. Polyeucte, according to his version, is a man who suddenly realizes that there is a far more glorious kingdom to conquer than any of a terrestrial kind, and that a particular technique exists for doing so. He immediately feels obliged to set out on this conquest, without giving a thought to anything else, and in the same frame of mind as when he used formerly to wage war in the service of the Emperor. Alexander wept, we are told, because he had only the terrestrial globe to conquer. Corneille apparently thought Christ had come down to earth to make up for this deficiency.

If patriotism acts invisibly as a dissolvent of morality, whether

Christian or lay, in time of peace, the contrary takes place in wartime; and this is perfectly natural. Where there is a moral duality, it is always the morality the actual circumstances require that suffers injury. The line of least resistance naturally gives the advantage to the type of morality which, in point of fact, there is no need to exercise: a war morality in peacetime, a peace morality in wartime.

In peacetime, justice and truth, because of the watertight compartment separating them individually from patriotism, are degraded to the rank of purely private virtues, such as for example politeness; but when the country demands the supreme sacrifice, this very separation deprives patriotism of that total validity which alone can call forth a total effort.

When one has got into the habit of considering as an absolute good, free of any shadow of doubt, this growth in the course of which France devoured and digested so many lands, is it surprising that propaganda inspired by precisely the same idea, and only substituting the name of Europe in place of that of France, should be able to penetrate into a corner of the mind? Present-day patriotism consists in an equation between absolute good and a collectivity corresponding to a given territorial area, namely France; anyone who changes in his mind the territorial term of the equation, and substitutes for it a smaller term, such as Brittany, or a larger term, such as Europe, is looked upon as a traitor. Why? It is all perfectly arbitrary. Habit makes it impossible for us to realize how exceedingly arbitrary it is. But at a time of supreme crisis, this arbitrary notion offers a hold to the manufacturer of sophistries inside us.

The present collaborators have as regards the new Europe, which a German victory would create, the same attitude the inhabitants of Provence, Brittany, Alsace, and Franche-Comté are expected to have toward the past, so far as the conquest of their country by the king of France is concerned. Why should the difference between these two historical periods change what is good and what is bad? Between 1918 and 1919 one would frequently hear worthy people who looked forward to peace argue as follows: "Formerly, provinces used to go to war with one another, then they became united and formed themselves into nations. In the same way, the nations are going to unite in

each continent, then throughout the whole world, and that will be
the end of all war." It was a very widely held platitude, and derived
from that type of reasoning by extrapolation which exercised such an
influence in the nineteenth century and was carried over into the
twentieth. The good people who talked thus had a general idea of the
history of France, but they didn't pause to think, when they were
speaking, that the national unity had been brought about almost exclusively by the most brutal conquests. Yet if they did remember this
in 1939, they must also have remembered that those conquests had always seemed to them a good thing. Is it surprising, therefore, that
with a part at least of their mind they should have thought, "For the
purposes of progress and the fulfillment of history, it may be we have
to pass through this experience"? They can well have said to themselves, "France was victorious in 1918; she was unable to bring about
European unity. Now Germany is trying to do so; we mustn't inter-
fere with her." The cruelties accompanying the German system ought,
it is true, to have stopped them. But they may either not have heard
anything about them, or supposed them to have been invented by a
lying propaganda, or regarded them as of little importance, because
the victims were people of inferior category. Is it not just as easy to
be ignorant of the cruelties of the Germans toward the Jews or the
Czechs as it is of those of the French toward the Annamites?

Péguy used to say: Blessed are they who die in a just war. It
must follow that those who kill them unjustly are cursed. If it is true
that the French soldiers of 1914 died in a just war, then it must
certainly also be true, to at least the same extent, for Vercingetorix.
If one thinks thus, what must one's feelings be toward the man who
kept him chained up in a dungeon, in complete darkness, for six
years, and then offered him as a public spectacle to the Romans before
finally cutting his throat? But Péguy was a fervent admirer of the
Roman Empire. If one admires the Roman Empire, why be angry with
Germany, which is trying to reconstitute it on a vaster scale by the
use of almost identical methods? This didn't stop Péguy from going
to his death in 1914. But it is this contradiction, though unformulated,
unrecognized, which stopped a good many young men in 1940 from
facing the enemy fire in the same spirit as Péguy.

Either conquest is always an evil thing, or it is always a good thing, or again it is sometimes a good, sometimes an evil thing. In this last case, a criterion is needed for judging. To suggest as a criterion that conquest is a good thing when it increases the power of the nation to which one belongs by the accident of birth, an evil thing when it diminishes this power, is something so entirely contrary to reason that it can only be acceptable to people who, of their own accord and once and for all, have banished reason altogether, as is the case with Germany. But Germany is able to do this, because she lives by a romantic tradition. France is not, because her attachment to reason forms part of the national heritage. A certain proportion of Frenchmen may well declare themselves hostile toward Christianity; but, before as after 1789, all movements in the realm of ideas which have taken place in France have claimed to be based on reason. It is impossible for France to set aside reason in the name of patriotism.

That is why France feels uncomfortable in her patriotism, in spite of the fact that it was she who, in the eighteenth century, invented the modern form of patriotism. It must not be imagined that what has been called the universal vocation of France renders a conciliation between patriotism and universal values easier for Frenchmen than for other people. It is, indeed, the contrary which is true. It is more difficult for Frenchmen, because they are unable completely to succeed in either suppressing the second term of the contradiction, or separating the two terms by a watertight compartment. They find this contradiction within their own patriotism. But because of this they are as it were obliged to invent a new sort of patriotism. If they do so, they will be fulfilling what has been up to a point, in the past, the function of France, namely, to think out what it is the world requires. The world requires at the present time a new patriotism. And it is now that this inventive effort must be made, just when patriotism is something that is causing bloodshed. We mustn't wait until it has become once more just a subject for conversation in drawing rooms, learned societies, and open-air cafés.

It is easy to say, with Lamartine, *"Ma patrie est partout où rayonne la France. . . . La vérité, c'est mon pays."* Unfortunately, this would only make sense if France and truth were synonymous. France

sometimes resorts to lying and committing injustice; this has happened, is happening, and will happen again. For France is not God, not
by a long chalk. Christ alone was able to say, "I am the truth." No
one else on this earth has the right to say that, whether speaking as an
individual or in the name of a collectivity, but with far less reason still
in the latter case. For it is possible for a man to attain such a degree
of holiness that it is no longer he who lives, but Christ in him.
Whereas there is no such thing as a holy nation.

There was once a nation which believed itself to be holy, with
the direst consequences for its well-being; and in connection with this,
it is strange indeed to reflect that the Pharisees were the resisters in
this nation, and the publicans the collaborators, and then to remind
oneself what were Christ's relations with each of these two national
groups.

This would seem to oblige us to consider that our resistance
would be a spiritually dangerous, even a spiritually harmful, position,
if amidst the motives which inspire it we did not manage to restrain
the patriotic motive within the necessary bounds. It is precisely this
danger that, in the extremely clumsy phraseology of our time, is
meant by those who, sincerely or not, say they are afraid this movement may turn into something Fascist; for Fascism is always intimately connected with a certain variety of patriotic feeling.

France's vocation in the universe cannot, unless we lie to ourselves, be recalled with unmixed pride. If we lie to ourselves, we
betray it in the very words with which we seek to recall it; if we
remind ourselves of the truth, shame should always temper our pride,
for every historical example of it, which is offered to us, has its em-
barrassing side. In the thirteenth century, France was a center of inspiration for the whole of Christendom. Yet it was, nevertheless, at the
beginning of this century that she utterly destroyed, south of the
Loire, a budding civilization, which already shone with a remarkable
splendor; and it was in the course of this military operation, and in co-
operation with the military power, that the Inquisition first became
established. That is certainly an ineradicable blot on her reputation.
The thirteenth century was the one in which Gothic replaced Romanesque, polyphonic music the Gregorian chant, and, in theology, con-

structions derived from Aristotle replaced Platonic sources of inspiration, hence one is at liberty to doubt whether French influence in this century amounted to any real progress. In the seventeenth century, once more, France shed her light over Europe. But the military prestige connected with this spiritual radiance was obtained by methods which any lover of justice is ashamed to mention; besides, just in the same degree as the French classical conception produced marvelous works in the French language, so was its influence destructive in other countries. In 1789, the hopes of all peoples were centered on France. But three years later she started going to war, and from her earliest victories onward, her liberating expeditions became transformed into conquering ones. Without England, Russia, and Spain to oppose her, she would have imposed on Europe a unity perhaps hardly less stifling than the one Germany is seeking to impose today. In the latter half of the last century, when people began to realize that Europe was not the whole world, and that there were quite a few continents on this planet, France was again seized with the desire to play a universal role. But all she managed to do was to carve out for herself a colonial empire copied from the British model, and in the hearts of not a few colored peoples her name is now linked with feelings which it is unbearable to have to think about.

Thus the contradiction inherent in French patriotism is visible also throughout the whole of French history. It must not be concluded from this that just because France has gone on living so long with this contradiction, she can go on doing so indefinitely. In the first place, once one has recognized a contradiction, it is disgraceful to put up with it. Then, as a matter of brute fact, France very nearly died from a crisis in French patriotism. Everything leads one to suppose that she *would* have died from it, but for the fact that British patriotism was, fortunately, made of sterner stuff. But we cannot transfer the latter over to France. It is our own kind we have to remake. It is waiting to be remade. It is again showing signs of life because German soldiers on French soil are the very best propaganda agents for French patriotism; only they won't always be there.

A terrible responsibility rests with us. For it is nothing less than a question of refashioning the soul of the country, and the temptation is so strong to do this by resorting to lies or half lies that it requires more than ordinary heroism to remain faithful to the truth.

The patriotic crisis took on a double aspect. In political parlance, one might say that there was both a Leftist and a Rightist crisis.

On the Right, among the younger middle-class generation, the break between patriotism and morals had, in conjunction with other causes, completely discredited all morality; but the prestige of patriotism was scarcely any greater. The attitude of mind expressed in the phrase "*Politique d'abord*" had spread considerably further than the actual influence of Maurras. The phrase was, of course, absurd; for politics are simply a technique, a specialized method of procedure. It is as if one were to say, "Mechanics first." The question which immediately poses itself is this, "Politics for what?" Richelieu would answer, "For the greater glory of the State." And why for this purpose and not for some other one? To this question, no answer is forthcoming.

That is the question which mustn't be asked. So-called realist politics, handed down from Richelieu to Maurras, not without being seriously impaired on the way, only make sense if this question is not put. A simple condition exists for it not to be. When the beggar said to Talleyrand, "Milord, I've got to live somehow," Talleyrand replied, "I don't see that that is necessary." But the beggar himself saw the necessity for it all right. In just the same way, Louis XIV saw well enough how necessary it was that the State should be served with blind devotion, because the State was, in fact, himself. Richelieu only looked upon himself as being the State's servant No. 1; all the same, in a sense he possessed it, and for that reason identified himself with it. Richelieu's political attitude only makes sense for those who, whether individually or collectively, feel either that they are masters of their country or else capable of becoming so.

The younger middle-class generation could no longer, from 1924 onward, have the feeling that France was their domain. The working classes made far too much noise for that. Besides which, it suffered from that mysterious exhaustion that swept over France after 1918, the causes of which were no doubt largely physical. Whether the fault is attributable to alcoholism, the nervous condition of the parents at the time their children were born and during their upbringing, or some other factor, the fact remains that for a long time now French youth has shown every indication of fatigue. German youth, even in 1932, when the authorities were doing nothing for them, gave evidence of an incomparably greater vitality, in spite of the very hard and long-drawn-out privations they had been through.

This fatigue prevented middle-class youth in France from feeling in a condition to impose themselves on the country. Hence, to the question, "Politics for what?" the necessary answer was, "For the purpose of being placed in power in this country by other people" —that is to say, people from abroad, foreigners. There was nothing in the moral code of these young people to stop them having such a desire. The shock they received in 1936 only sharpened this desire in them to an irreparably acute degree. Nobody had done them any harm; but they had received a nasty fright, been made to eat humble pie, and, what was an unpardonable crime in their eyes, precisely by those whom they regarded as their social inferiors. In 1937, the Italian press quoted an article from a French students' review in which a French girl expressed the hope that, surrounded as he was by innumerable cares of State, Mussolini would somehow find time to come and restore order in France.

Whatever antipathy we may feel toward people of this class, however criminal their subsequent attitude may have been, they are human creatures, and unhappy human creatures, too. The problem in their case presents itself in these terms: How to reconcile them with France without delivering her into their hands?

On the Left, that is to say, above all among the workmen and the intellectuals who lean in their direction, there are two absolutely distinct currents of opinion, although occasionally, but by no means necessarily, the two currents are found in the same person. One of these is the current emanating from French working-class tradition, which can clearly be traced back to the eighteenth century, when so many workmen read Jean-Jacques Rousseau, but which maybe has underground connections linking it up with the first movements on behalf of communal freedom. Those who are influenced by this current alone, devote themselves entirely to the thought of justice. Unfortunately, nowadays, such a thing is rare enough among the workmen and extremely rare among the intellectuals.

There are people of this sort to be found in all so-called Leftist groups—Christian, trade-unionist, anarchist, socialist, and particularly among Communist workmen, for Communist propaganda talks a lot about justice. In this it carries out the teachings of Lenin and Marx, strange as this may seem to those who have not studied all the ins and outs of the doctrine.

These men all feel profoundly internationalist in time of peace, for they know that justice recognizes no national boundaries. They often feel the same even in wartime, so long as their country escapes being defeated. But their country's defeat immediately causes a pure, steady flame of patriotism to light up in the depths of their consciousness. Men like this will be permanently reconciled with their country if they are offered a type of patriotism subordinated to the cause of justice.

The other current is a retort to the middle-class attitude. Marxism, by offering to the working class the supposedly scientific certainty that they will shortly become the lords and masters of the terrestrial globe, has created a working-class imperialism very similar to the nationalist imperialisms. Russia has provided, as it were, the experimental proof of this, and furthermore she is being relied upon to undertake the most arduous part of the action which is to result in the overthrow of established institutions.

For people who are morally exiled and in the position of immigrants, in contact above all with the repressive side of the State, and who for generations have found themselves on the border line of those social categories which provide fair game for the police, and are themselves treated as such each time the State swings over toward reaction, this offers an irresistible temptation. A huge, powerful, sovereign State, governing a territory much vaster than that of their own country, says to them, "I am yours, I am your possession, your property. I exist only to serve you, and before long I will make you the undisputed masters in your own country."

On their side, to refuse such a friendly offer would be just about

as easy as to refuse a cup of water when you haven't had anything
to drink for two days. Some, who made a terrific effort of self-
control in order to do this, so exhausted themselves in the process
that they immediately succumbed to the first exercise of pressure on
the part of Germany. Many of the others are only resisting in appearance, and in reality are simply standing on one side, for fear
of the risks which action necessarily brings in its train once a formal
engagement has been entered into. Such people, whether numerous
or otherwise, can never make up a force.

The U.S.S.R., outside Russia, is really the spiritual home of the
working class, their "country." In order to realize this, all one had to
do was to watch the French workmen's eyes as they gathered round
the newsstands and scanned the headlines announcing the first big
Russian reverses. It was not the thoughts of the repercussions these
defeats might have on Franco-German relations which filled their eyes
with despair, for British reverses never affected them in this way. They
felt they were threatened with the loss of more than France. They felt
rather in the same way as the early Christians would have felt if
some one had supplied them with material proofs showing Christ's
resurrection to have been a fiction. In a general way, there is no doubt
quite a lot of resemblance between the state of mind of the early
Christians and that of many Communist workmen. The latter, too,
are looking forward to some approaching Day of Judgment, which
shall establish absolute righteousness at one single stroke and forever
on this earth, and at the same time their own glory. Martyrdom came
easier to the early Christians than to those of succeeding centuries,
and infinitely easier than to Christ's immediate disciples, who, at the
moment of supreme crisis, were unable to face it. So today, sacrifice
is easier for a Communist than for a Christian.

Since the U.S.S.R. is a State, patriotic feeling for it is subject
to the same contradictions as is patriotic feeling anywhere. But it
doesn't result in the same weakening. Quite the reverse. The presence
of a contradiction, when it is felt, even in a dull sort of way, wears
down the feelings; when it isn't felt at all, the feelings are thereby in-
tensified, since they derive benefit at the same time from incompatible
motives. Thus the U.S.S.R. has all the prestige attaching to a State,

and to that cold brutality which permeates the politics of a State, especially a totalitarian one; while at the same time it has all the prestige attaching to a champion of justice. If the contradiction is not felt, this is partly because of its remoteness, partly because it promises absolute power to all who faithfully love it. Such an expectation doesn't diminish the need for justice, but renders it a blind one. As each of us considers himself sufficiently capable of practicing justice, each of us naturally thinks that a system under which he wielded power would be a reasonably just one. This is the temptation Christ underwent at the hands of the devil. Men are continually succumbing to it.

Although these workmen, animated by working-class imperialism, are very different from young middle-class Fascists, and make up a finer variety of humanity, the problem they pose is a similar one. How are they to be made to love their country sufficiently, without handing it over to them? For it can't be handed over to them, nor can they be given a privileged position in it; this would be a crying injustice toward the rest of the population, and more especially the peasants.

The present attitude of these workmen toward Germany must not blind us to the gravity of the problem. Germany happens to be the enemy of the U.S.S.R. Before she became so, agitation was already rife among them, it being a vital necessity for the Communist party always to maintain agitation; and it took the form of agitation "against German Fascism and British Imperialism." France didn't appear in the picture at all. Furthermore, throughout a whole year, which was a decisive one, from the summer of 1939 to the summer of 1940, Communist influence in France was entirely directed against the country. It will not be an easy thing to induce these workmen to turn their hearts toward their country.

Among the rest of the population, the crisis in the matter of patriotism has not been so acute; it hasn't gone so far as a renunciation in favor of something different; there has merely been a sort of melting away. In the case of the peasants, this was no doubt due to the fact that they felt they were of no account in the country, except in the shape of cannon fodder to serve interests that were alien to theirs; in that of the *petits bourgeois*, it must have been above all due to ennui.

To all such individual causes of want of patriotism there was added a very general cause which forms as it were the reverse side of idolatry. The State had ceased to be, under the title of nation or country, something infinitely valuable in the sense of something valuable enough to be served with devotion. On the other hand, it had become in everybody's eyes of unlimited value as something to be exploited. The quality of absoluteness, which is bound up with idolatry, remained with it, once the idolatry had ceased, and assumed this new aspect. The State appeared like an inexhaustible horn of plenty, pouring out its treasures in direct proportion to the pressure put upon it. So people always had a grudge against it for not providing more. Whatever it didn't supply seemed to be as a result of a deliberate refusal on its part. When it made demands, such insistence appeared paradoxical. When it imposed its will, this became at once an intolerable act of coercion. People's attitude toward the State was that of children, not toward their parents, but toward adults who are neither loved nor feared; children always demanding something and never wanting to obey.

How could people be expected to pass straightway from such an attitude to that of unlimited devotion demanded by war? For even after war had begun, the French believed that the State had victory tucked away somewhere in a safe place, side by side with other treasures, which it wasn't going to give itself the trouble to bring out. Everything was done to encourage this idea, as a slogan of the time testifies, "We shall win because we're the stronger."

Victory is going to liberate a country in which everyone will have been almost exclusively occupied in disobeying, from either good or bad motives. People will have listened in to London, read and distributed forbidden literature, traveled without a permit, hidden away supplies of corn, worked as badly as possible, done some black marketing, and will have boasted about all this to their friends and relations. How are people going to be made to understand that all this is finished, that henceforward they have to obey?

People will also have spent these years dreaming about eating their fill. Such dreams are the kind indulged in by beggars, in the sense that all one thinks about is receiving plenty of good things without giving anything in return. In point of fact, the authorities will have to guarantee proper distribution; how are we then to avoid this cheeky beggar's attitude, which already before the war was that of the public toward the State, becoming infinitely more accentuated? And if this attitude is adopted toward a foreign country, America for example, the danger becomes very much more serious still.

Another dream, and a very widespread one, is to kill; to kill invoking the highest possible motives, but in an underhand way and without any risk. Whether the State breaks up under the pressure of this diffused terrorism, as is to be feared, or whether it attempts to control it, in either case the repressive and police-ridden aspect of the State, which traditionally is so hated and despised in France, will occupy the forefront.

The government, which arises in France after the liberation of the country, will have to face a triple danger caused by this blood lust, this mendicity complex, and this inability to obey.

As for a remedy, there is only one: To give French people something to love; and, in the first place, to give them France to love; to conceive the reality corresponding to the name of France in such a way that as she actually is, in her very truth, she can be loved with the whole heart.

The essence of the contradiction inherent in patriotism is that one's country is something limited whose demands are unlimited. In times of extreme peril, it demands everything. Why should one accord everything to something which is limited? On the other hand, not to be resolved to give it everything in case of need is to abandon it entirely, for its preservation cannot be assured at any lesser price. So one always seems to be either on the debit or the credit side of what is due to it, and if one remains too long on the credit side, one swings later on with all the greater force back onto the debit side, through a process of reaction.

The contradiction is only one in appearance. Or, to be more precise, it is a real one, but when thoroughly examined is seen to be one of those basic contradictions belonging to our human condition, which must be recognized, accepted, and used as a footboard for hoisting oneself above what is simply human. Never in this world can there be any dimensional equality between an obligation and its subject. The obligation is something infinite, the subject of it is not. This contradiction presses down upon the daily lives of all men, without exception, including those who would be quite incapable of formulating it even confusedly in words. All the devices men have thought they had discovered for avoiding it have turned out to be lies.

One of them consists in only being prepared to recognize obligations toward what is not of this world. One variety of this particular device is spurious mysticism, spurious contemplation. Another is the practice of good works carried out in a certain spirit, "for the love of God," as they say, the unfortunate objects of compassion being but the raw material for the action, an anonymous means whereby one's love of God can be manifested. In either case there is a lie, for "he who loveth not his brother whom he hath seen, how should he love God whom he hath not seen?" It is only through things and individual beings on this earth that human love can penetrate to that which lies beyond.

Another device consists in admitting that there are on this earth one or more objects enshrining this absolute value, this infinitude, this perfection which are essentially bound up with the obligation as such. That is the lie propagated by idolatry.

The third device consists in denying any sort of obligation. You cannot prove this by a mathematical demonstration to be an error, for obligation belongs to an order of certainty very superior to that of formal proof. Actually, such a negation is impossible. It amounts to spiritual suicide. And Man is so made that in him spiritual death is accompanied by psychological diseases in themselves fatal. So that, in fact, the instinct of self-preservation prevents the soul from doing more than draw closer to such a state; and even so it is seized with a *taedium vitae*, which turns it into a desert. Almost always, or rather, almost certainly always, he who denies all obligations lies to others and to himself; in actual fact, he recognizes some among them. There isn't a man on earth who doesn't at times pronounce an

opinion on good and evil, even if it be only to find fault with somebody else.

We have to accept the situation provided for us, and which subjects us to absolute obligations in regard to things that are relative,
limited, and imperfect. So as to be able to discern what these things
are and the form in which their demands upon us are likely to be
made, we need only to see clearly what their actual relationship is to
goodness.

So far as our country is concerned, the conceptions of rootedness, of vital medium, suffice in this connection. They have no need
to be established by documentary proof, for of late years they have
been verified experimentally. Just as there are certain culture beds for
certain microscopic animals, certain types of soil for certain plants,
so there is a certain part of the soul in everyone and certain ways
of thought and action communicated from one person to another
which can only exist in a national setting, and disappear when a
country is destroyed.

Today every Frenchman knows what it was he missed as soon
as France fell. He knows it as well as he knows what is missing when
one is forced to go hungry. He knows that one part of his soul sticks
so closely to France, that when France is taken away it remains stuck
to her, as the skin does to some burning object, and is thus pulled
off. There is something, then, to which a part of every Frenchman's soul sticks, and is the same for all, unique, real though impalpable, and real in the sense of something one is able to touch. Hence,
what threatens France with destruction—and in certain circumstances
an invasion is a threat of destruction—is equivalent to a threat of
physical mutilation for all Frenchmen, and for their children and
grandchildren, and for their descendants to the end of time. For
there are peoples which have never recovered after having once been
conquered.

That is sufficient for the obligation owed to one's country to
impose itself as something self-evident. It coexists with other obligations. It does not require that we should give everything always;
but that we should give everything sometimes. Just as a miner has
sometimes to give everything, when an accident happens in the mine

and his companions are in danger of death. It is an accepted, a recognized thing. The obligation owed to one's country is every bit as clear, once the country is actually felt as something real and tangible— as it is being felt today. All Frenchmen have come to feel the reality of France through being deprived of her.

People have never ventured to deny the obligation toward one's country otherwise than by denying the reality of the country. Extreme pacifism of the type advocated by Gandhi is not a denial of this obligation, but a particular method for discharging it. This method has never yet been applied, so far as we know; it has certainly not been applied by Gandhi, who is far too much of a realist. If it had been applied in France, the French would not have used any armed force to resist the invader; but they would never have been prepared to do anything, of any kind, which might assist the army of occupation; they would have done everything possible to hinder it, and they would have persisted indefinitely, inflexibly in that attitude. It is clear that, in so doing, far greater numbers would have perished, and in far more frightful circumstances. This would be an imitation of Christ's passion realized on a national scale.

If there were any nation, in the aggregate, sufficiently close to perfection for one to be able to suggest to it that it should imitate Christ's passion, such a thing would certainly be well worth doing. As a nation it would disappear; but this disappearance would be worth infinitely more than the most glorious survival. However, it isn't that way these things are done. Most likely, almost certainly, they cannot be done that way. It can only be given to the individual soul, in its most secret manifestations, to follow the path leading to such perfection.

At the same time, if there are men whose vocation it is to bear witness to this unattainable perfection, the authorities are in duty bound not to obstruct them, and, in fact, to give them every assistance. In England, conscientious objectors are recognized.

But that is not enough. For men like these, we should go to the trouble of inventing something which, without constituting any direct or indirect participation in strategic operations, would involve being present in some way at the actual scene of war, and present in

UPROOTEDNESS AND NATIONHOOD

a much more arduous and more perilous fashion than is demanded of the soldiers themselves.

That is the unique remedy for the inconveniences arising out of pacifist propaganda. For that would make it possible, without being unjust, to bring discredit on those who, while professing an out-and-out pacifism, or what amounts to the same, refused to stand up for their principles in this way. Pacifism is only capable of causing harm when a confusion arises between two sorts of aversion; the aversion to kill, and the aversion to be killed. The former is honorable, but very weak; the latter, almost impossible to acknowledge, but very strong. When mixed together, they supply a motive force of extraordinary power, which is not restrained by any feeling of shame, and where the latter sort of aversion is alone operative. French pacifists of recent years had an aversion to being killed, but none to killing; otherwise they would not have rushed so hastily, in July 1940, to collaborate with Germany. The very few who were among them out of a real aversion to killing were sadly deceived.

By separating these two aversions, we eliminate all danger. The influence of the aversion to kill is not dangerous; in the first place, it is a good influence, for it has its origin in goodness; secondly, it is weak, and, unfortunately, there is no chance that it should ever be otherwise. As for those whom the fear of death renders weak, they should be treated with compassion, for every human being, unless he has been turned into a fanatic, is, at any rate at times, liable to this weakness; but if they turn their weakness into a doctrine to be propagated, that is criminal, and it is then necessary, and not difficult, to discredit them.

In defining one's native country as a certain particular vital medium, one avoids the contradictions and lies that corrode the idea of patriotism. There is one's own particular vital medium; but there are others besides. It has been produced by a network of causes in which good and evil, justice and injustice have been mixed up together, and so it cannot be the best possible one. It may have arisen at the expense of some other combination richer in vital properties, and if such has been the case, it would be right to regret the fact; but past events are over and done with; the particular medium happens to be in existence, and, such as it is, deserves to be guarded like a treasure for the good it contains.

The peoples conquered by the soldiers of the king of France in many cases suffered a wrong. But so many organic ties have grown up in the course of centuries that a surgical operation would but add a further wrong to the wrong already done. It is only possible partially to repair the past, and this can only be done through a recognized local and regional life receiving the unreserved encouragement of the authorities within the setting of the French nation. Moreover, the disappearance of the French nation, far from repairing in the slightest bit the wrong resulting from past conquest, would aggravate it in a far more serious manner. Admitting that certain peoples underwent, a few centuries ago, a loss of vitality as a result of French aggression, they would be altogether morally destroyed by a further wound brought about by German aggression. In this sense only is the commonplace true, according to which no incompatibility exists between the love for one's native heath and that for one's native land. For in this way a man from Toulouse can passionately regret the fact that his city should some centuries ago have become French; that so many marvelous Romanesque churches should have been destroyed to make way for a second-rate imported Gothic; that the Inquisition should have cut short a spiritual blossoming there; and can still more passionately vow never to permit that this same city of his should ever become German.

The same thing applies to relations with foreign countries. If one's native land is regarded as a vital medium, there is no need for it to be protected from foreign influences, save only in so far as that may be necessary for it to be able to remain such, that is to say, not in any rigorous fashion. The State could cease to be the absolute ruler by divine right over the territories under its control; and a reasonable and limited authority over these territories exercised by international organizations dealing with essential problems whose scope is an international one would cease to wear the appearance of a crime of *lèse-majesté*. Nucleuses could also be established for the free circulation of ideas, on a vaster scale than France and incorporating France, or connecting certain bits of French territory with certain bits of non-French territory. For instance, wouldn't it be a natural thing for Brittany, Wales, Cornwall, and Ireland to feel themselves, in regard to certain things, to be parts of the same environment?

But once again, the more attachment one shows for such non-nation nucleuses, the more one will want to preserve the national liberty; for this sort of intercourse over frontier boundaries doesn't exist for enslaved peoples. That is why the cultural exchanges between Mediterranean countries were incomparably greater and more vital before than after the Roman conquest; whereas all these countries, when reduced to the unfortunate state of provinces, fell into a dull uniformity. Exchange is only possible where each one preserves his own genius, and that is not possible without liberty.

In a general way, if the existence of a great number of life-giving nucleuses is recognized, one's own particular country only constituting one among them, nevertheless, should the latter be threatened with annihilation, all the obligations implied by loyalty toward all these separate nucleuses unite in the single obligation to go to the assistance of one's country. For the members of a population which is enslaved to a foreign State are deprived of all these nucleuses at once, and not merely of the national one. Thus, when a nation finds itself in peril to this extent, the military obligation becomes the unique way of expressing all one's loyalties in this world. This is true even for conscientious objectors, if sufficient trouble is taken to find for them an equivalent to actual participation in fighting.

Once this is recognized, certain modifications in the manner of considering war ought to follow where peril threatens the nation. In the first place, the distinction between soldiers and civilians, which the pressure of circumstances has already almost obliterated, should be entirely abolished. This was what had, to a large extent, brought about the antipatriotic reaction after 1918. Every individual in the population owes his country the whole of his strength, his resources, and his life itself, until the danger has been removed. It is desirable that the sufferings and perils should be shared by all categories of the population, young and old, men and women, the healthy and the sick, to the full extent to which this is technically possible, and even a bit more besides. Lastly, personal honor is so intimately bound up with the performance of this obligation, and external means of compulsion are so contrary to principles of honor, that all those who desire to escape it should be allowed to do so; they would be made to lose their nationality, and, in addition, either banished and forbidden ever to set foot in the country again, or be made to suffer some permanent form of indignity as a public mark that they had forfeited their right to personal honor.

It is shocking that want of personal honor should be punished in the same way as robbery or assassination. Those who don't want to defend their country should be made to lose, not life or liberty, but purely and simply their country.

If the state of the country is such that for a great many the latter is but a trifling punishment, then the military code also proves itself to be without efficacy. We cannot be ignorant of the fact.

If at certain times the military obligation comprehends all earthly loyalties, the State is under the reciprocal duty, at all times, to protect every nucleus, whether in or outside national territory, from which a part of the population, large or small, draws some of its spiritual life.

The State's most obvious duty is to keep efficient watch at all times over the security of the national territory. Security doesn't mean absence of danger, for in this world danger is ever present; it means a reasonable change of being able to weather any storms which should arise. But that is only the State's most elementary duty. If it does no more than that, it is as though it did nothing at all; for if that *is* all it does, it cannot even succeed in doing that.

The State's duty is to make the country, in the highest possible degree, a reality. The country was not a reality for very many Frenchmen in 1939. It has again become one as a result of deprivation. It must be made to remain so in possession, and for that to happen it must really become, in fact, a life-giving agent, really be turned into good, root-fixing ground. It must also be made a favorable setting for participation in and loyal attachment to all other sorts of environmental expression.

Today, while Frenchmen have recovered the feeling that France is a reality, they have at the same time become far more conscious than before of local differences. The dividing up of France into separate portions, the censorship of correspondence, which limits exchanges of thought to a restricted area, have each played their part, and paradoxically enough, the forcible throwing together of the population has also greatly contributed to this. People have now in a much sharper, more permanent form than before the feeling that they belong to Brittany, Lorraine, Provence, or Paris. There is an element of hostility in this feeling which we should try to get rid of; just as it is urgent also to get rid of xenophobia. But this feeling in itself ought not to be discouraged; on the contrary. It would be disastrous to declare it antipatriotic. In the atmosphere of anguish, confusion, solitude, uprootedness in which the French find themselves, all loyalties, all attachments are worth preserving like treasures of infinite value and rarity, worth tending like the most delicate plants.

That the Vichy Government should have put forward a regionalist doctrine is neither here nor there. Its only mistake in this connection has been in not applying it. Far from always preaching the exact opposite of its various battle cries, we ought to adopt many of the ideas launched by the propaganda services of the National Revolution, but turn them into realities.

In the same way, the French, because of their isolation, have come to realize that France is a small country, that shut up inside her it is stifling and they require a wider range. The idea of Europe, of European unity contributed a good deal toward the success of collaborationist propaganda in the early days. We cannot do too much to encourage, nourish such sentiments as these. It would be disastrous to create any opposition between them and patriotic sentiments.

Lastly, we cannot do too much to encourage the existence of progressive associations not forming wheels within the wheels of public administration; for that is the only condition on which they won't just become corpses. The trade-unions are a case in point, when they are not burdened with day-to-day responsibilities in the matter of economic organization. The same can be said of Christian associations, Protestant or Catholic, and particularly of organizations like the J.O.C.; but should the State allow itself to be influenced the least little bit by clerical inclinations, it would assuredly kill them on the spot. The same can also be said of associations which arose after the defeat in 1940, some of them officially, like the *chantiers de jeunesse* and *camps de compagnons*, others clandestinely, like the resistance groups. The former possess a certain amount of life, in spite of their official character, thanks to an exceptional conjunction of circumstances; but if their official role were to be maintained, they would just lose every spark of vitality. The latter have arisen in opposition to the State, and if one were to yield to the temptation to grant them an official existence in the public life of the country, such a thing would have the very gravest moral consequences on them.

On the other hand, if associations of this sort are out of contact with public affairs, they cease to exist. It is necessary, therefore, that while not forming part of the public administration, they should yet at the same time not lose all contact with it. A method of effecting this might be, for example, for representatives of such associations to be frequently chosen by the State to carry out special missions on a temporary basis. But the State would, on the one hand, have to select these representatives itself, and, on the other hand, all their associates would have to regard their having been selected as a matter for pride. Such a method could gradually develop into an institution.

Here again, while every effort is made to eliminate violent antagonisms, differences should be encouraged. In a country like ours, the perpetual stirring of ideas can never do any harm. It is mental inertia which is fatal to it.

The duty, which falls to the State, to ensure that the people are provided with a country to which they really feel they belong can never be regarded as a condition precedent to the carrying out of the military obligation by the population in times of national peril. For if the State fails in its duty, if the country is allowed to fall into ruin, nevertheless, while national independence subsists, there is always hope of a resurrection; if we look closely, we find in the history of all countries the most surprising ups and downs, sometimes following quite swiftly upon one another. But if the country is subdued by foreign arms, there is nothing left to hope for, save the possibility of a rapid liberation. This hope alone, when nothing else is left, it is worth dying for to preserve.

Thus, although one's country is a fact, and as such, subject to external conditions, to hazards of every kind, in times of mortal danger there is none the less an unconditional obligation to go to its assistance. But it is obvious that, in fact, the people will show all the greater ardor in its defense the more they will have been made to feel its reality.

The patriotic conception as defined above is incompatible with present-day views about the country's history, its national grandeur, and above all with the way in which one talks at present about the Empire.

France possesses an empire, and consequently, whatever attitude one may adopt with regard to it, it poses certain factual problems, which are highly complex and vary considerably according to the different localities. But we mustn't mix everything up together. First of all, there is a question of principle, and even something less definite than that, a question of sentiment. On the whole, has a Frenchman the right to be proud that France possesses an empire, and to think and talk about it with pride and joy, and in the tones of a legitimate owner?

Certainly, if he happens to be a French patriot after the style of Richelieu, Louis XIV, or Maurras. But not if the Christian ethic and the spirit of 1789 are indissolubly mixed into the actual substance of his patriotism. Every other nation might possibly have had the right to carve out an empire for itself, but not France; for the same reason which made the temporal sovereignty of the Pope a scandal in the eyes of Christendom. When one takes upon oneself, as France did in 1789, the function of thinking on behalf of the world, of defining justice for the world, one may not become an owner of human flesh and blood. Even if it be true that if we hadn't done so, others would have got hold of these unfortunate native peoples and would have treated them still worse, that was not a legitimate motive; when all is said and done, the total amount of harm would have been less. Motives of this kind are more often than not bad ones.

It is not for a priest to become the owner of a brothel on the supposition that its inmates would be worse treated by some bully. It was not for France to surrender her self-respect out of compassion. Besides, that isn't what she did. Nobody would seriously venture to claim that she went out to conquer these peoples to prevent other countries ill-treating them: all the less so since it was she who, in the nineteenth century, was largely responsible for bringing these colonial adventures back into fashion.

Among those she has reduced to submission, there are some who feel very keenly how scandalous it is that she of all countries should have done this; their resentment toward us is aggravated by a terribly grievous kind of bitterness and by a sort of bewilderment.

It may be that France now has to choose between her attachment to her Empire and the need to have a soul of her own again; or, in more general terms, between having a soul of her own and the Roman or Corneille-esque conception of greatness.

If she chooses wrongly, if we ourselves force her to choose wrongly, which is only too likely, she will have neither the one nor the other, but only the most appalling adversity, which she will undergo with astonishment, without anybody being able to discover any reason for it. And all those who are now in a position to get up and speak or to wield a pen will be eternally responsible for having committed a crime.

Bernanos has understood and declared that Hitlerism is a return to pagan Rome. But has he forgotten, have we forgotten, what an influential part Rome has played in our history, our culture, and still plays today in our everyday thoughts? If, out of horror for a certain form of evil, we have taken the terrible decision to make war, with all the atrocities war necessarily involves, can we be forgiven if we make less pitiless war against the same form of evil in our own hearts? If all the grandeur after the style of Corneille attracts us by its heroic glamour, Germany can equally well attract us too, for the German soldiers are undoubtedly "heroes." In the present confusion of thought and feeling over the subject of patriotism, is there any guarantee at all that a French soldier in Africa is inspired by a purer ideal of sacrifice than a German soldier in Russia? Actually, there isn't any. If we do not feel what a terrible responsibility this places on us, we cannot remain innocent in the midst of this unleashing of crime throughout the world.

If there is one thing for which it is necessary to face everything, set everything at naught for love of the truth, it is that one. We are all brought together in the name of patriotism. What is the use of us, what scorn shall we not deserve, if in our thoughts on this subject the least vestige of a lie is found?

But if feelings of a Corneille-esque type don't inspire our patriotism, one may well ask what motive there is to replace them.

Yet, there is one, no less vital, absolutely pure, and corresponding exactly to present circumstances. It is compassion for our country. We have a glorious respondent. It was Joan of Arc who used to say she felt pity for the kingdom of France.

But we can quote an infinitely higher authority. In the Gospels, there is not the least indication that Christ experienced anything resembling love for Jerusalem and Judea, save only the love which goes wrapped in compassion. He never showed any other kind of attachment to his country. But his compassion he expressed on more than one occasion. He wept over the city, foreseeing, as it was not difficult to do at that time, the destruction which should shortly fall upon it. He spoke to it as to a person. "Oh, Jerusalem, Jerusalem . . . how often would I have gathered . . ." Even as He was carrying the cross, He showed once again the pity He felt for it.

Let no one imagine that compassion for one's country excludes warlike energy. It fired the Carthaginians to perform one of the most prodigious deeds of heroism in the whole of history. After being conquered and reduced to very little by Scipio Africanus, they subsequently underwent over the course of fifty years a process of demoralization compared with which the French capitulation at Munich is as nothing at all. They were mercilessly exposed to whatever injuries the Numidians cared to inflict on them, and, having renounced by treaty the right to go to war, they vainly implored Rome for permission to defend themselves. When they finally did so without permission, their army was utterly wiped out. They then had to implore the pardon of the Romans. They agreed to hand over three hundred children of the nobility and all the arms they possessed. Then their delegates were ordered to evacuate the city entirely and definitively, so that it could be razed to the ground. They burst into cries of indignation, then into the bitterest tears. "They called upon their native city by name, and, addressing it as though it were a person, uttered the most heart-rending things." Then they begged the Romans, if they were determined to do them injury, only to spare their city, its stones, its temples, to which no possible guilt could be attached, and instead, if necessary, exterminate the entire population; they declared that such a course would bring less shame upon the Romans and would be infinitely preferable for the people of Carthage. The Romans remained inflexible; whereupon the city rose in rebellion, although devoid of resources, and it took Scipio Africanus, at the head of a large army, three whole years to reduce it and lay it waste.

This poignantly tender feeling for some beautiful, precious, fragile, and perishable object has a warmth about it which the sentiment of national grandeur altogether lacks. The vital current, which inspires it, is a perfectly pure one, and is charged with an extraordinary intensity. Isn't a man easily capable of acts of heroism to protect his children, or his aged parents? And yet no vestige of grandeur is attached to these. A perfectly pure love for one's country bears a close resemblance to the feelings which his young children, his aged parents, or a beloved wife inspire in a man. The thought of weakness can inflame love in just the same way as can the thought of strength, but in the former case the flame is of an altogether different order of purity. The compassion felt for fragility is always associated with love for real beauty, because we are keenly conscious of the fact that the existence of the really beautiful things ought to be assured forever, and is not.

One can either love France for the glory which would seem to ensure for her a prolonged existence in time and space; or else one can love her as something which, being earthly, can be destroyed, and is all the more precious on that account.

These are two distinct ways of loving; perhaps, most probably, incompatible with each other, although in speech they become mixed up together. Those whose hearts are made so as to experience the latter way can yet find themselves sometimes, through force of habit, using forms of speech which are really only suitable in the case of the former.

But the latter is alone legitimate for a Christian, for it alone wears the Christian badge of humility. It alone belongs to that species of love which can be given the name of charity. Nor should it be supposed that the object of such love need necessarily be confined to an unhappy country. Happiness is as much an object for compassion as unhappiness, because it belongs to the earth, in other words is incomplete, frail, and fleeting. Moreover, there is, unfortunately, always a certain amount of unhappiness in the life of any country.

Let no one imagine either that a love of this nature would run the risk of ignoring or rejecting what there is of pure and genuine grandeur in the past history of France, or in the country's present hopes and ideals. Quite the opposite. Compassion is all the more tender, all the more poignant, the more good one is able to discern in the being who forms the object of it, and it predisposes one to discern the good. When a Christian represents to himself Christ on the Cross, his compassion is not diminished by the thought of the latter's perfection, nor the other way about. But, on the other hand, such a love can keep its eyes open on injustices, cruelties, mistakes, falsehoods, crimes, and scandals contained in the country's past, its present, and in its ambitions in general, quite openly and fearlessly, and without being thereby diminished; the love being only rendered thereby more painful. Where compassion is concerned, crime itself provides a reason, not for withdrawing oneself, but for approaching, not with the object of sharing the guilt, but the shame. Mankind's crimes didn't diminish Christ's compassion. Thus compassion keeps both eyes open on both the good and the bad and finds in each sufficient reasons for loving. It is the only love on this earth which is true and righteous.

Just now it is the only sort of love that is suitable for the French. If the events we have recently been living through are not sufficient warning to us of the need to change our way of loving our country, what sort of lesson is there that could teach us? What more can one receive to awaken one's interest than a heavy blow with a club on the head?

Compassion for our country is the only sentiment which doesn't strike a false note at the present time, suits the situation in which the souls and bodies of Frenchmen actually find themselves, and possesses at once the humility and dignity appropriate to misfortune, and also that simplicity which misfortune required above everything else. To call up before people's minds at this time France's historic greatness, her past and future glories, the splendor which has surrounded her existence, none of that is possible without a sort of inward contraction which gives something forced to one's tone. Nothing that in any way resembles pride can be suitable for those in misfortune.

For the French who are suffering, recollections of this sort fall into the category of compensations. To seek compensations in misfortune is a bad thing. If the past is recalled too often, if it is turned into the unique source of comfort, such proceedings can cause immeasurable harm. The French are being starved of greatness. But for the unfortunate, greatness after the Roman manner is not what is wanted; for either it seems to them a mockery, or else their minds become poisoned by it, as was the case in Germany.

Compassion for France is not a compensation for, but a spiritualization of, the sufferings being undergone; it is able to transfigure even the most purely physical sufferings, such as cold and hunger. Whoever feels cold and hunger, and is tempted to pity himself, can, instead of doing that, from out of his own shrunken frame, direct his pity toward France; the very cold and hunger themselves then cause the love of France to enter into the body and penetrate to the depths of the soul. And this same compassion is able, without hindrance, to cross frontiers, extend itself over all countries in misfortune, over all countries without exception; for all peoples are subjected to the wretchedness of our human condition. Whereas pride in national glory is by its nature exclusive, nontransferable, compassion is by its nature universal; it is only more potential where distant and unfamiliar things are concerned, more real, more physical, more charged with blood, tears, and effective energy where things close at hand are concerned.

National pride is far removed from the affairs of daily life. In France, its only means of expression is through the Resistance; but there are many who either have not the opportunity to take any effective part in the Resistance, or can only devote some of their time to it. Compassion for France is an incentive charged with at least as much active value for the purposes of the Resistance; but one which can besides find daily, uninterrupted expression, on every possible sort of occasion, in a fraternal note marking the relations between Frenchmen. Fraternal feelings flourish readily in the midst of compassion for misfortune, which, while inflicting on each his share of suffering, endangers something far more precious than the well-being of each. National pride, whether it be in good times or in bad, is incapable of creating any real, ardent sense of fraternity. This didn't exist among the Romans. They didn't know what really tender feelings were.

A patriotism inspired by compassion gives the poorest part of the population a privileged moral position. National glory only acts as a stimulant among the lower orders of society at times when everyone can, while looking forward to his country's glory, look forward at the same time to having as large a personal share therein as he can wish for. Such was the case at the beginning of Napoleon's reign. Any little French lad, no matter where he hailed from, could legitimately carry in his heart any sort of dreams as to the future; no ambition could be regarded as great enough to be absurd. Every one knew that all ambitions would not be realized, but each one in particular had a chance of being, and many of them could be partially so. A noteworthy document of the period states that Napoleon's popularity was due, less to the devotion Frenchmen felt for his person, than to the possibilities of advancement, the opportunities of carving out a career for themselves, which he offered them. That is exactly the feeling which appears in *Le Rouge et le Noir*. The Romantics were children who felt bored because they no longer had before them the prospect of unrestricted social advancement. They sought literary glory as a substitute.

But this particular stimulant is only found in times of upheaval. Nor can one say that it ever takes the form of an invitation to the people as such. Every man of the people who partakes of it, dreams of emerging from among the people, leaving behind him the anonymity which characterizes humanity in the mass. This ambition, when it is widely held, is the result of a disturbed social condition, and the cause of more serious disturbances to follow; for it sees in social stability an obstacle. Although it happens to be a stimulant, it cannot be said that it is a healthy one, either for the individual soul or for the country. It is quite likely that this stimulant plays a large part in the present Resistance movement; for as far as France's future is concerned, hopes are readily entertained; and as for the individual's own future, anyone, no matter who it is, who has proved his mettle in the midst of danger, can look forward to no matter what in the state of latent revolution in which the country finds itself. But if this is so, it presents a terrible danger for the period of reconstruction, and another stimulant needs to be discovered immediately.

In times of social stability, in which, save in exceptional cases, those who form part of the anonymous mass remain in it more or less, never even seeking to emerge therefrom, the people cannot feel themselves at home in a patriotism founded upon pride and pomp and glory. It is as strange and unfamiliar to them as are the salons of Versailles, which constitute one of its expressions. Glory is the reverse of anonymity. If to military glory we add literary, scientific, and other sorts of glory, the people will continue to feel themselves strangers. The knowledge that certain Frenchmen who have covered themselves with glory have come out of their ranks will not, in stable periods, afford the people any comfort; for if the former have come out of the people, they have ceased to form part of the people.

On the other hand, if their country is presented to them as something beautiful and precious, but which is, in the first place, imperfect, and secondly, very frail and liable to suffer misfortune, and which it is necessary to cherish and preserve, they will rightly feel themselves to be more closely identified with it than will other classes of society. For the people have a monopoly of a certain sort of knowledge, perhaps the most important of all, that of the reality of misfortune; and for that very reason, they feel all the more keenly the preciousness of those things which deserve to be protected from it, and how incumbent it is on each of us to cherish and protect them. Melodrama reflects this popular state of feeling. Why it happens to be such a dreadful literary form would be worth while taking the trouble to examine. But far from being a false form of expression, it is very close, in a certain sense, to reality.

Were such a relationship to be established between the people and the country, the former would no longer regard their own personal sufferings as crimes committed by the country against themselves, but as ills suffered by the country in and through themselves. The difference is immense. In another sense, it is slight, and very little would be required to effect the change. But that little would have to come from another world. This presupposes a dissociation between the country and the State. Which is possible if grandeur in the Corneille style is abolished. But it would involve anarchy if, to compensate for this, the State were unable to manage to inspire of its own accord an increased public esteem.

To do that, it ought certainly not to return to the old methods of parliamentary life and party struggle. But what is most important of all, perhaps, is a complete overhaul of the police system. Circumstances would lend themselves to this. The English police system might be studied with advantage. At all events, the liberation of the country will, it is to be hoped, bring with it the liquidation of the personnel composing the police force, except for those who have taken a personal part against the enemy. They must be replaced by men who enjoy public esteem, and since that is, unfortunately, chiefly founded nowadays on money and diplomas, a fairly high standard of education must be demanded even beginning with ordinary policemen and inspectors, and further up really high qualifications, with correspondingly high pay. It would even be necessary, if the vogue for having *Grandes Ecoles* continues in France—which is perhaps not to be desired—to have one for the police, candidates being selected by examination. These are certainly clumsy methods; but something of the kind is indispensable. Furthermore—and this is still more important—we must do away entirely with social categories like those of prostitutes and ex-convicts, which play officially the part of a defenseless herd delivered over to the whims of the police, and providing the latter at the same time with both victims and accomplices; for a mutual contamination is under such conditions inevitable, collaboration having a debasing effect on both sides. We must abolish, in law, both these two categories of persons.

Criminal dishonesty in matters connected with the State on the part of men in public life must also be effectively punished, and more severely so than armed robbery.

The State in its administrative function should appear as the manager of the country's resources; a more or less capable manager, who is expected to be on the whole rather less capable than otherwise, because his task is a difficult one and carried out under morally unfavorable conditions. Obedience is none the less obligatory, not because of any particular right to issue commands possessed by the State, but because obedience is essential for the country's preservation and tranquillity. We must obey the State, however it happens to be, rather like loving children left by their parents, gone abroad, in the charge of some mediocre governess, but who obey her nevertheless out of love for their parents. If the State happens not to be mediocre, so much the better; besides, the pressure of public opinion must always be exercised in the manner of a stimulant encouraging it to leave the path of mediocrity; but whether mediocre or not, the obligation of obedience remains the same.

It is certainly not an unlimited obligation, but its only valid limit is a revolt on the part of conscience. No criterion can be offered indicating exactly what this limit is; it is even impossible for each of us to prescribe one for himself once and for all: when you feel you can't obey any longer, you just have to disobey. But there is at least one necessary condition, although insufficient of itself, making it possible to disobey without being guilty of crime; this is to be urged forward by so imperious an obligation that one is constrained to scorn all risks of whatever kind. If one feels inclined to disobey, but one is dissuaded by the excessive danger involved, that is altogether unpardonable, whether it be because one contemplated an act of disobedience, or else because one failed to carry it out, as the case may be. Besides, whenever one isn't strictly obliged to disobey, one is under the strict obligation to obey. A country cannot possess liberty unless it is recognized that disobedience toward the authorities, every time it doesn't proceed from an overriding sense of duty, is more dishonorable than theft. That means to say that public order ought to be regarded as more sacred than private property. The authorities could popularize this way of looking at things by means of education and other suitable methods, which would have to be thought out.

But it is only compassion for our country, the watchful and tender concern to keep it out of harm's way, which can give to peace, and especially to civil peace, what civil or foreign war possesses, unfortunately, of itself—something stirring, touching, poetic, and sacred. This compassion alone can give us back that feeling we have lacked for so long, and so rarely experienced throughout the course of history, and which Théophile expressed in the beautiful line, *"La sainte majesté des lois."*

When Théophile wrote that line, it was perhaps the last time such a feeling was deeply experienced in France. Afterward came Richelieu, then the Fronde, then Louis XIV, and so on. Montesquieu vainly sought to re-establish it in the public imagination by means of a book. The men of 1789 laid claim to it, but they didn't really feel it in their hearts, otherwise the country wouldn't have slithered so easily into war, both domestic and foreign.

Since then, even our language has become unsuitable to express it. It is, nevertheless, the sentiment that people are trying to revive, or its pale counterpart, when they talk about *"légitimité."* But giving a sentiment a name is not sufficient to call it to life. That is a fundamental truth that we are too apt to forget.

Why lie to ourselves? In 1939, just before the war, under the regime of decree laws, republican *légitimité* already no longer existed. It had departed like Villon's youth *"qui son partement m'a celé,"* noiselessly, without any warning, and without any one having done or said anything to stop it. As for the feeling for *légitimité*, it was completely dead. That it should now reappear in the thoughts of those in exile, that it should occupy a certain place, in company with other feelings in fact incompatible with it, in dreams for curing a sick people, all that means nothing at all, or very little. If it was dead in 1939, how

should it suddenly become effective again after years of systematic disobedience?

On the other hand, the Constitution of 1875 can no longer serve
as a basis for *légitimité*, after having come crashing down in 1940 amid
general public indifference and even contempt, after being abandoned
to its fate by the French people. For that is exactly what they did do.
Neither the Resistance groups nor the French in London can do anything about it. If a shadow of regret was expressed, it was not by any
section of the people, but by parliamentary men in whom their
profession kept alive an interest in republican institutions, elsewhere
nonexistent. Once again, it makes no difference that some considerable
time afterward the feeling for *légitimité* should have reappeared to
a certain extent. At the present moment, hunger invests the Third
Republic with all the poetry associated with a time when there was
enough to eat. It is a fugitive kind of poetry. Moreover, the disgust
felt for so many years and which attained its maximum in 1940 still
persists.

It is nevertheless certain that as and when the Vichy business
falls to pieces, and to the extent to which revolutionary, possibly
Communist, institutions don't arise, a return will be made to the political structure of the Third Republic. But that will only be because
there is a void that has to be filled with something. That is a question
of necessity, not of *légitimité*, and corresponds to the people's attitude, which is not one of loyal enthusiasm, but of dull resignation.
On the other hand, the date 1789 certainly awakens a really deep
echo; but all there is attached to it is an inspiration, there are no
institutions.

Seeing that we have, in fact, recently experienced a break in
historical continuity, constitutional legality can no longer be regarded
as having an historical basis; it must be made to derive from the
eternal source of all legality. The men who offer their services to
the country to govern it will have to publicly recognize certain
obligations corresponding to essential aspirations of the people eternally inscribed in the depths of popular feeling; the people must have
confidence in the word and in the capacity of these men, and be
provided with means of expressing the fact; they must also be made to

feel that, in accepting these men, they give an undertaking to obey them.

Since the people's obedience toward the public authorities is a necessity for the country, this obedience becomes a sacred obligation, and one that confers on the public authorities themselves, seeing that they form the object of it, the same sacred character. This doesn't mean an idolizing of the State in association with patriotism in the Roman style. It is the exact opposite of this. The State is sacred, not in the way an idol is sacred, but in the way common objects serving a religious purpose, like the altar, the baptismal water, or anything else of the kind, are sacred. Everybody knows they are only material objects; but material objects which are regarded as sacred because they serve a sacred purpose. That is the sort of majesty appropriate for the State.

If we are unable to inspire the people of France with a conception of this nature, they will have only the choice between anarchy and idolatry. Idolatry might take a Communist form. That is probably what would happen. It might also take a nationalist form, in which case it would presumably have as its object the pair of idols so characteristic of our age, composed of a man acclaimed as leader and at his side the ironbound machine of State. But we mustn't forget that, first, publicity is able to manufacture leaders, and secondly, if circumstances place a man of genuine ability in such a situation, he rapidly becomes a prisoner of his role. In other words, in the language of today, the absence of a pure source of inspiration would leave the French people no other alternatives than anarchy, Communism, or Fascism.

There are some people in America for example, who ask themselves whether the French in London might not have leanings toward Fascism. That is not putting the question in the proper way. Intentions, by themselves, are not of any great importance, save when their aim is directly evil, for to do evil the necessary means are always within easy reach. But good intentions only count when accompanied by the corresponding means for putting them into effect. St. Peter hadn't the slightest intention of denying Christ; but he did so because the grace was not in him which, had it been there,

would have enabled him not to do so. And even the energy, the categorical tone he employed to underline the contrary intention, helped
to deprive him of this grace. It is a case that is worth pondering in
all the trials life sets before us.

The thing is to know whether the French in London possess
the necessary means to prevent the people of France from sliding
into Fascism, and at the same time stop them from falling into either
Communism or anarchy. Fascism, Communism, and anarchy being all
scarcely different, almost equivalent, expressions of the self-same evil,
what we want to know is whether they have any remedy for this
evil.

If they haven't one, their *raison d'être*, which is to keep France
in the war, is brought entirely to an end by victory, which will
then plunge them back again among the mass of their fellow-country-
men. If they have one, they should already have begun applying it
to a great extent, and efficiently so, long before victory. For a treatment of this description cannot be started in the midst of all the
nervous tension, which will, both in each individual and in the mass,
necessarily accompany the liberation of the country. Still less can it
be started once people's nerves have quieted down again—supposing
one day such a thing should happen; it would be much too late: any
sort of treatment would then be entirely out of the question.

The important thing, then, is not for them to assert before the
world their right to govern France; any more than it is for a doctor
to publicly assert his right to prescribe treatment for a patient. The
essential thing is to have rightly diagnosed the case, conceived a cure,
chosen the right medicaments, and made sure the patient is supplied
with them. When a doctor knows how to do all that, not without a
certain risk of making mistakes, but with a reasonable chance of being
right, then, if other people try to prevent him exercising his function,
and to put a charlatan in his place, it is his duty to oppose them with
all his might. But if, in some place where there isn't a doctor, a lot of
ignoramuses busy themselves about the bedside of a sick man whose
condition calls for the most precise, most up-to-date form of treatment, what does it matter in whose particular hands among that lot he
happens to be when it comes to dying, or else being saved by a

stroke of luck? No doubt, it must in any case always be better that he should find himself in the hands of those who love him. But those who love him won't inflict on him the additional suffering of a battle royal raging at his pillow, unless they know themselves to be in possession of a likely means of saving his life.

III

LANGUAGE AND THOUGHT

Justice, truth, and beauty are sisters and comrades. With three such beautiful words we have no need to look for any others.

Critical, no less than religious, standards of discrimination inform the demands Simone Weil makes of her own as of all human thought. Her critical thought shows astonishing consistency in fusing reverence and discipline, in creating a reverent discipline. In her writings, through a common allegiance to standards, the critic and the mystic religious philosopher come together. Unfailingly, her criticism is founded on a vision of spiritual order and never stops seeking for clarity of expression and balance of thought. The critical function is a close ally of spiritual life. A failure in either one dimension is detrimental to the other, causing a breakdown in the total process of making responsible judgments. Intelligent thought requires a constant discipline if it is to avoid the pitfalls of what is sloppy and sentimental and disorderly. When the critical process retreats before such adversaries, the total effect on intelligence, and consequently on civilization, is lamentable, for, as Simone Weil writes, "when the intelligence is ill-at-ease the whole soul is sick." In her writings the critical process emerges from, and is simultaneously molded and refined by, the application of a firm and constant pressure on the need to mediate and to conjoin intellect and soul. Her essays, at once critical and religious, illustrate the goals of the evaluative process of critical thought that becomes transcendent and impersonal in that ultimate sense that Simone Weil is aware of when she observes: "The human being can only escape from the collective by raising himself above the personal and entering into the impersonal." Yet there is a tendency to ignore or to dismiss her view of the critical function, or to subordinate it to the mystical dimension of her life and thought. This leads to misreading and misunderstanding the critical powers of analysis that she brings to bear on all her writings.

A modern saint, she was also a modern critic when one considers the questions, the doubts, the concerns, and the issues that preoccupied her; the religious and cultural criteria she formulated; and the relevance and truth of her diagnosis of and prescriptions for "man in the modern world." In her critical thought she was to insist on both communication and transcendence. And she also steadfastly insisted that critical concepts that refused to acknowledge the interdependence of the physical and the spiritual nature of man were categorically incomplete. The failure to acknowledge this interdependence is tantamount to the failure to recognize, and hence to discriminate between, good and evil. "In all crucial problems of human existence the only choice is between supernatural good on the one hand and evil on the other." Her thought never loses sight of this criterion, which becomes for her a pivotal moral and critical centrality in the light of which all human problems, accomplishments, and aspirations are to be viewed and judged. Critical judgment is for her spiritual judgment. Any separation of them must result in a fictionalization of the direst consequences. In her religious, sociological, and literary reflections she never fails to speak to the intellect in order to reach the soul. Her criticism both expresses and advances a spiritual principle of unity. To some readers and commentators, no doubt, such criticism may sound conservative, even reactionary. To Simone Weil it was criticism with deep roots in Hellenism—in the Greek view of life that she especially admired and that she saw as being increasingly absent in the modern world: "Real genius is nothing else but the supernatural virtue of humility in the domain of thought."

Her concern with and her own careful use of language are always apparent. "Where there is a grave error of vocabulary it is almost certainly the sign of a grave error of thought," she emphasizes. In the debasement of language she detected one of the serious causes of modern breakdown. Indiscipline, formlessness, nihilism, blasphemy she associates with the careless use of language. The adverse effects of this on human thought, as she clearly indicates in her exquisite essay "The Power of Words," are immense: "To clarify thought, to discredit the intrinsically meaningless words, and to define the use of others by precise analysis—to do this, strange though it may appear, might be a way of saving human lives." She was not too hopeful of improvement or reform insofar as "our age seems almost entirely unfitted for such a task. The glossy surface of our civilization hides a real intellectual decadence." Problems of language cannot be detached from political problems, as she brings out in a sentence that rings with recurring truth in the social-political arena: "On inspection, almost all the words and phrases of our political vocabulary turn out to be hollow." Her perception of the corruption of language was intrinsically a moral (and a religious) one. The more blatant and callous the secular state becomes, the more decayed language itself becomes. And the more, too, is language separated from its intrinsic connection of responsibility to human worth. Hence, as Simone Weil laments, "language is no longer equipped for legitimately praising a man's character." Moral loss—moral immobilization—is the consequential, far-reaching loss of such a destructive process: "In every sphere, we seem to have lost the elements of intelligence: the ideas of limit, measure, proportion, relation, comparison, contingency, interdependence, interrelation of means and ends."

Other modern writers, critics, philosophers, and theologians have perceived the deteriorating life of language in society and culture. The remarkable diagnoses and continuing warnings of George Steiner come especially to mind at this point. But their concerns are, for the most part, humanistic, positivistic, rationalistic, existential, or academic, confined to and, in the end, circumscribed by a labyrinthine secularity that makes the modernist impasse all the more evident. Their solutions are not much better. In contrast, in her examination of the problems of language and thought, Simone Weil concentrates judgmentally on the accelerating loss of the spiritual idea of value in the twentieth century. Her concern, first and finally and always, revolves around the total effect of spiritual bankruptcy and of the profanation of "the good" in the religious sense that she identifies with it when she asserts: "The good is the only source of the sacred. There is nothing sacred except the good and what pertains to it." The enfeeblement and the disappearance of the criterion of value, she stresses in her essay "The Responsibility of Writers," are pervasive in all aspects of society and culture. "Such words as spontaneity, sincerity, gratuitousness, richness, enrichment—words which imply an almost total indifference to contrasts of value—have come more often from their pens than words which contain a reference to good and evil," she says of modern writers. Words particularly related to the sacramental concept of the good—virtue, nobility, honor, honesty, generosity—have been so twisted and debased that they have become almost impossible to use. The degradation of language is concomitant with and reflective of the despiritualization of man: "The fate of words is a touchstone of the progressive weakening of the idea of value, and although the fate of words does not depend upon writers one cannot help attributing a special responsibility to them, since words are their business."

Literary creativity cannot be absolved from moral and spiritual responsibility. Because the connection between literature and morality is equally endemic and binding she believed it impossible to exempt literature from those categories of good and evil to which all human actions are referable. Creative writers even if they bear the burden of imagination must also bear a burden of responsibility to the moral values of which they have been immemorially the guardians and which they have lost in various degrees of seriousness. Singling out the surrealists, she underlines their "non-oriented thought" and their dangerous and portentous choice of "the total absence of value as their supreme value." There has not always been a literary sacking of towns, she says, but "surrealism is such an equivalent." Many writers, she goes on to claim, have in one way or another surrendered the value of the spiritual principle of unity. They have converted twentieth-century literature into what is essentially psychological, "and psychology consists in describing states of the soul by displaying them all on the same plane without any discrimination of value." Her main, most vigorous complaint, and one that lacks neither legitimacy nor examples, she expresses in words that can hardly be dismissed except by those who, negating the idea of value, preach "the absolute absence of the absolute" (as Samuel Beckett expresses the moderns' spiritual malaise): "Writers do not have to be professors of morals, but they do have to express the human condition. And nothing concerns human life so essentially, for every man at every moment, as good and evil. When literature becomes deliberately indifferent to the opposition of good and evil, it betrays its function and forfeits all claim to excellence."

In her critical and aesthetic views, Simone Weil was severe, morally severe. Unhesitantly she can state: "I believe in the responsibility of the writers of recent years for the disaster of our time." We have in this statement an instance of the kind of sternness that one commentator equates with her total outlook, "half icy intellectual, half mystic." Yet, it is always the primary need to recognize the difference between good and evil which she demands that we confront, whatever the consequences. In much of modern literature, she observes, values are reversed so that evil becomes attractive, good tedious. She distinguishes between literary genius oriented towards the good—Homer, Aeschylus, Sophocles, Racine, Villon—and "demoniacal geniuses," of whom Rimbaud is an example and symbol. A writer who shirks his moral responsibility, who in effect refuses to give meaning to human action, refuses to recognize the difference between good and evil. This refusal constitutes a fundamental failure of responsibility. And insofar as he has occasion to influence human behavior, she claims, "it ought to be recognized that the moment a writer fills a role among the influences directing public opinion, he cannot claim to exercise unlimited freedom." She especially laments the loss of spiritual direction since the time of the Enlightenment with the usurpation of spiritual and moral authority by those men of letters who introduce "into literature a Messianic afflatus wholly detrimental to its artistic purity." With the waning of sharply defined moral standards, discriminating judgments and critical intelligence have been incalculably blunted. Writers must satisfy the standards of moral vision. When they do, then "their contemplation is the everflowing source of an inspiration which may legitimately guide us. For this inspiration, if we know how to receive it, tends—as Plato said—to make us grow wings to overcome gravity."

The value of a work of art must be judged according to the way it both discloses the moral real and relates to the human soul. In what can be called her metaphysics of art Simone Weil returns to this aesthetic principle. "Art is an attempt to transport into a limited quantity of matter," she points out, "modeled by man, an image of the infinite beauty of the entire universe." An artist who continuously attempts to make connection with the depths of mystery discovers that grace and nature are inseparable and indivisible. It is the Catholic sacramental view of life that she doubtlessly has in mind when she writes: "Every true artist has had real, direct, and immediate contact with the beauty of the world, contact that is of the nature of a sacrament." (A modern Catholic novelist, Flannery O'Connor, is saying something analogous to this when she writes: "The artist penetrates the concrete world in order to find at its depths the image of its source, the image of ultimate reality.") For Simone Weil the artist who distances himself from the ultimate divine source dissociates himself from the "permanent things" and falls into sin. Such artists become, in T. S. Eliot's phrase, "promoters of personality," seekers "after strange gods." These artists Simone Weil finds unworthy, for they defile the sacred consciousness and banish man's religious need. (Here admiration of *The Brothers Karamazov* is closely tied to Dostoevsky's perception of man's inexhaustible and indispensable religious needs.) The artist as *homo viator* must travel on the road to transcendence. His achievement must be an achievement in transcendence, beyond himself and beyond personality. "Perfection is impersonal," she emphasizes in one of her most astute essays, "Human Personality." "Our personality is the part of us which belongs to error and sin." Truth and beauty thus reside in the impersonal and anonymous, "in the realm of the sacred." An artist of the very highest genius is a spiritual artist. But, she exclaims, "there are not very many of them."

An artist, and anyone whose function it is to advise the public what to praise or to admire, should strive to plant in man "the invisible seed of pure good." Artists who think of their work as a manifestation of personality are "the most in bondage of public taste" and hence captives of collectivity. Artists who respect and affirm the clear and present existence of standards higher than their personal selves and talents recognize limits that are finally resolved in absolutes: "Justice, truth, and beauty are the image in our world of this impersonal and divine order of the universe. Nothing inferior to them is worthy to be the inspiration of men who accept the fact of death." Simone Weil was clear in her mind and firm in her conviction that art must visibilize the journey towards the absolute, the courage of belief, the operation of grace, the vindication of the holy, the salvation of the soul. Not unlike all the needs of life, art must have a constant reference to the theological truths, as well as to the eternal standard that "in all crucial problems of human existence the only choice is between supernatural good on the one hand and evil on the other."

THE POWER OF
WORDS

*Simone Weil applies to language the same austere stan-
dards that she applies to spiritual life. Language should
serve as a discipline of rational thought, though she admits
in this essay, as relevant today as it was when it appeared
in 1937, that the intellectual climate of the age favors the
growth of vacuous entities and abstractions, and that social
and political vocabulary contributes to creating a world of
myths and monsters.*

The relative security we enjoy in this age, thanks to a technology
which gives us a measure of control over nature, is more than can-
celled out by the dangers of destruction and massacre in conflicts
between groups of men. If the danger is grave it is no doubt partly
because of the power of the destructive weapons supplied by our techniques; but these weapons do not fire themselves, and it is dishonest to
blame inert matter for a situation in which the entire responsibility is
our own. Common to all our most threatening troubles is one characteristic which might appear reassuring to a superficial eye, but which
is in reality the great danger: *they are conflicts with no definable objective.* The whole of history bears witness that it is precisely such
conflicts that are the most bitter. It may be that a clear recognition of

this paradox is one of the keys to history; that it is the key to our own period there is no doubt.

In any struggle for a well-defined stake each combatant can weigh the value of the stake against the probable cost of the struggle and decide how great an effort it justifies; indeed, it is generally not difficult to arrive at a compromise which is more advantageous to both contending parties than even a successful battle. But when there is no objective there is no longer any common measure or proportion; no balance or comparison of alternatives is possible, and compromise is inconceivable. In such circumstances the importance of the battle can only be measured by the sacrifices it demands, and from this it follows that the sacrifices already incurred are a perpetual argument for new ones. Thus there would never be any reason to stop killing and dying, except that there is fortunately a limit to human endurance. This paradox is so extreme as to defy analysis. And yet the most perfect example of it is known to every so-called educated man, but, by a sort of taboo, we read it without understanding.

The Greeks and Trojans massacred one another for ten years on account of Helen. Not one of them except the dilettante warrior Paris cared two straws about her; all of them agreed in wishing she had never been born. The person of Helen was so obviously out of scale with this gigantic struggle that in the eyes of all she was no more than the symbol of what was really at stake; but the real issue was never defined by anyone, nor could it be, because it did not exist. For the same reason it could not be calculated. Its importance was simply imagined as corresponding to the deaths incurred and the further massacres expected; and this implied an importance beyond all reckoning. Hector foresaw that his city would be destroyed, his father and brothers massacred, his wife degraded to a slavery worse than death; Achilles knew that he was condemning his father to the miseries and humiliations of a defenceless old age; all were aware that their long absence at the war would bring ruin on their homes; yet no one felt that the cost was too great, because they were all in pursuit of a literal non-entity whose only value was in the price paid for it. When the Greeks began to think of returning to their homes it seemed to Minerva and Ulysses that a reminder of the sufferings of their dead comrades was a sufficient argument to put them to shame. They used, in fact, exactly the same arguments as three thousand years later were employed by Poincaré to castigate the proposal for a negotiated peace. Nowadays the popular mind has an explanation for this sombre zeal in piling up useless ruin; it imagines the machinations of economic interests. But there is no need to look so far. In the time of Homer's Greeks there were no organized bronze manufacturers or international cartels. The truth is that the role which we attribute to mysterious economic oligarchies was attributed by Homer's contemporaries to the gods of the Greek mythology. But there is no need of gods or conspiracies to make men rush headlong into the most absurd disasters. Human nature suffices.

For the clear-sighted, there is no more distressing symptom of this truth than the unreal character of most of the conflicts that are taking place today. They have even less reality than the war between Greeks and Trojans. At the heart of the Trojan War there was at least a woman and, what is more, a woman of perfect beauty. For our contemporaries the role of Helen is played by words with capital letters. If we grasp one of these words, all swollen with blood and tears, and squeeze it, we find it is empty. Words with content and meaning are not murderous. If one of them occasionally becomes associated with bloodshed, it is rather by chance than by inevitability, and the resulting action is generally controlled and efficacious. But when empty words are given capital letters, then, on the slightest pretext, men will begin shedding blood for them and piling up ruin in their name, without effectively grasping anything to which they refer, since what they refer to can never have any reality, for the simple reason that they mean nothing. In these conditions the only definition of success is to crush a rival group of men who have a hostile word on their banners; for it is a characteristic of these empty words that each of them has its complementary antagonist. It is true, of course, that not all of these words are intrinsically meaningless; some of them do have meaning if one takes the trouble to define them properly. But when a word is properly defined it loses its capital letter and can no longer serve either as a banner or as a hostile slogan; it becomes simply a sign, helping us to grasp some concrete reality, or concrete objective, or method of activity. To clarify thought, to discredit the intrinsically meaningless words, and to define the use of others by precise analysis—to do this, strange though it may appear, might be a way of saving human lives.

Our age seems almost entirely unfitted for such a task. The glossy surface of our civilization hides a real intellectual decadence. There is no area in our minds reserved for superstition, such as the Greeks had in their mythology; and superstition, under cover of an abstract vocabulary, has revenged itself by invading the entire realm of thought. Our science is like a store filled with the most subtle intellectual devices for solving the most complex problems, and yet we are almost incapable of applying the elementary principles of rational thought. In every sphere, we seem to have lost the very elements of intelligence: the ideas of limit, measure, degree, proportion, relation, comparison, contingency, interdependence, interrelation of means and ends. To keep to the social level, our political universe is peopled exclusively by myths and monsters; all it contains is absolutes and abstract entities. This is illustrated by all the words of our political and social vocabulary: nation, security, capitalism, communism, fascism, order, authority, property, democracy. We never use them in phrases such as: There is democracy *to the extent that* . . . or: There is capitalism *in so far as* . . . The use of expressions like 'to the extent that' is beyond our intellectual capacity. Each of these words seems to represent for us an absolute reality, unaffected by conditions, or an absolute objective, independent of methods of action, or an absolute evil; and at the same time we make all these words mean, successively or simultaneously, anything whatsoever. Our lives are lived, in actual fact, among changing, varying realities, subject to the casual play of external necessities, and modifying themselves according to specific conditions within specific limits; and yet we act and strive and sacrifice ourselves and others by reference to fixed and isolated abstractions which cannot possibly be related either to one another or to any concrete facts. In this so-called age of technicians, the only battles we know how to fight are battles against windmills.

So it is easy to find examples of lethal absurdity wherever one looks. The prime specimen is the antagonism between nations. People often try to explain this as a simple cover for capitalist rivalries; but in so doing they ignore a glaringly obvious fact, namely, that the world-wide and complex system of capitalist rivalries and wars and alliances in no way corresponds to the world's division into nations. Two French groups, in the form of limited companies, for example, may find themselves opposed to one another while each of them is in alliance with a German group. The German steel industry may be regarded with hostility by producers of steel goods in France; but it makes little difference to the mining companies whether the iron of Lorraine is worked in France or Germany; and the wine-growers, manufacturers of Parisian articles, and others have an interest in the prosperity of German industry. In the light of these elementary truths the current explanation of international rivalry breaks down. Whoever insists that nationalism is always a cover for capitalist greed should specify whose greed. The mining companies'? The electricity companies'? The steel magnates'? The textile industry's? The banks'? It cannot be all of them, because their interests do not coincide; and if one is referring only to a minority of them, then one must show how it is that this minority has got control of the State. It is true that the policy of a State at any given moment always coincides with the interests of some sector of capitalism, and this offers an explanation whose very superficiality makes it applicable everywhere. But in view of the international circulation of capital it is not clear why a capitalist should look to his own State for protection rather than to some foreign State, or why he should not find it as easy to use pressure and influence with foreign statesmen as with those of his own country. The world's economic structure coincides with its political structure only in so far as States exert their authority in economic affairs; and, moreover, the way they use this authority is not explicable solely in terms of economic interest. If we examine the term 'national interest' we find it does not even mean the interest of capitalist business. 'A man thinks he is dying for his country,' said Anatole France, 'but he is dying for a few industrialists.' But even that is saying too much. What one dies for is not even so substantial and tangible as an industrialist.

The national interest cannot be defined as a common interest of the great industrial, commercial, and financial companies of a country, because there is no such common interest; nor can it be defined as the

life, liberty, and well-being of the citizens, because they are continually being adjured to sacrifice their well-being, their liberty, and
their lives to the national interest. In the end, a study of modern history leads to the conclusion that the national interest of every State
consists in its capacity to make war. In 1911 France nearly went to war
for Morocco; but why was Morocco so important? Because the
populations of North Africa would make a reserve of cannon fodder;
and because, for the purpose of war, a country needs to make its
economy as self-supporting as possible in raw materials and markets.
What a country calls its vital economic interests are not the things
which enable its citizens to live, but the things which enable it to make
war; petrol is much more likely than wheat to be a cause of international conflict. Thus when war is waged it is for the purpose of safeguarding or increasing one's capacity to make war. International politics are wholly involved in this vicious circle. What is called national
prestige consists in behaving always in such a way as to demoralize
other nations by giving them the impression that, if it comes to war,
one would certainly defeat them. What is called national security is an
imaginary state of affairs in which one would retain the capacity to
make war while depriving all other countries of it. It amounts to this,
that a self-respecting nation is ready for anything, including war, except for a renunciation of its option to make war. But why is it so
essential to be able to make war? No one knows, any more than the
Trojans knew why it was necessary for them to keep Helen. That is
why the good intentions of peace-loving statesmen are so ineffectual.
If the countries were divided by a real opposition of interests, it would
be possible to arrive at satisfactory compromises. But when economic
and political interests have no meaning apart from war, how can they
be peacefully reconciled? It is the very concept of the nation that
needs to be suppressed—or rather, the manner in which the word is
used. For the word national and the expressions of which it forms part
are empty of all meaning; their only content is millions of corpses, and
orphans, and disabled men, and tears and despair.

Another good example of murderous absurdity is the opposition
between fascism and communism. The fact that this opposition constitutes today a double threat of civil war and world war is perhaps the

gravest of all our symptoms of intellectual atrophy, because one has only to examine the present-day meaning of the two words to discover two almost identical political and social conceptions. In each of them the State seizes control of almost every department of individual and social life; in each there is the same frenzied militarization, and the same artificial unanimity, obtained by coercion, in favour of a single party which identifies itself with the State and derives its character from this false identification, and finally there is the same serfdom imposed upon the working masses in place of the ordinary wage system. No two nations are more similar in structure than Germany and Russia, each threatening an international crusade against the other and each pretending to see the other as the Beast of the Apocalypse. Therefore one can safely assert that the opposition between fascism and communism is strictly meaningless. Victory for fascism can only mean extermination of the communists and victory for communism extermination of the fascists. In these circumstances it follows, of course, that anti-fascism and anti-communism are also meaningless. The anti-fascist position is this: Anything rather than fascism; anything, including fascism, so long as it is labelled communism. And the anti-communist position: Anything rather than communism; anything, including communism, so long as it is labelled fascism. For such a noble cause everyone in either camp is resolved to die, and above all to kill. In Berlin, in the summer of 1932, it was common to see a little group of people gather around two workmen or two petty *bourgeois*, one a communist and the other a Nazi, who were arguing. After a time it always became clear to both disputants that they were defending exactly the same programme; and this made their heads swim, but it only exacerbated in each of them his hatred for an opponent separated from him by such a gulf as to remain an enemy even when expressing the same ideas. That was four and a half years ago; the Nazis are still torturing German communists in the concentration camps today, and it is possible that France is threatened with a war of extermination between anti-fascists and anti-communists. If such a war took place it would make the Trojan war look perfectly reasonable by comparison; for even if the Greek poet was wrong who said that there was only Helen's phantom at Troy, a phantom Helen is a substantial reality compared to the distinction between fascism and communism.

The distinction between dictatorship and democracy, however, which is related to that between order and freedom, is indeed an example of a real opposition. Nevertheless, it loses its meaning if we see each of the two terms as a thing-in-itself, as is usually done nowadays, instead of seeing it as a point of reference for judging the character of a social structure. It is clear that neither absolute dictatorship nor absolute democracy exists anywhere, and that every social organism everywhere is always a compound of democracy and dictatorship in different proportions; it is clear, too, that the extent to which there is democracy is defined by the relations between different parts of the social mechanism and upon the conditions which control its functioning; it is therefore upon these relations and these conditions that we should try to act. Instead of which we generally imagine that dictatorship or democracy are intrinsically inherent in certain groups of men, whether nations or parties, so that we become obsessed with the desire to crush one or other of these groups, according to whether we are temperamentally more attached to order or to liberty. Many Frenchmen, for example, believe in all good faith that a military victory for France over Germany would be a victory for democracy. As they see it, freedom inheres in the French nation and tyranny in the German, in much the same way that for Molière's contemporaries there was a dormitive virtue inherent in opium. If a day comes when the requirements of so-called 'national defence' transform France into a fortified camp in which the whole nation is totally subjected to the military authority, and if this transformed France goes to war with Germany, then these Frenchmen will allow themselves to be killed, having first killed as many Germans as possible, in the touching belief that their blood is being shed for democracy. It does not occur to them that dictatorship arose in Germany as the result of certain conditions and that an alteration of those conditions, in such a way as to make possible some relaxation of the State authority in Germany, might be more effective than killing the young men of Berlin and Hamburg.

Another example: suppose one dared to suggest to any party man the idea of an armistice in Spain. If he is a man of the right he will indignantly reply that the fight must continue until the forces of order are triumphant and anarchy is crushed; if he is a man of the left he will reply with equal indignation that the fight must continue until the people's freedom and well-being are assured and the oppressors and exploiters crushed. The man of the right forgets that no political régime, of whatever kind, involves disorders remotely comparable to those of a civil war, with its deliberate destruction, its non-stop massacre in the firing-line, its slowing down of production, and the hundreds of crimes it permits every day, on both sides, by the fact that any hooligan can get hold of a gun. The man of the left, for his part, forgets that even on his own side liberty is suppressed far more drastically by the necessities of civil war than it would be by the coming to power of a party of the extreme right; in other words, he forgets that there is a state of siege, that militarization is in force both at the front and behind it, that there is a police terror, and that the individual has no security and no protection against arbitrary injustice; he forgets, too, that the cost of the war, and the ruin it causes, and the slowing down of production condemn the people to a long period of far more cruel privation than their exploiters would. And both of them forget that during the long months of civil war an almost identical régime has grown up on both sides. Each of them has unconsciously lost sight of his ideal and replaced it by an entity without substance. For each, the victory of what he still calls his idea can no longer mean anything except the extermination of the enemy; and each of them will scorn any suggestion of peace, replying to it with the same knockout argument as Minerva in Homer and Poincaré in 1917: 'The dead do not wish it.'

Of all the conflicts which set groups of men against one another the most legitimate and serious—one could perhaps say, the only serious one—is what is called today the *class struggle* (an expression which needs clarifying). But this is only true in so far as it is not confused by imaginary entities which obstruct controlled action, lead efforts astray, and entail the risk of ineradicable hatred, idiotic destructiveness, and senseless butchery. What is well founded, vital, and essential is the eternal struggle of those who obey against those who command when the mechanism of social power involves a disregard for the human dignity of the former. It is an eternal struggle because those who command are always inclined, whether they know it or not, to trample on the human dignity of those below them. The function of command cannot, except in special cases, be exercised in a way that respects the personal humanity of those who carry out orders. When exercised as though men were objects, and unresisting ones at that, it inevitably acts upon them as exceptionally pliable objects; for a man exposed to the threat of death, which is really the final sanction of all authority, can become more pliable than inert matter. So long as there is a stable social hierarchy, of whatever form, those at the bottom must struggle so as not to lose all the rights of a human being. But the resistance of those at the top, although it usually appears unjust, is also inspired by concrete motives. First, personal motives; for except in rather rare cases of generosity the privileged hate to lose any of their material and moral privileges. But there are also higher motives. To those in whom the functions of command are vested it seems to be their duty to defend order, without which no social life can survive; and the only order they conceive is the existing one. Nor are they entirely wrong, for until a different order has been, in fact, established no one can say with certainty that it is possible. It is just for this reason that social progress depends upon a pressure from below sufficient to change effectively the relations of power and thus to compel the actual establishment of new social relationships. The tension between pressure from below and resistance from above creates and maintains an unstable equilibrium, which defines at each moment the structure of a society. This tension is a struggle but not a war; and although it may in certain circumstances turn into a war, it does not inevitably do so. The story of the interminable and useless massacres around Troy is not our only legacy from antiquity; there is also the vigorous and concerted action of the Roman plebeians who, without shedding a drop of blood, escaped from a condition verging upon slavery and obtained the institution of tribunes to guarantee their new rights. In exactly the same way the French workers, by occupying the factories, without violence, enforced the recognition of certain elementary rights and obtained elected delegates to guarantee them.

But early Rome had one important advantage over modern France. In social matters she knew nothing of abstract entities, or words in capitals, or words ending in -ism; nor any of those things

which, with us, are liable to stultify the most serious efforts or to degrade the social struggle into a war as ruinous, as bloody, and as irrational in every way as a war between nations. On inspection, almost all
the words and phrases of our political vocabulary turn out to be hollow. What, for example, can be the meaning of that slogan which was so
popular at the recent elections—'the fight against the trusts'? A trust is
an economic monopoly in the hands of financial powers, which is used
by them not in the public interest but in such a way as to increase
their own influence. What is it that is wrong about this? The fact that
a monopoly is serving as the instrument of a will-to-power unin-
terested in the public good. But it is not this fact that is attacked; what
is attacked is the fact, which is in itself morally indifferent, that the
will-to-power belongs to an economic oligarchy. The aim is to replace
economic oligarchies by the State, which has a will-to-power of its
own and is quite as little concerned with the public good; and a will-
to-power, moreover, which is not economic but military and therefore
much more dangerous to any good folk who have a taste for staying
alive. And on the *bourgeois* side what on earth is the sense of objecting
to State control in economic affairs if one accepts private monopolies
which have all the economic and technical disadvantages of State
monopolies and possibly some others as well? One could make a long
list of pairs of complementary slogans of this kind, all of them equally
unreal. The two considered above are relatively harmless, but this is
not true of all of them.

For example, whatever can be in the heads of those for whom the
word 'capitalism' signifies the absolute of evil? The society in which we
live includes forms of coercion and oppression by which those who
suffer from them are all too often overwhelmed; it includes the most
grievous inequalities and unnecessary miseries. On the other hand,
the economic character of this society consists in certain methods of
production, consumption, and exchange, which are continually varying, however, and which depend upon certain fundamental relationships: between the production and the circulation of goods, between
the circulation of goods and money, between money and production, between money and consumption. This whole interplay of varied
and changing economic phenomena is arbitrarily converted into an

abstraction, which defies all definition, and is then made responsible, under the name of capitalism, for every hardship endured by oneself or others. After that, it is only natural that any man of character should devote his life to the destruction of capitalism, or rather (it comes to the same thing) to revolution—for the negative meaning is the only one possessed today by the word revolution.

Since the 'destruction of capitalism' has no meaning—capitalism being an abstraction—and since it does not refer to any precise modifications that might be applied to the régime (such modifications are contemptuously dismissed as 'reforms'), the slogan can only imply the destruction of capitalists and, more generally, of everyone who does not call himself an opponent of capitalism. Apparently it is easier to kill, and even to die, than to ask ourselves a few quite simple questions like the following: Can the laws and conventions which control our present economic life be said to constitute a system? To what extent is this or that feature of our economic life necessarily connected with the others? To what extent would the modification of this or that economic law produce repercussions among the others? How far can the ills arising from the social relations which exist today be attributed to this or that convention and how far are they attributable to the totality of conventions of our economic life? How far are they attributable to other factors, either permanent factors which would persist after the transformation of the economic system or, on the contrary, factors which could be eliminated without putting an end to what is called the régime? What kind of hardships, either transitory or permanent, would necessarily be involved by the chosen method for transforming the régime? What new hardships might be introduced by the proposed new organization of society? If we gave serious thought to these problems we might reach the point where we could give some meaning to the assertion that capitalism is an evil; but we should mean only a relative evil, and the proposal to transform the régime would be only for the purpose of substituting a lesser evil. And the proposed transformation would be a clearly defined and limited one.

The same criticism is applicable in its entirety to those in the opposite camp, except that the concern for maintaining order replaces the concern about the sufferings of the depressed social classes and the instinct of conservation replaces the desire for change. The *bourgeois* always tend to regard anyone who wishes to put an end to capitalism, and sometimes even anyone who wants to reform it, as an agent of disorder; and they do so because they are ignorant as to what extent and in what circumstances the various economic relations, which are subsumed today under the general name of capitalism, are factors in preserving order. Many of them are in favour of changing nothing, because they do not know what modifications of the system may or may not be dangerous; they fail to realize that, since conditions are always changing, the refusal to modify the system is itself a modification which may be productive of disorders. Most of them appeal to economic laws as religiously as if they were the unwritten laws invoked by Antigone, and this although they can see them changing day by day in front of their eyes. The preservation of the capitalist régime is a meaningless expression, in their mouths, because they do not know what ought to be preserved, nor how much of it; all they can mean, in practice, is the suppression of everyone who wants to put an end to the régime. The struggle between the opponents and the defenders of capitalism is a struggle between innovators who do not know what innovation to make and conservatives who do not know what to conserve; it is a battle of blind men struggling in a void, and for that very reason it is liable to become a war of extermination. The same situation exists on a smaller scale in the struggle within any industrial firm. In general, the worker instinctively blames his employer for all the hardships of work in a factory; he does not ask himself whether under any other property system the management would not inflict some of the same hardships on him, or indeed exactly the same ones, or even perhaps some worse ones; nor does he ask himself how many of these hardships might be abolished, by abolishing their causes, without any alteration of the existing property system. He identifies the struggle 'against the boss' with the undying protest of the human being oppressed by too many hardships. The head of the firm, for his part, is rightly concerned to maintain his authority. But his authority is strictly limited to overall direction, to the due co-ordination of the branches of production, and to ensuring, with some compulsion if necessary, that the work is properly executed. Any industrial régime,

of whatever kind, in which these functions of co-ordination and control can be effectively exercised is allowing sufficient authority to the
heads of the firms. But the feeling of authority, in these men's minds,
is especially connected with a certain atmosphere of deference and
subservience which has no necessary connexion with a high standard
of work; and, above all, when they become aware of latent or overt
opposition among their personnel they always attribute it to certain
individuals, whereas in reality a spirit of revolt, whether loud or
silent, aggressive or despairing, is always present wherever life is
physically or morally oppressive. In the worker's mind the struggle
'against the boss' is confused with the assertion of human dignity, and
in the manager's mind the struggle against the 'ringleaders' is confused
with his duty to the job and his professional conscience. Both of them
are tilting at windmills, so their efforts cannot be confined to reasonable objectives. When strikes are undertaken for clearly defined claims a
settlement is attainable without too great difficulty, as we have sometimes seen; but we have also seen strikes which resembled wars, in the
sense that neither side had any objective, strikes in which there were
no real or tangible issues—apart from arrested production, deteriorating machines, destitution, want, weeping women, and hungry children; and such bitterness on both sides that any agreement seemed impossible. In events like these there are the seeds of civil war.

If we analysed in this way all the words and formulas which have
served throughout history to call forth the spirit of self-sacrifice and
cruelty combined, we should doubtless discover them all to be just as
empty. And yet, all these bloodthirsty abstractions must have some
sort of connexion with real life; and indeed they have. It may be
that there was only Helen's phantom at Troy, but the Greek and
Trojan armies were not phantoms; and in the same way although there
is no meaning in the word nation and the slogans in which it occurs,
the different States with their offices, prisons, arsenals, barracks, and
customs are real enough. The theoretical distinction between the two
forms of totalitarian régime, fascism and communism, is imaginary,
but in Germany in 1932 there existed very concretely two political
organizations each of which wanted to achieve complete power and
consequently to exterminate the other. A democratic party may

gradually change into a party of dictatorship but it still remains distinct from the dictatorial party it is striving to suppress. France, for the purpose of defence against Germany, may submit in her turn to a totalitarian régime, but the French State and the German State will not cease to be two separate States. Both the destruction and the preservation of capitalism are meaningless slogans, but these slogans are supported by real organizations. Corresponding to each empty abstraction there is an actual human group, and any abstraction of which this is not true remains harmless. Conversely, any group which has not secreted an abstract entity will probably not be dangerous. This particular kind of secretion is superbly illustrated by the 'Dr. Knock' of Jules Romains with his maxim: 'Above the interest of the patient and the interest of the doctor stands the interest of Medicine.' It is pure comedy, because the medical profession has not so far secreted such an entity; it is always by organizations concerned with guarding or acquiring power that these entities are secreted. All the absurdities which make history look like a prolonged delirium have their root in one essential absurdity, which is the nature of power. The necessity for power is obvious, because life cannot be lived without order; but the allocation of power is arbitrary because all men are alike, or very nearly. Yet power must not seem to be arbitrarily allocated, because it will not then be recognized as power. Therefore prestige, which is illusion, is of the very essence of power. All power is based, in fact, upon the interrelation of human activities; but in order to be stable it must appear as something absolute and sacrosanct, both to those who wield and those who submit to it and also to other external powers. The conditions which ensure order are essentially contradictory, and men seem to be compelled to choose between the anarchy which goes with inadequate power and the wars of every kind which go with the preoccupation of prestige.

All the absurdities we have enumerated cease to appear absurd when translated into the language of power. Is it not natural that every State should define the national interest as the capacity to make war, when it is surrounded by States capable of subduing it by arms if it is weak? One must either join the race to prepare for war or else be resigned to enduring whatever some other armed State may choose to inflict; no third choice seems possible. Nothing but complete and universal disarmament could resolve this dilemma, and that is hardly conceivable. And, further, a State cannot appear weak in its external relations without the risk of weakening its authority with its own subjects. If Priam and Hector had delivered Helen to the Greeks this might merely have increased the Greeks' inclination to sack a town that seemed so ill prepared to defend itself; and they would also have risked a general uprising in Troy—not because the Trojans would have been upset by the surrender of Helen, but because it would have suggested to them that their chiefs could not be so very powerful. In Spain, if one of the two sides gave the impression of wanting peace this would first have the effect of encouraging its enemies and stimulating their aggressiveness, and then it would involve the risk of uprisings among its own supporters. Again, for a man who is outside both the anti-communist and the anti-fascist blocs the clash between two almost identical ideologies may appear ridiculous; but since these two blocs exist the members of one of them are bound to see absolute evil in the other, because it will exterminate them if they are the weaker. The leaders on each side must seem prepared to annihilate the enemy, in order to maintain their authority with their own troops; and once these blocs have achieved a certain degree of power, neutrality becomes an almost untenable position. In the same way, when those at the bottom of any social hierarchy begin to fear that unless they dispossess those above them they will be completely crushed, then, so soon as either side becomes strong enough to have nothing to fear, it will yield to the intoxication of power mixed with spite. Power, in general, is always essentially vulnerable; and therefore it is bound to defend itself, for otherwise society would lack the necessary minimum of stability. But it is nearly always believed, with or without reason, by all parties, that the only defence is attack. And it is natural that the most implacable conflicts should arise out of imaginary disputes, because these take place solely on the level of power and prestige. It would probably be easier for France to cede raw materials to Germany than a few acres of ground with the title of 'colony', and easier for Germany to do without raw materials than without the title of 'colonial power'. The essential contradiction in human society is that every social *status quo* rests upon an equilibrium of forces or pressures, similar to the equilibrium of fluids; but between one prestige and another there can be no equilibrium. Prestige has no bounds and its satisfaction always involves the infringement of someone else's prestige or dignity. And prestige is inseparable from power. This seems to be an impasse from which humanity can only escape by some miracle. But human life is made up of miracles. Who would believe that a Gothic cathedral could remain standing if we did not see it every day? Since the state of war is not, in fact, continuous, it is not impossible that peace might continue indefinitely. Once all the real data of a problem have been revealed the problem is well on the way to solution. The problem of peace, both international and social, has never yet been completely stated.

What prevents us from seeing the data of the problem is the swarm of vacuous entities or abstractions; they even prevent us from seeing that there is a problem to be solved, instead of a fatality to be endured. They stupefy the mind; they not only make men willing to die but, infinitely worse, they make them forget the value of life. To sweep away these entities from every department of political and social life is an urgently necessary measure of public hygiene. But the operation is not an easy one; the whole intellectual climate of our age favours the growth and multiplication of vacuous entities. Perhaps we should begin with a reform of our methods of scientific education and popularization, abolishing the artificial vocabulary which those methods crudely and superstitiously encourage. By reviving the intelligent use of expressions like *to the extent that, in so far as, on condition that, in relation to,* and by discrediting all those vicious arguments which amount to proclaiming the dormitive virtue of opium, we might be rendering a highly important practical service to our contemporaries. A general raising of the intellectual level would greatly assist any educational attempt to deflate the imaginary causes of strife. As things are, there is certainly no shortage of preachers of appeasement in every sphere; but their sermons, as a rule, are not intended to awaken intelligence and eliminate unreal conflicts, but rather, by inducing somnolence, to obscure real conflicts. There are no more dangerous enemies of international and social peace than those spellbinders whose talk about peace between nations means simply an indefinite prolongation of the *status quo* for the exclusive advantage of the French State or those whose advocacy of social peace presupposes safeguarding of privilege, or at least the right of the privileged to veto any change they dislike. The relations between social forces are essentially variable, and the underprivileged will always seek to alter them; it is wrong to enforce an artificial stabilization. What is required is discrimination between the imaginary and the real, so as to diminish the risks of war, without interfering with the struggle between forces which, according to Heraclitus, is the condition of life itself.

THE RESPONSIBILITY
OF WRITERS

Writers, Simone Weil insists, must be held morally accountable for their works. She believes that, no less than modern political and religious leaders, they have abandoned their sacred trust by failing to honor and preserve the idea of value. In the following letter she censures writers indifferent or even hostile to the eternal struggle between good and evil. In this indifference or hostility she sees an irresponsibility that leads to betrayal and to disaster.

The allusion by Gros to the controversy about the responsibility of writers impels me to return to the subject, in defense of a point of view opposed to that of the review and of almost everyone I sympathize with, and seeming, unfortunately, to resemble the one held by people for whom I feel no sympathy at all.

I believe in the responsibility of the writers of recent years for the disaster of our time. By that I don't mean only the defeat of France; the disaster of our time extends much further. It extends to the whole world, that is to say, to Europe, to America, and to the other continents in so far as Western influence has penetrated them.

It is true, as Mauriac has observed, that the best contemporary books are very little read. But the responsibility of writers cannot be measured by circulation figures. For literature has immense prestige.

This was shown by the efforts which used to be made by certain political bodies to obtain the support of well-known writers' names for demagogic purposes. And even those who have never heard the celebrated writers' names feel the prestige of the literature which is unknown to them. People have never read so much as today. They don't read books but they read mediocre or bad periodicals. These periodicals penetrate everywhere, in village and suburb; and, thanks to the literary customs of our time, there is no break of continuity between the worst of these periodicals and the best of our writers. This fact, which is known or, rather, confusedly felt by the public, endows the basest publicity rackets in their eyes with all the prestige of high literature. In recent years there have been some unbelievable degradations; for example, advice on love affairs by well-known writers. Of course they didn't all degrade themselves in this way; far from it. But those who did so degrade themselves were not disowned or repulsed by the others; they continued to enjoy the esteem accorded to their profession. Such easy morals in literature, such tolerance of baseness, involve our most eminent writers in responsibility for demoralizing little country girls who have never left their villages and have never heard the writers' names.

But writers have a more direct responsibility.

The essential characteristic of the first half of the twentieth century is the growing weakness, and almost the disappearance, of the idea of value. This is one of those rare phenomena which seem, as far as one can tell, to be really new in human history, though it may be, of course, that it has occurred before during periods which have since vanished in oblivion, as may also happen to our own period. It has appeared in many domains outside literature, and even in all of them. In industry, the substitution of quantity for quality; among the workers, the discrediting of skilled workmanship; among students, the substitution of diplomas for culture as the aim of education. Even in science there is no longer any criterion of value since classical science was discarded. But above all it was the writers who were the guardians of the treasure that has been lost; and some of them now take pride in having lost it.

Dadaism and surrealism are extreme cases; they represented the intoxication of total licence, the intoxication in which the mind wallows when it has made a clean sweep of value and surrendered to the immediate. The good is the pole towards which the human spirit is necessarily oriented, not only in action but in every effort, including the effort of pure intelligence. The surrealists have set up non-oriented thought as a model; they have chosen the total absence of value as their supreme value. Men have always been intoxicated by licence, which is why, throughout history, towns have been sacked. But there has not always been a literary equivalent for the sacking of towns. Surrealism is such an equivalent.

The other writers of the same and the preceding period have gone less far, but almost all of them—with perhaps three or four exceptions—have been more or less affected by the same disease, the enfeeblement of the sense of value. Such words as spontaneity, sincerity, gratuitousness, richness, enrichment—words which imply an almost total indifference to contrasts of value—have come more often from their pens than words which contain a reference to good and evil. Moreover, this latter class of words has become degraded, especially those which refer to the good, as Valéry remarked some years ago. Words like virtue, nobility, honour, honesty, generosity, have become almost impossible to use or else they have acquired bastard meanings; language is no longer equipped for legitimately praising a man's character. It is slightly, but only slightly, better equipped for praising a mind; the very word mind, and the words intelligence, intelligent, and others like them, have also become degraded. The fate of words is a touchstone of the progressive weakening of the idea of value, and although the fate of words does not depend upon writers one cannot help attributing a special responsibility to them, since words are their business.

The work of Bergson has been much and rightly praised in our day, and a lot has been said about its influence on the thought and literature of the period. Now, at the centre of the philosophy on which his first three books are based there is a conception which is totally alien to any considerations of value, namely, the conception of Life. The attempt to make this philosophy a foundation for Catholicism was very ill-judged, and in any case it was unnecessary because Catholicism has older foundations. And then there is the work of Proust, which makes many attempts to analyse non-oriented states of the soul; in his work the good only appears at those rare moments when, by the effect either of memory or of beauty, we are allowed a glimpse of eternity through the veil of time. One could make similar comments on many writers before and still more after 1914. In a general way, the literature of the twentieth century is essentially psychological; and psychology consists in describing states of the soul by displaying them all on the same plane without any discrimination of value, as though good and evil were external to them, as though the effort towards the good could be absent at any moment from the thought of any man.

Writers do not have to be professors of morals, but they do have to express the human condition. And nothing concerns human life so essentially, for every man at every moment, as good and evil. When literature becomes deliberately indifferent to the opposition of good and evil it betrays its function and forfeits all claim to excellence. Racine laughed at the Jansenists in his youth, but he was no longer laughing at them when he wrote *Phèdre*, and *Phèdre* is his masterpiece. From this point of view it is not true that French literature possesses continuity. It is not true that Rimbaud and those who have followed him (if we except certain passages of the *Saison en Enfer*) are a continuation of Villon. What if Villon did steal? In his case the act of stealing was perhaps the result of necessity or perhaps a sin; it was not a thrill or a gratuitous act. The sense of good and evil permeates all his verse, as its permeates all work that is not irrelevant to man's destiny.

It is true that there is a certain kind of morality which is even more alien to good and evil than amorality is. Those who are now blaming the eminent writers are worth infinitely less than they, and the 'moral revival' which certain people wish to impose would be much worse than the condition it is meant to cure. If our present suffering ever leads to a revival, this will not be brought about through slogans but in silence and moral loneliness, through pain, misery, and terror, in the profoundest depths of each man's spirit.

MORALITY
AND LITERATURE

In this essay Simone Weil defines her aesthetic with admirable forthrightness. She argues that immorality is inseparable from imaginative literature. Writers and readers will insist that immorality is not an aesthetic criterion. Rejecting such an insistence, in a passage that contains the kernel of her aesthetic perspective, she writes: "Every activity is related to good and evil twice over: by its performance and by its principle. Thus a book may on the one hand be well or badly written and on the other hand it may originate from good or from evil."

Nothing is so beautiful and wonderful, nothing is so continually fresh and surprising, so full of sweet and perpetual ecstasy, as the good. No desert is so dreary, monotonous, and boring as evil. This is the truth about authentic good and evil. With fictional good and evil it is the other way round. Fictional good is boring and flat, while fictional evil is varied and intriguing, attractive, profound, and full of charm.

This is because there are necessities and impossibilities in reality which do not obtain in fiction, any more than the law of gravity to which we are subject controls what is represented in a picture. In the space that separates heaven from earth things fall easily and indeed

290

inevitably whenever they are not supported; they never rise, or only a
very little and by painful contrivance. A man coming down a ladder,
who misses a step and falls, is either a sad or an uninteresting sight,
even the first time we see it. But if a man were walking in the sky as
though it were a ladder, going up into the clouds and coming down
again, he could do it every hour of every day and we would never be
tired of watching. It is the same with pure good; for a necessity as
strong as gravity condemns man to evil and forbids him any good, or
only within the narrowest limits and laboriously obtained and soiled
and adulterated with evil; except when the supernatural appears on
earth, which suspends the operation of terrestrial necessity. But if I
paint a picture of a man walking up into the air it has no interest.
That is a thing which is only interesting if it really happens. Unreality
takes away all value from the good.

A man walking in the ordinary way is a sight of no interest,
whereas men wildly jumping and leaping about would intrigue me for
a few minutes. But if I notice that both the one and the others are
going barefoot on red-hot coals my reactions change. The jumping
and leaping become frightful and unbearable to watch and, at the
same time, behind the horror, tedious and monotonous, whereas my
attention becomes passionately fixed upon the man who is walking
naturally. Thus it is that evil, so long as it is fictional, acquires interest
from the variety of forms it can assume, which then seem to spring
from pure fancy. But the necessity which is inseparable from reality
completely cancels this interest. The simplicity which makes the fictional good something insipid and unable to hold the attention becomes, in the real good, an unfathomable marvel.

It seems, therefore, that immorality is inseparable from literature,
which chiefly consists of the fictional. It is quite wrong to reproach
writers for being immoral unless one reproaches them at the same
time for being writers, as there were people in the seventeenth century with the courage to do. Writers with pretensions to high morality
are no less immoral than the others, they are merely worse writers. In
them as in the others, whatever they do and in spite of themselves,
good is tedious and evil is more or less attractive. One might, therefore, on these grounds, condemn the whole of literature *en bloc*. And
why not? Writers and devoted readers will cry out that immorality is

not an aesthetic criterion. But they must prove, as they have never done, that aesthetic criteria are the only ones applicable to literature. Since readers are not a separate animal species and since the people who read are the same ones who perform a great many other functions, it is impossible for literature to be exempted from the categories of good and evil to which all human activities are referred. Every activity is related to good and evil twice over: by its performance and by its principle. Thus a book may on the one hand be well or badly written and on the other hand it may originate either from good or from evil.

But it is not only in literature that fiction generates immorality. It does it also in life itself. For the substance of our life is almost exclusively composed of fiction. We fictionalize our future; and, unless we are heroically devoted to truth, we fictionalize our past, refashioning it to our taste. We do not study other people; we invent what they are thinking, saying, and doing. Reality provides us with some raw material, just as novelists often take a theme from a news item, but we envelop it in a fog in which, as in all fiction, values are reversed, so that evil is attractive and good is tedious. If reality administers a hard enough shock to awaken us for an instant, by contact with a saint, for example, or by falling into the world of destitution or crime, or some other such experience, it is then and only then that we feel for a moment the horrible monotony of evil and the unfathomable marvel of good. But we soon relapse into the waking dream peopled by our fictions.

There is something else which has the power to awaken us to the truth. It is the works of writers of genius, or at least of those with genius of the very first order and when it has reached its full maturity. They are outside the realm of fiction and they release us from it. They give us, in the guise of fiction, something equivalent to the actual density of the real, that density which life offers us every day but which we are unable to grasp because we are amusing ourselves with lies.

Although the works of these men are made out of words there is present in them the force of gravity which governs our souls. It is present and manifest. In our souls, although this gravity is often felt, it is disguised by the very effects it produces; submission to evil is always accompanied by error and falsehood. The man falling down the slope of cruelty or terror cannot discern what is the force that impels him nor the relations between it and all the other external conditions. In the words assembled by genius several slopes are simultaneously visible and perceptible, placed in their true relations, but the listener or reader does not descend any of them. He feels gravity in the way we feel it when we look over a precipice, if we are safe and not subject to vertigo. He perceives the unity and the diversity of its forms in this architecture of the abyss. It is in this way that in the *Iliad* the slope of victory and the slope of defeat are manifest and simultaneously perceptible, as they never are for a soldier occupied in fighting. This sense of gravity, which only genius can impart, is found in the drama of Aeschylus and Sophocles, in certain plays of Shakespeare, in Racine's *Phèdre* alone among French tragedies, in several comedies of Molière, in the *Grand Testament* of Villon. There, good and evil appear in their truth. Those poets had genius, and it was a genius oriented towards the good. There are also demoniacal geniuses; and they too have their maturity. But since the maturity of genius is conformity to the true relations of good and evil, the work which represents maturity of demoniacal genius is silence. Rimbaud is its example and symbol.

The sole *raison d'être* of all those writers who are not possessed by a genius of the very highest order in its full maturity is to constitute the milieu within which such a genius will one day appear. It is this function alone that justifies their existence, which ought otherwise to be prevented because of the immorality to which the nature of things condemns them. To reproach a writer for his immorality is to reproach him for having no genius, or only genius of the second order, if such an expression makes sense, or a still undeveloped genius. If he lacks genius it is not his fault, in a sense; but in another sense it is his one crime. It is completely vain to seek a remedy for the immorality of literature. The only remedy is genius, and the source of genius is beyond the scope of our efforts.

But what can and ought to be corrected, in view of this very fact of irremediable immorality, is the usurpation by writers of the function of spiritual guidance, for which they are totally unsuited. Only writers of the highest order of genius in their full maturity are fit to exercise those functions. As for all the other writers, unless they have a philosophic bent in addition to a literary one, which is rare, their conceptions about life and the world and their opinions on current problems can have no interest at all, and it is absurd that they should be called upon to express them. This abuse dates from the eighteenth century, and especially from romanticism, and it has introduced into literature a Messianic afflatus wholly detrimental to its artistic purity. Formerly, writers were domestics in great men's households, and although this position sometimes caused very painful situations it was much more favourable than the Messianic delusion, not only to the moral health of writers and public, but also to the art of literature itself.

It is only within the last fifty or twenty-five years that we have seen the gravest possible effects of this usurpation, because it is only since then that it has extended to the masses. No doubt there has always been a slight diffusion of bad literature, oral or written, among the people. But formerly it had an antidote in the things of pure beauty which impregnated popular life—religious ceremonies, prayer, song, story, and dance. And above all, it was without authority. But during the last quarter of a century all the authority associated with the function of spiritual guidance, usurped by men of letters, has seeped down into the lowest publications. Because from these publications up to the highest literary production there was continuity, and the public knew it. In the one milieu of literary men, in which no one ever refused to shake anyone else's hand, were to be found those who occupied themselves exclusively with the lowest publications, and their occasional collaborators, and also our greatest names. Between a poem by Valéry and an advertisement for a beauty cream promising a rich marriage to anyone who used it there was at no point a breach of continuity. So as a result of literature's spiritual usurpation a beauty cream advertisement possessed, in the eyes of little village girls, the authority that was formerly attached to the words of priests. Is it surprising that we should have sunk to where we now are? To have permitted that state of affairs is a crime for which all who can hold a pen should bear the responsibility as a remorse.

For centuries the function of director of conscience had been exclusively in the hands of priests. They often performed it atrociously badly, as witness the fires of the Inquisition, but at least they had some title to it. In reality it is only the greatest saints who can perform it, as it is only the greatest geniuses among writers. But all priests, in virtue of their profession, speak in the name of the saints and look to them for inspiration and try to imitate and follow them, and principally the one veritable saint, who is Christ. Or if they do not, as in fact often happens, they are failing in their duty. But in so far as they do it they are able to communicate more good than they themselves possess. A writer, on the other hand, has only himself to fall back on; he may be influenced by a number of other writers, but he cannot draw his inspiration from them.

When, as a result of what was called Enlightenment in the eighteenth century, the priests had in fact almost entirely lost this function of guidance, their place was taken by writers and scientists. In both cases it is equally absurd. Mathematics, physics, and biology are as remote from spiritual guidance as the art of arranging words. When that function is usurped by literature and science it proves that there is no longer any spiritual life. Numerous signs today seem to indicate that this usurpation by writers and scientists has come to an end, although the appearance of it still lingers. This should be a matter for rejoicing, were there not reason to fear that they will be replaced by something much worse than themselves.

But the works of authentic genius from past ages remain, and are available to us. Their contemplation is the ever-flowing source of an inspiration which may legitimately guide us. For this inspiration, if we know how to receive it, tends—as Plato said—to make us grow wings to overcome gravity.

SCIENTISM –
A REVIEW

Simone Weil wrote a number of essays on science. The following review is a cogent example of her understanding and clarity—and of that religious conception about human destiny that scientific thinkers so often neglect or scorn. Modern science, as she notes here, has lost all its rigidity but is paradoxically as narrow as ever. That scientism "is perfectly compatible with anti-nationalism, with anti-intellectualism, with surrealism—in fact with absolutely everything except what is authentically spiritual" is a charge that underlines an ongoing crisis.

This book is directed against what is known as scientism. Strictly speaking, there are two distinct types of scientism; the nineteenth-century type, represented by the lamentable trinity of Taine, Renan, and Berthelot, from which Bergson has helped to deliver us but which is still very much alive in the masses, among the successors of M. Homais and Bouvard and Pécuchet, and even among a great many decent people; and the scientism of today, which has lost all its rigidity but by a strange paradox is still as narrow as ever. It is perfectly compatible with anti-nationalism, with anti-intellectualism, with surrealism—in fact with absolutely everything except what is authentically spiritual. This is particularly the case in France, where there is a school of sociology which makes it possible to study myth and folklore and the civilizations of antiquity and of the coloured peoples without finding any trace of spirituality anywhere. The 1937 Exhibition, already so far away from us, was to some extent a manifestation of contemporary scientism; an extremely cultured man, high in the university hierarchy, seriously wished after visiting it that in every village in France the church might be replaced by a miniature Palace of Discovery.

As is well known, the collection *Présences* in which this book appears is of Catholic inspiration. It is fitting that Catholics should relegate the Palace of Discovery to its proper place in relation to the Church. They have been all too slow about it and are too much permeated by the very atmosphere they wish to dissipate; so strong is the spirit of the age in which one lives. Thus the Rev. Père Sertillanges, in an essay full of good sense, points out that no man of talent has ever been altogether a scientist, because the limitations of science are obvious. But he adds: 'Renan was right when he said: "The great reign of the spirit will only begin when the material world is entirely subject to man." And that is the task of science.' Very probably Father Sertillanges means no more than to say that the contemplative life demands leisure and that technology is one of the preconditions for leisure. But what he actually says is something quite different; and one is tempted to ask him whether the domination of the world by the human spirit was not the definition of the earthly Paradise and whether man's subjection to flesh and matter, which imposes work upon him among other burdens, did not begin at the moment when he became a sinner, and whether the effects of sin can be undone by anything except grace.

Daniel-Rops expounds once again, very clearly and ably, the ideas formerly diffused by the group of 'Ordre Nouveau'. They are simple. Present-day techniques are tending to reduce to almost nothing the part played by human labour in the production of manufactured articles, and in doing so they equally reduce the profit on capital and the value of mass-produced goods. Let us encourage this development; let us abolish all manual labour except for a short spell of civic duty imposed on the entire population; let the production of necessary goods be socialized and the products be distributed free. People will employ their leisure freely in qualified work which will still be regulated by the law of supply and demand. In this sketch of the future Daniel-Rops employs verbs in the future tense, just like any Marxist. A Moslem would warn him of the imprudence of using the future tense without adding 'insh' Allah', 'if God wills'. If passion played so small a part in social organization as this scheme presupposes, it would be possible to obtain an equitable system even with poorly developed techniques. The members of 'Ordre Nouveau', an extremely sympathetic group, forget that in all human affairs the problem of incentive is vital, is as important as fuel for a motor. And yet they ought to have learnt this when they tried to organize a model of voluntary civilian service, and failed. They failed because there was nothing to give people an incentive to follow them. A people subjected to a short period of compulsory unpaid labour will not really work except under pressure from a despotic central power and under the threat of severe punishments, unless other truly effective stimulants can be discovered; and for this a real effort of discovery is needed. And as for the long years of leisure, one must be naïve, especially today, not to reflect that some people would devote them to the one sport which really inflames men, the sport whose objective is the domination of others; having once taken up this sport it is not easy to drop it, and, since it calls for unlimited resources, in armaments and other things, the period of compulsory labour would soon be prolonged to a whole life-time. Daniel-Rops, yielding unconsciously to the prestige of Marxism although it forms part of the scientism which he is combating, believes that wars are the result of economic maladjustments; but the economic maladjustments are primarily the result of that will to power of which war is one of the aspects. These problems call for the closest examination because, if Daniel-Rops' hopes are in fact illusory, these illusions are extremely dangerous at the present time.

André Thérive contributes some amusing pages on the different kinds of scientific romance, from Cyrano de Bergerac to Huxley. Pierre Devaux gives a panorama of past and future inventions, of great value as regards the past. Raymond Charmet, writing on what he calls 'the modern myth of science', gives a number of quotations among which several are pearls of pure idiocy; this, for example, from J. Perrin in his introduction to *Atoms*: 'The conquest of Destiny seems to authorise at last an unbounded Hope'.

Naturally, the most interesting essay in the book is Louis de Broglie's. It is compact, clear, perfectly precise, and every word is instructive. In a general way, the comparison between contemporary scientists, so far as one can judge them from their more popular writings, and thinkers like Lavoisier, Lagrange, Ampère, not to mention Galileo and Archimedes, is profoundly depressing; but a scientist like Louis de Broglie brings some consolation.

And yet what he says about philosophy is of a naïveté which is typically contemporary. All of what he believes to be the contributions of science to philosophy are illusory, in the sense that what he takes to be new is not new. It is true that quantum mechanics finally delivered philosophy from the fashionable scientism of the nineteenth century; but with a little intelligence philosophers could have delivered themselves without the help of quanta.

It was suspected before the appearance of quanta that there is not only continuity in the universe but also discontinuity; the Pythagoreans, for example, already in their day attached importance to numbers. The notion of qualitative change has always implied certain actions 'impossible to represent within our usual spatio-temporal frame'. It is only a physicist who can speak of 'the apparent determinism of the macroscopic scale'; on the scale of our senses there is no appearance of determinism except in the laboratory. Ask a meteorologist or a peasant if they see much determinism in storms or rain; look at the sea, and say if the shapes of the waves appear to reveal a very rigorous necessity! The truth is that nineteenth-century physicists believed there were no more things in heaven and earth than in their laboratory—and indeed in their laboratory only at the moment when an experiment succeeded. Their excuse was their professional obsession but those who shared their belief without that excuse were fools. Physicists today have lost that illusion; so much the better, but they are wrong to think that this means they are contributing something new. Determinism, says M. de Broglie, can no longer be maintained except as a 'metaphysical postulate'. But it was never anything else for a man of any intelligence. It was nothing else for Lucretius.

Quantum mechanics has also cleared up a confusion about the very important conception of the 'negligible' which, once again, the slightest critical effort would have sufficed to clear up equally well. One neglects in fact what is very small compared to the object of one's research. Physicists have tried to make negligible by right what they have treated as negligible in fact, by assimilating it to the infinitely small of mathematics. The smoother a metal surface is, the more slowly the speed decreases of a ball rolling horizontally across it. I cannot make the metal surface as smooth as I would like, but having procured the smoothest available I can imagine that in twenty years' time smoother ones will be produced. In mathematics, the further I carry the series 1.9999 etc., the less the quantity obtained differs from 2; and for this reason I say that 1.999 . . . 9 is equal to 2, and by analogy I say also that a ball rolls on a smooth surface at a uniform speed. But there is in reality a great difference between the two limiting cases. The quantity which mathematicians call infinitely small can be diminished at any moment, by calculation, exactly as much as may be desired; but the quantity which physicists call negligible cannot be diminished at the present moment any further than present technical resources permit, and to diminish it further requires a technical progress which cannot at this moment be taken as certain. So there cannot be an infinitely small in physics. This fact is obvious, but it had been forgotten and quantum mechanics compelled its recognition.

It has recently been perceived that the processes of observing and measuring exert an action upon the phenomena observed, so that it is impossible to know a phenomenon as it would be if we were not observing it. This obvious truth has always been known, but it was thought that the interfering action could be indefinitely diminished through the improvement of experimental technique, and in this way it was assimilated *de jure* to the infinitely small. Today, however, it is postulated in quantum mechanics, rightly or wrongly, that there is an insuperable limit to technical progress in accuracy; which means that there is a source of error which cannot be reduced. But even if the limit imposed today by quantum mechanics were some day to be surpassed it would still remain true that observation disturbs the phenomenon observed, and that the disturbance is not infinitesimal.

M. de Broglie points to a new philosophical idea invented by physicists, or rather by a physicist, M. Niels Bohr. This has been called 'complementarity' by M. Bohr and he gives as examples of it the 'wave' aspect and the 'corpuscle' aspect of matter, and the vital aspect and the physico-chemical aspect in the description of living beings. The nearer we approach to precision in regard to one of these aspects, the further from it we get in regard to the complementary aspect, and reciprocally.

This complementarity is nothing other than the old correlation of contraries which is basic in the thought of Heraclitus and Plato. From the philosophical point of view it has no novelty, but that does not make it the less interesting, because nothing is so interesting in philosophy as a recent discovery of an eternal idea. From the scientific point of view, however, it has great novelty, because from the Renaissance onwards an attempt has been made to impose unity upon the whole of science. This was a mad ambition, and today it has become necessary to introduce the correlation of contraries. A fortunate necessity, because no human thought is valid unless it recognizes this relation. But it is a difficult relation to handle properly, and if scientists want to begin to make use of it they will need a serious philosophical grounding. Heraclitus, Plato, and Kant could instruct them, but not any contemporary authors.

The progress of science, on the other hand, can bring nothing new to philosophy; and this for two reasons. First, science cannot be anything for the philosopher except matter for reflection. The philosopher can find something to learn from scientists, as he can from blacksmiths, painters, or poets; but not more, and above all not in a different way. But the main reason is that there is not, strictly speaking, the possibility of anything new in philosophy. When a man introduces a new thought into philosophy it can hardly be anything except a new accent upon some thought which is not only eternal by right but ancient in fact. Novelties of this kind, which are infinitely valuable, are the result only of long meditation by a great mind. But, as for novelties in the ordinary sense of the word, there are none. Philosophy does not progress nor evolve; and philosophers are uncomfortable today, for they must either betray their vocation or be out of fashion. The fashion today is to progress, to evolve. It is indeed something even more compulsive than a fashion. If the great public were aware that philosophy is not susceptible to progress, there would no doubt be resentment at its getting any public funds. To find a place in the budget for the eternal is not in the spirit of our age. So the majority of philosophers keep quiet about that eternity which is their privilege. And that is why, when we find that the ideas of Louis de Broglie about the contributions of science to philosophy are not worthy of a mind like his, it is not him that we should blame but the philosophers whom he has happened to meet.

In any case, this book is a source of encouragement. It shows that even today it is still possible to reflect, and to publish books which stimulate reflection.

FREEDOM OF
OPINION

"There has been a lot of freedom of thought over the past few years, but no thought." This sentence hints at some of the reasons behind "Freedom of Opinion." Here, Simone Weil shows her irritation with writers who claim and exercise the role of directors of conscience and yet seek to escape any moral accountability. The puritanical austerity (and, to some, absurdity) of her suggestions for dealing with those who play this "double game" will hardly endear her to ideologues of enlightenment.

Freedom of opinion and freedom of association are usually classed together. It is a mistake. Save in the case of natural groupings, association is not a need, but an expedient employed in the practical affairs of life.

On the other hand, complete, unlimited freedom of expression for every sort of opinion, without the least restriction or reserve, is an absolute need on the part of the intelligence. It follows from this that it is a need of the soul, for when the intelligence is ill-at-ease the whole soul is sick. The nature and limits of the satisfaction corresponding to this need are inscribed in the very structure of the various faculties of the soul. For the same thing can be at once limited and unlimited, just as one can produce the length of a rectangle indefinitely without it ceasing to be limited in width.

In the case of a human being, the intelligence can be exercised in three ways. It can work on technical problems, that is to say, discover means to achieve an already given objective. It can provide light when a choice lies before the will concerning the path to be followed. Finally, it can operate alone, separately from the other faculties, in a purely theoretical speculation where all question of action has been provisionally set aside.

When the soul is in a healthy condition, it is exercised in these three ways in turn, with different degrees of freedom. In the first function, it acts as a servant. In the second function, it acts destructively and requires to be reduced to silence immediately it begins to supply arguments to that part of the soul which, in the case of any one not in a state of perfection, always places itself on the side of evil. But when it operates alone and separately, it must be in possession of sovereign liberty; otherwise something essential is wanting to the human being.

The same applies in a healthy society. That is why it would be desirable to create an absolutely free reserve in the field of publication, but in such a way as for it to be understood that the works found therein did not pledge their authors in any way and contained no direct advice for readers. There it would be possible to find, set out in their full force, all the arguments in favor of bad causes. It would be an excellent and salutary thing for them to be so displayed. Anybody could there sing the praises of what he most condemns. It would be publicly recognized that the object of such works was not to define their authors' attitudes vis-à-vis the problems of life, but to contribute, by preliminary researches, toward a complete and correct tabulation of data concerning each problem. The law would see to it that their publication did not involve any risk of whatever kind for the author.

On the other hand, publications destined to influence what is called opinion, that is to say, in effect, the conduct of life, constitute acts and ought to be subjected to the same restrictions as are all acts. In other words, they should not cause unlawful harm of any kind to any human being, and above all, should never contain any denial, explicit or implicit, of the eternal obligations toward the human being, once these obligations have been solemnly recognized by law.

The distinction between the two fields, the one which is outside action and the one which forms part of action, is impossible to express on paper in juridical terminology. But that doesn't prevent it from being a perfectly clear one. The separate existence of these two fields is not difficult to establish in fact, if only the will to do so is sufficiently strong.

It is obvious, for example, that the entire daily and weekly press comes within the second field; reviews also, for they all constitute, individually, a focus of radiation in regard to a particular way of thinking; only those that were to renounce this function would be able to lay claim to total liberty.

The same applies to literature. It would solve the argument which arose not long ago on the subject of literature and morals, and which was clouded over by the fact that all the talented people, through professional solidarity, were found on one side, and only fools and cowards on the other.

But the attitude of the fools and cowards was none the less, to a large extent, consistent with the demands of reason. Writers have an outrageous habit of playing a double game. Never so much as in our age have they claimed the role of directors of conscience and exercised it. Actually, during the years immediately preceding the war, no one challenged their right to it except the savants. The position formerly occupied by priests in the moral life of the country was held by physicists and novelists, which is sufficient to gauge the value of our progress. But if somebody called upon writers to render an account of the orientation set by their influence, they barricaded themselves indignantly behind the sacred privilege of art for art's sake.

There is not the least doubt, for example, that André Gide has always known that books like the *Nourritures Terrestres* and the *Caves du Vatican* have exercised an influence on the practical conduct of life of hundreds of young people, and he has been proud of the fact. There is, then, no reason for placing such books behind the inviolable barrier of art for art's sake, and sending to prison a young fellow who pushes somebody off a train in motion. One might just as well claim the privileges of art for art's sake in support of crime. At one time the Surrealists came pretty close to doing so. All that has been repeated by so many idiots *ad nauseam* about the responsibility of our writers in the defeat of France in 1940 is, unfortunately, only too true.

If a writer, thanks to the complete freedom of expression accorded to pure intelligence, publishes written matter that goes contrary to the moral principles recognized by law, and if later on he becomes a notorious focus of influence, it is simple enough to ask him if he is prepared to state publicly that his writings do not express his personal attitude. If he is not prepared to do so, it is simple enough to punish him. If he lies, it is simple enough to discredit him. Moreover, it ought to be recognized that the moment a writer fills a role among the influences directing public opinion, he cannot claim to exercise unlimited freedom. Here again, a juridical definition is impossible; but the facts are not really difficult to discern. There is no reason at all why the sovereignty of the law should be limited to the field of what can be expressed in legal formulas, since that sovereignty is exercised just as well by judgments in equity.

Besides, the need of freedom itself, so essential to the intellect, calls for a corresponding protection against suggestion, propaganda, influence by means of obsession. These are methods of constraint, a special kind of constraint, not accompanied by fear or physical distress, but which is none the less a form of violence. Modern technique places extremely potent instruments at its service. This constraint is, by its very nature, collective, and human souls are its victims.

Naturally, the State is guilty of crime if it makes use of such methods itself, save in cases where the public safety is absolutely at stake. But it should, furthermore, prevent their use. Publicity, for example, should be rigorously controlled by law and its volume very considerably reduced; it should also be severely prohibited from ever dealing with subjects which belong to the domain of thought.

Likewise, repression could be exercised against the press, radio broadcasts, or anything else of a similar kind, not only for offenses against moral principles publicly recognized, but also for baseness of tone and thought, bad taste, vulgarity, or a subtly corrupting moral atmosphere. This sort of repression could take place without in any way infringing on freedom of opinion. For instance, a newspaper could be suppressed without the members of its editorial staff losing the right to go on publishing wherever they liked, or even, in the less serious cases, remain associated to carry on the same paper under another name. Only, it would have been publicly branded with infamy and would run the risk of being so again. Freedom of opinion can be claimed solely—and even then with certain reservations —by the journalist, not by the paper; for it is only the journalist who is capable of forming an opinion.

Generally speaking, all problems to do with freedom of expression are clarified if it is posited that this freedom is a need of the intelligence, and that intelligence resides solely in the human being, individually considered. There is no such thing as a collective exercise of the intelligence. It follows that no group can legitimately claim freedom of expression, because no group has the slightest need of it.

In fact the opposite applies. Protection of freedom of thought requires that no group should be permitted by law to express an opinion. For when a group starts having opinions, it inevitably tends to impose them on its members. Sooner or later, these individuals find themselves debarred, with a greater or lesser degree of severity, and on a number of problems of greater or lesser importance, from expressing opinions opposed to those of the group, unless they care to leave it. But a break with any group to which one belongs always involves suffering—at any rate of a sentimental kind. And just as danger, exposure to suffering are healthy and necessary elements in the sphere of action, so are they unhealthy influences in the exercise of the intelligence. A fear, even a passing one, always provokes either a weakening or a tautening, depending on the degree of courage, and that is all that is required to damage the extremely delicate and fragile instrument of precision that constitutes our intelligence. Even friendship is, from this point of view, a great danger. The intelligence is defeated as soon as the expression of one's thoughts is preceded, explicitly or implicitly, by the little word "we." And when the light of the intelligence grows dim, it is not very long before the love of good becomes lost.

The immediate, practical solution would be the abolition of political parties. Party strife, as it existed under the Third Republic, is intolerable. The single party, which is, moreover, its inevitable outcome, is the worst evil of all. The only remaining possibility is a public life without parties. Nowadays, such an idea strikes us as a novel and daring proposition. All the better, since something novel is what is wanted. But, in point of fact, it is only going back to the tradition of 1789. In the eyes of the people of 1789, there was literally no other possibility. A public life like ours has been over the course of the last half century would have seemed to them a hideous nightmare. They would never have believed it possible that a representative of the people should so divest himself of all personal dignity as to allow himself to become the docile member of a party.

Moreover, Rousseau had clearly demonstrated how party strife automatically destroys the Republic. He had foretold its effects. It would be a good thing just now to encourage the reading of the *Contrat Social*. Actually, at the present time, wherever there were political parties, democracy is dead. We all know that the parties in England have a certain tradition, spirit, and function making it impossible to compare them to anything else. We all know, besides, that the rival teams in the United States are not political parties. A democracy where public life is made up of strife between political parties is incapable of preventing the formation of a party whose avowed aim is the overthrow of that democracy. If such a democracy brings in discriminatory laws, it cuts its own throat. If it doesn't, it is just as safe as a little bird in front of a snake.

A distinction ought to be drawn between two sorts of associations: those concerned with interests, where organization and discipline would be countenanced up to a certain point, and those concerned with ideas, where such things would be strictly forbidden. Under present conditions, it is a good thing to allow people to group themselves together to defend their interests, in other words, their wage receipts and so forth, and to leave these associations to act within very narrow limits and under the constant supervision of the authorities. But such associations should not be allowed to have anything to do with ideas. Associations in which ideas are being canvassed should be not so much associations as more or less fluid social mediums. When some action is contemplated within them, there is no reason why it need be put into execution by any person other than those who approve of it.

In the working-class movement, for example, such a distinction would put an end to the present inextricable confusion. In the period before the war, the workingman's attention was being continually pulled in three directions at once. In the first place, by the struggle for higher wages; secondly, by what remained—growing ever feebler, but still showing some signs of life—of the old trade-union spirit of former days, idealist and more or less libertarian in character; and, lastly, by the political parties. Very often, when a strike was on, the workmen who struggled and suffered would have been quite incapable of deciding for themselves whether it was all a matter of wages, a revival of the old trade-union spirit, or a political maneuver conducted by a party; and nobody looking on from the outside was in any better position to judge.

That is an impossible state of affairs. When the war broke out, the French trade-unions were dead or moribund, in spite of their millions of members—or because of them. They again took on some semblance of life, after a prolonged lethargy, when the Resistance against the invader got under way. That doesn't prove that they are viable. It is perfectly clear that they had been all but destroyed by two sorts of poison, each of which by itself is deadly.

Trade-unions cannot flourish if at their meetings the workmen are obsessed by their earnings to the same extent as they are in the factory, when engaged in piecework. To begin with, because the result is that sort of moral death always brought about by an obsession in regard to money. Next, because the trade-union, having become, under present social conditions, a factor continually acting upon the economic life of the country, ends up inevitably by being transformed into a single, compulsory, professional organization, obliged to toe the line in public affairs. It has then been changed into the semblance of a corpse.

Besides, it is no less evident that trade-unions cannot live in intimate contact with political parties. There is something resulting from the normal play of mechanical forces that makes such a thing quite impossible. For an analogous reason, moreover, the Socialist party cannot live side by side with the Communist party, because the latter's party character is, as it were, marked to a so much greater degree.

Furthermore, the obsession about wages strengthens Communist influence, because questions to do with money, however closely they may affect the majority of men, produce at the same time in all men a sensation of such deadly boredom that it requires to be compensated by the apocalyptic prospect of the Revolution, according to Communist tenets. If the middle classes haven't the same need of an apocalypse, it is because long rows of figures have a poetry, a prestige which tempers in some sort the boredom associated with money; whereas, when money is counted in sixpences, we have boredom in its pure, unadulterated state. Nevertheless, that taste shown by bourgeois, both great and small, for Fascism, indicates that, in spite of everything, they too can feel bored.

Under the Vichy Government single and compulsory professional organizations for workmen have been created. It is a pity that they have been given, according to the modern fashion, the name of corporation, which denotes, in reality, something so very different and so beautiful. But it is a good thing that such dead organizations should be there to take over the dead part of trade-union activity. It would be dangerous to do away with them. It is far better to charge them with the day-to-day business of dealing with wages and what are called immediate demands. As for the political parties, if they were all strictly prohibited in a general atmosphere of liberty, it is to be hoped their underground existence would at any rate be made difficult for them.

In that event, the workmen's trade-unions, if they still retain a spark of any real life, could become again, little by little, the expression of working-class thought, the instrument of working-class integrity. According to the traditions of the French working-class movement, which has always looked upon itself as responsible for the whole world, they would concern themselves with everything to do with justice—including, where necessary, questions about wages; but only at long intervals and to rescue human beings from poverty.

Naturally, they would have to be able to exert an influence on professional organizations, according to methods of procedure defined by law.

There would, perhaps, only be advantages to be gained by making it illegal for professional organizations to launch a strike, and allowing trade-unions—with certain restrictions—to do so, while at the same time attaching risks to this responsibility, prohibiting any sort of coercion, and safeguarding the continuity of economic life.

As for the lockout, there is no reason why it should not be entirely suppressed.

The authorized existence of associations for promoting ideas could be subject to two conditions. First, that excommunication may not be applied. Recruitment would be voluntary and as a result of personal affinity, without, however, making anybody liable to be invited to subscribe to a collection of assertions crystallized in written form. But once a member had been admitted, he could not be expelled except for some breach of integrity or undermining activities; which latter offense would, moreover, imply the existence of an illegal organization, and consequently expose the offender to a more severe punishment.

This would, in fact, amount to a measure of public safety, experience having shown that totalitarian states are set up by totalitarian parties, and that these totalitarian parties are formed by dint of expulsions for the crime of having an opinion of one's own.

The second condition could be that ideas must really be put into circulation, and tangible proof of such circulation given in the shape of pamphlets, reviews, or typed bulletins in which problems of general interest were discussed. Too great a uniformity of opinion would render any such association suspect.

For the rest, all associations for promoting ideas would be authorized to act according as they thought fit, on condition that they didn't break the law or exert any sort of disciplinary pressure on their members.

As regards associations for promoting interests, their control would, in the first place, involve the making of a distinction, namely, that the word "interest" sometimes expresses a need and at other times something quite different. In the case of a poor workingman, interest means food, lodging, and heating. For an employer, it means something of a different kind. When the word is taken in its first sense, the action of the authorities should be mainly to stimulate, uphold, and defend the interests concerned. When used in its second sense, the action of the authorities should be continually to supervise, limit,

and, whenever possible, curb the activities of the associations representing such interests. It goes without saying that the severest restrictions and the hardest punishments should be reserved for those
which are, by their nature, the most powerful.

What has been called freedom of association has been, in fact, up
to now, freedom for associations. But associations have not got to be
free; they are instruments, they must be held in bondage. Only
the human being is fit to be free.

As regards freedom of thought, it is very nearly true to say that
without freedom there *is* no thought. But it is truer still to say that
when thought is nonexistent, it is nonfree into the bargain. There has
been a lot of freedom of thought over the past few years, but no
thought. Rather like the case of a child who, not having any meat,
asks for salt with which to season it.

HUMAN
PERSONALITY

This definitive essay covers the entire range of Simone Weil's thought, as the title on her own manuscript clearly suggests: "Collectivity. Person. Impersonal. Right. Justice." It has also been accurately translated under the title "Beyond Personalism." Critical of any attainment that is a manifestation of personality, she emphasizes that the highest things are impersonal and anonymous. These point to a great spiritual transformation, whereby the personality transcends the world of sin and error and becomes part of the realm of the sacred. This should be the goal of all artists (and nonartists). Only then does the supernatural virtue of humility become a spiritual reality.

'You do not interest me.' No man can say these words to another without committing a cruelty and offending against justice.

'Your person does not interest me.' These words can be used in an affectionate conversation between close friends, without jarring upon even the tenderest nerve of their friendship.

In the same way, one can say without degrading oneself, 'My person does not count', but not 'I do not count'.

This proves that something is amiss with the vocabulary of the

modern trend of thought known as Personalism. And in this domain,
where there is a grave error of vocabulary it is almost certainly the
sign of a grave error of thought.

There is something sacred in every man, but it is not his person.
Nor yet is it the human personality. It is this man; no more and no
less.

I see a passer-by in the street. He has long arms, blue eyes,
and a mind whose thoughts I do not know, but perhaps they are
commonplace.

It is neither his person, nor the human personality in him, which
is sacred to me. It is he. The whole of him. The arms, the eyes, the
thoughts, everything. Not without infinite scruple would I touch
anything of this.

If it were the human personality in him that was sacred to me,
I could easily put out his eyes. As a blind man he would be exactly
as much a human personality as before. I should have destroyed
nothing but his eyes.

It is impossible to define what is meant by respect for human
personality. It is not just that it cannot be defined in words. That
can be said of many perfectly clear ideas. But this one cannot be
conceived either; it cannot be defined nor isolated by the silent operation of the mind.

To set up as a standard of public morality a notion which can
neither be defined nor conceived is to open the door to every kind
of tyranny.

The notion of rights, which was launched into the world in
1789, has proved unable, because of its intrinsic inadequacy, to fulfil
the role assigned to it.

To combine two inadequate notions, by talking about the rights
of human personality, will not bring us any further.

What is it, exactly, that prevents me from putting that man's
eyes out if I am allowed to do so and if it takes my fancy?

Although it is the whole of him that is sacred to me, he is not
sacred in all respects and from every point of view. He is not
sacred in as much as he happens to have long arms, blue eyes, or
possibly commonplace thoughts. Nor as a duke, if he is one; nor as a
dustman, if that is what he is. Nothing of all this would stay my hand.

What would stay it is the knowledge that if someone were to put out his eyes, his soul would be lacerated by the thought that harm was being done to him.

At the bottom of the heart of every human being, from earliest infancy until the tomb, there is something that goes on indomitably expecting, in the teeth of all experience of crimes committed, suffered, and witnessed, that good and not evil will be done to him. It is this above all that is sacred in every human being.

The good is the only source of the sacred. There is nothing sacred except the good and what pertains to it.

This profound and childlike and unchanging expectation of good in the heart is not what is involved when we agitate for our rights. The motive which prompts a little boy to watch jealously to see if his brother has a slightly larger piece of cake arises from a much more superficial level of the soul. The word justice means two very different things according to whether it refers to the one or the other level. It is only the former one that matters.

Every time that there arises from the depths of a human heart the childish cry which Christ himself could not restrain, 'Why am I being hurt?', then there is certainly injustice. For if, as often happens, it is only the result of a misunderstanding, then the injustice consists in the inadequacy of the explanation.

Those people who inflict the blows which provoke this cry are prompted by different motives according to temperament or occasion. There are some people who get a positive pleasure from the cry; and many others simply do not hear it. For it is a silent cry, which sounds only in the secret heart.

These two states of mind are closer than they appear to be. The second is only a weaker mode of the first; its deafness is complacently cultivated because it is agreeable and it offers a positive satisfaction of its own. There are no other restraints upon our will than material necessity and the existence of other human beings around us. Any imaginary extension of these limits is seductive, so there is a seduction in whatever helps us to forget the reality of the obstacles. That is why upheavals like war and civil war are so intoxicating; they empty human lives of their reality and seem to turn people into puppets. That is also why slavery is so pleasant to the masters.

In those who have suffered too many blows, in slaves for example, that place in the heart from which the infliction of evil evokes
a cry of surprise may seem to be dead. But it is never quite dead;
it is simply unable to cry out any more. It has sunk into a state of
dumb and ceaseless lamentation.

And even in those who still have the power to cry out, the cry
hardly ever expresses itself, either inwardly or outwardly, in coherent
language. Usually, the words through which it seeks expression are
quite irrelevant.

That is all the more inevitable because those who most often
have occasion to feel that evil is being done to them are those who
are least trained in the art of speech. Nothing, for example, is more
frightful than to see some poor wretch in the police court stammering
before a magistrate who keeps up an elegant flow of witticisms.

Apart from the intelligence, the only human faculty which has
an interest in public freedom of expression is that point in the heart
which cries out against evil. But as it cannot express itself, freedom
is of little use to it. What is first needed is a system of public education capable of providing it, so far as possible, with means of expression; and next, a régime in which the public freedom of expression is characterized not so much by freedom as by an attentive
silence in which this faint and inept cry can make itself heard; and
finally, institutions are needed of a sort which will, so far as possible,
put power into the hands of men who are able and anxious to hear
and understand it.

Clearly, a political party busily seeking, or maintaining itself in,
power can discern nothing in these cries except a noise. Its reaction
will be different according to whether the noise interferes with or contributes to that of its own propaganda. But it can never be capable
of the tender and sensitive attention which is needed to understand
its meaning.

The same is true to a lesser degree of organizations contaminated by party influences; in other words, when public life is dominated by a party system, it is true of all organizations, including,
for example, trade unions and even churches.

Naturally, too, parties and similar organizations are equally insensitive to intellectual scruples.

So when freedom of expression means in fact no more than freedom of propaganda for organizations of this kind, there is in fact no free expression for the only parts of the human soul that deserve it. Or if there is any, it is infinitesimal; hardly more than in a totalitarian system.

And this is how it is in a democracy where the party system controls the distribution of power; which is what we call democracy in France, for up to now we have known no other. We must therefore invent something different.

Applying the same criterion in the same way to any public institution we can reach equally obvious conclusions.

It is not the person which provides this criterion. When the infliction of evil provokes a cry of sorrowful surprise from the depth of the soul, it is not a personal thing. Injury to the personality and its desires is not sufficient to evoke it, but only and always the sense of contact with injustice through pain. It is always, in the last of men as in Christ himself, an impersonal protest.

There are also many cries of personal protests, but they are unimportant; you may provoke as many of them as you wish without violating anything sacred.

So far from its being his person, what is sacred in a human being is the impersonal in him.

Everything which is impersonal in man is sacred, and nothing else.

In our days, when writers and scientists have so oddly usurped the place of priests, the public acknowledges, with a totally unjustified docility, that the artistic and scientific faculties are sacred. This is generally held to be self-evident, though it is very far from being so. If any reason is felt to be called for, people allege that the free play of these faculties is one of the highest manifestations of the human personality.

Often it is, indeed, no more than that. In which case it is easy to see how much it is worth and what can be expected from it.

One of its results is the sort of attitude which is summed up in Blake's horrible saying: 'Sooner murder an infant in its cradle than nurse unacted desires', or the attitude which breeds the idea of the 'gratuitous act.' Another result is a science in which every possible standard, criterion, and value is recognized except truth.

Gregorian chant, Romanesque architecture, the *Iliad*, the invention of geometry were not, for the people through whom they were brought into being and made available to us, occasions for the manifestation of personality.

When science, art, literature, and philosophy are simply the manifestation of personality they are on a level where glorious and dazzling achievements are possible, which can make a man's name live for thousands of years. But above this level, far above, separated by an abyss, is the level where the highest things are achieved. These things are essentially anonymous.

It is pure chance whether the names of those who reach this level are preserved or lost; even when they are remembered they have become anonymous. Their personality has vanished.

Truth and beauty dwell on this level of the impersonal and the anonymous. This is the realm of the sacred; on the other level nothing is sacred, except in the sense that we might say this of a touch of colour in a picture if it represented the Eucharist.

What is sacred in science is truth; what is sacred in art is beauty. Truth and beauty are impersonal. All this is too obvious.

If a child is doing a sum and does it wrong, the mistake bears the stamp of his personality. If he does the sum exactly right, his personality does not enter into it at all.

Perfection is impersonal. Our personality is the part of us which belongs to error and sin. The whole effort of the mystic has always been to become such that there is no part left in his soul to say 'I'.

But the part of the soul which says 'We' is infinitely more dangerous still.

Impersonality is only reached by the practice of a form of attention which is rare in itself and impossible except in solitude; and not only physical but mental solitude. This is never achieved by a man who thinks of himself as a member of a collectivity, as part of something which says 'We'.

Men as parts of a collectivity are debarred from even the lower forms of the impersonal. A group of human beings cannot even add two and two. Working out a sum takes place in a mind temporarily oblivious of the existence of any other minds.

Although the personal and the impersonal are opposed, there is a way from the one to the other. But there is no way from the collective to the impersonal. A collectivity must dissolve into separate persons before the impersonal can be reached.

This is the only sense in which the person has more of the sacred than the collectivity.

The collectivity is not only alien to the sacred, but it deludes us with a false imitation of it.

Idolatry is the name of the error which attributes a sacred character to the collectivity; and it is the commonest of crimes, at all times, at all places. The man for whom the development of personality is all that counts has totally lost all sense of the sacred; and it is hard to know which of these errors is the worst. They are often found combined, in various proportions, in the same mind. But the second error is much less powerful and enduring than the first.

Spiritually, the struggle between Germany and France in 1940 was in the main not a struggle between barbarism and civilization or between evil and good, but between the first of these two errors and the second. The victory of the former is not surprising; it is by nature the stronger.

There is nothing scandalous in the subordination of the person to the collectivity; it is a mechanical fact of the same order as the inferiority of a gram to a kilogram on the scales. The person is in fact always subordinate to the collectivity, even in its so-called free expression.

For example, it is precisely those artists and writers who are most inclined to think of their art as the manifestation of their personality who are in fact the most in bondage to public taste. Hugo had no difficulty in reconciling the cult of the self with his role of 'resounding echo'; and examples like Wilde, Gide, and the Surrealists are even more obvious. Scientists of the same class are equally enslaved by fashion, which rules over science even more despotically than over the shape of hats. For these men the collective opinion of specialists is practically a dictatorship.

The person, being subordinate to the collective both in fact and by the nature of things, enjoys no natural rights which can be appealed to on its behalf.

It is said, quite correctly, that in antiquity there existed no notion of respect for the person. The ancients thought far too clearly to entertain such a confused idea.

The human being can only escape from the collective by raising himself above the personal and entering into the impersonal. The moment he does this, there is something in him, a small portion of his soul, upon which nothing of the collective can get a hold. If he can root himself in the impersonal good so as to be able to draw energy from it, then he is in a condition, whenever he feels the obligation to do so, to bring to bear without any outside help, against any collectivity, a small but real force.

There are occasions when an almost infinitesimal force can be decisive. A collectivity is much stronger than a single man; but every collectivity depends for its existence upon operations, of which simple addition is the elementary example, which can only be performed by a mind in a state of solitude.

This dependence suggests a method of giving the impersonal a hold on the collective, if only we could find out how to use it.

Every man who has once touched the level of the impersonal is charged with a responsibility towards all human beings: to safeguard, not their persons, but whatever frail potentialities are hidden within them for passing over to the impersonal.

It is primarily to these men that the appeal to respect the sacredness of the human being should be addressed. For such an appeal can have no reality unless it is addressed to someone capable of understanding it.

It is useless to explain to a collectivity that there is something in each of the units composing it which it ought not to violate. To begin with, a collectivity is not someone, except by a fiction; it has only an abstract existence and can only be spoken to fictitiously. And, moreover, if it were someone it would be someone who was not disposed to respect anything except himself.

Further, the chief danger does not lie in the collectivity's tendency to immolate himself in the collective. Or perhaps the first danger is only a superficial and deceptive aspect of the second.

Just as it is useless to tell the collectivity that the person is sacred, it is also useless to tell the person so. The person cannot believe it. It does not feel sacred. The reason that prevents the person from feeling sacred is that actually it is not.

If there are some people who feel differently, who feel something sacred in their own persons and believe they can generalize and attribute it to every person, they are under a double illusion.

What they feel is not the authentic sense of the sacred but its false imitation engendered by the collective; and if they feel it in respect of their own person it is because it participates in collective prestige through the social consideration bestowed upon it.

So they are mistaken in thinking they can generalize from their own case. Their motive is generous, but it cannot have enough force to make them really see the mass of people as anything but mere anonymous human matter. But it is hard for them to find this out, because they have no contact with the mass of people.

The person in man is a thing in distress; it feels cold and is always looking for a warm shelter.

But those in whom it is, in fact or in expectation, warmly wrapped in social consideration are unaware of this.

That is why it was not in popular circles that the philosophy of personalism originated and developed, but among writers, for whom it is part of their profession to have or hope to acquire a name and a reputation.

Relations between the collectivity and the person should be arranged with the sole purpose of removing whatever is detrimental to the growth and mysterious germination of the impersonal element in the soul.

This means, on the one hand, that for every person there should be enough room, enough freedom to plan the use of one's time, the opportunity to reach ever higher levels of attention, some solitude, some silence. At the same time the person needs warmth, lest it be driven by distress to submerge itself in the collective.

If this is the good, then modern societies, even democratic ones, seem to go about as far as it is possible to go in the direction of evil. In particular, a modern factory reaches perhaps almost the limit of horror. Everybody in it is constantly harassed and kept on edge by the interference of extraneous wills while the soul is left in cold and desolate misery. What man needs is silence and warmth; what he is given is an icy pandemonium.

Physical labour may be painful, but it is not degrading as such. It is not art; it is not science; it is something else, possessing an exactly equal value with art and science, for it provides an equal opportunity to reach the impersonal stage of attention.

To take a youth who has a vocation for this kind of work and employ him at a conveyor-belt or as a piece-work machinist is no less a crime than to put out the eyes of the young Watteau and make him turn a grindstone. But the painter's vocation can be discerned and the other cannot.

Exactly to the same extent as art and science, though in a different way, physical labour is a certain contact with the reality, the truth, and the beauty of this universe and with the eternal wisdom which is the order in it.

For this reason it is sacrilege to degrade labour in exactly the same sense that it is sacrilege to trample upon the Eucharist.

If the workers felt this, if they felt that by being the victim they are in a certain sense the accomplice of sacrilege, their resistance would have a very different force from what is provided by the consideration of personal rights. It would not be an economic demand but an impulse from the depth of their being, fierce and desperate like that of a young girl who is being forced into a brothel; and at the same time it would be a cry of hope from the depth of their heart.

This feeling, which surely enough exists in them, is so inarticulate as to be indiscernible even to themselves; and it is not the professionals of speech who can express it for them.

Usually, when addressing them on their conditions, the selected topic is wages; and for men burdened with a fatigue that makes any effort of attention painful it is a relief to contemplate the unproblematic clarity of figures.

In this way, they forget that the subject of the bargain, which they complain they are being forced to sell cheap and for less than the just price, is nothing other than their soul.

Suppose the devil were bargaining for the soul of some poor wretch and someone, moved by pity, should step in and say to the devil: 'It is a shame for you to bid so low; the commodity is worth at least twice as much.'

Such is the sinister farce which has been played by the working-class movement, its trade unions, its political parties, its leftist intellectuals.

This bargaining spirit was already implicit in the notion of rights which the men of 1789 so unwisely made the keynote of their deliberate challenge to the world. By so doing, they ensured its inefficacy in advance.

The notion of rights is linked with the notion of sharing out, of exchange, of measured quantity. It has a commercial flavour, essentially evocative of legal claims and arguments. Rights are always asserted in a tone of contention; and when this tone is adopted, it must rely upon force in the background, or else it will be laughed at.

There is a number of other notions, all in the same category, which are themselves entirely alien to the supernatural but nevertheless a little superior to brute force. All of them relate to the behaviour of the collective animal, to use Plato's language, while it still exhibits a few traces of the training imposed on it by the supernatural working of grace. If they are not continually revived by a renewal of this working, if they are merely survivals of it, they become necessarily subject to the animal's caprice.

To this category belong the notion of rights, and of personality, and of democracy. As Bernanos had the courage to point out, democracy offers no defence against dictatorship. By the nature of things, the person is subdued to the collectivity, and rights are dependent upon force. The lies and misconceptions which obscure this truth are extremely dangerous because they prevent us from appealing to the only thing which is immune to force and can preserve us from it: namely, that other force which is the radiance of the spirit. It is only in plants, by virtue of the sun's energy caught up by the green leaves and operating in the sap, that inert matter can find its way upward against the law of gravity. A plant deprived of light is gradually but inexorably overcome by gravity and death.

Among the lies in question is the eighteenth-century materialists'
notion of natural right. We do not owe this to Rousseau, whose lucid
and powerful spirit was of genuinely Christian inspiration, but to
Diderot and the Encyclopedists.

It was from Rome that we inherited the notion of rights, and
like everything that comes from ancient Rome, who is the woman
full of the names of blasphemy in the Apocalypse, it is pagan and un-
baptizable. The Romans, like Hitler, understood that power is not
fully efficacious unless clothed in a few ideas, and to this end they
made use of the idea of rights, which is admirably suited to it.
Modern Germany has been accused of flouting the idea; but she
invoked it *ad nauseam* in her role of deprived, proletarian nation.
It is true, of course, that she allows only one right to her victims:
obedience. Ancient Rome did the same.

It is singularly monstrous that ancient Rome should be praised
for having bequeathed to us the notion of rights. If we examine
Roman law in its cradle, to see what species it belongs to, we discover that property was defined by the *jus utendi et abutendi*. And
in fact the things which the property owner had the right to use or
abuse at will were for the most part human beings.

The Greeks had no conception of rights. They had no words
to express it. They were content with the name of justice.

It is extraordinary that Antigone's unwritten law should have
been confused with the idea of natural right. In Creon's eyes there
was absolutely nothing that was natural in Antigone's behaviour. He
thought she was mad.

And we should be the last people to disagree with him; we
who at this moment are thinking, talking, and behaving exactly as he
did. One has only to consult the text.

Antigone says to Creon: 'It was not Zeus who published that
edict; it was not Justice, companion of the gods in the other world,
who set such laws among men.' Creon tries to convince her that his
orders were just; he accuses her of having outraged one of her
brothers by honouring the other; so that the same honour has been
paid to the impious and the loyal, to the one who died in the attempt
to destroy his own country and the one who died defending it.

She answers: 'Nevertheless the other world demands equal laws.'

To which he sensibly objects: 'There can be no equal sharing between a brave man and a traitor', and she has only the absurd reply:
'Who knows whether this holds in the other world?'

Creon's comment is perfectly reasonable: 'A foe is never a friend,
not even in death.' And the little simpleton can only reply: 'I was
born to share, not hate, but love.'

To which Creon, ever more reasonable: 'Pass, then, to the other
world, and if thou must love, love those who dwell there.'

And, truly, this was the right place for her. For the unwritten
law which this little girl obeyed had nothing whatsoever in common
with rights, or with the natural; it was the same love, extreme and
absurd, which led Christ to the Cross.

It was Justice, companion of the gods in the other world, who
dictated this surfeit of love, and not any right at all. Rights have
no direct connexion with love.

Just as the notion of rights is alien to the Greek mind, so also
it is alien to the Christian inspiration whenever it is pure and un-
contaminated by the Roman, Hebraic, or Aristotelian heritage. One
cannot imagine St. Francis of Assisi talking about rights.

If you say to someone who has ears to hear: 'What you are
doing to me is not just', you may touch and awaken at its source
the spirit of attention and love. But it is not the same with words
like 'I have the right . . .' or 'you have no right to . . .' They evoke
a latent war and awaken the spirit of contention. To place the notion
of rights at the centre of social conflicts is to inhibit any possible
impulse of charity on both sides.

Relying almost exclusively on this notion, it becomes impossible
to keep one's eyes on the real problem. If someone tries to brow-
beat a farmer to sell his eggs at a moderate price, the farmer can
say: 'I have the right to keep my eggs if I don't get a good enough
price.' But if a young girl is being forced into a brothel she will
not talk about her rights. In such a situation the word would sound
ludicrously inadequate.

Thus it is that the social drama, which corresponds to the latter
situation, is falsely assimilated, by the use of the word 'rights', to the
former one.

Thanks to this word, what should have been a cry of protest

from the depth of the heart has been turned into a shrill nagging of claims and counter-claims, which is both impure and unpractical.

The notion of rights, by its very mediocrity, leads on naturally to that of the person, for rights are related to personal things. They are on that level.

It is much worse still if the word 'personal' is added to the word 'rights', thus implying the rights of the personality to what is called full expression. In that case the tone that colours the cry of the oppressed would be even meaner than bargaining. It would be the tone of envy.

For the full expression of personality depends upon its being inflated by social prestige; it is a social privilege. No one mentions this to the masses when haranguing them about personal rights. They are told the opposite; and their minds have not enough analytic power to perceive this truth clearly for themselves. But they feel it; their everyday experience makes them certain of it.

However, this is not a reason for them to reject the slogan. To the dimmed understanding of our age there seems nothing odd in claiming an equal share of privilege for everybody—an equal share in things whose essence is privilege. The claim is both absurd and base; absurd because privilege is, by definition, inequality; and base because it is not worth claiming.

But the category of men who formulate claims, and everything else, the men who have the monopoly of language, is a category of privileged people. They are not the ones to say that privilege is unworthy to be desired. They don't think so and, in any case, it would be indecent for them to say it.

Many indispensable truths, which could save men, go unspoken for reasons of this kind; those who could utter them cannot formulate them and those who could formulate them cannot utter them. If politics were taken seriously, finding a remedy for this would be one of its more urgent problems.

In an unstable society the privileged have a bad conscience. Some of them hide it behind a defiant air and say to the masses: 'It is quite appropriate that I should possess privileges which you are denied.'

Others benevolently profess: 'I claim for all of you an equal share in the privileges I enjoy.'

The first attitude is odious. The second is silly, and also too easy.

Both of them equally encourage the people down the road of evil, away from their true and unique good, which they do not possess, but to which, in a sense, they are so close. They are far closer than those who bestow pity on them to an authentic good, which could be a source of beauty and truth and joy and fulfilment. But since they have not reached it and do not know how to, this good might as well be infinitely far away. Those who speak for the people and to them are incapable of understanding either their distress or what an overflowing good is almost within their reach. And, for the people, it is indispensable to be understood.

Affliction is by its nature inarticulate. The afflicted silently beseech to be given the words to express themselves. There are times when they are given none; but there are also times when they are given words, but ill-chosen ones, because those who choose them know nothing of the affliction they would interpret.

Usually, they are far removed from it by the circumstances of their life; but even if they are in close contact with it or have recently experienced it themselves, they are still remote from it because they put it at a distance at the first possible moment.

Thought revolts from contemplating affliction, to the same degree that living flesh recoils from death. A stag advancing voluntarily step by step to offer itself to the teeth of a pack of hounds is about as probable as an act of attention directed towards a real affliction, which is close at hand, on the part of a mind which is free to avoid it.

But that which is indispensable to the good and is impossible naturally is always possible supernaturally.

Supernatural good is not a sort of supplement to natural good, as we are told, with support from Aristotle, for our greater comfort. It would be nice if this were true, but it is not. In all the crucial problems of human existence the only choice is between supernatural good on the one hand and evil on the other.

To put into the mouth of the afflicted words from the vocabulary of middle values, such as democracy, rights, personality, is to
offer them something which can bring them no good and will inevitably do them much harm.

These notions do not dwell in heaven; they hang in the middle
air, and for this very reason they cannot root themselves in earth.

It is the light falling continually from heaven which alone gives
a tree the energy to send powerful roots deep into the earth. The tree
is really rooted in the sky.

It is only what comes from heaven that can make a real impress
on the earth.

In order to provide an armour for the afflicted, one must put
into their mouths only those words whose rightful abode is in heaven,
beyond heaven, in the other world. There is no fear of its being
impossible. Affliction disposes the soul to welcome and avidly drink
in everything which comes from there. For these products it is not
consumers but producers who are in short supply.

The test for suitable words is easily recognized and applied.
The afflicted are overwhelmed with evil and starving for good. The
only words suitable for them are those which express nothing but
good, in its pure state. It is easy to discriminate. Words which can be
associated with something signifying an evil are alien to pure good.
We are criticizing a man when we say: 'He puts his person forward';
therefore the person is alien to good. We can speak of an abuse of
democracy; therefore democracy is alien to good. To possess a right
implies the possibility for making good or bad use of it; therefore
rights are alien to good. On the other hand, it is always and everywhere good to fulfil an obligation. Truth, beauty, justice, compassion are always and everywhere good.

For the aspirations of the afflicted, if we wish to be sure of using
the right words, all that is necessary is to confine ourselves to those
words and phrases which always, everywhere, in all circumstances
express only the good.

This is one of the only two services which can be rendered to
the afflicted with words. The other is to find the words which express the truth of their affliction, the words which can give reso-

nance, through the crust of external circumstances, to the cry which is always inaudible: 'Why am I being hurt?'

For this, they cannot count upon men of talent, personality, celebrity, or even genius in the sense in which the word is usually employed, which assimilates it to talent. They can count only upon men of the very highest genius: the poet of the *Iliad*, Aeschylus, Sophocles, Shakespeare as he was when he wrote *Lear*, or Racine when he wrote *Phèdre*. There are not very many of them.

But there are many human beings only poorly or moderately endowed by nature, who seem infinitely inferior not merely to Homer, Aeschylus, Sophocles, Shakespeare, and Racine but also to Virgil, Corneille, and Hugo, but who nevertheless inhabit the realm of impersonal good where the latter poets never set foot.

A village idiot in the literal sense of the word, if he really loves truth, is infinitely superior to Aristotle in his thought, even though he never utters anything but inarticulate murmurs. He is infinitely closer to Plato than Aristotle ever was. He has genius, while only the word talent applies to Aristotle. If a fairy offered to change his destiny for one resembling Aristotle's he would be wise to refuse unhesitatingly. But he does not know this. And nobody tells him. Everybody tells him the contrary. But he must be told. Idiots, men without talent, men whose talent is average or only a little more, must be encouraged if they possess genius. We need not be afraid of making them proud, because love of truth is always accompanied by humility. Real genius is nothing else but the supernatural virtue of humility in the domain of thought.

What is needed is to cherish the growth of genius, with a warm and tender respect, and not, as the men of 1789 proposed, to encourage the flowering of talents. For it is only heroes of real purity, the saints and geniuses, who can help the afflicted. But the help is obstructed by a screen which is formed between the two by the men of talent, intelligence, energy, character, or strong personality. The screen must not be damaged, but put aside as gently and imperceptibly as possible. The far more dangerous screen of the collective must be broken by abolishing every part of our institutions and customs which harbours the party spirit in any form whatsoever.

Neither a personality nor a party is ever responsive either to truth or to affliction.

There is a natural alliance between truth and affliction, because both of them are mute suppliants, eternally condemned to stand speechless in our presence.

Just as a vagrant accused of stealing a carrot from a field stands before a comfortably seated judge who keeps up an elegant flow of queries, comments, and witticisms while the accused is unable to stammer a word, so truth stands before an intelligence which is concerned with the elegant manipulation of opinions.

It is always language that formulates opinions, even when there are no words spoken. The natural faculty called intelligence is concerned with opinion and language. Language expresses relations; but it expresses only a few, because its operation needs time. When it is confused and vague, without precision or order, when the speaker or listener is deficient in the power of holding a thought in his mind, then language is empty or almost empty of any real relational content. When it is perfectly clear, precise, rigorous, ordered, when it is addressed to a mind which is capable of keeping a thought present while it adds another to it and of keeping them both present while it adds a third, and so on, then in such a case language can hold a fairly rich content of relations. But like all wealth, this relative wealth is abject poverty compared with the perfection which alone is desirable.

At the very best, a mind enclosed in language is in prison. It is limited to the number of relations which words can make simultaneously present to it; and remains in ignorance of thoughts which involve the combination of a greater number. These thoughts are outside language, they are unformulatable, although they are perfectly rigorous and clear and although every one of the relations they involve is capable of precise expression in words. So the mind moves in a closed space of partial truth, which may be larger or smaller, without ever being able so much as to glance at what is outside.

If a captive mind is unaware of being in prison, it is living in error. If it has recognized the fact, even for the tenth of a second, and then quickly forgotten it in order to avoid suffering, it is living in falsehood. Men of the most brilliant intelligence can be born, live, and die in error and falsehood. In them, intelligence is neither a good, nor even an asset. The difference between more or less intelligent men is like the difference between criminals condemned to life imprisonment in smaller or larger cells. The intelligent man who is proud of his intelligence is like a condemned man who is proud of his large cell.

A man whose mind feels that it is captive would prefer to blind himself to the fact. But if he hates falsehood, he will not do so; and in that case he will have to suffer a lot. He will beat his head against the wall until he faints. He will come to again and look with terror at the wall, until one day he begins afresh to beat his head against it; and once again he will faint. And so on endlessly and without hope. One day he will wake up on the other side of the wall.

Perhaps he is still in a prison, although a larger one. No matter. He has found the key; he knows the secret which breaks down every wall. He has passed beyond what men call intelligence, into the beginning of wisdom.

The mind which is enclosed within language can possess only opinions. The mind which has learned to grasp thoughts which are inexpressible because of the number of relations they combine, although they are more rigorous and clearer than anything that can be expressed in the most precise language, such a mind has reached the point where it already dwells in truth. It possesses certainty and unclouded faith. And it matters little whether its original intelligence was great or small, whether its prison cell was narrow or wide. All that matters is that it has come to the end of its intelligence, such as it was, and has passed beyond it. A village idiot is as close to truth as a child prodigy. The one and the other are separated from it only by a wall. But the only way into truth is through one's own annihilation; through dwelling a long time in a state of extreme and total humiliation.

It is the same barrier which keeps us from understanding affliction. Just as truth is a different thing from opinion, so affliction is a different thing from suffering. Affliction is a device for pulverizing the soul; the man who falls into it is like a workman who gets caught up in a machine. He is no longer a man but a torn and bloody rag on the teeth of a cog-wheel.

The degree and type of suffering which constitutes affliction in the strict sense of the word varies greatly with different people. It depends chiefly upon the amount of vitality they start with and upon their attitude towards suffering.

Human thought is unable to acknowledge the reality of affliction. To acknowledge the reality of affliction means saying to oneself: 'I may lose at any moment, through the play of circumstances over which I have no control, anything whatsoever that I possess, including those things which are so intimately mine that I consider them as being myself. There is nothing that I might not lose. It could happen at any moment that what I am might be abolished and replaced by anything whatsoever of the filthiest and most contemptible sort.'

To be aware of this in the depth of one's soul is to experience non-being. It is the state of extreme and total humiliation which is also the condition for passing over into truth. It is a death of the soul. This is why the naked spectacle of affliction makes the soul shudder as the flesh shudders at the proximity of death.

We think piously of the dead when we evoke them in memory, or when we walk among graves, or when we see them decently laid out on a bed. But the sight of corpses lying about as on a battle-field can sometimes be both sinister and grotesque. It arouses horror. At the stark sight of death, the flesh recoils.

When affliction is seen vaguely from a distance, either physical or mental, so that it can be confused with simple suffering, it inspires in generous souls a tender feeling of pity. But if by chance it is suddenly revealed to them in all its nakedness as a corrosive force, a mutilation or leprosy of the soul, then people shiver and recoil. The afflicted themselves feel the same shock of horror at their own condition.

To listen to someone is to put oneself in his place while he is speaking. To put oneself in the place of someone whose soul is corroded by affliction, or in near danger of it, is to annihilate oneself. It is more difficult than suicide would be for a happy child. Therefore the afflicted are not listened to. They are like someone whose tongue has been cut out and who occasionally forgets the fact. When they move their lips no ear perceives any sound. And they themselves soon sink into impotence in the use of language, because of the certainty of not being heard.

That is why there is no hope for the vagrant as he stands before the magistrate. Even if, through his stammerings, he should utter a cry to pierce the soul, neither the magistrate nor the public will hear it. His cry is mute. And the afflicted are nearly always equally deaf to one another; and each of them, constrained by the general indifference, strives by means of self-delusion or forgetfulness to become deaf to his own self.

Only by the supernatural working of grace can a soul pass through its own annihilation to the place where alone it can get the sort of attention which can attend to truth and to affliction. It is the same attention which listens to both of them. The name of this intense, pure, disinterested, gratuitous, generous attention is love.

Because affliction and truth need the same kind of attention before they can be heard, the spirit of justice and the spirit of truth is nothing else but a certain kind of attention, which is pure love.

Thanks to an eternal and providential decree, everything produced by a man in every sphere, when he is ruled by the spirit of justice and truth, is endowed with the radiance of beauty.

Beauty is the supreme mystery of this world. It is a gleam which attracts the attention and yet does nothing to sustain it. Beauty always promises, but never gives anything; it stimulates hunger but has no nourishment for the part of the soul which looks in this world for sustenance. It feeds only the part of the soul that gazes. While exciting desire, it makes clear that there is nothing in it to be desired, because the one thing we want is that it should not change. If one does not seek means to evade the exquisite anguish it inflicts, then desire is gradually transformed into love; and one begins to acquire the faculty of pure and disinterested attention.

In proportion to the hideousness of affliction is the supreme beauty of its true representation. Even in recent times one can point to *Phèdre*, *L'École des femmes*, *Lear*, and the poems of Villon; but far better examples are the plays of Aeschylus and Sophocles, and far better still, the *Iliad*, the book of Job and certain folk poems; and far beyond these again are the accounts of the Passion in the

Gospels. The radiance of beauty illumines affliction with the light of the spirit of justice and love, which is the only light by which human thought can confront affliction and report the truth of it.

And it sometimes happens that a fragment of inexpressible truth is reflected in words which, although they cannot hold the truth that inspired them, have nevertheless so perfect a formal correspondence with it that every mind seeking that truth finds support in them. Whenever this happens a gleam of beauty illumines the words.

Everything which originates from pure love is lit with the radiance of beauty.

Beauty can be perceived, though very dimly and mixed with many false substitutes, within the cell where all human thought is at first imprisoned. And upon her rest all the hopes of truth and justice, with tongue cut out. She, too, has no language; she does not speak; she says nothing. But she has a voice to cry out. She cries out and points to truth and justice who are dumb, like a dog who barks to bring people to his master lying unconscious in the snow.

Justice, truth, and beauty are sisters and comrades. With three such beautiful words we have no need to look for any others.

Justice consists in seeing that no harm is done to men. Whenever a man cries inwardly: 'Why am I being hurt?' harm is being done to him. He is often mistaken when he tries to define the harm, and why and by whom it is being inflicted on him. But the cry itself is infallible.

The other cry, which we hear so often: 'Why has somebody else got more than I have?', refers to rights. We must learn to distinguish between the two cries and to do all that is possible, as gently as possible, to hush the second one, with the help of a code of justice, regular tribunals, and the police. Minds capable of solving problems of this kind can be formed in a law school.

But the cry 'Why am I being hurt?' raises quite different problems, for which the spirit of truth, justice, and love is indispensable.

In every soul the cry to be delivered from evil is incessant. The Lord's Prayer addresses it to God. But God has power to deliver from evil only the eternal part of the soul of those who have made real and direct contact with him. The rest of the soul, and the entire soul of whoever has not received the grace of real and direct contact with God, is at the mercy of men's caprice and the hazards of circumstance.

Therefore it is for men to see that men are preserved from harm.

When harm is done to a man, real evil enters into him; not merely pain and suffering, but the actual horror of evil. Just as men have the power of transmitting good to one another, so they have the power to transmit evil. One may transmit evil to a human being by flattering him or giving him comforts and pleasures; but most often men transmit evil to other men by doing them harm.

Nevertheless, eternal wisdom does not abandon the soul entirely to the mercy of chance and men's caprice. The harm inflicted on a man by a wound from outside sharpens his thirst for the good and thus there automatically arises the possibility of a cure. If the wound is deep, the thirst is for good in its purest form. The part of the soul which cries 'Why am I being hurt?' is on the deepest level and even in the most corrupt of men it remains from earliest infancy perfectly intact and totally innocent.

To maintain justice and preserve men from all harm means first of all to prevent harm being done to them. For those to whom harm has been done, it means to efface the material consequences by putting them in a place where the wound, if it is not too deep, may be cured naturally by a spell of well-being. But for those in whom the wound is a laceration of the soul it means further, and above all, to offer them good in its purest form to assuage their thirst.

Sometimes it may be necessary to inflict harm in order to stimulate this thirst before assuaging it, and that is what punishment is for. Men who are so estranged from the good that they seek to spread evil everywhere can only be reintegrated with the good by having harm inflicted upon them. This must be done until the completely innocent part of their soul awakens with the surprised cry 'Why am I being hurt?' The innocent part of the criminal's soul must then be fed to make it grow until it becomes able to judge and condemn his past crimes and at last, by the help of grace, to forgive them. With this the punishment is completed; the criminal has been reintegrated with the good and should be publicly and solemnly reintegrated with society.

That is what punishment is. Even capital punishment, although it excludes reintegration with society in the literal sense, should be the same thing. Punishment is solely a method of procuring pure good for men who do not desire it. The art of punishing is the art of awakening in a criminal, by pain or even death, the desire for pure good.

But we have lost all idea of what punishment is. We are not aware that its purpose is to procure good for a man. For us it stops short with the infliction of harm. That is why there is one, and only one, thing in modern society more hideous than crime—namely, repressive justice.

To make the idea of repressive justice the main motive of war or revolt is inconceivably dangerous. It is necessary to use fear as a deterrent against the criminal activity of cowards; but that repressive justice, as we ignorantly conceive it today, should be made the motive of heroes is appalling.

All talk of chastisement, punishment, retribution, or punitive justice nowadays always refers solely to the basest kind of revenge.

The treasure of suffering and violent death, which Christ chose for himself and which he so often offers to those he loves, means so little to us that we throw it to those whom we least esteem, knowing that they will make nothing of it and having no intention of helping them to discover its value.

For criminals, true punishment; for those whom affliction has bitten deep into the soul, such help as may bring them to quench their thirst at the supernatural springs; for everyone else, some well-being, a great deal of beauty, and protection from those who would harm him; in every sphere, a strict curb upon the chatter of lies, propaganda, and opinion, and the encouragement of a silence in which truth can germinate and grow; this is what is due to men.

To ensure that they get it, we can only count upon those who have passed beyond a certain barrier, and it may be objected that they are too few in number. Probably there are not many of them, but they are no object for statistics, because most of them are hidden. Pure good from heaven only reaches the earth in imperceptible quantities, whether in the individual soul or in society. The grain of mustard seed is 'the least of all seeds'. Persephone ate only one grain of the pomegranate. A pearl buried deep in a field is not visible; neither is the yeast in dough.

But just as the catalysts of bacteria, such as yeast, operate by their mere presence in chemical reactions, so in human affairs the invisible seed of pure good is decisive when it is put in the right place.

How is it to be put there?

Much could be done by those whose function it is to advise the public what to praise, what to admire, what to hope and strive and seek for. It would be a great advance if even a few of these makers of opinion were to resolve in their hearts to eschew absolutely and without exception everything that is not pure good, perfection, truth, justice, love.

It would be an even greater advance if the majority of those who possess today some fragments of spiritual authority were aware of their obligation never to hold up for human aspiration anything but the real good in its perfect purity.

By the power of words we always mean their power of illusion and error. But, thanks to a providential arrangement, there are certain words which possess, in themselves, when properly used, a virtue which illumines and lifts up towards the good. These are the words which refer to an absolute perfection which we cannot conceive. Since the proper use of these words involves not trying to make them fit any conception, it is in the words themselves, as words, that the power to enlighten and draw upward resides. What they express is beyond our conception.

God and *truth* are such words; also *justice, love,* and *good*.

It is dangerous to use words of this kind. They are like an ordeal. To use them legitimately one must avoid referring them to anything humanly conceivable and at the same time one must associate with them ideas and actions which are derived solely and directly from the light which they shed. Otherwise, everyone quickly recognizes them for lies.

They are uncomfortable companions. Words like *right, democracy* and *person* are more accommodating and are therefore naturally preferred by even the best intentioned of those who assume public functions. Public functions have no other meaning except the possibility of doing good to men, and those who assume them with good intentions do in fact want to procure good for their contemporaries; but they usually make the mistake of thinking they can begin by getting it at bargain prices.

Words of the middle region, such as *right, democracy, person,* are valid in their own region, which is that of ordinary institutions. But for the sustaining inspiration of which all institutions are, as it were, the projection, a different language is needed.

The subordination of the person to the collectivity is in the nature of things, like the inferiority of a gram to a kilogram on the scales. But there can be a scales on which the gram outweighs the kilogram. It is only necessary for one arm to be more than a thousand times as long as the other. The law of equilibrium easily overcomes an inequality of weight. But the lesser will never outweigh the greater unless the relation between them is regulated by the law of equilibrium.

In the same way, there is no guarantee for democracy, or for the protection of the person against the collectivity, without a disposition of public life relating it to the higher good which is impersonal and unrelated to any political form.

It is true that the word person is often applied to God. But in the passage where Christ offers God himself as an example to men of the perfection which they are told to achieve, he uses not only the image of a person but also, above all, that of an impersonal order: 'That ye may be like the children of your Father which is in heaven; for he maketh his sun to rise on the evil and on the good, and sendeth rain on the just and on the unjust.'

Justice, truth, and beauty are the image in our world of this impersonal and divine order of the universe. Nothing inferior to them is worthy to be the inspiration of men who accept the fact of death.

Above those institutions which are concerned with protecting rights and persons and democratic freedoms, others must be invented for the purpose of exposing and abolishing everything in contemporary life which buries the soul under injustice, lies, and ugliness.

They must be invented, for they are unknown, and it is impossible to doubt that they are indispensable.

IV

CRITERIA OF WISDOM

The sin against the Spirit consists of knowing a thing to be good and hating it because it is good.

How does one pass from critical intelligence into the beginning of wisdom? This is a question that Simone Weil never stops asking. Nor does she hesitate to provide hints and suggestions challenging both believer and unbeliever. Hers is not the mere voice of a religious apologist. What distinguishes her writings and thought is an interiorizing spiritual strength, which is equally distinguished by manifest qualities of certainty and of judgment. In some ways she is a tantalizing propagandist who, using all her powers of strategy, of tact and tactic, knows that she must engage anyone willing to listen to her. She can be likened to a religious artist who strives to trap and bribe one's attention. ("All art is propaganda," writes the charismatic English sculptor, engraver, and essayist Eric Gill, "for it is in fact impossible to do anything, to make anything, which is not expressive of 'value.'") She knows that she is playing for the highest of stakes, the fate of the value of the soul. One finds in the tone of her appeal the inevitable traits (and habits) of a dedicated didactician. If on occasion she seems unreasonable in her demands and relentless in her judgments, for she is always driving towards a perfect Christianity,

343

she at the same time conveys complete sincerity. This sincerity has
the final virtue of redemption. Simone Weil, speaking of and to herself,
speaks of and to others. Her writings are dialogues with her soul
and with those of other men and women. Her inner life contains the
outer world. A mystic without a church, she knows that there are
countless others who share her affliction. She also knows that affliction
is by its very nature inarticulate. "Thought revolts from contemplating affliction, to the same degree that living flesh recoils from death."
To this affliction she seeks to lend a contemplative voice. This
voice must be convincing if it is to be believed. And belief must
have substance since it must seek to satisfy a test, a principle, a rule,
a canon, or a standard by which value is valued. One's spiritual life,
in both its limitation and its possibility, must be continuously judged;
and the spiritual life continuously posits criteria. In her writings
Simone Weil provides criteria for contemplation.

Criteria of themselves are never adequate. They need refining,
metastasizing, so as to take on that added dimension which mere intellectual fact and fate preclude. A really positive understanding of
criteria must lead to an internalizing transformation of life and faith.
Wisdom is the revealed spiritual zenith of this transformation. It is part
of, a reflex of, the divine and as such is always alive. Wisdom is
not only the world-thought, it is God. It is God and Man, for it is
Christ, as one theologian predicates. For Simone Weil this signifies divine wisdom. The faculty of judging attains its spiritualization
in wisdom. Wisdom transforms criteria by turning them from a finite
towards an infinite direction. It has precisely those powers of transcendence that, in her spiritual vocabulary, distinguish gravity from
grace. Gravity is the evil which drags down and cloys the human
soul; it can be both an oppressive and a repressive force. Grace is the
opposing force of good which makes possible the release and ascent
of the soul. When criteria lose sight of wisdom it is the pull of
gravity that predominates. Human experience is in a state of crisis
as these two forces remain in perpetual contention. The human condition is ever in the throes of descent and yet at the edge of ascent.
When grasped in their full meaning and fatefulness, spiritual criteria
enable one to measure his perilous situation, and specifically what

existentialists term the limit-situation. Wisdom is cognition, profound insight into the meaning and tasks of life. It is the revelation of and the main emanation from God, a radiation of his eternal light, a half-celestial, half-terrestrial being, a mediatrix between God and man, to use an apocryphal image. Acquiring wisdom is no easy job for the catechumen. Criteria, Simone Weil believes, stipulate the recognition of value precedent to the realization of God. "Earthly things are the criterion of spiritual things. This is what we generally don't want to recognize, because we are frightened of a criterion."

Connect: this is her unceasing admonition. Separations can become links. Breaks can be healed. Barriers can be surmounted. Distances can be overcome. Streams can be crossed. She writes: "The essence of created things is to be intermediaries. They are intermediaries leading from one to the other, and there is no end to this. They are intermediaries leading to God. We have to experience them as such." The connection—the intermediary—that she sees existing between criteria and wisdom is one that defies division and produces spiritual unity. Once man accepts the meaning of this connection he is able to see what hitherto he has not seen; he is capable of understanding the true relationship of things. The criteria of wisdom can serve as doorways to the eternal, but only at that point where interconnection is made. "To re-establish order is to undo the creature in us." "We have to be nothing in order to be in our right place in the whole." "Belief in the existence of other human beings as such is *love*." Knowledge such as this is the revelation of wisdom. In learning something about ourselves, she is saying, we begin to approach the divine. In wisdom, then, beginning and ending harmonize. "It is a fault to wish to be understood before we have made ourselves clear to ourselves." The *sophia* of Christian Hellenism informs in the most decisive ways her ideas of making connection between the secular and the sacred. Her otherworldliness is rarely without a sense of that same refining proportion which she appeals to when she writes: "Proportion can be defined as the combination of equality with inequality, and everywhere throughout the universe it is the sole factor making for balance." The criteria of wisdom that recur in her "thorny creed," as it has been described, serve as qualitative guidelines to matters of life and faith. The goal is understanding that crystallizes into purgation. Simone Weil carefully, strictly, plotted her criteria in the light of wisdom. Wisdom is the final criterion, its consummation.

Her criteria of wisdom point the way towards one's spiritual development. They have a quintessentially active goal: life's acquisition of virtues, which become links to God himself. Friendship, of which she writes in the best tradition of Hellenism, is for her one of the greatest paradigms of virtue. Her essay of the same title is an illustration of the way in which she amalgamates Hellenism, Platonism, and Christianity. It is also an illustration of the criterionic method of her thought as it blends with those forms of knowledge leading to wisdom. It is a perfect illustration of her Christian Hellenism. Here the strictness, the purity, of her contextual thought—the trenchancy and rigor of the criterion that she is arguing—is made clear in her definition: "Friendship is a supernatural harmony, a union of opposites." Her stress on clarity and precision of language and critical thought informs her criteria of friendship: "There is no friendship where there is inequality." "Friendship has something universal about it. It consists of loving a human being as we should like to be able to love each soul in particular of all those who go to make up the human race." Her intellectual grasp and delineation of criteria make her intuitive insights into the realities of interpersonal relations sharp and unsentimental: "When the necessity which brings people together has nothing to do with the emotions, when it is simply due to circumstances, hostility often makes its appearance from the start." Against that necessity which is the principle of impurity she constantly warns. Criteria identify moral and spiritual guides that must translate into an ethos of life and faith. The full meaning of what Simone Weil is pronouncing, and of the wisdom she is finally communicating in her view of friendship as a sacrament, is essentialized in these faithful, prevenient words: "Pure friendship is an image of the original and perfect friendship that belongs to the Trinity and is the very essence of God. It is impossible for two human beings to be one while scrupulously respecting the distance that separates them, unless God is present in each of them. The point at which parallels meet is infinity."

Simone Weil helps us not only to approach wisdom but also to contemplate it. In contemplation, pervaded by the attitude of looking and waiting, the real presence of God is felt. It is a form of contact with the beautiful, a sacramental experience by which one passes from the flesh to the soul. "The beautiful is the experimental proof that the incarnation is possible," she writes. The beautiful and the good irradiate the realm of wisdom. As such it touches infinity. When the act of judgment coheres with the grace of wisdom a spiritual entity is born. And at this point of juncture one is made more aware of the vices that are subject to gravity. When such an awareness is attained, spiritualized so to speak, it is possible for one to fathom the crisis of meaning encountered in Simone Weil's distinction between evil and good: "Evil is multifarious and fragmentary, good is one; evil is apparent, good is mysterious; evil consists in action, good in non-action, in activity which does not act." The recognition of the power of evil, as a necessity and a duty, is tantamount to the transcendence of a criterion of wisdom. It is a point of arrival at which one can say that one must live for one's soul. Now the attendant experience of suffering can be apprehended in its true, or pure, significance: "The false God changes suffering into violence. The true God changes violence into suffering. Expiatory suffering is the shock in return for the evil we have done. Redemptive suffering is the shadow of the pure good we desire." And now, too, we are ready to see the good that is good and the sin that is sin. This knowledge "leads to a knowledge of the distance between good and evil and the commencement of a painful effort of assimilation." Divine wisdom proclaims this ineradicable and universal criterion: "Evil has to be purified—or life is not possible. God alone can do that." The fearsomeness of evil can never be underestimated: "We cannot contemplate without terror the extent of the evil which man can do and endure."

Insofar as the Devil governs the social order, says Simone Weil, all that man can do is to limit the evil of it. Man wants the absolute good; but "that which is within our reach is the good which is correlated to evil." Only in the idea of relationship can one break out of the social: "To relate belongs to the solitary spirit. No crowd can conceive relationship." Man must have the courage to test, to judge, and to meditate on the social order in order to detach himself from it. "To contemplate the social is as good a way of detachment as to retire from the world," she writes. "That is why I have not been wrong to rub

shoulders with politics for so long." The social element is one in which
the pull of gravity is supreme. She identifies Rome, a society "absolutely without mysticism," with this gravity, as she also does the
Hebrews, since "their God was heavy." The distinction between "social morality" and "supernatural morality" is equivalent to that between gravity and grace, as also between knowledge and wisdom.
Rootedness must be centered in something other than the social. "A
nation as such cannot be the object of supernatural love. It has
no soul. It is a Great Beast." For Simone Weil the Great Beast, "the
only *ersatz* of God," is the Devil disguised. Submission to the former
is submission to the latter. The consequences of the social are forbidding: Conscience is deceived. Judgment falters. Meditation, as a
phase of purification, ceases. Wisdom vanishes. And the soul is deprived
of life and death. The power of Satan is unassailable in the abyss of
gravity. "It is only by entering the transcendental, the supernatural,
the authentically spiritual order that man rises above the social. Until
then, whatever he may do, the social is transcendent in relation to
him."

Simone Weil's contemplations consist of spiritual directions, spiritual counsels, spiritual exercises. But beyond, or, better, along with
these, they transmute into spiritual life. A glimpse of beauty, a purity of
soul, a realization of wisdom, a sense of the holy: these are the encountered constituents of this experience. Her thoughts are never
without a higher purpose. In their formulation they necessarily impose
a discipline of attention, of a devotional rather than an essentially
ascetical character. Not the laceration of the self but the "decreation"
of the self is the goal. "May that which is low in us go downward so
that which is high can go upward. For we are wrong side upward. We
are born thus. To re-establish order is to undo the creature in us."
Human misery is at the core of human experience: "The curtain is
human misery: there was a curtain even for Christ." The anguish of
Job and the symbol of the Cross are constants of her religious vision.
So that the love of God may penetrate the depths of what she calls
"vegetative energy," nature must undergo the ultimate violence. The
acceptance of this spiritual fact is the recognition of "this world, the
realm of necessity, [which] offers us absolutely nothing except
means." No violence, she believed, can make purity less pure, though

it can inflict suffering on it. Hence, the consequences of suffering can be dangerous, leading to imbalance, distortion, degradation. The virtue of patience, an innermost essence of wisdom, is indispensable to spiritual warfare, visible or invisible: "Patience consists in not transforming suffering into crime. That in itself is enough to transform crime into suffering." The need for patience, like the need for roots, is a divine need. To ignore or to reject this need is to glorify a broken world. "We are like barrels with no bottom to them so long as we have not understood that we rest on a foundation."

DECREATION

If there is one doctrine to which Simone Weil held unswerv-
ingly it is that of decreation, of disincarnation, through
which man renounces and purifies the self. Decreation is a
spiritual act devastating the "I" in us, a stripping away and
renunciation of the ego; an ultimate transfiguration, humil-
ity, communion with the infinite: and Grace.

Decreation: To make something created pass into the uncreated.

Destruction: To make something created pass into nothingness. A blameworthy substitute for decreation.

Creation is an act of love and it is perpetual. At each moment our existence is God's love for us. But God can only love himself. His love for us is love for himself through us. Thus, he who gives us our being loves in us the acceptance of not being.

Our existence is made up only of his waiting for our acceptance not to exist. He is perpetually begging from us that existence which he gives. He gives it to us in order to beg it from us.

Relentless necessity, wretchedness, distress, the crushing burden of poverty, and of labor which wears us out, cruelty, torture, violent

death, constraint, disease—all these constitute divine love. It is God
who in love withdraws from us so that we can love him. For if we
were exposed to the direct radiance of his love, without the protection of space, of time, and of matter, we should be evaporated like
water in the sun; there would not be enough "I" in us to make it possible to surrender the "I" for love's sake. Necessity is the screen set
between God and us so that we can be. It is for us to pierce through
the screen so that we cease to be.

There exists a "deifugal" force. Otherwise all would be God.

An imaginary divinity has been given to man so that he may strip
himself of it as Christ did of his real divinity.

Renunciation. Imitation of God's renunciation in creation. In a
sense, God renounces being everything. We should renounce being
something. That is our only good.

We are like barrels with no bottom to them so long as we have
not understood that we rest on a foundation.

Elevation and abasement. A woman looking at herself in a mirror
and adorning herself does not feel the shame of reducing the self, that
infinite being which surveys all things, to a small space. In the same
way every time that we raise the ego (the social ego, the psychological ego, etc.) as high as we raise it, we degrade ourselves to an infinite
degree by confining ourselves to being more than that. When the ego is
abased (unless energy tends to raise it by desire), we know that we are
not that.

A very beautiful woman who looks at her reflection in the mirror can very well believe that she is that. An ugly woman knows that
she is not that.

Everything which is grasped by our natural faculties is hypothetical. It is only supernatural love that establishes anything. Thus we
are co-creators.

We participate in the creation of the world by decreating
ourselves.

We only possess what we renounce; what we do not renounce escapes from us. In this sense we cannot possess anything whatever unless it passes through God.

Catholic communion. God did not only make himself flesh for us once, every day he makes himself matter in order to give himself to man and to be consumed by him. Reciprocally, by fatigue, affliction, and death, man is made matter and is consumed by God. How can we refuse this reciprocity?

He emptied himself of his divinity. We should empty ourselves of the false divinity with which we were born.

Once we have understood we are nothing, the object of all our efforts is to become nothing. It is for this that we suffer with resignation, *it is for this that we act*, it is for this that we pray.

May God grant that I become nothing.

In so far as I become nothing, God loves himself through me.

There is a resemblance between the lower and the higher. Hence slavery is an image of obedience to God, humiliation an image of humility, physical necessity an image of the irresistible pressure of grace, the saints' abandonment from day to day an image of the frittering away of time among criminals, prostitutes, etc.

On this account, it is necessary to seek out what is lowest as an image.

May that which is low in us go downward so that which is high can go upward. For we are wrong side upward. We are born thus. To re-establish order is to undo the creature in us.

Reversal of the objective and the subjective.

Similarly reversal of the positive and the negative. That is also the meaning of the philosophy of the Upanishads.

We are born and live in an inverted fashion, for we are born and live in sin which is an inversion of the hierarchy. The first operation is one of reversal. Conversion.

Except the seed die . . . It has to die in order to liberate the energy it bears within it, so that with this energy new forms may be developed.

So we have to die in order to liberate a *tied up* energy, in order to possess an energy which is free and capable of understanding the true relationship of things.

The extreme difficulty which I often experience in carrying out the slightest action is a favor granted to me. For thus, by ordinary actions and without attracting attention, I can cut some of the roots of the tree. However indifferent we may be as to the opinion of others, extraordinary actions contain a stimulus which cannot be separated from them. This stimulus is quite absent from ordinary actions. To find extraordinary difficulty in doing an ordinary action is a favor which calls for gratitude. We must not ask for the removal of such a difficulty; we must beg for grace to make good use of it.

In general, we must not wish for the disappearance of any of our troubles, but grace to transform them.

For men of courage, physical sufferings (and privations) are often a test of endurance and of strength of soul. But there is a better use to be made of them. For me, then, may they not be that. May they rather be a testimony, lived and felt, of human misery. May I endure them in a completely passive manner. Whatever happens, how could I ever think an affliction too great, since the wound of an affliction, and the abasement to which those whom it strikes are condemned, opens to them the knowledge of human misery, knowledge which is the door of all wisdom?

But pleasure, happiness, prosperity, if we know how to recognize in them all that comes from outside (chance, circumstances, etc.), likewise bear testimony to human misery. They should be used in the same way. This applies even to grace, in so far as it is a sensible phenomenon.

We have to be nothing in order to be in our right place in the whole.

Renunciation demands that we should pass through anguish equivalent to that which would be caused in reality by the loss of all loved beings and all possessions, including our faculties and attainments in the order of intelligence and character, our opinions, beliefs concerning what is good, what is stable, etc. And we must not lay these things down of ourselves but lose them—like Job. Moreover, the energy thus cut off from its object should not be wasted in oscillations and degraded. The anguish should therefore be still greater than in real affliction, it should not be cut up and spread over time nor oriented toward a hope.

When the passion of love goes as far as vegetative energy, then we have cases like Phèdre, Arnolphe, etc. *"Et je sens là-dedans qu'il faudra que je crève . . ."*

Hippolyte is really more necessary to the life of Phèdre, in the most literal sense of the word, than food.

In order that the love of God may penetrate as far down as that, nature has to undergo the ultimate violence. Job, the cross . . .

The love of Phèdre or of Arnolphe is impure. A love which should descend as low as theirs and yet remain pure. . . .

We must become nothing, we must go down to the vegetative level; it is then that God becomes bread.

If we consider what we are at a definite moment—the present moment, cut off from the past and the future—we are innocent. We cannot at that instant be anything but what we are: all progress implies duration. It is in the order of the world, at this instant, that we should be such as we are.

To isolate a moment in this way implies pardon. But such isolation is detachment.

There are only two instants of perfect nudity and purity in human life: birth and death. It is only when newly born or on our deathbed that we can adore God in human form without sullying the divinity.

Death. An instantaneous state, without past or future. Indispensable for entering eternity.

If we find fullness of joy in the thought that God is, we must find the same fullness in the knowledge that we ourselves are not, for it is the same thought. And this knowledge is extended to our sensibility only through suffering and death.

Joy within God. Perfect and infinite joy really exists within God. My participation can add nothing to it, my non-participation can take nothing from the reality of this perfect and infinite joy. Of what importance is it then, whether I am to share in it or not? Of no importance whatever.

Those who wish for their salvation do not truly believe in the reality of the joy within God.

Belief in immortality is harmful because it is not in our power to conceive of the soul as really incorporeal. So this belief is in fact a belief in the prolongation of life, and it robs death of its purpose.

The presence of God. This should be understood in two ways. As Creator, God is present in everything that exists as soon as it exists. The presence for which God needs the co-operation of the creature is the presence of God, not as Creator but as Spirit. The first presence is the presence of creation. The second is the presence of de-creation. (He who created us without our help will not save us without our consent. St. Augustine.)

God could create only by hiding himself. Otherwise there would be nothing but himself.

Holiness should then be hidden too, even from consciousness in a certain measure. And it should be hidden in the world.

Being and having. Being does not belong to man, only having. The being of man is situated behind the curtain, on the supernatural side. What he can know of himself is only what is lent him by circumstances. My "I" is hidden for me (and for others); it is on the side of God, it is in God, it is God. To be proud is to forget that one is God . . . The curtain is human misery: there was a curtain even for Christ.

Job. Satan to God: "Doth he love thee for thyself alone?" It is a question of the level of love. Is love situated on the level of sheep, fields of corn, numerous children? Or is it situated further off, in the third dimension, behind? However deep this love may be, there is a breaking point when it succumbs, and it is this moment which transforms, which wrenches us away from the finite toward the infinite, which makes the soul's love for God *transcendent in the soul*. It is the death of the soul. Woe to him for whom the death of the body precedes that of the soul. The soul which is not full of love dies a bad death. Why is it necessary that such a death should happen without distinction? It must indeed be so. It is necessary that anything falling should happen without distinction.

Appearance clings to being, and pain alone can tear them from each other.

For whoever is in possession of being there can be no appearance. Appearance chains being down.

Time in its course tears appearance from being and being from appearance, by violence. Time makes it manifest that it is not eternity.

It is necessary to uproot oneself. To cut down the tree and make of it a cross, and then to carry it every day.

It is necessary not to be "myself," still less to be "ourselves."
The city gives one the feeling of being at home.
We must take the feeling of being at home into exile.
We must be rooted in the absence of a place.

To uproot oneself socially and vegetatively.
To exile oneself from every earthly country.
To do all that to others, from the outside is a substitute [*ersatz*] for decreation. It results in unreality.
But by uprooting oneself one seeks greater reality.

LOVE

Love, for Simone Weil, is both a sacramental and a reciprocal experience. It is based on the belief in the existence of other human beings. It is also, and finally, a recognition of Divine Otherness. Grace without love is meaningless. "What is not love is not relationship with God." Love is a purifying stage of disincarnation in which contemplation ultimately replaces the possession of objects, and brings one closer to the God who is perfect.

Love is a sign of our wretchedness. God can only love himself. We can only love something else.

God's love for us is not the reason for which we should love him. God's love for us is the reason for us to love ourselves. How could we love ourselves without this motive?

It is impossible for man to love himself except in this roundabout way.

If my eyes are blindfolded and if my hands are chained to a stick, this stick separates me from things, but I can explore them by means of it. It is only the stick which I feel, it is only the wall which I perceive.

It is the same with creatures and the faculty of love. Supernatural love touches only creatures and goes only to God. It is only creatures that it loves (what else have we to love?), but it loves them as intermediaries. For this reason it loves all creatures equally, itself included. To love a stranger as oneself implies the reverse: to love oneself as the stranger.

Love of God is pure when joy and suffering inspire an *equal* degree of gratitude.

Love on the part of someone who is happy is the wish to share the suffering of the beloved who is unhappy.

Love on the part of someone who is unhappy is to be filled with joy by the mere knowledge that his beloved is happy, without sharing in this happiness or even wishing to do so.

In Plato's eyes carnal love is a degraded image of true love. Chaste human love (conjugal fidelity) is a less degraded image of it. Only in the stupidity of the present day could the idea of sublimation arise.

The Love of Phaedrus. He neither exercises force, nor submits to it. That constitutes the only purity. Contact with the sword causes the same defilement, whether it be through the handle or the point. For him who loves, its metallic coldness will not destroy love, but will give the impression of being abandoned by God. Supernatural love has no contact with force, but at the same time it does not protect the soul against the coldness of force, the coldness of steel. Only an earthly attachment, if it has in it enough energy, can afford protection from the coldness of steel. Armor, like the sword, is made of metal. Murder freezes the soul of the man who loves only with pure love, whether he be the author or the victim, so likewise does everything which, without going so far as actual death, constitutes violence. If we want to have a love which will protect the soul from wounds, we must love something other than God.

Love tends to go ever further and further, but there is a limit. When the limit is passed love turns to hate. To avoid this change love has to become different.

Among human beings, only the existence of those we love is fully recognized.

Belief in the existence of other human beings as such is *love*.

The mind is not forced to believe in the existence of anything (subjectivism, absolute idealism, solipsism, skepticism: cf. the Upanishads, the Taoists, and Plato, who, all of them, adopt this philosophical attitude by way of purification). That is why the only organ of contact with existence is acceptance, love. That is why beauty and reality are identical. That is why joy and the sense of reality are identical.

This need to be the creator of what we love is a need to imitate God. But the divinity toward which it tends is false unless we have recourse to the model seen from the other, the heavenly side. . . .

Pure love of creatures is not love in God, but love which has passed through God as through fire. Love which detaches itself completely from creatures to ascend to God, and comes down again associated with the creative love of God.

Thus the two opposites which rend human love are united: to love the beloved being just as he is and to want to re-create him.

Imaginary love of creatures. We are attached by a cord to all the objects of attachment, and a cord can always be cut. We are also attached by a cord to the imaginary God, the God for whom love is also an attachment. But to the real God we are not attached, and that is why there is no cord which can be cut. He enters into us. He alone can enter into us. All other things remain outside, and our knowledge of them is confined to the tensions of varying degree and direction which affect the cord when there is a change of position on their part or on ours.

Love needs reality. What is more terrible than the discovery that through a bodily appearance we have been loving an imaginary being? It is much more terrible than death, for death does not prevent the beloved from having lived.

That is the punishment for having fed love on imagination.

It is an act of cowardice to seek from (or to wish to give) the people we love any other consolation than that which works of art give us, which help us through the mere fact that they *exist*. To love and to be loved only serve mutually to render this existence more concrete, more constantly present to the mind. But it should be present as the source of our thoughts not as their object. If there are grounds for wishing to be understood, it is not for ourselves but for the other, in order that we may exist for him.

Everything which is vile or second-rate in us revolts against purity and needs, in order to save its own life, to soil this purity.

To soil is to modify, it is to touch. The beautiful is that which we cannot wish to change. To assume power over is to soil. To possess is to soil.

To love purely is to consent to distance, it is to adore the distance between ourselves and that which we love.

The imagination is always united with a desire, that is to say a value. Only desire without an object is empty of imagination. There is the real presence of God in everything which imagination does not veil. The beautiful takes our desire captive and empties it of its object, giving it an object which is present and thus forbidding it to fly off toward the future.

Such is the price of chaste love. Every desire for enjoyment belongs to the future and the world of illusion, whereas if we desire only that a being should exist, he exists: what more is there to desire? The beloved being is then naked and real, not veiled by an imaginary future. The miser never looks at his treasure without imagining it n times larger. It is necessary to be dead in order to see things in their nakedness.

Thus in love there is chastity or the lack of chastity, according to whether the desire is or is not directed toward the future.

In this sense, and on condition that it is not turned toward a pseudo-immortality conceived on the model of the future, the love we devote to the dead is perfectly pure. For it is the desire for a life which is finished that can no longer give anything new. We desire that the dead man should have existed, and he has existed.

Wherever the spirit ceases to be a principle it also ceases to be an end. Hence the close connection between collective "thought" under all its forms and the loss of the sense of and respect for souls. The soul is the human being considered as having a value in itself. To love the soul of a woman is not to think of her as serving one's own pleasure, etc. Love no longer knows how to contemplate, it wants to possess (disappearance of Platonic love).

It is a fault to wish to be understood before we have made ourselves clear to ourselves. It is to seek pleasures in friendship, and pleasures which are not deserved. It is something which corrupts even more than love. You would sell your soul for friendship.

Learn to thrust friendship aside, or rather the dream of friendship. To desire friendship is a great fault. Friendship should be a gratuitous joy like those afforded by art or life. We must refuse it so that we may be worthy to receive it; it is of the order of grace ("Depart from me, O Lord . . ."). It is one of those things which are added unto us. *Every* dream of friendship deserves to be shattered. It is not by chance that you have never been loved. . . . To wish to escape from solitude is cowardice. Friendship is not to be sought, not to be dreamed, not to be desired; it is to be exercised (it is a virtue). We must have done with all this impure and turbid border of sentiment. *Schluss!*

Or rather (for we must not prune too severely within ourselves), everything in friendship which does not pass into real exchanges should pass into considered thoughts. It serves no useful purpose to do without the inspiring virtue of friendship. What should be severely forbidden is to dream of its sentimental joys. That is corruption. Moreover, it is as stupid as to dream about music or painting. Friendship cannot be separated from reality any more than the beautiful. It is a miracle, like the beautiful. And the miracle consists simply in the fact that it *exists*. At the age of twenty-five, it is high time to have done with adolescence once and for all. . . .

Do not allow yourself to be imprisoned by any affection. Keep your solitude. The day, if it ever comes, when you are given true affection there will be no opposition between interior solitude and friendship, quite the reverse. It is even by this infallible sign that you will recognize it. Other affections have to be severely disciplined.

The same words (e.g., a man says to his wife, "I love you") can be commonplace or extraordinary according to the manner in which they are spoken. And this manner depends on the depth of the region in a man's being from which they proceed without the will being able to do anything. And by a marvelous agreement they reach the same region in him who hears them. Thus the hearer can discern, if he has any power of discernment, what is the value of the words.

Benefaction is permissible precisely because it constitutes a humiliation still greater than pain, a still more intimate and undeniable proof of dependence. And gratitude is prescribed for the same reason, since therein lies the use to be made of the received benefit. The dependence, however, must be on fate and not on any particular human being. That is why the benefactor is under an obligation to keep himself entirely out of the benefaction. Moreover, the gratitude must not in any degree constitute an attachment, for that is the gratitude proper to dogs.

Gratitude is first of all the business of him who helps if the help is pure. It is only by virtue of reciprocity that it is due from him who is helped.

In order to feel true gratitude (the case of friendship being set aside), I have to think that it is not out of pity, sympathy, or caprice that I am being treated well, it is not as a favor or privilege, nor as a natural result of temperament, but from a desire to do what justice demands. Accordingly, he who treats me thus wishes that all who are in my situation may be treated in the same way by all who are in his own.

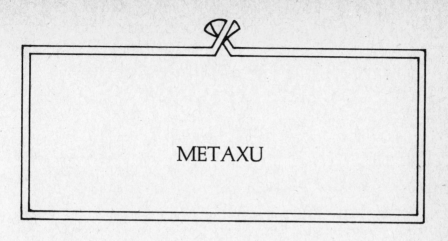

METAXU

Simone Weil never fails to affirm the existence of bridges,
of the Platonic metaxu, *or intermediaries, between temporal*
becoming and fullness of being, between nature and super-
nature, between man and God. Her own words vividly
image this eternalizing process: "Two prisoners whose cells
adjoin communicate with each other by knocking on the
wall. The wall is the thing which separates them but it is
also their means of communication. It is the same with us
and God. Every separation is a link."

All created things refuse to be for me as ends. Such is God's extreme mercy toward me. And that very thing is what constitutes evil. Evil is the form which God's mercy takes in this world.

This world is the closed door. It is a barrier. And at the same time it is the way through.

Two prisoners whose cells adjoin communicate with each other by knocking on the wall. The wall is the thing which separates them but it is also their means of communication. It is the same with us and God. Every separation is a link.

By putting all our desire for good into a thing, we make that thing a condition of our existence. But we do not, on that account, make of it a good. Merely to exist is not enough for us.

The essence of created things is to be intermediaries. They are intermediaries leading from one to the other, and there is no end to this. They are intermediaries leading to God. We have to experience them as such.

The bridges of the Greeks. We have inherited them but we do not know how to use them. We thought they were intended to have houses built upon them. We have erected skyscrapers on them to which we ceaselessly add stories. We no longer know that they are bridges, things made so that we may pass along them, and that by passing along them we go toward God.

Only he who loves God with a supernatural love can look upon means simply as means.

Power (and money, power's master key) is a means at its purest. For that very reason it is the supreme end for all those who have not understood.

This world, the realm of necessity, offers us absolutely nothing except means. Our will is forever sent from one means to another like a billiard ball.

All our desires are contradictory, like the desire for food. I want the person I love to love me. If, however, he is totally devoted to me he does not exist any longer and I cease to love him. And as long as he is not totally devoted to me he does not love me enough. Hunger and repletion.

Desire is evil and illusory, yet without desire we should not seek for that which is truly absolute, truly boundless. We have to have experienced it. Misery of those beings from whom fatigue takes away that supplementary energy which is the source of desire.

Misery also of those who are blinded by desire.

We have to fix our desire to the axis of the poles.

What is it a sacrilege to destroy? Not that which is base, for that is of no importance. Not that which is high, for, even should we want to, we cannot touch that. The *metaxu*. The *metaxu* form the region of good and evil.

No human being should be deprived of his *metaxu*, that is to say of those relative and mixed blessings (home, country, traditions, culture, etc.) which warm and nourish the soul and without which, short of sainthood, a *human* life is not possible.

The true earthly blessings are *metaxu*. We can respect those of others only in so far as we regard those we ourselves possess as *metaxu*. This implies that we are already making our way toward the point where it is possible to do without them. For example, if we are to respect foreign countries, we must make of our own country not an idol, but a steppingstone toward God.

All the faculties being freely exercised without becoming mixed, starting from a single, unique principle. It is the microcosm, the imitation of the world. Christ according to St. Thomas. The just man of the *Republic*. When Plato speaks of specialization he speaks of the specialization of man's faculties and not of the specialization of men; the same applies to hierarchy. The temporal having no meaning except by and for the spiritual, but not being mixed with the spiritual. Leading to it by nostalgia, by reaching beyond itself. It is the temporal seen as a bridge, a *metaxu*. It is the Greek and Provençal vocation.

Civilization of the Greeks. No adoration of force. The temporal was only a bridge. Among the states of the soul they did not seek intensity, but purity.

FRIENDSHIP

Simone Weil's comments on friendship must surely rank with the noblest that have been written on the subject. She raises friendship to the highest level, including and yet transcending mere reciprocal necessity or motivation. Pure friendship, as a criterion of universal love, "is a miracle by which a person consents to view from a certain distance, and without coming any nearer, the very being who is necessary to him as food."

There is however a personal and human love which is pure and which enshrines an intimation and a reflection of divine love. This is friendship, provided we keep strictly to the true meaning of the word.

Preference for some human being is necessarily a different thing from charity. Charity does not discriminate. If it is found more abundantly in any special quarter, it is because affliction has chanced to provide an occasion there for the exchange of compassion and gratitude. It is equally available for the whole human race, inasmuch as affliction can come to all, offering them an opportunity for such an exchange.

Preference for a human being can be of two kinds. Either we are seeking some particular good in him, or we need him. In a

general way all possible attachments come under one of these heads.
We are drawn toward a thing, either because there is some good we are
seeking from it, or because we cannot do without it. Sometimes the
two motives coincide. Often however they do not. Each is distinct
and quite independent. We eat distasteful food, if we have nothing
else, because we cannot do otherwise. A moderately greedy man looks
out for delicacies, but he can easily do without them. If we have no
air we are suffocated; we struggle to get it, not because we expect to
get some advantage from it but because we need it. We go in search of
sea air without being driven by any necessity, because we like it. In
time it often comes about automatically that the second motive takes
the place of the first. This is one of the great misfortunes of our
race. A man smokes opium in order to attain to a special condition,
which he thinks superior; often, as time goes on, the opium reduces
him to a miserable condition which he feels to be degrading, but he is
no longer able to do without it. Arnolphe bought Agnes from her
adopted mother, because it seemed to him it would be an advantage to
have a little girl with him, a little girl whom he would gradually
make into a good wife. Later on she ceased to cause him anything but
a heart-rending and degrading torment. But with the passage of time
his attachment to her had become a vital bond which forced this terrible line from his lips:

"Mais je sens là-dedans qu'il faudra que je crève—"

Harpagon started by considering gold as an advantage. Later it
became nothing but the object of a haunting obsession, yet an object
of which the loss would cause his death. As Plato says, there is a great
difference between the essence of the Necessary and that of the
Good.

There is no contradiction between seeking our own good in a
human being and wishing for his good to be increased. For this very
reason, when the motive that draws us toward anybody is simply
some advantage for ourselves, the conditions of friendship are not fulfilled. Friendship is a supernatural harmony, a union of opposites.

When a human being is in any degree necessary to us, we cannot
desire his good unless we cease to desire our own. Where there is
necessity there is constraint and domination. We are in the power of
that of which we stand in need, unless we possess it. The central good

for every man is the free disposal of himself. Either we renounce it, which is a crime of idolatry, since it can be renounced only in favor of God, or we desire that the being we stand in need of should be deprived of this free disposal of himself.

Any kind of mechanism may join human beings together with bonds of affection which have the iron hardness of necessity. Mother love is often of such a kind; so at times is paternal love, as in *Père Goriot* of Balzac; so is carnal love in its most intense form, as in *L'Ecole des Femmes* and in *Phèdre;* so also, very frequently, is the love between husband and wife, chiefly as a result of habit. Filial and fraternal love are more rarely of this nature.

There are moreover degrees of necessity. Everything is necessary in some degree if its loss really causes a decrease of vital energy. (This word is here used in the strict and precise sense that it might have if the study of vital phenomena were as far advanced as that of falling bodies.) When the degree of necessity is extreme, deprivation leads to death. This is the case when all the vital energy of one being is bound up with another by some attachment. In the lesser degrees, deprivation leads to a more or less considerable lessening of energy. Thus a total deprivation of food causes death, whereas a partial deprivation only diminishes the life force. Nevertheless the necessary quantity of food is considered to be that required if a person is not to be weakened.

The most frequent cause of necessity in the bonds of affection is a combination of sympathy and habit. As in the case of avarice or drunkenness, that which was at first a search for some desired good is transformed into a need by the mere passage of time. The difference from avarice, drunkenness, and all the vices, however, is that in the bonds of affection the two motives—search for a desired good, and need—can very easily coexist. They can also be separated. When the attachment of one being to another is made up of need and nothing else it is a fearful thing. Few things in this world can reach such a degree of ugliness and horror. There is always something horrible whenever a human being seeks what is good and only finds necessity. The stories that tell of a beloved being who suddenly appears with a death's head best symbolize this. The human soul possesses a whole arsenal of lies with which to put up a defense against this ugliness and, in imagination, to manufacture sham advantages where there is only necessity.

It is for this very reason that ugliness is an evil, because it conduces to lying.

Speaking quite generally, we might say that there is affliction whenever necessity, under no matter what form, is imposed so harshly that the hardness exceeds the capacity for lying of the person who receives the impact. That is why the purest souls are the most exposed to affliction. For him who is capable of preventing the automatic reaction of defense, which tends to increase the soul's capacity for lying, affliction is not an evil, although it is always a wounding and in a sense a degradation.

When a human being is attached to another by a bond of affection which contains any degree of necessity, it is impossible that he should wish autonomy to be preserved both in himself and in the other. It is impossible by virtue of the mechanism of nature. It is, however, made possible by the miraculous intervention of the supernatural. This miracle is friendship.

"Friendship is an equality made of harmony," said the Pythagoreans. There is harmony because there is a supernatural union between two opposites, that is to say, necessity and liberty, the two opposites God combined when he created the world and men. There is equality because each wishes to preserve the faculty of free consent both in himself and in the other.

When anyone wishes to put himself under a human being or consents to be subordinated to him, there is no trace of friendship. Racine's Pylades is not the friend of Orestes. There is no friendship where there is inequality.

A certain reciprocity is essential in friendship. If all good will is entirely lacking on one of the two sides, the other should suppress his own affection, out of respect for the free consent which he should not desire to force. If on one of the two sides there is not any respect for the autonomy of the other, this other must cut the bond uniting them out of respect for himself. In the same way, he who consents to be enslaved cannot gain friendship. But the necessity contained in the bond of affection can exist on one side only, and in this case there is only friendship on one side, if we keep to the strict and exact meaning of the word.

A friendship is tarnished as soon as necessity triumphs, if only for a moment, over the desire to preserve the faculty of free consent on both sides. In all human things, necessity is the principle of impurity. All friendship is impure if even a trace of the wish to please or the contrary desire to dominate is found in it. In a perfect friendship these two desires are completely absent. The two friends have fully consented to be two and not one, they respect the distance which the fact of being two distinct creatures places between them. Man has the right to desire direct union with God alone.

Friendship is a miracle by which a person consents to view from a certain distance, and without coming any nearer, the very being who is necessary to him as food. It requires the strength of soul that Eve did not have; and yet she had no need of the fruit. If she had been hungry at the moment when she looked at the fruit, and if in spite of that she had remained looking at it indefinitely without taking one step toward it, she would have performed a miracle analogous to that of perfect friendship.

Through this supernatural miracle of respect for human autonomy, friendship is very like the pure forms of compassion and gratitude called forth by affliction. In both cases the contraries which are the terms of the harmony are necessity and liberty, or in other words subordination and equality. These two pairs of opposites are equivalent.

From the fact that the desire to please and the desire to command are not found in pure friendship, it has in it, at the same time as affection, something not unlike a complete indifference. Although it is a bond between two people it is in a sense impersonal. It leaves impartiality intact. It in no way prevents us from imitating the perfection of our Father in heaven who freely distributes sunlight and rain in every place. On the contrary, friendship and this distribution are the mutual conditions one of the other, in most cases at any rate. For, as practically every human being is joined to others by bonds of affection that have in them some degree of necessity, he cannot go toward perfection except by transforming this affection into friendship. Friendship has something universal about it. It consists of loving a human being as we should like to be able to love each soul in particular of all those who go to make up the human race. As a geometrician looks at a particular figure in order to deduce the universal properties of the triangle, so he who knows how to love directs upon a particular human being a universal love. The consent to preserve an autonomy within ourselves and in others is essentially of a universal order. As soon as we wish for this autonomy to be respected in more than just one single being we desire it for everyone, for we cease to arrange the order of the world in a circle whose center is here below. We transport the center of the circle beyond the heavens.

Friendship does not have this power if the two beings who love each other, through an unlawful use of affection, think they form only one. But then there is not friendship in the true sense of the word. That is what might be called an adulterous union, even though it comes about between husband and wife. There is not friendship where distance is not kept and respected.

The simple fact of having pleasure in thinking in the same way as the beloved being, or in any case that fact of desiring such an agreement of opinion, attacks the purity of the friendship at the same time as its intellectual integrity. It is very frequent. But at the same time pure friendship is rare.

When the bonds of affection and necessity between human beings are not supernaturally transformed into friendship, not only is the affection of an impure and low order, but it is also combined with hatred and repulsion. That is shown very well in *L'Ecole des Femmes* and in *Phèdre*. The mechanism is the same in affections other than carnal love. It is easy to understand this. We hate what we are dependent upon. We become disgusted with what depends on us. Sometimes affection does not only become mixed with hatred and revulsion; it is entirely changed into it. The transformation may sometimes even be almost immediate, so that hardly any affection has had time to show; this is the case when necessity is laid bare almost at once. When the necessity which brings people together has nothing to do with the emotions, when it is simply due to circumstances, hostility often makes its appearance from the start.

When Christ said to his disciples: "Love one another," it was not attachment he was laying down as their rule. As it was a fact that there were bonds between them due to the thoughts, the life, and the habits they shared, he commanded them to transform these bonds into friendship, so that they should not be allowed to turn into impure attachment or hatred.

Since, shortly before his death, Christ gave this as a new commandment to be added to the two great commandments of the love of
our neighbor and the love of God, we can think that pure friendship,
like the love of our neighbor, has in it something of a sacrament.
Christ perhaps wished to suggest this with reference to Christian
friendship when he said: "Where there are two or three gathered together in my name there am I in the midst of them." Pure friendship
is an image of the original and perfect friendship that belongs to the
Trinity and is the very essence of God. It is impossible for two human
beings to be one while scrupulously respecting the distance that separates them, unless God is present in each of them. The point at which
parallels meet is infinity.

EQUALITY

Equality is the recognition of the same amount of respect for all men and women, for all brothers and sisters, as Simone Weil would call them. Equality must be made compatible with individuating differentiation: "Where there is only a difference in kind, not in degree, there is no inequality at all." Equality must be the outgrowth of a humility that triumphs over the cruel urge to humiliate.

Equality is a vital need of the human soul. It consists in a recognition, at once public, general, effective, and genuinely expressed in institutions and customs, that the same amount of respect and consideration is due to every human being because this respect is due to the human being as such and is not a matter of degree.

It follows that the inevitable differences among men ought never to imply any difference in the degree of respect. And so that these differences may not be felt to bear such an implication, a certain balance is necessary between equality and inequality.

A certain combination of equality and inequality is formed by equality of opportunity. If no matter who can attain the social rank corresponding to the function he is capable of filling, and if education is sufficiently generalized so that no one is prevented from developing any capacity simply on account of his birth, the prospects are the same for every child. In this way, the prospects for each man are the same as for any other man, both as regards himself when young, and as regards his children later on.

But when such a combination acts alone, and not as one factor among other factors, it ceases to constitute a balance and contains great dangers.

To begin with, for a man who occupies an inferior position and suffers from it to know that his position is a result of his incapacity and that everybody is aware of the fact is not any consolation, but an additional motive of bitterness; according to the individual character, some men can thereby be thrown into a state of depression, while others can be encouraged to commit crime.

Then, in social life, a sort of aspirator toward the top is inevitably created. If a descending movement does not come to balance this ascending movement, the social body becomes sick. To the extent to which it is really possible for the son of a farm laborer to become one day a minister, to the same extent should it really be possible for the son of a minister to become one day a farm laborer. This second possibility could never assume any noticeable proportions without a very dangerous degree of social constraint.

This sort of equality, if allowed full play by itself, can make social life fluid to the point of decomposing it.

There are less clumsy methods of combining equality with differentiation. The first is by using proportion. Proportion can be defined as the combination of equality with inequality, and everywhere throughout the universe it is the sole factor making for balance.

Applied to the maintenance of social equilibrium, it would impose on each man burdens corresponding to the power and well-being he enjoys, and corresponding risks in cases of incapacity or neglect. For instance, an employer who is incapable or guilty of an offense against his workmen ought to be made to suffer far more, both in the spirit and in the flesh, than a workman who is incapable or guilty of an offense against his employer. Furthermore, all workmen ought to know that this is so. It would imply, on the one hand, certain rearrangement with regard to risks, on the other hand, in criminal law, a conception of punishment in which social rank, as an aggravating circumstance, would necessarily play an important part in deciding what the penalty was to be. All the more reason, therefore, why the exercise of important public functions should carry with it serious personal risks.

Another way of rendering equality compatible with differentiation would be to take away as far as possible all quantitative character from differences. Where there is only a difference in kind, not in degree, there is no inequality at all.

But making money the sole, or almost the sole, motive of all actions, the sole, or almost the sole, measure of all things, the poison of inequality has been introduced everywhere. It is true that this inequality is mobile; it is not attached to persons, for money is made and lost; it is none the less real.

There are two sorts of inequality, each with its corresponding stimulant. A more or less stable inequality, like that of ancient France, produces an idolizing of superiors—not without a mixture of repressed hatred—and a submission to their commands. A mobile, fluid inequality produces a desire to better oneself. It is no nearer to equality than is stable inequality, and is every bit as unwholesome. The Revolution of 1789, in putting forward equality, only succeeded in reality in sanctioning the substitution of one form of inequality for another.

The more equality there is in a society, the smaller is the action of the two stimulants connected with the two forms of inequality, and hence other stimulants are necessary.

Equality is all the greater in proportion as different human conditions are regarded as being, not more nor less than one another, but simply as other. Let us look on the professions of miner and minister simply as two different vocations, like those of poet and mathematician. And let the material hardships attaching to the miner's condition be counted in honor of those who undergo them.

In wartime, if an army is filled with the right spirit, a soldier is proud and happy to be under fire instead of at headquarters; a general is proud and happy to think that the successful outcome of the battle depends on his forethought; and at the same time the soldier admires the general and the general the soldier.

Such a balance constitutes an equality. There would be equality in social conditions if this balance could be found therein. It would mean honoring each human condition with those marks of respect which are proper to it, and are not just a hollow pretense.

BEAUTY

Beauty is a redeeming experience, according to Simone Weil, that makes life endurable. "Beauty captivates the flesh in order to obtain permission to pass right to the soul." It contains and syncretizes unions of contraries: the union of the instantaneous and the eternal, of the personal and the impersonal, of the sensorial and the spiritual, of the painful and the joyful. In the authentic feeling of beauty God is.

Beauty is the harmony of chance and the good.

Beauty is necessity which, while remaining in conformity with its own law and with that alone, is obedient to the good.

The subject of science is the beautiful (that is to say order, proportion, harmony) in so far as it is suprasensible and necessary.

The subject of art is sensible and contingent beauty discerned through the network of chance and evil.

The beautiful in nature is a union of the sensible impression and of the sense of necessity. Things must be like that (in the first place), and precisely, they are like that.

Beauty captivates the flesh in order to obtain permission to pass right to the soul.

Among other unions of contraries found in beauty there is that of the instantaneous and the eternal.

The beautiful is that which we can contemplate. A statue, a picture which we can gaze at for hours.
The beautiful is something on which we can fix our attention.
Gregorian music. When the same things are sung for hours each day and every day, whatever falls even slightly short of supreme excellence becomes unendurable and is eliminated.
The Greeks looked at their temples. We can endure the statues in the Luxembourg because we do not look at them.
A picture, such as one could place in the cell of a criminal sentenced to solitary confinement for life, without its being an atrocity, to the contrary.

Only drama without movement is truly beautiful. Shakespeare's tragedies are second class, with the exception of *Lear*. Those of Racine third class, except for *Phèdre*. Those of Corneille of the nth class.

A work of art has an author and yet, when it is perfect, it has something which is essentially anonymous about it. It imitates the anonymity of divine art. In the same way the beauty of the world proves there to be a God who is personal and impersonal at the same time, and is neither the one nor the other separately.

The beautiful is a carnal attraction which keeps us at a distance and implies a renunciation. This includes the renunciation of that which is most deep-seated, the imagination. We want to eat all the other objects of desire. The beautiful is that which we desire without wishing to eat it. We desire that it should be.

We have to remain quite still and unite ourselves with that which we desire yet do not approach.

We unite ourselves to God in this way: We cannot approach him. Distance is the soul of the beautiful.

The attitude of looking and waiting is the attitude which corresponds with the beautiful. As long as one can go on conceiving, wishing, longing, the beautiful does not appear. That is why in all beauty we find contradiction, bitterness, and absence which are irreducible.

Poetry: *impossible* pain and joy. A poignant touch, nostalgia. Such is Provençal and English poetry. A joy which by reason of its unmixed purity hurts, a pain which by reason of its unmixed purity brings peace.

Beauty is a fruit which we look at without trying to seize it.
The same with an affliction which we contemplate without drawing back.

A double movement of descent: to do again, out of love, what gravity does. Is not the double movement of descent the key to all art?

This movement of descent, the mirror of grace, is the essence of all music. All the rest only serves to enshrine it.
The rising of the notes is a purely sensorial rising. The descent is at the same time a sensorial descent and a spiritual rising. Here we have the paradise which every being longs for: where the slope of nature makes us rise toward the good.

In everything which gives us the pure authentic feeling of beauty there is really the presence of God. There is, as it were, an incarnation of God in the world, and it is indicated by beauty.
The beautiful is the experimental proof that the incarnation is possible.
Hence all art of the highest order is religious in essence. (That is what people have forgotten today.) A Gregorian melody is as powerful a witness as the death of a martyr.

If the beautiful is the real presence of God in matter, and if contact with the beautiful is a sacrament in the full sense of the word, how is it that there are so many perverted aesthetes? Nero. Is it like the hunger of those who frequent black masses for the consecrated hosts? Or is it, more probably, because these people do not devote themselves to what is genuinely beautiful, but to a bad imitation? For, just as there is an art which is divine, so there is one which is demoniacal. It was no doubt the latter that Nero loved. A great deal of our art is of the devil.

A person who is passionately fond of music may quite well be a perverted person—but I should find it hard to believe this of anyone who thirsted for Gregorian chanting.

We must certainly have committed crimes which have made us accursed, since we have lost all the poetry of the universe.

Art has no immediate future because all art is collective and there is no more collective life (there are only dead collections of people), and also because of this breaking of the true pact between the body and the soul. Greek art coincided with the beginning of geometry and with athleticism, the art of the Middle Ages with the craftsmen's guilds, the art of the Renaissance with the beginning of mechanics, etc. . . . Since 1914 there has been a complete cut. Even comedy is almost impossible: there is only room for satire (when was it easier to understand Juvenal?) Art will never be reborn except from amidst a general anarchy—it will be epic, no doubt, because affliction will have simplified a great many things. . . . It is therefore quite useless for you to envy Leonardo or Bach. Greatness in our times must take a different course. Moreover, it can only be solitary, obscure, and without an echo. . . . (but without an echo, no art).

EVIL

The created world contains the whole range of good and evil. As a phenomenon subject to the movement of gravity, evil objectifies baseness and can have no depth or transcendence. That which endows beings and things with a greater reality is good, Simone Weil declares. "The unreality which takes the goodness from the good: this is what constitutes evil." Evil must be purified, or life is not possible.

Creation: good broken up into pieces and scattered throughout evil.

Evil is limitless, but it is not infinite. Only the infinite limits the limitless.

Monotony of evil: never anything new, everything about it is *equivalent*. Never anything real, everything about it is imaginary.

It is because of this monotony that quantity plays so great a part. A host of women (Don Juan) or of men (Célimène), etc. One is condemned to false infinity. That is hell itself.

Evil is license and that is why it is monotonous: everything has to be drawn from ourselves. But it is not given to man to create, so it is a bad attempt to imitate God.

Not to recognize and accept this impossibility of creating is the source of many an error. We are obliged to imitate the act of creation, and there are two possible imitations—the one real and the other apparent—preserving and destroying.

There is no trace of "I" in the act of preserving. There is in that of destroying. The "I" leaves its mark on the world as it destroys.

Literature and morality. Imaginary evil is romantic and varied; real evil is gloomy, monotonous, barren, boring. Imaginary good is boring; real good is always new, marvelous, intoxicating. Therefore "imaginative literature" is either boring or immoral (or a mixture of both). It only escapes from this alternative if in some way it passes over to the side of reality through the power of art—and only genius can do that.

A certain inferior kind of virtue is good's degraded image, of which we have to repent, and of which it is more difficult to repent than it is of evil. The Pharisee and the Publican.

Good as the opposite of evil is, in a sense, equivalent to it, as is the way with all opposites.

It is not good which evil violates, for good is inviolate: only a degraded good can be violated.

That which is the direct opposite of an evil never belongs to the order of higher good. It is often scarcely any higher than evil! Examples: theft and the bourgeois respect for property; adultery and the "respectable woman"; the savings bank and waste; lying and "sincerity."

Good is essentially other than evil. Evil is multifarious and fragmentary, good is one; evil is apparent, good is mysterious; evil consists in action, good in non-action, in activity which does not act, etc.— Good considered on the level of evil and measured against it as one opposite against another is good of the penal code order. Above there is a good which, in a sense, bears more resemblance to evil than to this low form of good. This fact opens the way to a great deal of demagogy and many tedious paradoxes.

Good which is defined in the way that one defines evil should be rejected. Evil does reject it. But the way it rejects it is evil.

Is there a union of incompatible vices in beings given over to evil? I do not think so. Vices are subject to gravity, and that is why there is no depth or transcendence in evil.

We experience good only by doing it.

We experience evil only by refusing to allow ourselves to do it, or, if we do it, by repenting of it.

When we do evil we do not know it, because evil flies from the light.

Does evil, as we conceive it to be when we do not do it, exist? Does not the evil that we do seem to be something simple and natural which compels us? Is not evil analogous to illusion? When we are the victims of an illusion we do not feel it to be an illusion but a reality. It is the same perhaps with evil. Evil when we are in its power is not felt as evil but as a necessity, or even a duty.

As soon as we do evil, the evil appears as a sort of duty. Most people have a sense of duty about doing certain things that are bad and others that are good. The same man feels it to be a duty to sell for the highest price he can and not to steal, etc. Good for such people is on the level of evil, it is a good without light.

The sensitivity of the innocent victim who suffers is like felt crime. True crime cannot be felt. The innocent victim who suffers knows the truth about his executioner, the executioner does not know it. The evil which the innocent victim feels in himself is in his executioner, but he is not sensible of the fact. The innocent victim can only know the evil in the shape of suffering. That which is not felt by the criminal is his own crime. That which is not felt by the innocent victim is his own innocence.

It is the innocent victim who can feel hell.

The sin which we have in us emerges from us and spreads outside ourselves, setting up a contagion of sin. Thus, when we are in a temper, those around us grow angry. Or again, from superior to inferior: anger produces fear. But at the contact of a perfectly pure being there is a transmutation, and the sin becomes suffering. Such is the function of the just servant of Isaiah, of the Lamb of God. Such is redemptive suffering. All the criminal violence of the Roman Empire ran up against Christ, and in him it became pure suffering. Evil beings, on the other hand, transform simple suffering (sickness, for example) into sin.

It follows, perhaps, that redemptive suffering has to have a social origin. It has to be injustice, violence on the part of human beings.

The false God changes suffering into violence. The true God changes violence into suffering.

Expiatory suffering is the shock in return for the evil we have done. Redemptive suffering is the shadow of the pure good we desire.

A hurtful act is the transference to others of the degradation which we bear in ourselves. That is why we are inclined to commit such acts as a way of deliverance.

All crime is a transference of the evil in him who acts, to him who undergoes the result of the action. This is true of unlawful love as well as murder.

The apparatus of penal justice has been so contaminated with evil, after all the centuries during which, without any compensatory purification, it has been in contact with evil-doers, that a condemnation is very often a transference of evil from the penal apparatus itself to the condemned man; and that is possible even when he is guilty and the punishment is not out of proportion. Hardened criminals are the only people to whom the penal apparatus can do no harm. It does terrible harm to the innocent.

When there is a transference of evil, the evil is not diminished but increased in him from whom it proceeds. This is a phenomenon of multiplication. The same is true when the evil is transferred to things.

Where, then, are we to put the evil?

We have to transfer it from the impure part to the pure part of ourselves, thus changing it into pure suffering. The crime which is latent in us we must inflict on ourselves.

In this way, however, it would not take us long to sully our own point of inward purity, if we did not renew it by contact with an unchangeable purity placed beyond all possible attack.

Patience consists in not transforming suffering into crime. That in itself is enough to transform crime into suffering.

To transfer evil to what is exterior is to distort the relationship between things. That which is exact and fixed, number, proportion, harmony, withstands this distortion. Whatever my state, whether vigorous or exhausted, in three miles there are three milestones. That is why number hurts when we are suffering: it interferes with the operation of transference. To fix my attention on what is too rigid to be distorted by my interior modifications is to make possible within myself the apparition of something changeless and an access to the eternal.

We must accept the evil done to us as a remedy for that which we have done.

It is not the suffering we inflict on ourselves, but that which comes to us from outside which is the true remedy. Moreover, it has to be unjust. When we have sinned by injustice it is not enough to suffer what is just, we have to suffer injustice.

Purity is absolutely invulnerable as purity, in the sense that no violence can make it less pure. It is, however, highly vulnerable in the sense that every attack of evil makes it suffer, that every sin which touches it turns it into suffering.

If someone does me an injury I must desire that this injury shall not degrade me. I must desire this out of love for him who inflicts it, in order that he may not really have done evil.

The saints (those who are nearly saints) are more exposed than others to the devil, because the real knowledge they have of their wretchedness makes the light *almost* intolerable.

The sin against the Spirit consists of knowing a thing to be good and hating it because it is good. We experience the equivalent of it in the form of resistance every time we set our faces in the direction of good. For every contact with good leads to a knowledge of the distance between good and evil and the commencement of a painful effort of assimilation. It is something which hurts, and we are afraid. This fear is perhaps the sign of the reality of the contact. The corresponding sin cannot come about unless a lack of hope makes the consciousness of the distance intolerable, and changes the pain into hatred. Hope is a remedy in this respect. But a better remedy is indifference to ourselves, and being happy because the good is good, although we are far from it and may even suppose that we are destined to remain separated from it forever.

Once an atom of pure good has entered the soul, the most criminal weakness is infinitely less dangerous than the very slightest treason, even though this should be confined to a purely inward movement of thought, lasting no more than an instant but to which we have given our consent. That is a participation in hell. So long as the soul has not tasted of pure goodness it is separated from hell as it is from paradise.

It is only possible to choose hell through an attachment to salvation. He who does not desire the joy of God, but is satisfied to know that there really is joy in God, falls but does not commit treason.

When we love God through evil as such, it is really God whom we love.

We have to love God through evil as such: to love God through the evil we hate, while hating this evil: to love God as the author of the evil which we are actually hating.

Evil is to love, what mystery is to the intelligence. As mystery compels the virtue of faith to be supernatural, so does evil the virtue of charity. Moreover, to try to find compensation or justification for evil is just as harmful for charity, as to try to expose the heart of the mysteries on the plane of human intelligence.

Speech of Ivan in the *Karamazovs:* "Even though this immense factory were to produce the most extraordinary marvels and were to cost only a single tear from a single child, I refuse."

I am in complete agreement with this sentiment. No reason whatever which anyone could produce to compensate for a child's tear, would make me consent to that tear. Absolutely none which the mind can conceive. There is just one, however, but it is intelligible only to supernatural love: "God willed it." And for that reason I would consent to a world which was nothing but evil as readily as to a child's tear.

The death agony is the supreme dark night which is necessary even for the perfect if they are to attain to absolute purity, and for that reason it is better that it should be bitter.

The unreality which takes the goodness from good, this is what constitutes evil. Evil is always the destruction of tangible things in which there is the real presence of good. Evil is carried out by those who have no knowledge of this real presence. In that sense it is true that no one is wicked voluntarily. The relations between forces give to absence the power to destroy presence.

We cannot contemplate without terror the extent of the evil which man can do and endure.

How could we believe it possible to find a compensation for this evil since, because of it, God suffered crucifixion?

Good and evil. Reality. That which gives more reality to beings and things is good, that which takes it from them is evil.

The Romans did evil by robbing the Greek towns of their statues, because the towns, the temples, and the life of the Greeks had less reality without the statues, and because the statues could not have as much reality in Rome as in Greece.

The desperate, humble supplication of the Greeks to be allowed to keep some of their statues: a desperate attempt to make their own notion of value pass into the mind of others. Understood thus, there is nothing base in their behavior. But it was almost bound to be ineffectual. There is a duty to understand and weigh the system of other people's values with our own, on the same balance. To forge the balance.

To allow the imagination to dwell on what is evil implies a certain cowardice; we hope to enjoy, to know, and to grow through what is unreal.

Even to dwell in imagination on certain things as possible (quite a different thing from clearly conceiving the possibility of them, which is essential to virtue) is to commit ourselves to them already. Curiosity is the cause of it. We have to forbid ourselves certain things (not the conception of them but the dwelling on them); we must not think about them. We believe that thought does not commit us in any way, but it alone commits us, and license of thought includes all license. Not to think about a thing, supreme faculty. Purity, negative virtue. If we have allowed our imagination to dwell on an evil thing, if we meet other men who make it objective through their words and actions and thus remove the social barrier, we are already nearly lost. And what is easier? There is no sharp division. When we see the ditch we are already over it. With good it is quite otherwise; the ditch is visible when it has still to be crossed, at the moment of the wrench and the rending. One does not fall into good. The word baseness expresses this property of evil.

Even when it is an accomplished fact evil keeps the character of unreality; this perhaps explains the simplicity of criminals; everything is simple in dreams. This simplicity corresponds to that of the highest virtue.

Evil has to be purified—or life is not possible. God alone can do that. This is the idea of the Gita. It is also the idea of Moses, of Mahomet, of Hitlerism. . . .

But Jehovah, Allah, Hitler are earthly Gods. The purification they bring about is imaginary.

That which is essentially different from evil is virtue accompanied by a clear perception of the possibility of evil, and of evil appearing as something good. The presence of illusions which we have abandoned, but which are still present in the mind, is perhaps the criterion of truth.

We cannot have a horror of doing harm to others unless we have reached a point where others can no longer do harm to us (then we love others, carrying things to the farthest limit, like our past selves).

The contemplation of human misery wrenches us in the direction of God, and it is only in others whom we love as ourselves that we can contemplate it. We can neither contemplate it in ourselves as such, nor in others as such.

The extreme affliction which overtakes human beings does not create human misery, it merely reveals it.

Sin and the glamour of force. Because the soul in its entirety has not been able to know and accept human misery, we think that there is a difference between human beings, and in this way we fall short of justice, either by making a difference between ourselves and others, or by making a selection among others.

This is because we do not know that human misery is a constant and irreducible quantity, which is as great as it can be in each man, and that greatness comes from the one and only God, so that there is identity between one man and another in this respect.

We are surprised that affliction does not have an ennobling effect. This is because when we think of the afflicted person it is the affliction we have in mind. Whereas he himself does not think of his affliction: he has his soul filled with no matter what paltry comfort he may have set his heart on.

How could there be no evil in the world? The world has got to be foreign to our desires. If this were so, without its containing evil, our desires would then be entirely bad. That must not happen.

There is every degree of distance between the creature and God. A distance where the love of God is impossible. Matter, plants, animals. Here, evil is so complete that it destroys itself; there is no longer any evil: mirror of divine innocence. We are at the point where love is just possible. It is a great privilege since the love which unites is in proportion to the distance.

God has created a world which is not the best possible, but which contains the whole range of good and evil. We are at the point where it is as bad as possible. For beyond is the stage where evil becomes innocence.

THE GREAT BEAST

The Great Beast symbolizes for Simone Weil a transcendent social idolatry necessary to man who lives in the cave. "A pharisee is someone who is virtuous out of obedience to the Great Beast," she concludes. When the "power of the social element" usurps God's place in the soul, the collective soul is ascendant. "The collective is the object of all idolatry, this it is which chains us to the earth." Could there be, Simone Weil asks, a worse prison than this?

The great beast is the only object of idolatry, the only *ersatz* of God, the only imitation of something which is infinitely far from me and which is I myself.

If we could be egoistical it would be very pleasant. It would be a rest. But literally we cannot.

It is impossible for me to take myself as an end, or, in consequence, my fellow man as an end, since he is my fellow. Nor can I take any material thing, because matter is still less capable of having finality conferred upon it than human beings are.

Only one thing can be taken as an end, for in relation to the human person it possesses a kind of transcendence: this is the collective.

The collective is the object of all idolatry, this it is which chains us to the earth. In the case of avarice: gold is of the social order. In the case of ambition: power is of the social order. Science and art are full of the social element also. And love? Love is more or less an exception: that is why we can go to God through love, not through avarice or ambition. Yet the social element is not absent from love (passions excited by princes, celebrated people, all those who have prestige. . .)

There are two goods of the same denomination but radically different from each other: one which is the opposite of evil and one which is the absolute. The absolute has no opposite. The relative is not the opposite of the absolute; it is derived from it through a relationship which is not commutative. That which we want is the absolute good. That which is within our reach is the good which is correlated to evil. We betake ourselves to it by mistake, like the prince who starts to make love to the maid instead of the mistress. The error is due to the clothes. It is the social which throws the color of the absolute over the relative. The remedy is in the idea of relationship. Relationship breaks its way out of the social. It is the monopoly of the individual. Society is the cave. The way out is solitude.

To relate belongs to the solitary spirit. No crowd can conceive relationship. "This is good or bad in relation to. . . ." "in so far as . . ." That escapes the crowd. A crowd cannot add things together.

He who is above social life returns to it when he wishes; not so he who is below. It is the same with everything. A relationship which is not commutative between what is better and what is less good.

The vegetative and the social are the two realms where the good does not enter.

Christ redeemed the vegetative, not the social. He did not pray for the world.

The social order is irreducibly that of the prince of this world. Our only duty with regard to the social is to try to limit the evil of it. (Richelieu: The salvation of states lies only in this world).

A society, like the Church, which claims to be divine is perhaps more dangerous on account of the *ersatz* good which it contains than on account of the evil which sullies it.

Something of the social labeled divine; an intoxicating mixture which carries with it every sort of license. Devil disguised.

Conscience is deceived by the social. Our supplementary energy (imaginative) is to a great extent taken up with the social. It has to be detached from it. That is the most difficult of detachments.

Meditation on the social mechanism is in this respect a purification of the first importance.

To contemplate the social is as good a way of detachment as to retire from the world. That is why I have not been wrong to rub shoulders with politics for so long.

It is only by entering the transcendental, the supernatural, the authentically spiritual order that man rises above the social. Until then, whatever he may do, the social is transcendent in relation to him.

On the nonsupernatural plane, society is that which keeps evil (certain forms of it) away by forming, as it were, a barrier. A society of criminals or people given over to vice, even if only composed of a handful of men, destroys this barrier.

But what is it that impels people to enter such a society? Either necessity, or laxity, or, usually, a mixture of the two. They do not think they are becoming involved, for they do not know that, apart from the supernatural, it is only society which prevents us from falling naturally into the most fearful vice and crime. They do not know that they are going to become different, for they do not know the extent of the region within themselves which can be changed by environment. They always become involved without knowing.

Rome is the Great Beast of atheism and materialism, adoring nothing but itself. Israel is the Great Beast of religion. Neither the one nor the other is likable. The Great Beast is always repulsive.

Would a society in which only gravity reigned be able to exist, or is a little of the supernatural element a vital necessity?

In Rome, perhaps, there was only gravity.
With the Hebrews, too, perhaps. Their God was heavy.

Perhaps there was only one ancient people absolutely without
mysticism: Rome. By what mystery? It was an artificial city, made up
of fugitives, just as Israel was.

The Great Beast of Plato. The whole of Marxism, in so far as it
is true, is contained in the page of Plato on the Great Beast; and its
refutation is there too.

The power of the social element. Agreement between several men
brings with it a feeling of reality. It brings with it also a sense of duty.
Divergence, where this agreement is concerned, appears as a sin.
Hence *all* returns to the fold are possible. The state of conformity is
an imitation of grace.

By a strange mystery—which is connected with the power of the
social element—quite ordinary men gain virtues through their profession, in dealing with the objects connected with it, which virtues, if
extended to all circumstances of life, would make of them heroes or
saints.
But the power of the social element makes these virtues *natural.*
Accordingly they need a compensation.

Pharisees: "Verily I say unto you, they have received their reward." Inversely, Christ could have said of the publicans and prostitutes: "Verily I say unto you, they have received their punishment"—
that is to say, social reprobation. In so far as they have received this,
the Father who is in secret does not punish them. Whereas the sins
which are not accompanied by social reprobation receive their full
measure of punishment from the Father who is in secret. Thus social
reprobation is a favor on the part of destiny. It turns into a supplementary evil, however, for those who, under the pressure of this
reprobation, manufacture for themselves eccentric social surroundings, within which they have full license. Criminal and homosexual circles, etc.

The service of the false God (of the social Beast under whatever form it may be) purifies evil by eliminating its horror. Nothing seems evil to those who serve it, except failure in its service. The service of the true God, on the other hand, allows the horror of evil to remain and even makes it more intense. While this evil horrifies us, we yet love it as emanating from the will of God.

Those who think today that one of the adversaries is on the side of the good, think also that that side will be victorious.

To watch a good, loved as such, condemned as it were by the oncoming tide of events is an intolerable suffering.

The idea that that which does not exist any more may be a good, is painful and we thrust it aside. That is submission to the Great Beast.

The force of soul of the Communists comes from the fact that they are going not only toward what they believe to be the good, but toward what they believe will surely and soon be brought about. Thus without being saints—they are a long way from that—they can endure dangers and sufferings which only a saint would bear for justice alone.

In some respects the state of mind of the Communists is very analogous to that of the early Christians.

That eschatological propaganda explains very well the persecutions of the first period.

"He to whom little is forgiven, the same loveth little." This concerns someone with whom social virtue occupies a very large place. Grace finds little room to spare in him. Obedience to the Great Beast, which conforms to the good—that is social virtue.

A pharisee is someone who is virtuous out of obedience to the Great Beast.

Charity can and should love in all countries all that is a condition of the spiritual development of individuals, that is to say, on the one hand, social order, even if it is bad, as being less bad than disorder; on the other hand the language, ceremonies, customs—all that contains beauty—all the poetry which the life of a country embraces.

But a nation as such cannot be the object of supernatural love. It has no soul. It is a Great Beast.

And yet a city . . .

But that is not social; it is a human environment of which one is no more conscious than of the air one breathes. A contact with nature, the past, tradition.

Rootedness lies in something other than the social.

Patriotism. We must not have any love other than charity. A nation cannot be an object of charity. But a country can be such, as an environment bearing traditions which are eternal. Every country can be that.

V

PATHS
OF MEDITATION

The mysteries of the faith cannot be either affirmed or denied; they must be placed above that which we affirm or deny.

Simone Weil chose to remain "a stranger and an exile" at the threshold of the Church. And yet she did pass through the sacred doors of infinity. Ultimately, miraculously, her life and thought instance a spiritual victory that is perhaps unparalleled in the twentieth century. The paths of her unceasing meditations led her out of herself to God. Destiny made it impossible for her not to bear "the mark of the experience of God." To judge by the allegory of her life, written a few months before her death, her encounter with the divine seems foreordained: "He entered my room and said: 'Poor creature, you who understood nothing, who know nothing. Come with me and I will teach you things which you do not suspect.' I followed him." In its unalterable direction and in its shaping form her lifework is itself a divine meditation, which is her passageway to God. "God is attention without distraction," she writes. Action and contemplation seek for and find a point of perfect harmony and unity in God. "The silent presence of the supernatural here below is that point of leverage. That is why, in the early centuries of Christianity, the Cross was compared to a balance." Any true relationship between means and ends must exist in God. This relationship must be one of reciprocal forgiveness: "God's great crime against us is to have created us, is the fact of our existence. And in our existence is our great crime against God. When we forgive God for our existence, he forgives us for our existing." One's spiritual transformation depends on the attainment of this reciprocity. The value of one's conception of life is now completely altered, illuminated, for the soul has now, too, "passed through the fire of the love of God": "When a man's way of behaving towards things and men, or simply his way of regarding them, reveals supernatural virtues, one knows that his soul is no longer virgin, it has slept with God; perhaps even without knowing it, like a girl violated in her sleep."

Since God is not in time, Simone Weil specifies, man is abandoned in time. Creation itself is an abdication; God, then, must wait patiently for man to love him. God is the good, and "the good which is nothing but good can only stand waiting." Whatever speaks to man of time conveys God's supplication to man. "God waits like a beggar who stands motionless and silent before someone who will perhaps give him a piece of bread. Time is that waiting." The very nature of creation hinders the drawing closer together of God and man. "Time, which is our one misery, is the very touch of his hand. It is the abdication by which he lets us exist." In the grip of this paradox, in which the possibility of divine mystery inheres, one can make contact that helps to place oneself in what Simone Weil calls "the third dimension": "Contact with human creatures is given to us through the sense of absence. Compared with this absence, presence becomes more than absence." Indeed, one should not dare to speak about God, or to pronounce the word, "except when one is not able to do otherwise." But precisely at that point when "one is not able to do otherwise," when, that is, infinite possibility becomes divine certainty, and one has truly imitated the patience and humility of God, one's experience of God transcends both affirmation and denial. "We can only know one thing about God: that he is what we are not. Our misery alone is the image of this. The more we contemplate it, the more we contemplate him."

Simone Weil's meditations on the Cross belong to the highest expression of her mystic genius and of her "supernatural knowledge." In the Passion of Christ she saw a correlation with and expres-

sion of a suffering humanity. Christ is proof that human affliction is
irreducible, "that it is as great in the absolutely sinless man as in the
sinner." He also essentializes abandonment. Man, in his misery, shares
in the distance placed between the Son and his Father. It signals participation in the Cross of Christ, which should become the very substance of life. "The Trinity and the Cross are the two poles of Christianity"—she asserts in one of the most astonishing, if not the greatest,
of her meditations, "The Love of God and Affliction"—"the two essential truths: the first perfect joy; the second perfect affliction. It is
necessary to know both the one and the other and their mysterious
unity, but the human condition in this world places us infinitely far
from the Trinity, at the very foot of the Cross." The contemplation
of Christ's Cross alone enables man to accept and endure affliction.
This contemplation should also teach man not to feel compassion for
himself or even others, but rather to extend compassion to slaugh-
tered innocence, to the Christ "across the centuries." Only Christ is
capable of compassion. And only by looking upon the symbol of the
Cross can man love God. "The Cross of Christ is the only source of
light that is bright enough to illumine affliction. Wherever there is
affliction, in any age or any country, the Cross of Christ is the truth
of it." Repeatedly she identifies the Cross and necessity. Human
destiny and the Passion of Christ are one. "There is not, there cannot
be, any human activity in whatever sphere, of which Christ's Cross is
not the supreme and secret truth."

If the knowledge of affliction is, as Simone Weil contends, the
key to Christianity, it is also the key to her religious meditations. In
his acceptance of affliction man consents to God's grace and accepts
the decreative process of "expiation": "to want not to be any longer,"
to know that "we are totally mistaken" in the presumption, the
arrogance, "that the world is created and controlled by ourselves."
Decreation, a purgative inner state of soul, indicates progress in
man's self-knowledge of his nothingness. Affliction and decreation,
in terms of acceptance, the acceptance of humility really, are inter-
dependent spiritual states. In the act of accepting suffering, man accepts the gift of grace and begins to climb the ladder of transcendence, or as Simone Weil writes: "Affliction, when it is consented to
and accepted and loved, is truly a baptism." As such, it is an up-

rooting of life, "a more or less attenuated equivalent of death" that takes possession of the soul. In the course of this possession God is absent. This absence accentuates death, darkness, horror, lovelessness, accursedness, inertia. Men who are struck down by affliction are at the foot of the Cross, the point of the greatest possible distance from God. "One can only accept the existence of affliction by considering it as a distance," she reflects. But, for those who love, this distance is only separation, and separation, though painful, is a good because it is love. "This universe where we are living," she continues, "and of which we form a minute particle, is the distance put by the divine Love between God and God." Man can never escape obedience to God. He must learn to feel in all things the obedience of the universe to God: "As soon as we feel this obedience with our whole being, we see God." Simone Weil equates this process with an apprenticeship, involving not only time and effort but also, inevitably and indispensably, joy and suffering.

Perhaps more than any of her great meditations, her meditation on God, whatever its theological sources, or validity, or orthodoxy, breathes a coalescent inspiration and profundity. It is as if a divine passion possesses and overwhelms her every word and thought as she probes the divine questions: "How can we seek for him? How can we go towards him?" The very essence, the justification of her fate, is caught in those two obsessive questions. The paths of her meditation, of her mystic quest, lead her to and merge with them. Her answers to them are an intermediary between divine passion and divine revelation: "We are incapable of progressing vertically," she confesses. "We cannot take one step towards the heavens. God crosses the universe and comes to us. Over the infinity of space and time the infinitely more infinite love of God comes to possess us." To those who refuse, God returns again and again, like a beggar, until "one day he stops coming." "If we consent, God places a little seed in us and he goes away again. From that moment God has no more to do; neither have we, except to wait." She does not hesitate, nevertheless, to stress that "the growth of seed within us is painful." There are always weeds to pull up and grass to cut: "This gardening amounts to a violent operation." But when the seed does grow of itself there comes a time when the soul belongs to God. It is now the soul's turn to cross the universe to go to God. And now too the love within the soul is divine and uncreated; "it is the love of God for God which is passing through it. God alone is capable of loving God." A tremendous transformation is effected in us, for the soul comes into the actual presence of God. "It is at the point of intersection between creation and Creator. This point is the point of intersection of the two branches of the Cross."

Always it is the right orientation of the soul towards God that counts for Simone Weil. This orientation contains the divine possibility of transfiguration. It also clarifies and, in the end, divinizes affliction, which she considers "a marvel of divine technique." She likens extreme affliction, consisting of physical pain, spiritual distress, and social degradation, to a nail being struck by a hammer. The shock, which is ultimately religious, spiritual, and infinite, travels from the nail's head to the point. "The point of the nail is applied to the very centre of the soul, and its head is the whole of necessity throughout all space and time." This nail pierces through creation, through the veil, or screen, separating the soul from God. And the soul enters a different, a totally other dimension. "The man whose soul remains oriented towards God while a nail is driven through it finds himself nailed to the very centre of the universe; the true centre, which is not in the middle, which is not in space and time, which is God." Affliction serves both as spiritual opportunity and revelation. We pass through the divine fire. We have things disclosed to us that hitherto have been divine secrets. A divine synthesis in purgation transpires; our spiritual blindness is lifted; the laws of gravitation are put aside by divine grace. Affliction is a supernatural process. To pass through the experience of affliction is "to know it in the depths of one's being." It is to know, that is, the death of the soul, as well as the acceptance of that death, by finally placing one's treasure and heart not merely "outside one's person but outside all one's thoughts and feelings and outside everything knowable, in the hands of our Father who is in secret."

Simone Weil's theological-metaphysical meditations never fail to attain a point of balance. In its totality her thought is identified, and identifiable, by its intrinsic sense of harmony. In this she is a true Christian Hellenist. If she emphasizes "the love of God and affliction,"

she equally emphasizes the "love of the order of the world." Her
sensuous vision of living life, of "the country of here below," "the
city of the world," is not as denuded, or as harsh, or as one-dimen-
sionally dialectical as some of her commentators like to think. Affliction is not her last or only word, or if it is, it is mediated by her
supreme appreciation of beauty, in which she sees a redemptive incarnational capacity. Beauty is another indicator of the divine, or as
she notes: "Beauty is eternity here below." It assists us in finding
answers to the divine questions and in making us more perceptive
of our sense of time, values, and being. Beauty can conduce spiritual
transformation in the sacred forms that Simone Weil underscores
when she writes: "By loving our neighbour we imitate the divine
love which created us all and all our fellows. By loving the order
of the world we imitate the divine love which created this universe
of which we are a part." She especially singles out for praise the
beauty of the world as it is expressed by Greek Stoicism, by parts of
the Old Testament (the Psalms, the Book of Job, Isaiah, and the Book
of Wisdom), by Saint John of the Cross, and by Saint Francis, who
"stripped himself naked in order to have immediate contact with the
beauty of the world." But for the most part, she complains, the beauty
of the world, as a central inspiration, is absent from the Christian
tradition. Her criticism is not, in our present impoverished circumstances, without either its sociological or its ecological validity or
relevance; she observes in that prophetic vein that recalls a D. H.
Lawrence: "Today one might think that the white races had almost
lost all feeling for the beauty of the world, and that they had taken
upon them the task of making it disappear from all the continents
where they have penetrated with their armies, their trade and their
religion."

   Her sense of beauty can hardly be overestimated. It underlines
her most intense feelings about, her "filial piety" towards, the tangible world. Any estimation of her thought has to take these feelings,
in all their sensuous reverence, into full account since they comprise
an essential dimension of her thought. What she has to say about
beauty arises not so much, or only, from some rapturous, ecstatic
inner source of vibration, but from a deep and sensitive passion for
creation. Ultimately she writes of the beauty of the world from a

religious imagination. It can be said that in her appreciation and evocation of the beautiful she writes as a great artist who sees beauty as the most natural approach to God. Though the modern secular world has debased beauty, she affirms its wondrous sacramental potentiality. "If it were made true and pure, it would sweep all secular life in a body to the feet of God; it would make the total incarnation of the faith possible." Beauty, a mysterious emanation of the divine, is also a "divine enticement," a "labyrinth," a "trap": "The soul's natural inclination to love beauty is the trap God most frequently uses in order to win it and open it to the breath from on high." An attribute of matter, beauty is a supernal essence of the world to human sensibility: "The beauty of the world is the co-operation of divine wisdom in creation." At the same time beauty, she stresses, can be painfully tantalizing, drawing us towards it without our knowing what to ask of it. Even when we possess it, we still desire something more of it, even to feed on it. But looking and eating are two different operations, except "in the country inhabited by God," where they are one and the same. "It may be," she thinks, "that vice, depravity, and crime are nearly always, or even perhaps always, in their essence, attempts to eat beauty, to eat what we should only look at." Our love of beauty, if it is to transcend the slavery of matter, must intersect with our pursuit of wisdom, at last breaking through the curtain that separates us from the ultimate Real. It is this truth that we must contemplate: "We cannot contemplate without a certain love. The contemplation of this image of the order of the world constitutes a certain contact with the beauty of the world. The beauty of the world is the order of the world that is loved."

What Simone Weil has to say about carnal love having the beauty of the world as its object shows a profound sympathy of compassion. In her judgments she can be hard, but she is never heartless. How can we diminish and transcend our coarseness, our vulgarity, our cruelty? She helps us to confront this question, to come to grips with it—and with ourselves. One could say that she arouses in us the redemptive process in all of its possibilities. Her special relevance to the modern human predicament is inestimable when one reflects on statements such as these: "The longing to love the beauty of the world in a human being is essentially the longing for the Incarnation." "The different kinds of vice, the use of drugs, in the literal or metaphorical sense of the word, all such things constitute the search for the state where the beauty of the world will be tangible. The mistake lies precisely in the search for a special state." "The only true beauty, the only beauty that is the real presence of God, is the beauty of the universe. Nothing less than the universe is beautiful." "To destroy cities, either materially or morally, or to exclude human beings from a city, thrusting them down to the state of social outcasts, this is to sever every bond of poetry and love between human beings and the universe. It is to plunge them forcibly into the horror of ugliness. There can scarcely be a greater crime." Her understanding of the human condition is always characterized by control and order; sentimentalism in no way subverts her view of the created universe in which, "under a thousand different forms, grace and mortal sin are everywhere." A purity of thought, conveyed with absolute sincerity and sympathy, informs and shapes her judgments, her deeper vision, of the supernatural presence in all life.

"Concerning the Our Father" marks the culmination of her meditations. It is her spiritual epitome, the final resolution and the final consecration of her life's thought. All approaches to Simone Weil end in her approach to God. Passage from time into eternity and release from the prison of self are gained in this meditation. Consent to grace eternalizes in the supreme supplication, "Our Father." We arrive at the highest spiritual moment when we ask for "supernatural bread." Divine possibility is realized. "The prayer began with the word 'Father,' " she points out in a paradigmatic passage; "it ends with the word 'evil.' We must go from confidence to fear. Confidence alone can give us strength enough not to fall as a result of fear. After having contemplated the name, the kingdom, and the will of God, after having received the supernatural bread and having been purified from evil, the soul is ready for the true humility which crowns all virtues." Her meditation on the most sacred of prayers, the source of all prayers according to Saint Augustine, is the sacred point at and in which all her paths of meditation converge. It is the point when a modern saint gives her final testimony. Her concluding sentences summarize the worth of her meditation, in its depth and warmth, even as they can confirm for us why, in the history of spirituality, it is comparable to some of the greatest works on the Our Father, including that of Origen in the third century or of Saint Teresa in the sixteenth century: "The Our Father contains all possible petitions; we cannot conceive of any prayer not already contained in it. It is to prayer what Christ is to humanity. It is impossible to say it once through, giving the fullest possible attention to each word, without a change, infinitesimal perhaps but real, taking place in the soul."

Simone Weil's life was a gesture of spiritual destiny. Her devotion was unhesitant. Her faith was unshakable. "My heart, I hope, is transferred forever into the Holy Eucharist," she wrote a year before she died. In her meditations we are in the presence of a modern saint, a mystic and religious philosopher, who seeks for and attains unity across the gulf of "infinite separation." In the end we must stand before this spiritual attainment deeply humbled. Our experience of her vision, a vision which is surely one of the great miracles of the twentieth century, becomes a lesson in humility that allows us to enter the "warm silence," the "true silence," when, as she believes, God's love can speak and be heard.

TWO POEMS

These two poems belong to the period in 1938 when, in the course of following the liturgical services during Holy Week at the Benedictine monastery of Solesmes, "the thought of the Passion of Christ entered into my being once and for all," as Simone Weil later said of her conversion. In both poems she evokes man's approach to the supernatural, "The Threshold" describing the soul's painful journey of purification, "The Stars" emphasizing man's need to wait in patience for divine grace.

THE THRESHOLD

Open the door to us, and we will see the orchards,
We will drink their cold water where the moon
      has left its trace.
The long road burns, hostile to strangers.
We wander without knowing and find no place.

We want to see flowers. Here thirst grips us.
Waiting and suffering, we are here before the door.

If we must, we will break this door with our fists.
We press and push, but the barrier still holds.

One must weaken, must wait and look vainly.
We look at the door: it is closed, unbreachable.
We fix our eyes there; we weep under the torment;
We see it always; the weight of time crushes us.

Before us is the door; what use for us to wish?
Better to turn away, abandoning hope.
We will never enter. We are weary of seeing it . . .
The door, opening, let so much silence escape

That neither the orchards appeared nor any flower;
Only the immense space where emptiness and
        light are
Was suddenly everywhere present, overflowed
        the heart,
And washed our eyes almost blind under the dust.

THE STARS

Fiery stars peopling the night the far skies,
Mute stars turning without seeing always icy,
You tear from our hearts the days past
And hurl us into tomorrow, our cries lost at your
        height.

Since we must, we follow you, with arms tied,
With eyes raised toward your pure but bitter light.
On your face all traces matter little.
We hold our tongues, we stagger on the highways.

It is there, in the heart suddenly, their fire divine.

COME WITH ME

The description of the mystical experience given below appears at the end of the second volume of THE NOTEBOOKS OF SIMONE WEIL. *She wrote it a few months before her death; it can serve as a key to her religious thought. Contact with the divine, she shows, can be a decisive, lightning moment of "pure intuition," of "acceptance of the moral void." "Whoever for an instant can endure the void either receives the supernatural bread or else falls," she records. "Terrible risk; but we have got to run it."*

He entered my room and said: 'Poor creature, you who understand nothing, who know nothing. Come with me and I will teach you things which you do not suspect'. I followed him.

He took me into a church. It was new and ugly. He led me up to the altar and said: 'Kneel down'. I said 'I have not been baptized'. He said 'Fall on your knees before this place, in love, as before the place where lies the truth'. I obeyed.

He brought me out and made me climb up to a garret. Through the open window one could see the whole city spread out, some wooden scaffoldings, and the river on which boats were being unloaded. The garret was empty, except for a table and two chairs. He bade me be seated.

We were alone. He spoke. From time to time someone would enter, mingle in the conversation, then leave again.

Winter had gone; spring had not yet come. The branches of the trees lay bare, without buds, in the cold air full of sunshine.

The light of day would arise, shine forth in splendour, and fade away; then the moon and the stars would enter through the window. And then once more the dawn would come up.

At times he would fall silent, take some bread from a cupboard, and we would share it. This bread really had the taste of bread. I have never found that taste again.

He would pour out some wine for me, and some for himself—wine which tasted of the sun and of the soil upon which this city was built.

At other times we would stretch ourselves out on the floor of the garret, and sweet sleep would enfold me. Then I would wake and drink in the light of the sun.

He had promised to teach me, but he did not teach me anything. We talked about all kinds of things, in a desultory way, as do old friends.

One day he said to me: 'Now go'. I fell down before him, I clasped his knees, I implored him not to drive me away. But he threw me out on the stairs. I went down unconscious of anything, my heart as it were in shreds. I wandered along the streets. Then I realized that I had no idea where this house lay.

I have never tried to find it again. I understood that he had come for me by mistake. My place is not in that garret. It can be any-where—in a prison cell, in one of those middle-class drawing-rooms full of knick-knacks and red plush, in the waiting-room of a station—anywhere, except in that garret.

Sometimes I cannot help trying, fearfully and remorsefully, to repeat to myself a part of what he said to me. How am I to know if I remember rightly? He is not there to tell me.

I know well that he does not love me. How could he love me? And yet deep down within me something, a particle of myself, can-not help thinking, with fear and trembling, that perhaps, in spite of all, he loves me.

CONTEMPLATION OF
THE DIVINE

*Supernatural insight defines the power and significance of
Simone Weil's contemplation of the Divine as found in
these startling pages from her notebooks. Some of the radical essences of her theology recur here, as this particular
and symptomatic remark demonstrates: "Religion in so far
as it is a sense of consolation is a hindrance to true faith;
and in this sense atheism is a purification."*

Lever. Tears the being away from appearance. Λόγος—Knowledge of
the second kind? Already of the third kind?—Tears the will away from
desire, or desire away from perspective—Third dimension.

Sin and virtue are not acts, but states. Acts are only the automatic
consequence of a state. But we are only able to represent them to
ourselves in the form of acts. Whence the symbol of sin *prior to all
act*. We are born in a state of sin. Has there been a time when man
was not in a state of sin? But he did not possess knowledge.

Blood on snow. Innocence and evil. That evil itself may be
pure. It can only be pure in the form of suffering, and the suffering
of someone innocent. An innocent being who suffers sheds the light
of salvation upon evil. He is the visible image of the innocent God.

412

That is why a God who loves man and a man who loves God have to suffer.

Happy innocence. Violetta. Something also infinitely precious. But it is a frail, precarious happiness, a fortuitous happiness. Apple blossom. Such happiness is not securely linked to innocence.

The woman who wishes for a child white as snow and red as blood, gets it; but she dies, and the child is handed over to a stepmother.

'Judge not.' Christ himself does not judge. He is judgment. Suffering innocence as measuring-rod.

Judgment, perspective. In this sense, every judgment judges him who pronounces it. Not to judge. It is not indifference or abstention, it is transcendent judgment, the imitation of divine judgment, which is impossible for us; but 'Be ye perfect, even as your heavenly Father is perfect.'

The drawing closer together of God and man is prohibited by the very nature of creation, by the gulf separating being from appearance. Upanishads: the gods do not wish it. It means an unmaking of creation, and creation unmakes itself in suffering.

Loss of the sense of reality when the mind submits itself to a perspective. Slavery; the perspective of the master. Other people's perspective. Underneath perspective. Disorder underneath order. But for this very reason slavery is the image of the relationship between man and God.

Not to speak about God (not in the inner language of the soul either); not to pronounce this word, *except when one is not able to do otherwise* ('able' is obviously used here in a particular sense).

Connection between the tree of earthly Paradise and knowledge, and between the tree of the cross and divine Wisdom. What mystery lies in this correspondence? (And whence comes the expression 'tree of the cross'?)

Human misery, and not pleasure, contains (with respect to ourselves) the secret of divine Wisdom. All pleasure-seeking is the search for an artificial paradise, for a more intense state (higher because more intense), for an intoxication, an enlargement. But it gives us nothing, except the experience that it is vain. Only the contemplation of our limitations and our misery places us on a higher plane. (Rajas–Sattva.)

'Whosoever humbleth himself shall be exalted.' Adam and Eve wanted to exalt themselves.

Fresco by Masaccio.

Their disobedience consisted in wanting without God to become *sicut dei*.

[Man has sinned in trying to become God (on the imaginary plane), and God has redeemed this sin by becoming man. By which means man can really become *sicut deus*. Thus the serpent had spoken truly.]

The ascending movement is vain (and worse than vain) if it does not spring from a descending movement.

'*Eritis sicut dei, scientes bonum et malum*': that is strictly true through the redemption.

(Why should one be reluctant to think that God willed Adam's sin?)

It is as if man's approach toward an imaginary divinity were an appeal to God for this desire to be crowned by punishment and redemption. He was driven out of Paradise so that he should know that he is not *sicut deus*. (That is why we have to suffer; otherwise we forget the fact too easily.)

Our thought, which gives us dominion over the universe, makes us be *sicut dei* at all times when we are not being gnawed by necessity.

Adam and Eve sought for divinity in vital energy—in a tree, a fruit. But it is prepared for us on some dead wood, geometrically squared, upon which hangs a corpse. We must look for the secret of our kinship with God in our mortality.

The knowledge of our misery is the only thing in us which is not miserable.

Sin is nothing else but the failure to recognize human misery— it is unconscious misery and for that very reason guilty misery. The story of Christ is the experimental proof that human misery is irreducible, that it is as great in the absolutely sinless man as in the sinner. Only it is enlightened. But this misery cannot be separated from the state of sin; the story of Christ is bound up with that of Adam.

In the same way that, in a sense, God is infinitely more than the whole universe, and, in a sense, manifests himself through a part of the universe, namely, good—so, in a sense, human misery is defined by the state of sin, and, in a sense, is independent of sin. Thus it is true to say that the Incarnation and the Passion are and are not consequences of Adam's disobedience.

Man's misery consists in the fact that he is not God. He is continually forgetting this.

Prometheus. God has given man fire—fire, the arts, writing, etc., all the material conditions for man's separation from the animals— and is punished for it by suffering, for, penetrating into the human soul, he there suffers human misery.

We can only know one thing about God: that he is what we are not. Our misery alone is the image of this. The more we contemplate it, the more we contemplate Him.

'He to whom much is forgiven, the same loveth much': sin (at the moment of repentance) is like an equivalent of suffering. The good *and* happy man cannot find room in himself for divine love (unless he has a supernatural insight into the fragile nature of goodness and happiness). He takes for an essential part of his nature that which is granted to him by circumstances. He confuses the 'I' with character.

For men of courage physical sufferings (and privations) are often a test of endurance and of strength of soul. But there is a better use to be made of them. For me, then, let them not be that. Let them be a sensible testimony of human misery. Let me endure them in a completely passive manner. Whatever happens to me, how could I ever come to regard affliction as too heavy, since the wound of affliction and the abasement to which those whom it strikes are condemned opens to them the knowledge of human misery, knowledge which is the door, the passage leading to all wisdom?

But pleasure, happiness, prosperity, if we know how to recognize in them what comes from outside (chance, circumstances), likewise bear testimony to human misery. The same use should be made of them. Milarepa and the food. (This applies even to grace, in so far as it is a sensible phenomenon.)

We must be nothing in order to be in our true place in the whole.

Sin and knowledge of our misery. If one knows with all one's soul that one is mortal and one accepts it with all one's soul, one cannot kill (except, supposing such a thing to be possible, under the exigencies of justice).

Sin and the prestige of force. Owing to the fact that the whole soul has not managed to know and accept human misery, we think there must be a difference between human beings, and consequently we fail to be just, either by drawing a distinction between our advantage and that of other people, or else by marking a preference for certain individuals from among other people.

This comes from the fact that we do not know that human misery represents a constant and irreducible quantity and exists in each man in the largest possible form; and that greatness comes from a one and only God, so that every man is identical with every other man.

Error as an incentive. Error as a source of energy. I think I see a friend. I run towards him. When I get a little nearer I perceive that it is someone else towards whom I am running—a stranger. The splash of colour formed by this face, these clothes, etc., which a moment before was a source of motor energy is so no longer. Some energy has been liberated.

Bad actions are those where the energy for them has been derived from an error.

All particular incentives are errors. Only that energy which is not derived from any incentive is good. Obedience to God, that is to say, since God is beyond all that we can imagine or conceive, to nothing. This is at the same time impossible and necessary—in other words it is supernatural.

Love of God is pure when joy and suffering *equally* inspire gratitude.

The handshake of a friend on meeting again after a long absence. I do not even notice whether it gives pleasure or pain to my sense of touch; just as a blind man feels objects directly at the end of his stick, so I feel the presence of my friend directly. The same applies to life's circumstances, whatever they may be, and God.

This implies that we must never seek consolation for pain. For felicity is beyond the realm of consolation and pain, outside it. We apprehend it through a sense of another kind, just as the perception of objects at the end of a stick or an instrument is of another kind to that of touch in the strict sense of the word. This other sense is formed by a shifting of the attention through an apprenticeship in which the entire soul and the body participate.

That is why we read in the Gospel: 'I say unto you that these have received their reward'. There must be no compensation. It is the void in sensible impression which carries me beyond sensible impression.

Religion in so far as it is a source of consolation is a hindrance to true faith; and in this sense atheism is a purification. I have to be an atheist with that part of myself which is not made for God. Among those in whom the supernatural part of themselves has not been awakened, the atheists are right and the believers wrong.

The mysteries of the Catholic faith—and those of other religious or metaphysical traditions—are not designed in order to be believed by all parts of the soul. The presence of Christ in the host is not a fact in the same way that the presence of my friend Paul in Paul's body is a fact; otherwise it would not be supernatural. (Both facts are, moreover, equally incomprehensible—but not in the same way.) The Eucharist should not then be an object of belief for the part of me which apprehends facts. That is where Protestantism is true (or, with respect to the incarnation, where Deism is true). But this presence of Christ in the host is not a symbol either, for a symbol is the combination of an abstraction and an image; it is something which human intelligence can represent to itself; it is not supernatural. There the Catholics are right, not the Protestants. Only that part of myself which is made for the supernatural should adhere to these mysteries. But this adherence is more a matter of love than of belief. What is, then, the distinction between love and faith?

The rôle of the intelligence—that part of us which affirms and denies, formulates opinions—is solely one of submission. All that I conceive of as true is less true than these things of which I cannot conceive

the truth, but which I love. That is why St. John of the Cross calls
faith a night. With those who have received a Christian education, the
lower parts of the soul become attached to these mysteries when they
have no right at all to do so. That is why such people need a purification of which St. John of the Cross describes the stages. Atheism and
incredulity constitute an equivalent of such a purification.

We should not seize upon these mysteries as truths, for that is
impossible, but recognize the subordination to these mysteries which
we love of all that we seize upon as truths. The intelligence can
recognize this subordination by feeling that the love of these mysteries is the source of conceptions which it can seize upon as truths.
Such would seem to be the relationship between faith and love.

In the sphere of the relationship between man and the supernatural we must seek a more than mathematical precision, something
even more precise than science. Such is also one of the uses to which
science should be put.

The mysteries of the faith cannot be either affirmed or denied;
they must be placed above that which we affirm or deny.

Since we are, in fact, in an age of incredulity, why neglect the
purificatory use of incredulity? I have had experimental knowledge
of its use.

Necessity enters into contact with the intelligence through knowledge of the second kind and with the sensibility through affliction.
There is only purification if we recognize it as being identical under
these two forms.

Affliction degrades when it abolishes knowledge of the second
kind. Nothing is more difficult than to preserve the latter in affliction
(for that it is necessary to pass to the third kind?).

The will of God. Composition upon several planes. A plurality
of distinct and convergent motives places the will in contact with
what is above the sphere of particular motives.

Μεταξύ.

It is always a question of rising above perspectives through the
composition of perspectives, of placing oneself in the *third dimension*.

'The breadth and depth of the love of Christ.'

Not to take one step, *even in the direction of good*, beyond that to which one is irresistibly impelled by God, this applying to action, word and thought. But to be willing to go anywhere under his impulsion, to the extreme limit, if there is one. (The Cross . . .) To be willing to go to the maximum length is to pray to be impelled, but without knowing whither.

Humility; believing oneself to be beneath others. This in itself does not make any sense. It is an operation similar to that by which Descartes denies in order to bring himself round to the point where he doubts. One must believe oneself to be beneath others in order to bring oneself round to the point where one regards oneself as their equal and does not prefer oneself. Since it is impossible to prevent oneself from imagining a hierarchical order, a ladder amongst human beings (and perfection consists in not imagining it), one must place oneself on the lowest rung so as to avoid being situated above any other human being in one's own estimation. By dint of maintaining oneself on the lowest rung, the ladder disappears.

Contact with human creatures is given to us through the sense of presence. Contact with God is given to us through the sense of absence. Compared with this absence, presence becomes more absent than absence.

We should examine very closely the notion of *possibility*, for it is the key to a great number of mysteries which surround the human condition.

What is not truth can be above or below truth. It is above when it is a source of truths.

Faith is the experience that the intelligence is lighted up by love. Truth as the light coming from good—the good which lies above essences. The organ in us through which we see truth is the intelligence; the organ in us through which we see God is love.

'The eyes of the soul—these are the demonstrations themselves.' In the case of truths. But the eye of the soul for the contemplation of the divine is love.

Only the intelligence must recognize by those means which are proper to it, namely, verification and demonstration, the preeminence of love. It must only submit itself when it knows in a perfectly clear and precise manner why. Otherwise submission is an error, and that to which it submits itself, in spite of the label attached, is something other than supernatural love. (It is social influence for example.)

'When two or three are gathered together in my name.' Not just one. But not a hundred either. Two or three.

Why (setting aside confession and direction of conscience) have colloquies between two or three never been recognized among religious exercises? Not talks, but colloquies pursued with the maximum concentration of attention. This would no doubt be of as much value (at any rate for those with a corresponding vocation for it) as reciting the breviary.

Beauty. Impossible to define it psychologically, because the fulness of aesthetic contemplation excludes introspection. One cannot therefore define aesthetic order as the condition of existence for the production of the aesthetic sentiment (. . . but as the condition for contemplation). It is an order which does not constitute a condition of existence.

The proof of the existence of God by the order of the world, in the manner in which it is usually put forward, is a wretched one. But we can say: the fact that man can pass into a state of aesthetic contemplation before a spectacle of nature as before a Greek statue is a proof of God.

A work of art has an author, and yet, when it is perfect, there is something essentially anonymous about it. It imitates the anonymity of divine art. Thus the beauty of the world proves that there is a God who is at the same time personal and impersonal, and neither just one nor the other.

Author and order. Necessity also (mathematical and mechanical relationships) represents an order without an author.

Mathematics as μεταξύ leading towards the impersonal aspect of God.

If the 'I', in the personal sense, fades away in proportion and in so far as man imitates God, how could it be sufficient to conceive of a personal God? The image of a personal God is a hindrance to such an imitation.

Faith. It is for the intelligence to discern what forms the object of supernatural love. For it must perfectly discern all that which is at the level of intelligible truth and all that which is below it. All that which is neither the one nor the other is the object of supernatural love. Discrimination on the part of the intelligence is essential in order to separate supernatural love from attachment. For we can be attached to something which we name God.

Love (ἀγάπη) is a disposition of the supernatural part of the soul. Faith is a disposition of *all* the parts of the soul—and of the body as well—each one assuming with regard to the object of love the attitude suitable to its nature. Justice, according to Plato. (In the Scriptures, too, faith is continually assimilated to justice.)

Hope, this is faith in so far as it is oriented in Time towards the future. It is the supernatural equivalent of the resolve to persevere in the path of virtue.

That which is below resembles that which is above. Hence slavery is an image of obedience to God, humiliation is an image of humility, etc.

This being so, it is necessary to seek out that which is lowest in its quality of image.

Let that which is base in us go to the bottom in order that that which is noble in us may go to the top. For we are reversed beings. We are born like this. Re-establishing order means unmaking the creature in us.

Order and disorder. All order presupposes a correlative disorder, in this sense that order is essentially partial, and thus the proof of the existence of God by the order of the world (in its commonly accepted form) is just as much a proof against the existence of God. But it is otherwise in the case of beauty; beauty is a perfect order. So, likewise, the absolutely obedient soul is in a perfect order.

The world is only beautiful for him who experiences *amor fati*, and consequently *amor fati* is, for whoever experiences it, an experimental proof of the reality of God.

An order implies a person as author of it, a particular end, a plan in view of such an end, material objects which constitute at the same time means and obstacles, and which are caught up in a host of relationships apart from their actual relationship to this order. For example, a clock.

All that disappears in the case of something beautiful, although the work of human hands. All that has no meaning at all when related to the world.

Faith is an attitude of all the parts of the soul other than supernatural love with respect to what they are unable to apprehend, and in so far as it goes unapprehended by them. If they do apprehend something, it is a question of something of a different order from faith, and the object does not correspond to the label. Dark night.

THE THINGS OF
THE WORLD

"The value of a religious or, more generally, a spiritual way of life is appreciated by the amount of illumination thrown upon the things of the world." Simone Weil's own words dispute the charge that she was an extreme ascetic who rejected or neutralized human life. One critic suggests that she was never anything more than a dead Cathar! Surely this attack ignores the heroism that impels responses such as these: *"To die for God is not a proof of faith in God. To die for an unknown and repulsive convict who is a victim of injustice, that is proof of faith in God." "The faith of a judge is not seen in his behaviour at church, but in his behaviour on the bench." "The Roman who died to save his slaves from torture loved God."*

God himself cannot prevent what has happened from having happened. What better proof that the creation is an abdication?

What greater abdication of God than is represented by time? We are abandoned in time.

God is not in time.

Creation and original sin are only two aspects, which are different for us, of a single act of abdication by God. And the Incarnation, the Passion, are also aspects of this act.

God emptied himself of his divinity and filled us with a false divinity. Let us empty ourselves of it. This act is the purpose of the act by which we were created.

At this very moment God, by his creative will, is maintaining me in existence, in order that I may renounce it.

God waits patiently until at last I am willing to consent to love him.

God waits like a beggar who stands motionless and silent before someone who will perhaps give him a piece of bread. Time is that waiting.

Time is God's waiting as a beggar for our love.

The stars, the mountains, the sea, and all the things that speak to us of time, convey God's supplication to us.

By waiting humbly we are made similar to God.

God is only the good. That is why he is waiting there in silence. Anyone who comes forward and speaks is using a little force. The good which is nothing but good can only stand waiting.

Beggars who are modest are images of Him.

Humility is a certain relation of the soul to time. It is an acceptance of waiting. That is why, socially, it is the mark of inferiors that they are made to wait. "I nearly had to wait" is the tyrant's word. But in ceremony, whose poetry makes all men equal, everybody has to wait.

Art is waiting. Inspiration is waiting.

He shall bear fruit in patience.

Humility partakes in God's patience. The perfected soul waits for the good in silence, immobility and humility like God's own. Christ nailed on the cross is the perfect image of the Father.

No saint has been able to obtain from God that the past should not have been, or that he himself should grow ten years older in one day or one day older in ten years, or that . . . No miracle can do anything against time. The faith that moves mountains is impotent against time.

God has left us abandoned in time.

God and humanity are like two lovers who have missed their rendezvous. Each is there before the time, but each at a different place, and they wait and wait and wait. He stands motionless, nailed to the spot for the whole of time. She is distraught and impatient. But alas for her if she gets tired and goes away. For the two places where they are waiting are at the same point in the fourth dimension...

The crucifixion of Christ is the image of the fixity of God.

God is attention without distraction.

One must imitate the patience and humility of God.

"Be ye holy because I am holy". Imitation of God. Doubtless borrowed by Moses from the Egyptian wisdom.

It is in time that we have our "I".

The acceptance of time and of whatever it may bring—without any exception—(*amor fati*)—that is the only disposition of the soul which is unconditioned in relation to time. It encloses the infinite. Whatever may happen ...

God has given his finite creatures this power of transporting themselves into the infinite.

Mathematics is its image.

If the pleasant or painful content of each minute (even those in which we sin) is regarded as a special caress from God, in what way does time separate us from Heaven?

The dereliction in which God leaves us is his own way of caressing us.

Time, which is our one misery, is the very touch of his hand. It is the abdication by which he lets us exist.

He stays far away from us, because if He approached He would cause us to disappear. He waits for us to go to him and disappear.

At death, some disappear into the absence of God and others disappear into the presence of God. We cannot conceive this difference. That is why the representations of heaven and hell have been elaborated, so as to have an approximation which the imagination can grasp.

Essence of faith: It is impossible really to desire the good and not obtain it.

Or reciprocally: anything which it is possible really to desire without obtaining it is not really the good.

It is impossible to receive the good when one has not desired it.

That is the meaning of the precept: confine your desires to things that depend upon yourself.

But that does not mean things which you have in yourself or which you can acquire by your will-power. For all that is wretched and valueless. It means an object of humble and desperate longing, of supplication.

The good is something which you can never get by your own effort, but neither can you desire it without getting it.

That is why our situation is just like that of little children who cry that they are hungry and who receive bread.

That is why suppliants of every kind are sacred, supplication is sacred.

One has the duty to give everything except what one has the duty to refuse.

Olive branch. Tree of the Holy Spirit, emblem of suppliants.

God has separated force and the good in this world, and kept the good for himself.

His commandments have the form of asking.

Everything we get for ourselves by our own will and our own efforts, and everything given or withheld by the chance of external circumstances, is absolutely without value. It may be bad or indifferent, but never good.

God leaves us in this world exposed to evil.

Nevertheless, if we desire that the eternal and non-sensible part of our soul should be preserved from all evil, it will be.

Everything that exists is subjected to necessity. But there is a carnal necessity into which the opposition of good and evil does not enter, and a spiritual necessity which is entirely subjected to this opposition.

The very idea of redemption implies a spiritual necessity.

Only necessity is an object of knowledge. Nothing else can be grasped by thought. Necessity is known through exploration, experiment, experience. Mathematics is experience of a certain kind. Necessity is the thing with which human thought has contact.

The only thing in us that is unconditioned is desire. It is ap-

propriate that it should be directed towards the unconditioned being,
God.

Nothing can be produced unless the conditions for its production are brought together.

Such and such a thing calls for such and such a condition. But
if one thinks: everything can be produced, given the conditions, and
everything is equivalent . . .

If one desires a particular thing one becomes enslaved to the
series of conditions. But if one desires the series itself, the satisfaction
of this desire is unconditioned.

That is why the one and only liberation is love of the order of
the world.

Christ on the cross, the greatest harm inflicted on the greatest
good: if one loves that, one loves the order of the world.

In water and blood. The public life of Christ commenced with
a baptism of water and ended with a baptism of blood.

On the cross he rendered unto Caesar what was Caesar's and
unto God what was God's.

You shall judge them by their fruits. There is no greater evil than
to do evil to men, and no greater good than to do good to men.

One cannot know what is in a man's mind when he speaks a
certain word (God, freedom, progress . . .). One can only judge
the good in his soul by the good in his actions, or in the expression
of his original thoughts.

One cannot perceive the presence of God in a man, but only
the reflection of that light in his manner of conceiving earthly life.
Thus, the true God is present in the *Iliad* and not in the book of
Joshua.

The author of the *Iliad* depicts life as only a man who loves
God can see it. The author of Joshua as only a man who does not
love God can see it.

One does not testify so well for God by speaking about Him as
by expressing, either in actions or words, the new aspect assumed
by the creation after the soul has experienced the Creator.

Indeed, the truth is that the latter is the only way.

To die for God is not a proof of faith in God. To die for an unknown and repulsive convict who is a victim of injustice, that is a proof of faith in God.

That is what Christ was explaining: "I was naked . . . I was hungry . . ."

The love of God is only an intermediary between the natural and the supernatural love of creatures.

It is solely because of the crucifixion that faith in Christ can be, as St. John says, a criterion. To accept as God a common convict, shamefully tortured and put to death, is truly to overcome the world. (And he says nothing about the resurrection.) It is to renounce all temporal safety. It is to accept and love necessity.

But who thinks of Christ today as a common convict, except his enemies? People worship the historic grandeur of the Church.

The black slaves overcame the world by faith in Christ: "They crucified my Lord".

God is present, Christ is present, wherever there is enacted between one man and another an act of supernatural virtue.

The soul's attitude towards God is not a thing that can be verified, even by the soul itself, because God is elsewhere, in heaven, in secret. If one thinks to have verified it, there is really some earthly thing masquerading under the label of God. One can only verify whether the behaviour of the soul as regards this world bears the mark of an experience of God.

In the same way, a bride's friends do not go into the nuptial chamber; but when she is seen to be pregnant they know she has lost her virginity.

There is not fire in a cooked dish, but one knows it has been on the fire.

On the other hand, even though one may think to have seen the flames under them, if the potatoes are raw it is certain they have not been on the fire.

It is not the way a man talks about God, but the way he talks about things of the world that best shows whether his soul has passed through the fire of the love of God. In this matter no deception is possible. There are false imitations of the love of God, but not of the transformation it effects in the soul, because one has no idea of this transformation except by passing through it oneself.

In the same way, the proof that a child can do division is not that he can recite the rule, but that he can divide. If he recites the rule, I don't know whether he understands it. If I give him some difficult sums in division and he gets the answers right, I have no need to make him explain the rule. It doesn't even matter if he is incapable of it, or doesn't know the name of the operation. I know that he understands it. If the child who could repeat the rule adds the numbers up instead of dividing them, I know he doesn't understand it.

In the same way, I know that the author of the *Iliad* knew and loved God and the author of the Book of Joshua did not.

When a man's way of behaving towards things and men, or simply his way of regarding them, reveals supernatural virtues, one knows that his soul is no longer virgin, it has slept with God; perhaps even without knowing it, like a girl violated in her sleep. That has no importance, it is only the fact that matters.

The only certain proof a young woman's friends have that she has lost her virginity is that she is pregnant. Otherwise there is no proof—not even if she should talk and behave lewdly. Her husband may be impotent.

In the same way, if a soul speaks of God with words of faith and love, either publicly or inwardly, this is no proof either for others or for itself. It may be that what it calls God is an impotent being, that is to say, a false God, and that it has never really slept with God.

What is a proof is the appearance of supernatural virtues in that part of its behaviour which is turned towards men.

The faith of a judge is not seen in his behaviour at church, but in his behaviour on the bench.

But, like a woman's pregnancy, this transformation is not effected by direct efforts, but by a union of love with God.

A woman may talk in the most lewd way and yet be a virgin. But if she is pregnant she is not a virgin, even though she may pretend to know nothing. It is the same with the Old Testament and the *Iliad*.

Iliad. Only the love of God can enable a soul to discern the horror of human misery so lucidly and so coolly without losing either tenderness or serenity.

The Roman who died to save his slaves from torture loved God.

Every master who believes that his slaves are his equals knows and loves God. And reciprocally.

A painter does not draw the spot where he is standing. But in looking at his picture I can deduce his position by relation to the things drawn.

On the other hand, if he puts himself into his picture I know for certain that the place where he shows himself is not the place where he is.

According to the conception of human life expressed in the acts and words of a man I know (I mean I would know if I possessed discernment) whether he sees life from a point in this world or from above in heaven.

On the other hand, when he talks about God I cannot discern (and yet sometimes I can . . .) whether he is speaking from within or externally.

If a man says he has been in an aeroplane, and has drawn the clouds, his picture is not a proof for me; I may believe it is a fantasy. If he brings me a bird's eye view of the town, it is a proof.

The Gospel contains a conception of human life, not a theology.

If I light an electric torch at night out of doors I don't judge its power by looking at the bulb, but by seeing how many objects it lights up.

The brightness of a source of light is appreciated by the illumination it projects upon non-luminous objects.

The value of a religious or, more generally, a spiritual way of life is appreciated by the amount of illumination thrown upon the things of this world.

Earthly things are the criterion of spiritual things.

This is what we generally don't want to recognize, because we are frightened of a criterion.

The virtue of anything is manifested outside the thing.

If, on the pretext that only spiritual things are of value, we refuse to take the light thrown on earthly things as a criterion, we are in danger of having a non-existent treasure.

Only spiritual things are of value, but only physical things have a verifiable existence. Therefore the value of the former can only be verified as an illumination projected on to the latter.

(That is the reason why the Kshatriyas instruct the Brahmins.)

God, who willed to create this world, willed that it should be so.

If a man took my left-hand glove, passed it behind his back, and returned it to me as a right-hand glove, I should know that he had access to the 4th dimension. No other proof is possible.

In the same way, if a man gives bread to a beggar in a certain way or speaks in a certain way about a defeated army, I know that his thought has been outside this world and sat with Christ alongside the Father who is in Heaven.

If a man describes to me at the same time two opposite sides of a mountain, I know that his position is somewhere higher than the summit.

It is impossible to understand and love at the same time both the victors and the vanquished, as the *Iliad* does, except from the place, outside the world, where God's Wisdom dwells.

THE FATHER'S
SILENCE

Humility, as the root of love, is antecedent to a state of grace. Its place in the religious conception of life, Simone Weil maintains, is central. Indeed, it is a sign of a recognition of limits, as well as of a self-recognition of the temper of the soul. "It is not easy to give with the same humility that is appropriate for receiving," she says. "To give in the spirit of one who begs." Humility is a supernatural virtue that is at the same time allied to the transcendent discipline of attention.

Mercy is a specifically divine attribute. There is no human mercy. Mercy implies an infinite distance. One does not feel pity for what is close at hand.

Jaffier.

Mercy comes down from what is not suffering to what suffers.

In order to be merciful, one must have a point of impassibility in one's soul.

And all the rest of it exposed defencelessly to the hazards of fortune.

The compassion one feels for the afflicted is the compassion felt, in affliction, by the impassible part of one's own soul for the part of it which feels. The compassion Christ felt for himself when he said: "Father, if thou be willing, remove this cup from me . . . My God, why hast thou forsaken me?" The silent compassion of the Father for Christ.

This self-compassion is what a pure soul feels in affliction. A pure soul feels the same compassion for the affliction of others.

The love which unites Christ abandoned on the Cross to his Father at an infinite distance dwells in every saintly soul. One point in this soul is always with the Father. "Where your treasure is, there will your heart be also." The sensitive part is always exposed to the torture of affliction. In such a soul the dialogue of Christ's cry and the Father's silence echoes perpetually in a perfect harmony.

Before an afflicted man, this soul immediately responds with the true note. "My Father, why have you forsaken him?" And in the centre of the soul the Father's silence replies.

"Why has it been allowed that he should go hungry?" While one's thought is occupied by this question, one proceeds automatically to find bread for him.

When the act is performed thus, the afflicted man is dispensed from gratitude, because it is Christ who thanks.

"Father, why . . . ?" God accuses himself for Christ's Passion. "He that delivered me unto thee hath the greater sin . . ."

One can only excuse men for evil by accusing God of it. If one accuses God one forgives, because God is the Good.

Amid the multitude of those who seem to owe us something, God is our only real debtor. But our debt to him is greater. He will release us from it if we forgive Him.

Sin is an offense offered to God from resentment at the debts he owes and does not pay us. By forgiving God we cut the root of sin in ourselves. At the bottom of every sin there is anger against God.

If we forgive God for his crime against us, which is to have made us finite creatures, He will forgive our crime against him, which is that we are finite creatures.

By accepting that we are creatures we win freedom from the past.

Just as God, through the mouth of Christ, accused himself of the Passion, so we should accuse God for every human affliction. And just as God replies with silence, so we should reply with silence.

Compassion presupposes that the spiritual part of the soul has transported itself to God and that the carnal part is left naked, without clothes of protection, exposed to every blow. Because of this nakedness, the mere presence of a man in affliction makes it sensitive to the possibility of affliction.

The imperfect use the spiritual part of their soul as clothing for the carnal part. When the spiritual part has transported itself to God, the rest is left naked.

Christ, nailed naked to the Cross, exposed to the spears.

To be no longer aware of oneself except as a thing vowed to obedience.

To live naked and nailed to the Tree of Life.

To act only under compulsion, or from natural necessity, or by a strict obligation, or by an irresistible order from God, or by a lively natural inclination. Then the "I" will perish of inanition.

Where no direction is imposed either by necessity or by obligation or by God, follow inclination.

Form the habit of always doing what one thinks one is obliged to.

I would like to achieve this without effort.

If I could find the point of emergence of the root of errors, and sever it at a blow. Then there would only remain the painful labour of overcoming bad habits. And there is also perversity.

ἀπεθάνετε, καὶ ἡ ζωὴ ὑμῶν κέκρυπται σὺν τῷ Χριστῷ ἐν τῷ θεῷ

One can only love one's neighbor with a compassionate love. It is the only just love.

Even in οὐαὶ ὑμῖν, there is compassion.

Love men as the sun would love us if it could see us.

δειλοῖσι βροτοῖσιν.

The sun as a thinking being is the model of perfection.

How many ways God has of giving himself!

Compassion makes love equal for everybody. Contempt for crime and admiration for greatness are balanced in compassion.

The dogma of the Trinity is necessary so that there may not be dialogue between us and God, but between God and himself within us. So that we may be absent.

God dwelling in food. Lamb, bread. In matter worked by human labour, bread, wine.

That ought to be the centre of peasant life. By his labour, if he so intends it, the peasant gives a little of his flesh so that it may become the flesh of Christ.

He should be a consecrated man.

Sanctity is a transmutation like the Eucharist.

For a man to be really inhabited by Christ like the host after consecration, the man's flesh and blood must first have become inert matter, and in addition nutritive for his fellows. Then, by a secret consecration, this matter can become flesh and blood of Christ. This second transmutation is only God's affair, but the first is partly ours.

It is sufficient to regard one's flesh and blood as inert matter, insensible, and nutritive for others.

"Don't heed yourself", "needs must"—there is the seed of this in the stoicism of the people.

If I grow thin from labour in the fields, my flesh really becomes wheat. If that wheat is used for the host it becomes Christ's flesh. Anyone who labours with this intention should become a saint.

God created me as a non-being which has the appearance of existing, in order that through love I should renounce this apparent existence and be annihilated by the plenitude of being.

Faith should be integrated with the people's stoicism. It has never been done. The least fortunate should be spiritually invested with the freedom of the Christian city.

Are there not more princes than peasants in the roll of the saints?

God created me as a non-being which has the appearance of existing, in order that through love I should renounce what I think is my existence and so emerge from non-being. Then there is no "I". The "I" belongs to non-being. But I have not the right to know this. If I knew it, where would be the renunciation? I shall never know it.

Other people are illusions of existence for themselves.

This way of regarding them makes their existence not less but more real for me. For I see them as they are related to themselves, and not to me.

In order to feel compassion for someone in affliction, the soul has to be divided in two. One part absolutely removed from all contamination and all danger of contamination. The other part contaminated to the point of identification. This tension is passion, com—passion. The Passion of Christ is this phenomenon in God.

Unless there is a point of eternity in one's soul which is proof against any contagion by affliction, one cannot have compassion for the afflicted. Either one is kept far away from them by difference of situation and lack of imagination, or else, if one really approaches them, pity is mixed with horror, disgust, fear, invincible repulsion.

Every movement of pure compassion in a soul is a new descent of Christ upon earth to be crucified.

Souls which are absorbed in God without feeling compassion for human misery are still climbing and have not reached the stage of descending again (even though they apply themselves to good works).

A single piece of bread given to a hungry man is enough to save a soul—if it is given in the right way.

It is not easy to give with the same humility that is appropriate for receiving. To give in the spirit of one who begs.

It is necessary at the same time to know that one does not exist and to wish not to exist.

Humility is the root of love.

Humility exerts an irresistible power upon God.

If God had not been humiliated, in the person of Christ, he would be inferior to us.

Hunger (thirst, etc.) and all carnal desire is an orientation of the body towards the future. The whole carnal part of our soul is oriented towards the future. Death freezes it. Privation is a distant likeness of death.

The life of the flesh is oriented towards the future. Concupiscence is life itself. Detachment is death.

"Terit carni superbiam—potus cibique parcitas." It is the pride of the flesh to believe that it draws its life from itself. Hunger and thirst oblige it to feel its dependence on what is outside. The feeling of dependence makes it humble.

Io, the wandering maiden, and the Gypsies' moon.

Find in Origen: Matthew, 5, 45–48 (be ye perfect . . .)

Postulate: what is inferior depends on what is superior.

There is only one unique source of light. Dim light does not consist of rays coming from another source, which is dim; it is the same light, degraded.

In the same way, mysticism should provide the key for all knowledge and all values.

The key is harmony (Philolaus).

Christ is the key.

All geometry proceeds from the Cross.

The beautiful is the contact of the good with the faculty of sense. (The real is the same thing.)

The true is the contact of the good with the intelligence.

All goods in this world, all beauties, all truths, are diverse and partial aspects of one unique good. Therefore they are goods which need to be ranged in order. Puzzle games are an image of this operation. Taken all together, viewed from the right point and rightly related, they make an architecture. Through this architecture the unique good, which cannot be grasped, becomes apprehensible.

All architecture is a symbol of this, an image of this.

The entire universe is nothing but a great metaphor.

In astrology, etc., we see a degraded reflection of this understanding of the universe as metaphor, and perhaps an attempt—but an illegitimate one (it seems to me)—to get material proof of it. Alchemy also.

To beseech, this means that one waits for life or death to be dealt by something outside oneself. Kneeling, with head bent so that the conqueror may more conveniently strike it off, hands touching his knees (but, more likely, originally raised above them) so as to receive from his compassion the gift of life, like the seed of a father.

A few minutes pass like this in silence. The heart empties itself of all its attachments, frozen by the imminent contact of death. A new life is received, which is made purely of mercy.

That is how one should pray to God.

Waiting patiently in expectation is the foundation of the spiritual life.

Filial piety is simply an image of the attitude to God.

If a soul cried to God its hunger for the bread of life, incessantly, indefatigably, like a new-born child whom its mother forgets to feed . . .

May those cries which I raised when I was a week or two old continue incessantly within me for that milk which is the seed of the Father.

The Virgin's milk, the Father's seed—I shall have it if I cry for it. The cry is the first resource granted to a human being. What we could never get by work, we cry for. The first nourishment flows from the mother and is given in response to the child's cry; there is no question of work.

The milk of the Virgin is the beauty of the world. In its aspect of beauty the world is perfectly pure.

Justice—when perceived as beautiful the world appears perfectly just. The Virgin is Justice. The Virgin of the Zodiac, holding an ear of corn. Cosmic Virgin in the Apocalypse. The Virgin is the creation, under the aspect of purity.

(Once a living woman was pure to the same extent as the purity of creation regarded as such. At least—perhaps . . .)

Truth—the beauty of the universe is the sign that it is real.

THE LOVE OF GOD
AND AFFLICTION

This essay systematizes the theological ideas scattered in Simone Weil's notebooks, to the same period of which writing it also belongs. Affliction, malheur, *she believes, is necessary so that "the human creature may un-create itself." Along with beauty, it is the only thing piercing and devastating enough to penetrate the soul. It marks the occasion of a supernatural process when one hears the Word of God and has a part in the Cross of Christ: "Affliction, when it is consented to and accepted and loved, is truly a baptism."*

In the realm of suffering, affliction is something apart, specific and irreducible. It is quite a different thing from simple suffering. It takes possession of the soul and marks it through and through with its own particular mark, the mark of slavery. Slavery as practised by ancient Rome is simply the extreme form of affliction. The men of antiquity, who knew a lot about the subject, used to say: 'A man loses half his soul the day he becomes a slave.'

Affliction is inseparable from physical suffering and yet quite distinct. In suffering, all that is not bound up with physical pain or something analogous is artificial, imaginary, and can be eliminated by a suitable adjustment of the mind. Even in the case of the absence or death of someone we love, the irreducible part of the sorrow is akin to physical pain, a difficulty in breathing, a constriction of the heart, or an unsatisfied need, a hunger, or the almost biological disorder caused by the brutal unloosing of an energy hitherto absorbed by an attachment and now left undirected. A sorrow which is not centered around an irreducible core of such a nature is mere romanticism or literature. Humiliation is also a violent condition of the whole physical being, which wants to rise up against the outrage but is forced, by impotence or fear, to hold itself in check.

On the other hand a pain which is only physical is of very little account, and leaves no mark on the soul. Toothache is an example. An hour or two of violent pain caused by a bad tooth is nothing once it is over.

It is another matter if the physical suffering is very prolonged or frequent, but this is often something quite different from an attack of pain; it is often an affliction.

Affliction is an uprooting of life, a more or less attenuated equivalent of death, made irresistibly present to the soul by the attack or immediate apprehension of physical pain. If there is complete absence of physical pain there is no affliction for the soul, because thought can turn itself away in any direction. Thought flies from affliction as promptly and irresistibly as an animal flies from death. Here below, physical pain and nothing else has the power to chain down our thoughts; provided that we count as physical pain certain phenomena which, though difficult to describe, are bodily and are strictly equivalent to it; in particular, for example, the fear of physical pain.

When thought is obliged by an attack of physical pain, however slight, to recognize the presence of affliction, this produces a state of mind as acute as that of a condemned man who is forced to look for hours at the guillotine which is going to behead him. Human beings can live twenty years, fifty years, in this acute state. We pass by them without noticing. What man is capable of discerning them unless Christ himself looks through his eyes? We notice only that they sometimes behave strangely, and we censure this behaviour.

There is not real affliction unless the event which has gripped and uprooted a life attacks it, directly or indirectly, in all its parts, social, psychological, and physical. The social factor is essential. There is not really affliction where there is not social degradation or the fear of it in some form or another.

There is both continuity and a separating threshold, like the boiling point of water, between affliction itself and all the sorrows which, even though they may be very violent, very deep, and very lasting, are not afflictions in the true sense. There is a limit; on the far side of it we have affliction but not on the near side. This limit is not purely objective; all sorts of personal factors have to be taken into account. The same event may plunge one human being into affliction and not another.

The great enigma of human life is not suffering but affliction. It is not surprising that the innocent are killed, tortured, driven from their country, made destitute or reduced to slavery, put in concentration camps or prison cells, since there are criminals to perform such actions. It is not surprising either that disease is the cause of long sufferings, which paralyse life and make it into an image of death, since nature is at the mercy of the blind play of mechanical necessities. But it *is* surprising that God should have given affliction the power to seize the very souls of the innocent and to possess them as sovereign master. At the very best, he who is branded by affliction will only keep half his soul.

As for those who have been struck the kind of blow which leaves the victim writhing on the ground like a half-crushed worm, they have no words to describe what is happening to them. Among the people they meet, those who have never had contact with affliction in its true sense can have no idea of what it is, even though they may have known much suffering. Affliction is something specific and impossible to compare with anything else, just as nothing can convey the idea of sound to the deaf and dumb. And, as for those who have themselves been mutilated by affliction, they are in no state to help anyone at all and are almost incapable of even wishing to do so. Thus compassion for the afflicted is an impossibility. When it is really found, it is a more astounding miracle than walking on water, healing the sick, or even raising the dead.

Affliction constrained Christ to implore that he might be spared, to seek consolation from man, to believe he was forsaken by the

Father. It constrained a just man to cry out against God; a just man as perfect as human nature can be; more so, perhaps, if Job is not so much a historical character as a figure of Christ. 'He laughs at the affliction of the innocent!' This is not blasphemy but a genuine cry of anguish. The Book of Job is a pure marvel of truth and authenticity from beginning to end. As regards affliction, all that departs from this model is more or less tainted with falsehood.

Affliction causes God to be absent for a time, more absent than a dead man, more absent than light in the utter darkness of a cell. A kind of horror submerges the whole soul. During this absence there is nothing to love. What is terrible is that if, in this darkness where there is nothing to love, the soul ceases to love, God's absence becomes final. The soul has to go on loving in the void, or at least to go on wanting to love, though it may be only with an infinitesimal part of itself. Then, one day, God will come to show himself to this soul and to reveal the beauty of the world to it, as in the case of Job. But if the soul stops loving it falls, even in this life, into something which is almost equivalent to hell.

That is why those who plunge men into affliction before they are prepared to receive it are killers of souls. On the other hand, in a time such as ours, where affliction is hanging over us all, help given to souls is only effective if it goes far enough really to prepare them for affliction. That is no small thing.

Affliction hardens and discourages because, like a red-hot iron, it stamps the soul to its very depths with the contempt, the disgust, and even the self-hatred and sense of guilt and defilement which crime logically should produce but actually does not. Evil dwells in the heart of the criminal without being felt there. It is felt in the heart of the man who is afflicted and innocent. Everything happens as though the state of soul appropriate for criminals had been separated from crime and attached to affliction; and it even seems to be in proportion to the innocence of those who are afflicted.

If Job cries out that he is innocent in such despairing accents it is because he himself is unable to believe so, it is because his soul within him is on the side of his friends. He implores God himself to bear witness, because he no longer hears the testimony of his own conscience; it is no longer anything but an abstract, lifeless memory for him.

Men have the same carnal nature as animals. If a hen is hurt, the others rush up and peck it. The phenomenon is as automatic as gravitation. Our senses attach to affliction all the contempt, all the revulsion, all the hatred which our reason attaches to crime. Except for those whose whole soul is inhabited by Christ, everybody despises the afflicted to some extent, although practically no one is conscious of it.

This law of sensibility also holds good with regard to ourselves. In the case of someone in affliction, all the contempt, revulsion, and hatred are turned inwards; they penetrate to the centre of his soul and from there they colour the whole universe with their poisoned light. Supernatural love, if it has survived, can prevent this second result from coming about, but not the first. The first is of the very essence of affliction; there is no affliction without it.

'Christ . . . being made a curse for us.' It was not only the body of Christ, hanging on the wood, which was accursed, it was his whole soul also. In the same way every innocent being in his affliction feels himself accursed. This even goes on being true for those who have been in affliction and have come out of it through a change in their fortunes, if the affliction has bitten deeply enough into them.

Another effect of affliction is, little by little, to make the soul its accomplice, by injecting a poison of inertia into it. In anyone who has suffered affliction for a long enough time there is a complicity with regard to his own affliction. This complicity impedes all the efforts he might make to improve his lot; it goes so far as to prevent him from seeking a way of deliverance, sometimes even to the point of preventing him from wishing for deliverance. Then he is established in affliction, and people may get the impression that he is quite contented. Even worse, this complicity may induce him, in spite of himself, to shun and flee from the means of deliverance; and for this it will resort to pretexts which are sometimes ridiculous. Even after a man has been relieved of his affliction, there will be something left in him which impels him to embrace it again, if it has pierced irrevocably into the depth of his soul. It is as though affliction had established itself in

him like a parasite and was directing him for its own purposes. Sometimes this impulse triumphs over all the impulses of the soul towards
happiness. If the affliction has been ended as the result of some kind-
ness, it may take the form of hatred for the benefactor; this is the
cause of certain apparently inexplicable acts of savage ingratitude. It
is sometimes easy to deliver an unhappy man from his present distress,
but it is difficult to set him free from his past affliction. Only God can
do it. And even the grace of God himself cannot cure irremediably
wounded nature in this world. The glorified body of Christ bore the
marks of nail and spear.

One can only accept the existence of affliction by considering it
as a distance.

God created through love and for love. God did not create anything except love itself, and the means to love. He created love in all its
forms. He created beings capable of love from all possible distances.
Because no other could do it, he himself went to the greatest possible
distance, the infinite distance. This infinite distance between God and
God, this supreme tearing apart, this incomparable agony, this marvel of love, is the crucifixion. Nothing can be further from God than
that which has been made accursed.

This tearing apart, over which supreme love places the bond of
supreme union, echoes perpetually across the universe in the depth of
the silence, like two notes, separate yet blending into one, like a pure
and heart-rending harmony. This is the Word of God. The whole creation is nothing but its vibration. When human music in its greatest
purity pierces our soul, this is what we hear through it. When we have
learnt to hear the silence, this is what we grasp, even more distinctly,
through it.

Those who persevere in love hear this note from the very lowest
depths into which affliction has thrust them. From that moment they
can no longer have any doubt.

Men struck down by affliction are at the foot of the Cross, almost
at the greatest possible distance from God. It must not be thought that
sin is a greater distance. Sin is not a distance, it is a turning of our eyes
in the wrong direction.

It is true that there is a mysterious connexion between this distance and an original disobedience. From the beginning, we are told,

humanity turned its eyes away from God and walked as far as it could in the wrong direction. That is because it was then able to walk. As for us, we are nailed down to the spot, free only to choose which way we will look, ruled by necessity. A blind mechanism, heedless of degrees of spiritual perfection, continually buffets men hither and thither and flings some of them at the very foot of the Cross. It rests with them only to keep or not to keep their eyes turned towards God through all the shocks. It is not that God's Providence is absent; it is by his Providence that God willed necessity as a blind mechanism.

If the mechanism were not blind there would not be any affliction. Affliction is above all anonymous; it deprives its victims of their personality and turns them into things. It is indifferent, and it is the chill of this indifference—a metallic chill—which freezes all those it touches, down to the depth of their soul. They will never find warmth again. They will never again believe that they are anyone.

Affliction would not have this power without the element of chance which it contains. Those who are persecuted for their faith and are aware of it are not afflicted, in spite of their suffering. They only fall into affliction if suffering or fear fills the soul to the point of making it forget the cause of the persecution. The martyrs who came into the arena singing as they faced the wild beasts were not afflicted. Christ was afflicted. He did not die like a martyr. He died like a common criminal, in the same class as thieves, only a little more ridiculous. For affliction is ridiculous.

Only blind necessity can throw men to the extreme point of distance, close to the Cross. Human crime, which is the cause of most affliction, is part of blind necessity, because criminals do not know what they are doing.

There are two forms of friendship: meeting and separation. They are indissoluble. Both of them contain the same good, the unique good, which is friendship. For when two beings who are not friends are near each other there is no meeting, and when friends are far apart there is no separation. As both forms contain the same good thing, they are both equally good.

God produces himself and knows himself perfectly, just as we in our miserable way make and know objects outside ourselves. But, before all things, God is love. Before all things, God loves himself. This love, this friendship of God, is the Trinity. Between the terms united by this relation of divine love there is more than nearness; there is infinite nearness or identity. But through the Creation, the Incarnation, and the Passion, there is also infinite distance. The interposed density of all space and all time sets an infinite distance between God and God.

Lovers or friends desire two things. The one is to love each other so much that they enter into each other and only make one being. The other is to love each other so much that, having half the globe between them, their union will not be diminished in the slightest degree. All that man vainly desires here below is perfectly realized in God. We have all those impossible desires within us as a mark of our destination, and they are good for us provided we no longer hope to fulfil them.

The love between God and God, which in itself *is* God, is this bond of double power; the bond which unites two beings so closely that they are no longer distinguishable and really form a single unity, and the bond which stretches across distance and triumphs over infinite separation. The unity of God, wherein all plurality disappears, and the abandonment wherein Christ believes he is left, while not ceasing to love his Father perfectly, these are two forms expressing the divine value of the same Love, the Love which is God himself.

God is so essentially love that the unity, which in a sense is his actual definition, is a pure effect of love. And corresponding to the infinite virtue of unification belonging to this love there is the infinite separation over which it triumphs, which is the whole creation spread throughout the totality of space and time, consisting of mechanically brutal matter and interposed between Christ and his Father.

As for us men, our misery gives us the infinitely precious privilege of sharing in this distance placed between the Son and his Father. This distance is only separation, however, for those who love. For those who love, separation, although painful, is a good, because it is love. Even the distress of the abandoned Christ is a good. There cannot be a greater good for us on earth than to share in it. God can never be perfectly present to us here below on account of our flesh. But he can be almost perfectly absent from us in extreme affliction. For us, on earth, this is the only possibility of perfection. That is why the Cross is our only hope. 'No forest bears such a tree, with this flower, this foliage and this seed.'

This universe where we are living, and of which we form a minute particle, is the distance put by the divine Love between God and God. We are a point in this distance. Space, time, and the mechanism that governs matter are the distance. Everything that we call evil is only this mechanism. God has provided that when his grace penetrates to the very centre of a man and from there illuminates all his being, he is able to walk on the water without violating the laws of nature. But when a man turns away from God he simply gives himself up to the law of gravity. He then believes that he is deciding and choosing, but he is only a thing, a falling stone. If we examine human society and souls closely and with real attention, we see that wherever the virtue of supernatural light is absent, everything is obedient to mechanical laws as blind and as exact as the laws of gravitation. To know this is profitable and necessary. Those whom we call criminals are only tiles blown off a roof by the wind and falling at random. Their only fault is the initial choice by which they became those tiles.

The mechanism of necessity can be transposed on to any level while still remaining true to itself. It is the same in the world of blind matter, in plants, in animals, among nations, and in souls. Seen from our present stand-point, and in human perspective, it is quite blind. If, however, we transport our hearts beyond ourselves, beyond the universe, beyond space and time, to where our Father dwells, and if we regard this mechanism from there, it appears quite different. What seemed to be necessity becomes obedience. Matter is entirely passive and in consequence entirely obedient to God's will. It is a perfect model for us. There cannot be any other being than God and that which obeys God. On account of its perfect obedience, matter deserves to be loved by those who love its Master, in the same way as a needle once used by his beloved who has died is cherished by a lover. The world's beauty gives us an intimation of its claim to a place in our heart. In the beauty of the world harsh necessity becomes an object of love. What is more beautiful than the effect of gravity on sea-waves as they flow in ever-changing folds, or the almost eternal folds of the mountains?

The sea is not less beautiful in our eyes because we know that ships are sometimes wrecked. On the contrary this adds to its beauty. If it altered the movement of its waves to spare a ship it would be a creature gifted with discernment and choice, and not this fluid perfectly obedient to every external pressure. It is this perfect obedience which makes the sea's beauty.

All the horrors which occur in this world are like the folds imposed upon the waves by gravity. That is why they contain an element of beauty. Sometimes a poem, such as the *Iliad*, makes this beauty perceptible.

Men can never escape from obedience to God. A creature cannot but obey. The only choice given to men, as intelligent and free creatures, is to desire obedience or not to desire it. If a man does not desire it, he obeys all the same, perpetually, in as much as he is a thing subject to mechanical necessity. If he does desire it, he is still subject to mechanical necessity, but a new necessity is added to it, a necessity constituted by the laws pertaining to supernatural things. Certain actions become impossible for him; others are accomplished by means of him, sometimes almost in spite of himself.

When we have the feeling that on some occasion we have disobeyed God, it simply means that we ceased for a time to desire to be obedient. But of course, other things being equal, a man does not perform the same actions if he gives his consent to obedience as if he does not; any more than a plant, other things being equal, grows in the same way if it is in the light as if it is in the dark. The plant does not have any control or choice in the matter of its own growth. We, however, are like plants which have the one choice of being in or out of the light.

Christ proposed the docility of matter to us as a model when he told us to consider the lilies of the field which neither toil nor spin. This means that they did not set out to clothe themselves in such or such a colour, they have not exercised their will nor made arrangements for such a purpose, they have received everything that natural necessity brought them. If they seem to us infinitely more beautiful than the richest stuffs it is not because they are richer but because of their docility. Materials are docile too, but docile to man, not to God. Matter is not beautiful when it obeys man, but only when it obeys God.

If sometimes in a work of art it seems almost as beautiful as in the sea or in mountains or in flowers it is because the light of God has filled the artist. In order to find beautiful those things which are made by men unenlightened by God, it is necessary to have understood with all one's soul that these men themselves are only matter which obeys without knowing it. For anyone who has reached this point, absolutely everything here below is perfectly beautiful. In everything which exists, in everything which happens, he discerns the mechanism of necessity and he recognizes in this necessity the infinite sweetness of obedience. For us, this obedience of things in relation to God is what the transparency of a window pane is in relation to light. As soon as we feel this obedience with our whole being, we see God.

When we hold a newspaper upside down, we see the odd shapes of the printed characters. When we turn it the right way up, we no longer see the characters, we see words. The passenger on a ship in a storm feels each shock as an inward upheaval. The captain is aware only of the complex combination of wind, current, and swell, with the ship's position and its shape, its sails, and its helm.

As one has to learn to read, or to practise a trade, so one must learn to feel in all things, first and almost solely, the obedience of the universe to God. It is truly an apprenticeship; and like every apprenticeship it calls for time and effort. For the man who has finished his training the differences between things or between events are no more important than those perceived by someone who knows how to read when he has before him the same sentence repeated several times, in red ink and blue, and printed in this, that, and the other kind of type. The man who cannot read sees only the differences. For the man who can read it all comes to the same thing, because the sentence is the same. Whoever has finished his apprenticeship recognizes things and events, everywhere and always, as vibrations of the same divine and infinitely sweet word. Which is not to say that he will not suffer. Pain is the colour of certain events. When a man who can and a man who cannot read look at a sentence written in red ink they both see something red; but the red colour is not so important for the one as for the other.

When an apprentice gets hurt or complains of fatigue, workmen and peasants have this fine expression: 'It's the trade getting into his body.' Whenever we have some pain to endure, we can say to ourselves that it is the universe, the order and beauty of the world, and the obedience of creation to God which are entering our body. After that how can we fail to bless with the tenderest gratitude the Love which sends us this gift?

Joy and suffering are two equally precious gifts which must both of them be fully tasted, each one in its purity and without trying to mix them. Through joy, the beauty of the world penetrates our soul. Through suffering it penetrates our body. We could no more become friends of God through joy alone than one becomes a ship's captain by studying books on navigation. The body plays a part in all apprenticeships. On the plane of physical sensibility, suffering alone gives us contact with that necessity which constitutes the order of the world, for pleasure does not involve an impression of necessity. It is on a higher plane of sensibility that the necessity in joy can be recognized, and then only indirectly through the sense of beauty. In order that our being may one day become wholly sensitive in every part to this obedience which is the substance of matter, in order that a new sense may be formed in us which allows us to hear the universe as the vibration of the word of God, the transforming power of suffering and of joy are equally indispensable. When either of them comes to us we have to open the very centre of our soul to it, as a woman opens her door to messengers from her beloved. What does it matter to a lover if the messenger is courteous or rough so long as he gives her a message?

But affliction is not suffering. Affliction is something quite different from a divine educational method.

The infinity of space and time separates us from God. How can we seek for him? How can we go towards him? Even if we were to walk for endless centuries we should do no more than go round and round the world. Even in an aeroplane we could not do anything else. We are incapable of progressing vertically. We cannot take one step towards the heavens. God crosses the universe and comes to us.

Over the infinity of space and time the infinitely more infinite love of God comes to possess us. He comes at his own time. We have the power to consent to receive him or to refuse. If we remain deaf he comes back again and again a beggar, but also, like a beggar, one day he stops coming. If we consent, God places a little seed in us and he goes away again. From that moment God has no more to do; neither have we, except to wait. We have only not to regret the consent we gave, the nuptial Yes. It is not as easy as it seems, for the growth of the seed within us is painful. Moreover, from the very fact that we accept this growth we cannot avoid destroying whatever gets in its way, pulling up the weeds, cutting the grasses; and unfortunately they are part of our very flesh, so that this gardening amounts to a violent operation. On the whole, however, the seed grows of itself. A day comes when the soul belongs to God, when it not only consents to love but when truly and effectively it loves. Then in its turn it must cross the universe to go to God. The soul does not love like a creature, with created love. The love within it is divine, uncreated, for it is the love of God for God which is passing through it. God alone is capable of loving God. We can only consent to give up our own feelings so as to allow free passage in our soul for this love. That is the meaning of denying oneself. We were created solely in order to give this consent.

The divine Love crossed the infinity of space and time to come from God to us. But how can it repeat the journey in the opposite direction, starting from a finite creature? When the seed of divine love placed in us has grown and become a tree, how can we, we who bear it, take it back to its origin? How can we make, in the opposite direction, the journey which God made when he came to us? How can we cross infinite distance?

It seems impossible, but there is a way. It is a way well known to us. We are quite well aware of the likeness in which this tree is made, this tree which has grown within us, this most beautiful tree where the birds of the air come and perch. We know what is the most beautiful of all trees. 'No forest bears its equal.' Something even a little more frightful than a gallows—that is the most beautiful of all trees. It was the seed of this tree that God placed within us, without our knowing what seed it was. If we had known, we should not have said Yes at the first moment. It is this tree which has grown within us and which has become ineradicable. Only a betrayal could uproot it.

When a hammer strikes a nail the shock travels, without losing any of its force, from the nail's large head to the point, although it is only a point. If the hammer and the nail's head were infinitely large the effect would still be the same. The point of the nail would transmit this infinite shock at the place where it was applied.

Extreme affliction, which means physical pain, distress of soul, and social degradation, all together, is the nail. The point of the nail is applied to the very centre of the soul, and its head is the whole of necessity throughout all space and time.

Affliction is a marvel of divine technique. It is a simple and ingenious device to introduce into the soul of a finite creature that immensity of force, blind, brutal, and cold. The infinite distance which separates God from the creature is concentrated into a point to transfix the centre of a soul.

The man to whom such a thing occurs has no part in the operation. He quivers like a butterfly pinned alive to a tray. But throughout the horror he can go on wanting to love. There is no impossibility in that, no obstacle, one could almost say no difficulty. Because no pain, however great, up to the point of losing consciousness, touches that part of the soul which consents to a right orientation.

It is only necessary to know that love is an orientation and not a state of the soul. Anyone who does not know this will fall into despair at the first onset of affliction.

The man whose soul remains oriented towards God while a nail is driven through it finds himself nailed to the very centre of the universe; the true centre, which is not in the middle, which is not in space and time, which is God. In a dimension which is not spatial and which is not time, a totally other dimension, the nail has pierced through the whole of creation, through the dense screen which separates the soul from God.

In this marvellous dimension, without leaving the time and place to which the body is bound, the soul can traverse the whole of space and time and come into the actual presence of God.

It is at the point of intersection between creation and Creator. This point is the point of intersection of the two branches of the Cross.

St. Paul was perhaps thinking about things of this kind when he said: 'That ye, being rooted and grounded in love, may be able to comprehend with all saints what is the breadth, and length, and depth, and height; and to know the love of Christ, which passeth knowledge.'

If the tree of life, and not simply the divine seed, is already formed in a man's soul at the time when extreme affliction strikes him, then he is nailed to the same cross as Christ.

Otherwise, there is the choice between the crosses on each side of Christ's.

We are like the impenitent thief if we seek consolation in contempt and hatred for our fellows in misfortune. This is the commonest effect of real affliction; it was so in the case of Roman slavery. People who are surprised when they observe such a state of mind in the afflicted would almost all fall into it themselves if affliction struck them.

To be like the good thief it is sufficient to remember that no matter what degree of affliction one is submerged in, one has deserved at least that much. Because it is certain that before being reduced to impotence by affliction one has been an accomplice, through cowardice, inertia, indifference, or culpable ignorance, in crimes which have plunged other human beings into an affliction at least as great. Generally, no doubt, we could not prevent those crimes, but we could express our reprobation of them. We neglected to do so, or even approved them, or at least we concurred in the expression of approval around us. For this complicity, the affliction we are suffering is not, in strict justice, too great a penalty. We have no right to feel compassion for ourselves. We know that at least once a perfectly innocent being suffered a worse affliction; it is better to direct our compassion to him across the centuries.

That is what everybody can and ought to say to himself. Because among our institutions and customs there are things so atrocious that nobody can legitimately feel himself innocent of this diffused complicity. It is certain that each of us is involved at least in the guilt of criminal indifference.

But in addition it is the right of every man to desire to have his part in Christ's own Cross. We have an unlimited right to ask God for everything that is good. In such demands there is no need for humility or moderation.

It is wrong to desire affliction; it is against nature, and it is a perversion; and moreover it is the essence of affliction that it is suffered unwillingly. So long as we are not submerged in affliction all we can do is to desire that, if it should come, it may be a participation in the Cross of Christ.

But what is in fact always present, and what it is therefore always permitted to love, is the possibility of affliction. All the three sides of our being are always exposed to it. Our flesh is fragile; it can be pierced or torn or crushed, or one of its internal mechanisms can be permanently deranged, by any piece of matter in motion. Our soul is vulnerable, being subject to fits of depression without cause and pitifully dependent upon all sorts of objects, inanimate and animate, which are themselves fragile and capricious. Our social personality, upon which our sense of existence almost depends, is always and entirely exposed to every hazard. These three parts of us are linked with the very centre of our being in such a way that it bleeds for any wound of the slightest consequence which they suffer. Above all, anything which diminishes or destroys our social prestige, our right to consideration, seems to impair or abolish our very essence—so much is our whole substance an affair of illusion.

When everything is going more or less well, we do not think about this almost infinite fragility. But nothing compels us not to think about it. We can contemplate it all the time and thank God for it unceasingly. We can be thankful not only for the fragility itself but also for that more intimate weakness which connects it with the very centre of our being. For it is this weakness which makes possible, in certain conditions, the operation by which we are nailed to the very centre of the Cross.

We can think of this fragility, with love and gratitude, on the occasion of any suffering, whether great or small. We can think of it at times when we are neither particularly happy nor unhappy. We can think of it whenever we experience any joy. This, however, we ought not to do if the thought were liable to cloud or lessen the joy. But it is not so. This thought only adds a more piercing sweetness to joy, in the same way that the flowers of the cherry are the more beautiful for being frail.

If we dispose our thought in this way, then after a certain time the Cross of Christ should become the very substance of our life. No doubt this is what Christ meant when he advised his friends to bear their cross each day, and not, as people seem to think nowadays, simply that one should be resigned about one's little daily troubles—which, by an almost sacrilegious abuse of language, people sometimes refer to as crosses. There is only one cross; it is the whole of that necessity by which the infinity of space and time is filled and which, in given circumstances, can be concentrated upon the atom that any one of us is, and totally pulverize it. To bear one's cross is to bear the knowledge that one is entirely subject to this blind necessity in every part of one's being, except for one point in the soul which is so secret that it is inaccessible to consciousness. However cruelly a man suffers, if there is some part of his being still intact and if he is not fully conscious that it has escaped only by chance and remains every moment at the mercy of chance, he has no part in the Cross. This is above all the case when the part of the soul which remains intact, or even relatively intact, is the social part; which is the reason why sickness profits nothing unless there is added to it the spirit of poverty in its perfection. It is possible for a perfectly happy man—if he recognizes, truly, concretely, and all the time, the possibility of affliction—to enjoy happiness completely and at the same time bear his cross.

But it is not enough to be aware of this possibility; one must love it. One must tenderly love the harshness of that necessity which is like a coin with two faces, the one turned towards us being domination, and the one turned towards God, obedience. We must embrace it closely even if it offers its roughest surface and the roughness cuts into us. Any lover is glad to clasp tightly some object belonging to an absent loved one, even to the point where it cuts into the flesh. We know that this universe is an object belonging to God. We ought to thank God from the depth of our hearts for giving us necessity, his mindless, sightless, and perfectly obedient slave, as absolute sovereign. She drives us with a whip. But being subject in this world to her tyranny, we have only to choose God for our treasure, and put our heart with it, and from that moment we shall see the other face of the tyranny, the face which is pure obedience. We are the slaves of necessity, but we are also the sons of her Master. Whatever she demands of us, we ought to love the sight of her docility, we who are the children of the house. When she does not do as we wish, when she compels us to suffer what we would not, it is given us by means of love to pass through to the other side and to see the face of obedience which she turns towards God. Lucky are those to whom this precious opportunity comes often.

Intense and long-drawn-out physical pain has this unique advantage, that our sensibility is so made as to be unable to accept it. We can get used to, make the best of, and adapt ourselves to anything else except that; and we make the adaptation, in order to have the illusion of power, in order to believe that we are in control. We play at imagining that we have chosen what is forced upon us. But when a human being is transformed, in his own eyes, into a sort of animal, almost paralysed and altogether repulsive, he can no longer retain that illusion. It is all the better if this transformation is brought about by human wills, as a result of social reprobation, provided that it is not an honourable persecution but, as it were, a blind, anonymous oppression. In its physical part, the soul is aware of necessity only as constraint and is aware of constraints only as pain. It is the same truth which penetrates into the senses through pain, into the intelligence through mathematical proof, and into the faculty of love through beauty. So it was that to Job, when once the veil of flesh had been rent by affliction, the world's stark beauty was revealed. The beauty of the world appears when we recognize that the substance of the universe is necessity and that the substance of necessity is obedience to a perfectly wise Love. The universe of which we are a fraction has no other essence than to be obedient.

In the joy of the senses there is a virtue analogous to that of physical pain, if the joy is so vivid and pure, if it so far exceeds expectation, that we immediately recognize our inability to procure anything like it, or to retain its possession, by our own efforts. Of such joys, beauty is always the essence. Pure joy and pure pain are two aspects of the same infinitely precious truth. Fortunately so, because it is this that gives us the right to wish joy rather than pain to those we love.

The Trinity and the Cross are the two poles of Christianity, the two essential truths: the first, perfect joy; the second, perfect affliction. It is necessary to know both the one and the other and their mysterious unity, but the human condition in this world places us infinitely far from the Trinity, at the very foot of the Cross. Our country is the Cross.

The knowledge of affliction is the key of Christianity. But that knowledge is impossible. It is not possible to know affliction without having been through it. Thought is so revolted by affliction that it is as incapable of bringing itself voluntarily to conceive it as an animal, generally speaking, is incapable of suicide. Thought never knows affliction except by constraint. Unless constrained by experience, it is impossible to believe that everything in the soul—all its thoughts and feelings, its every attitude towards ideas, people, and the universe, and, above all, the most intimate attitude of the being towards itself—that all this is entirely at the mercy of circumstances. Even if one recognizes it theoretically, and it is rare indeed to do so, one does not believe it with all one's soul. To believe it with all one's soul is what Christ called, not renunciation or abnegation, as it is usually translated, but denying oneself; and it is by this that one deserves to be his disciple. But when we are in affliction or have passed through it we do not believe this truth any more than before; one could almost say that we believe it still less. Thought can never really be constrained; evasion by falsehood is always open to it. When thought finds itself, through the force of circumstance, brought face to face with affliction it takes immediate refuge in lies, like a hunted animal dashing for cover. Sometimes in its terror it burrows very deep into falsehood and it often happens that people who are or have been in affliction become addicted to lying as a vice, in some cases to such a degree that they lose the sense of any distinction between truth and falsehood in anything. It is wrong to blame them. Falsehood and affliction are so closely linked that Christ conquered the world simply because he, being the Truth, continued to be the Truth in the very depth of extreme affliction. Thought is constrained by an instinct of self-preservation to fly from the sight of affliction, and this instinct is infinitely more essential to our being than the instinct to avoid physical death. It is comparatively easy to face physical death so long as circumstances or the play of imagination present it under some other aspect than that of afflic-

tion. But to be able to face affliction with steady attention when it is
close to him a man must be prepared, for the love of truth, to accept
the death of the soul. This is the death of which Plato spoke when
he said 'to philosophize is to learn to die'; it is the death which was
symbolized in the initiation rites of the ancient mysteries, and which is
represented by baptism. In reality, it is not a question of the soul's
dying, but simply of recognizing the truth that it is a dead thing, something analogous to matter. It has no need to turn into water; it is
water; the thing we believe to be our self is as ephemeral and automatic
a product of external circumstances as the form of a sea-wave.

It is only necessary to know that, to know it in the depth of
one's being. But to know humanity in that way belongs to God alone
and to those in this world who have been regenerated from on high.
For it is impossible to accept that death of the soul unless one possesses another life in addition to the soul's illusory life, unless one
has placed one's treasure and one's heart elsewhere—and not merely
outside one's person but outside all one's thoughts and feelings and
outside everything knowable, in the hands of our Father who is in
secret. Of those who have done this one can say that they have been
born of water and the Spirit; for they are no longer anything except a
two-fold obedience—on the one side to the mechanical necessity in
which their earthly condition involves them, and on the other to the
divine inspiration. There is nothing left in them which one could call
their own will, their person, their 'I'. They have become nothing other
than a certain intersection of nature and God. This intersection is the
name with which God has named them from all eternity; it is their
vocation. In the old baptism by immersion the man disappeared under
the water; this means to deny one's self, to acknowledge that one is
only a fragment of the inert matter which is the fabric of creation. He
only reappeared because he was lifted up by an ascending movement stronger than gravity; this is the image of the divine love in man.
Baptism contains the symbol of the state of perfection. The engagement it involves is the promise to desire that state and to beseech God
for it, incessantly and untiringly, for as long as one has not obtained
it—as a hungry child never stops asking his father for bread. But we
cannot know what this promise commits us to until we encounter
the terrible presence of affliction. It is only there, face to face with

affliction, that the true commitment can be made, through a more secret, more mysterious, more miraculous contact even than a sacrament.

The knowledge of affliction being by nature impossible both to
those who have experienced it and to those who have not, it is equally
possible for both of them by supernatural favour; otherwise Christ
would not have spared from affliction the man he cherished above all,
and after having promised that he should drink from his cup. In both
cases the knowledge of affliction is something much more miraculous
than walking on water.

Those whom Christ recognized as his benefactors are those whose
compassion rested upon the knowledge of affliction. The others give
capriciously, irregularly, or else too regularly, or from habit imposed
by training, or in conformity with social convention, or from vanity
or emotional pity, or for the sake of a good conscience—in a word,
from self-regarding motives. They are arrogant or patronizing or tact-
lessly sympathetic, or they let the afflicted man feel that they regard
him simply as a specimen of a certain type of affliction. In any case,
their gift is an injury. And they have their reward on earth, because
their left hand is not unaware of what their right hand gave. Their
contact with the afflicted must be a false one because the true understanding of the afflicted implies knowledge of affliction. Those who
have not seen the face of affliction, or are not prepared to, can only
approach the afflicted behind a veil of illusion or falsehood. If the look
of affliction itself is revealed by chance on the face of the afflicted,
they run away.

The benefactor of Christ, when he meets an afflicted man, does
not feel any distance between himself and the other. He projects all his
own being into him. It follows that the impulse to give him food is as
instinctive and immediate as it is for oneself to eat when one is hungry.
And it is forgotten almost at once, just as one forgets yesterday's meals.
Such a man would not think of saying that he takes care of the afflicted
for the Lord's sake; it would seem as absurd to him as it would be to
say that he eats for the Lord's sake. One eats because one can't help
it. Christ will thank the people who give in the way they eat.

They do for the afflicted something very different from feeding,
clothing, or taking care of them. By projecting their own being into
those they help they give them for a moment—what affliction has de-

prived them of—an existence of their own. Affliction is essentially a
destruction of personality, a lapse into anonymity. Just as Christ put
off his divinity for love, so the afflicted are stripped of their humanity
by misfortune. In affliction, that misfortune itself becomes a man's
whole existence and in every other respect he loses all significance, in
everybody's eyes including his own. There is something in him that
would like to exist, but it is continually pushed back into nothingness,
like a drowning man whose head is pushed under the water. He may
be a pauper, a refugee, a negro, an invalid, an ex-convict, or anything
of the kind; in any case, whether he is an object of ill usage or of charity he will in either case be treated as a cipher, as one item among
many others in the statistics of a certain type of affliction. So both
good treatment and bad treatment will have the same effect of compelling him to remain anonymous. They are two forms of the same
offence.

The man who sees someone in affliction and projects into him his
own being brings to birth in him through love, at least for a moment,
an existence apart from his affliction. For, although affliction is the occasion of this supernatural process, it is not the cause. The cause is the
identity of human beings across all the apparent distances placed between them by the hazards of fortune.

To project one's being into an afflicted person is to assume for a
moment his affliction, it is to choose voluntarily something whose
very essence consists in being imposed by constraints upon the unwilling. And that is an impossibility. Only Christ has done it. Only
Christ and those men whose whole soul he possesses can do it. What
these men give to the afflicted whom they succour, when they
project their own being into them, is not really their own being, because they no longer possess one; it is Christ himself.

Charity like this is a sacrament, a supernatural process by which a
man in whom Christ dwells really puts Christ into the soul of the
afflicted. If it is bread that is given, this bread is equivalent to the host.
And this is not speaking symbolically or by conjecture, it is a literal
translation of Christ's own words. He says: 'You have done it unto
me.' Therefore he is in the naked or starving man. But he is not there
in virtue of the nakedness or hunger, because affliction in itself contains no gift from above. Therefore Christ's presence can only be due

to the operation of charity. It is obvious that Christ is in the man whose charity is perfectly pure; for who could be Christ's benefactor except Christ himself? And it is easy to understand that only Christ's presence in a soul can put true compassion in it. But the Gospel reveals further than he who gives from true compassion gives Christ himself. The afflicted who receive this miraculous gift have the choice of consenting to it or not.

In affliction, if it is complete, a man is deprived of all human relationship. For him there are only two possible kinds of relation with men: the first, in which he figures only as a thing, is as mechanical as the relation between two contiguous drops of water, and the second is purely supernatural love. All relationships between these two extremes are forbidden him. There is no place in his life for anything except water and the Spirit. Affliction, when it is consented to and accepted and loved, is truly a baptism.

It is because Christ alone is capable of compassion that he received none while he was on earth. Being in the flesh in this world, he was not at the same time in the souls of those around him; and so there was no one to have pity on him. When suffering compelled him to seek pity, his closest friends refused it; they left him to suffer alone. Even John slept; and Peter, who had been able to walk on water, was incapable of pity when his master fell into affliction. So as to avoid seeing him, they took refuge in sleep. When Pity herself becomes affliction, where can she turn for help? It would have needed another Christ to have pity on Christ in affliction. In the centuries that followed, pity for Christ's affliction was one of the signs of sanctity.

The supernatural process of charity, as opposed to that of communion, for example, does not need to be completely conscious. Those whom Christ thanks reply: 'Lord, when . . . ?' They did not know whom they were feeding. In general, there is nothing even to show that they knew anything at all about Christ. They may or they may not have. The important thing is that they were just; and because of that the Christ within them gave himself in the form of almsgiving. Beggars are fortunate people, in that there is a possibility of their receiving once or twice in their life such an alms.

Affliction is truly at the centre of Christianity. Through it is accomplished the sole and two-fold commandment: 'Love God',

'Love your neighbour.' For, as regards the first, it was said by Christ: 'No man cometh unto the Father, but by me'; and he also said: 'As Moses lifted up the serpent in the wilderness, even so must the Son of man be lifted up: that whosoever believeth in him should not perish, but have eternal life.' The serpent is that serpent of bronze which it was sufficient to look upon to be saved from the effects of poison. Therefore it is only by looking upon the Cross that we can love God. And as regards our neighbour, Christ has said who is the neighbour whom we are commanded to love. It is the naked, bleeding, and senseless body which we see lying in the road. What we are commanded to love first of all is affliction: the affliction of man, the affliction of God.

People often reproach Christianity for a morbid preoccupation with suffering and grief. This is an error. Christianity is not concerned with suffering and grief, for they are sensations, psychological states, in which a perverse indulgence is always possible; its concern is with something quite different, which is affliction. Affliction is not a psychological state; it is a pulverization of the soul by the mechanical brutality of circumstances. The transformation of a man, in his own eyes, from the human condition into that of a half-crushed worm writhing on the ground is a process which not even a pervert would find attractive. Neither does it attract a sage, a hero, or a saint. Affliction is something which imposes itself upon a man quite against his will. Its essence, the thing it is defined by, is the horror, the revulsion of the whole being, which it inspires in its victim. And this is the very thing one must consent to, by virtue of supernatural love.

It is our function in this world to consent to the existence of the universe. God is not satisfied with finding his creation good; he wants it also to find itself good. That is the purpose of the souls which are attached to minute fragments of this world; and it is the purpose of affliction to provide the occasion for judging that God's creation is good. Because, so long as the play of circumstance around us leaves our being almost intact, or only half impaired, we more or less believe that the world is created and controlled by ourselves. It is affliction that reveals, suddenly and to our very great surprise, that we are totally mistaken. After that, if we praise, it is really God's creation that we are praising. And where is the difficulty? We are well aware that divine glory is in no way diminished by our affliction; therefore we are in no way prevented from praising God for his great glory.

Thus, affliction is the surest sign that God wishes to be loved by us; it is the most precious evidence of his tenderness. It is something altogether different from a paternal chastisement, and could more justly be compared to the tender quarrels by which a young couple confirm the depth of their love. We dare not look affliction in the face; otherwise we should see after a little time that it is the face of love. In the same way Mary Magdalene perceived that he whom she took to be the gardener was someone else.

Seeing the central position occupied in their faith by affliction, Christians ought to suspect that it is in a sense the very essence of creation. To be a created thing is not necessarily to be afflicted, but it is necessarily to be exposed to affliction. Only the uncreated is indestructible. Those who ask why God permits affliction might as well ask why God created. And that, indeed, is a question one may well ask. Why did God create? It seems so obvious that God is greater than God and the creation together. At least, it seems obvious so long as one thinks of God as Being. But that is not how one ought to think of him. So soon as one thinks of God as Love one senses that marvel of love by which the Father and the Son are united both in the eternal unity of the one God and also across the separating distance of space and time and the Cross.

God is love, and nature is necessity; but this necessity, through obedience, is a mirror of love. In the same way, God is joy, and creation is affliction; but it is an affliction radiant with the light of joy. Affliction contains the truth about our condition. They alone will see God who prefer to recognize the truth and die, instead of living a long and happy existence in a state of illusion. One must want to go towards reality; then, when one thinks one has found a corpse, one meets an angel who says: 'He is risen.'

The Cross of Christ is the only source of light that is bright enough to illumine affliction. Wherever there is affliction, in any age or any country, the Cross of Christ is the truth of it. Any man, whatever his beliefs may be, has his part in the Cross of Christ if he loves truth to the point of facing affliction rather than escape into the depths of falsehood. If God had been willing to withhold Christ from the men of any given country or epoch, we should know it by an infallible sign; there would be no affliction among them. We know of no such period in history. Wherever there is affliction there is the Cross —concealed, but present to anyone who chooses truth rather than falsehood and love rather than hate. Affliction without the Cross is hell, and God has not placed hell upon the earth.

Conversely, there are many Christians who have no part in Christ because they lack the strength to recognize and worship the blessed Cross in every affliction. There is no such proof of feebleness of faith as the way in which people, even including Christians, sidetrack the problem of affliction when they discuss it. All the talk about original sin, God's will, Providence and its mysterious plans (which nevertheless one thinks one can try to fathom), and future recompenses of every kind in this world and the next, all this only serves to conceal the reality of affliction, or else fails to meet the case. There is only one thing that enables us to accept real affliction, and that is the contemplation of Christ's Cross. There is nothing else. That one thing suffices.

A mother, a wife, or a fiancée, if they know that the person they love is in distress, will want to help him and be with him, and if that is impossible they will at least seek to lessen their distance from him and lighten the heavy burden of impotent sympathy by suffering some equivalent distress. Whoever loves Christ and thinks of him on the Cross should feel a similar relief when gripped by affliction.

By reason of the essential link between the Cross and affliction, no State has the right to dissociate itself from all religion except on the absurd hypothesis that it has succeeded in abolishing affliction. *A fortiori* it has no such right if it is itself creating affliction. A penal system entirely dissociated from any reference to God has a really infernal aura. Not on account of wrong verdicts or excessive punishments but, apart from all that, in itself. It defiles itself by contact with every defilement, and since it contains no purifying principle it becomes so polluted that it can further degrade even the most degraded criminal. Contact with it is hideous for anyone with any integrity or health of mind; and, as for the corrupt, they find an even more horribly corrupt sort of appeasement in the very punishments it inflicts. Nothing is pure enough to bring purity to the places reserved for crime and punishment except Christ, who was himself condemned by the law.

But it is only the Cross, and not the complications of dogma, that is needed by States; and it is disastrous that the Cross and dogma have become so closely linked. By this link, Christ has been drawn away from the criminals who are his brothers.

The idea of necessity as the material common to art, science, and every kind of labour is the door by which Christianity can enter profane life and permeate the whole of it. For the Cross is necessity itself brought into contact with the lowest and the highest part of us; with our physical sensibility by its evocation of physical pain and with supernatural love by the presence of God. It thus involves the whole range of contacts with necessity which are possible for the intermediate parts of our being.

There is not, there cannot be, any human activity in whatever sphere, of which Christ's Cross is not the supreme and secret truth. No activity can be separated from it without rotting or shrivelling like a cut vine-shoot. That is what is happening today, before our uncomprehending eyes, while we ask ourselves what has gone wrong. And Christians comprehend least of all because, knowing that the roots of our activities go back long before Christ, they cannot understand that the Christian faith is the sap in them.

But this would be no problem if we understood that the Christian faith, under veils which do not obscure its radiance, comes to flower and fruit at every time and every place where there are men who do not hate the light.

Never since the dawn of history, except for a certain period of the Roman Empire, has Christ been so absent as today. The separation of religion from the rest of social life, which seems natural even to the majority of Christians nowadays, would have been judged monstrous by antiquity.

The sap of Christianity should be made to flow everywhere in the life of society; but nevertheless it is destined above all for man in solitude. The Father is in secret, and there is no secret more inviolable than affliction.

There is a question which is absolutely meaningless and therefore, of course, unanswerable, and which we normally never ask ourselves, but in affliction the soul is constrained to repeat it incessantly like a sustained, monotonous groan. This question is: Why? Why are things as they are? The afflicted man naïvely seeks an answer, from men, from things, from God, even if he disbelieves in him, from anything or everything. Why is it necessary precisely that he should have nothing to eat, or be worn out with fatigue and brutal treatment, or be about to be executed, or be ill, or be in prison? If one explained to him the causes which have produced his present situation, and this is in any case seldom possible because of the complex interaction of circumstances, it will not seem to him to be an answer. For his question 'Why?' does not mean 'By what cause?' but 'For what purpose?' And it is impossible, of course, to indicate any purposes to him; unless we invent some imaginary ones, but that sort of invention is not a good thing.

It is singular that the affliction of other people, except sometimes, though not always, those very close to us, does not provoke this question. At the most, it may occur to us casually for a moment. But so soon as a man falls into affliction the question takes hold and goes on repeating itself incessantly. Why? Why? Why? Christ himself asked it: 'Why hast thou forsaken me?'

There can be no answer to the 'Why?' of the afflicted, because the world is necessity and not purpose. If there were finality in the world, the place of the good would not be in the other world. Whenever we look for final causes in this world it refuses them. But to know that it refuses, one has to ask.

The only things that compel us to ask the question are affliction, and also beauty; for the beautiful gives us such a vivid sense of the presence of something good that we look for some purpose there, without ever finding one. Like affliction, beauty compels us to ask: Why? Why is this thing beautiful? But rare are those who are capable of asking themselves this question for as long as a few hours at a time. The afflicted man's question goes on for hours, days, years; it ceases only when he has no strength left.

He who is capable not only of crying out but also of listening will hear the answer. Silence is the answer. This is the eternal silence for which Vigny bitterly reproached God; but Vigny had no right to say how the just man should reply to the silence, for he was not one of the just. The just man loves. He who is capable not only of listening but also of loving hears this silence as the word of God.

The speech of created beings is with sounds. The word of God is silence. God's secret word of love can be nothing else but silence. Christ is the silence of God.

Just as there is no tree like the Cross, so there is no harmony like the silence of God. The Pythagoreans discerned this harmony in the fathomless eternal silence around the stars. In this world, necessity is the vibration of God's silence.

Our soul is constantly clamorous with noise, but there is one point in it which is silence, and which we never hear. When the silence of God comes to the soul and penetrates it and joins the silence which is secretly present in us, from then on we have our treasure and our heart in God; and space opens before us as the opening fruit of a plant divides in two, for we are seeing the universe from a point situated outside space.

This operation can take place in only two ways, to the exclusion of all others. There are only two things piercing enough to penetrate our souls in this way; they are affliction and beauty.

Often, one could weep tears of blood to think how many unfortunates are crushed by affliction without knowing how to make use of it. But, coolly considered, this is not a more pitiful waste than the squandering of the world's beauty. The brightness of stars, the sound of sea-waves, the silence of the hour before dawn—how often do they not offer themselves in vain to men's attention? To pay no attention to the world's beauty is, perhaps, so great a crime of ingratitude that it deserves the punishment of affliction. To be sure, it does not always get it; but then the alternative punishment is a mediocre life, and in what way is a mediocre life preferable to affliction? Moreover, even in the case of great misfortune such people's lives are probably still mediocre. So far as conjecture is possible about sensibility, it would seem that the evil within a man is a protection against the external evil that attacks him in the form of pain. One must hope it is so, and that for the impenitent thief God has mercifully reduced to insignificance such useless suffering. In fact, it certainly is so, because that is the great temptation which affliction offers; it is always possible for an afflicted man to suffer less by consenting to become wicked.

The man who has known pure joy, if only for a moment, and who has therefore tasted the flavour of the world's beauty, for it is the same thing, is the only man for whom affliction is something devastating. At the same time, he is the only man who has not deserved this punishment. But, after all, for him it is no punishment; it is God himself holding his hand and pressing it rather hard. For, if he remains constant, what he will discover buried deep under the sound of his own lamentations is the pearl of the silence of God.

FORMS OF
THE IMPLICIT LOVE
OF GOD

Following and complementing "The Love of God and Affliction," in WAITING FOR GOD, *is the long essay "Forms of the Implicit Love of God," from which the two sections below are taken. In this essay Simone Weil stresses that the implicit love of God can have only these immediate objects, the only things "here below in which God is really though secretly present": religious ceremonies, the beauty of the world, our neighbor, friendship. These indirect loves, each of which has the virtue of a sacrament, belong to a period of preparation and "constitute an upward movement of the soul, not without some effort, toward higher things."*

LOVE OF THE ORDER OF THE WORLD

The love of the order and beauty of the world is thus the complement of the love of our neighbor.

It proceeds from the same renunciation, the renunciation that is an image of the creative renunciation of God. God causes this universe to exist, but he consents not to command it, although he has the power to do so. Instead he leaves two other forces to rule in his place. On the one hand there is the blind necessity attaching to matter, in-

cluding the psychic matter of the soul, and on the other the autonomy essential to thinking persons.

By loving our neighbor we imitate the divine love which
created us and all our fellows. By loving the order of the world we
imitate the divine love which created this universe of which we are a
part.

Man does not have to renounce the command of matter and
of souls, since he does not possess the power to command them. But
God has conferred upon him an imaginary likeness of this power, an
imaginary divinity, so that he also, although a creature, may empty
himself of his divinity.

Just as God, being outside the universe, is at the same time the
center, so each man imagines he is situated in the center of the world.
The illusion of perspective places him at the center of space; an illusion
of the same kind falsifies his idea of time; and yet another kindred
illusion arranges a whole hierarchy of values around him. This illusion
is extended even to our sense of existence, on account of the intimate
connection between our sense of value and our sense of being; being
seems to us less and less concentrated the farther it is removed from
us.

We relegate the spatial form of this illusion to the place where it
belongs, the realm of the imagination. We are obliged to do so; otherwise we should not perceive a single object; we should not even be
able to direct ourselves enough to take a single step consciously. God
thus provides us with a model of the operation which should transform all our soul. In the same way as in our infancy we learn to control
and check this illusion in our sense of space, we should control and
check it in our sense of time, values, and being. Otherwise from every
point of view except that of space we shall be incapable of discerning
a single object or directing a single step.

We live in a world of unreality and dreams. To give up our
imaginary position as the center, to renounce it, not only intellectually but in the imaginative part of our soul, that means to awaken
to what is real and eternal, to see the true light and hear the true
silence. A transformation then takes place at the very roots of our
sensibility, in our immediate reception of sense impressions and psy-

chological impressions. It is a transformation analogous to that which takes place in the dusk of evening on a road, where we suddenly discern as a tree what we had at first seen as a stooping man; or where we suddenly recognize as a rustling of leaves what we thought at first was whispering voices. We see the same colors; we hear the same sounds, but not in the same way.

To empty ourselves of our false divinity, to deny ourselves, to give up being the center of the world in imagination, to discern that all points in the world are equally centers and that the true center is outside the world, this is to consent to the rule of mechanical necessity in matter and of free choice at the center of each soul. Such consent is love. The face of this love, which is turned toward thinking persons, is the love of our neighbor; the face turned toward matter is love of the order of the world, or love of the beauty of the world which is the same thing.

In ancient times the love of the beauty of the world had a very important place in men's thoughts and surrounded the whole of life with marvelous poetry. This was the case in every nation—in China, in India, and in Greece. The Stoicism of the Greeks, which was very wonderful and to which primitive Christianity was infinitely close, especially in the writings of Saint John, was almost exclusively the love of the beauty of the world. As for Israel, certain parts of the Old Testament, the Psalms, the Book of Job, Isaiah, and the Book of Wisdom, contain an incomparable expression of the beauty of the world.

The example of Saint Francis shows how great a place the beauty of the world can have in Christian thought. Not only is his actual poem perfect poetry, but all his life was perfect poetry in action. His very choice of places for solitary retreats or for the foundations of his convents was in itself the most beautiful poetry in action. Vagabondage and poverty were poetry with him; he stripped himself naked in order to have immediate contact with the beauty of the world.

Saint John of the Cross also has some beautiful lines about the beauty of the world. But in general, making suitable reservations for the treasures that are unknown, little known, or perhaps buried among the forgotten remains of the Middle Ages, we might say that the beauty of the world is almost absent from the Christian tradition. This is strange. It is difficult to understand. It leaves a terrible gap. How can Christianity call itself catholic if the universe itself is left out?

It is true that there is little mention of the beauty of the world in the Gospel. But in so short a text, which, as Saint John says, is very far from containing all that Christ taught, the disciples no doubt thought it unnecessary to put anything so generally accepted.

It does, however, come up on two occasions. Once Christ tells us to contemplate and imitate the lilies of the field and the birds of the air, in their indifference as to the future and their docile acceptance of destiny; and another time he invites us to contemplate and imitate the indiscriminate distribution of rain and sunlight.

The Renaissance thought to renew its spiritual links with antiquity by passing over Christianity, but it hardly took anything but the secondary products of ancient civilization—art, science, and curiosity regarding human things. It scarcely touched the fringe of the central inspiration. It failed to rediscover any link with the beauty of the world.

In the eleventh and twelfth centuries there had been the beginning of a Renaissance which would have been the real one if it had been able to bear fruit; it began to germinate notably in Languedoc. Some of the Troubadour poems on spring lead one to think that perhaps Christian inspiration and the beauty of the world would not have been separated had it developed. Moreover the spirit of Languedoc left its mark on Italy and was perhaps not unrelated to the Franciscan inspiration. But, whether it be coincidence or more probably the connection of cause and effect, these germs did not survive the war of the Albigenses and only traces of the movement were found after that.

Today one might think that the white races had almost lost all feeling for the beauty of the world, and that they had taken upon them the task of making it disappear from all the continents where they have penetrated with their armies, their trade and their religion. As Christ said to the Pharisees: "Woe to you, for ye have taken away the key of knowledge; ye entered not in yourselves and them that were entering in ye hindered."

And yet at the present time, in the countries of the white races, the beauty of the world is almost the only way by which we can allow

God to penetrate us, for we are still farther removed from the other two. Real love and respect for religious practices are rare even among those who are most assiduous in observing them, and are practically never to be found in others. Most people do not even conceive them to be possible. As regards the supernatural purpose of affliction, compassion and gratitude are not only rare but have become almost unintelligible for almost everyone today. The very idea of them has almost disappeared; the very meaning of the words has been debased.

On the other hand a sense of beauty, although mutilated, distorted, and soiled, remains rooted in the heart of man as a powerful incentive. It is present in all the preoccupations of secular life. If it were made true and pure, it would sweep all secular life in a body to the feet of God; it would make the total incarnation of the faith possible.

Moreover, speaking generally, the beauty of the world is the commonest, easiest, and most natural way of approach.

Just as God hastens into every soul immediately it opens, even a little, in order through it to love and serve the afflicted, so he descends in all haste to love and admire the tangible beauty of his own creation through the soul that opens to him.

But the contrary is still more true. The soul's natural inclination to love beauty is the trap God most frequently uses in order to win it and open it to the breath from on high.

This was the trap which enticed Cora. All the heavens above were smiling at the scent of the narcissus; so was the entire earth and all the swelling ocean. Hardly had the poor girl stretched out her hand before she was caught in the trap. She fell into the hands of the living God. When she escaped she had eaten the seed of the pomegranate which bound her for ever. She was no longer a virgin; she was the spouse of God.

The beauty of the world is the mouth of a labyrinth. The unwary individual who on entering takes a few steps is soon unable to find the opening. Worn out, with nothing to eat or drink, in the dark, separated from his dear ones, and from everything he loves and is accustomed to, he walks on without knowing anything or hoping anything, incapable even of discovering whether he is really going forward or merely turning round on the same spot. But this affliction is as nothing compared with the danger threatening him. For if he does not lose courage, if he goes on walking, it is absolutely certain that he will finally arrive at the center of the labyrinth. And there God is waiting to eat him. Later he will go out again, but he will be changed, he will have become different, after being eaten and digested by God. Afterward he will stay near the entrance so that he can gently push all those who come near into the opening.

The beauty of the world is not an attribute of matter in itself. It is a relationship of the world to our sensibility, the sensibility that depends upon the structure of our body and our soul. The Micromegas of Voltaire, a thinking infusorian organism, could have had no access to the beauty on which we live in the universe. We must have faith that, supposing such creatures were to exist, the world would be beautiful for them too; but it would be beautiful in another way. Anyhow we must have faith that the universe is beautiful on all levels, and more generally that it has a fullness of beauty in relation to the bodily and psychic structure of each of the thinking beings that actually do exist and of all those that are possible. It is this very agreement of an infinity of perfect beauties that gives a transcendent character to the beauty of the world. Nevertheless the part of this beauty we experience is designed and destined for our human sensibility.

The beauty of the world is the co-operation of divine wisdom in creation. "Zeus made all things," says an Orphic line, "and Bacchus perfected them." This perfecting is the creation of beauty; God created the universe, and his Son, our first-born brother, created the beauty of it for us. The beauty of the world is Christ's tender smile for us coming through matter. He is really present in the universal beauty. The love of this beauty proceeds from God dwelling in our souls and goes out to God present in the universe. It also is like a sacrament.

This is true only of universal beauty. With the exception of God, nothing short of the universe as a whole can with complete accuracy be called beautiful. All that is in the universe and is less than the universe can be called beautiful only if we extend the word beyond its strict limits and apply it to things that share indirectly in beauty, things that are imitations of it.

All these secondary kinds of beauty are of infinite value as open-ings to universal beauty. But, if we stop short at them, they are, on the contrary, veils; then they corrupt. They all have in them more or less of this temptation, but in very different degrees.

There are also a number of seductive factors which have noth-ing whatever to do with beauty but which cause the things in which they are present to be called beautiful through lack of discernment; for these things attract love by fraud, and all men, even the most ig-norant, even the vilest of them, know that beauty alone has a right to our love. The most truly great know it too. No man is below or above beauty. The words which express beauty come to the lips of all as soon as they want to praise what they love. Only some are more and some less able to discern it.

Beauty is the only finality here below. As Kant said very aptly, it is a finality which involves no objective. A beautiful thing involves no good except itself, in its totality, as it appears to us. We are drawn toward it without knowing what to ask of it. It offers us its own exis-tence. We do not desire anything else, we possess it, and yet we still desire something. We do not in the least know what it is. We want to get behind beauty, but it is only a surface. It is like a mirror that sends us back our own desire for goodness. It is a sphinx, an enigma, a mystery which is painfully tantalizing. We should like to feed upon it but it is merely something to look at; it appears only from a certain distance. The great trouble in human life is that looking and eating are two different operations. Only beyond the sky, in the country in-habited by God, are they one and the same operation. Children feel this trouble already, when they look at a cake for a long time almost regretting that it should have to be eaten and yet are unable to help eating it. It may be that vice, depravity, and crime are nearly always, or even perhaps always, in their essence, attempts to eat beauty, to eat what we should only look at. Eve began it. If she caused hu-manity to be lost by eating the fruit, the opposite attitude, looking at the fruit without eating it, should be what is required to save it. "Two winged companions," says an Upanishad, "two birds are on the branch of a tree. One eats the fruit, the other looks at it." These two birds are the two parts of our soul.

It is because beauty has no end in view that it constitutes the only finality here below. For here below there are no ends. All the things that we take for ends are means. That is an obvious truth. Money is the means of buying, power is the means of commanding. It is more or less the same for all the things that we call good.

Only beauty is not the means to anything else. It alone is good in itself, but without our finding any particular good or advantage in it. It seems itself to be a promise and not a good. But it only gives itself; it never gives anything else.

Nevertheless, as it is the only finality, it is present in all human pursuits. Although they are all concerned with means, for everything that exists here below is only a means, beauty sheds a luster upon them which colors them with finality. Otherwise there could neither be desire, nor, in consequence, energy in the pursuit.

For a miser after the style of Harpagon, all the beauty of the world is enshrined in gold. And it is true that gold, as a pure and shining substance, has something beautiful about it. The disappearance of gold from our currency seems to have made this form of avarice disappear too. Today those who heap up money without spending it are desirous of power.

Most of those who seek riches connect the thought of luxury with them. Luxury is the finality of riches. Moreover luxury itself represents beauty for a whole class of men. It provides surroundings through which they can feel in a vague fashion that the universe is beautiful; just as Saint Francis needed to be a vagabond and a beggar in order to feel it to be beautiful. Either way would be equally legitimate if in each case the beauty of the world were experienced in an equally direct, pure, and full manner; but happily God willed that it should not be so. Poverty has a privilege. That is a dispensation of Providence without which the love of the beauty of the world might easily come into conflict with the love of our neighbor. Nevertheless, the horror of poverty—and every reduction of wealth can be felt as poverty, even its failure to increase—is essentially a horror of ugliness. The soul that is prevented by circumstances from feeling anything of the beauty of the world, even confusedly, even through what is false, is invaded to its very center by a kind of horror.

The love of power amounts to a desire to establish order among the men and things around oneself, either on a large or small scale, and this desire for order is the result of a sense of beauty. In this case, as in the case of luxury, the question is one of forcing a certain circle into a pattern suggestive of universal beauty; this circle is limited, but the hope of increasing it indefinitely may often be present. This unsatisfied appetite, the desire to keep on increasing, is due precisely to a desire for contact with universal beauty, even though the circle we are organizing is not the universe. It is not the universe and it hides it. Our immediate universe is like the scenery in a theater.

In his poem *Sémiramis*, Valéry succeeds very well in making us feel the connection between tyranny and the love of beauty. Apart from war, the instrument for increasing his power, Louis XIV was only interested in festivals and architecture. Moreover war itself, especially as conducted in the old days, stirs man's sense of beauty in a way that is vital and poignant.

Art is an attempt to transport into a limited quantity of matter, modeled by man, an image of the infinite beauty of the entire universe. If the attempt succeeds, this portion of matter should not hide the universe, but on the contrary it should reveal its reality to all around.

Works of art that are neither pure and true reflections of the beauty of the world nor openings onto this beauty are not strictly speaking beautiful; their authors may be very talented but they lack real genius. That is true of a great many works of art which are among the most celebrated and the most highly praised. Every true artist has had real, direct, and immediate contact with the beauty of the world, contact that is of the nature of a sacrament. God has inspired every first-rate work of art, though its subject may be utterly and entirely secular; he has not inspired any of the others. Indeed the luster of beauty that distinguishes some of those others may quite well be a diabolical luster.

Science has as its object the study and the theoretical reconstruction of the order of the world—the order of the world in relation to the mental, psychic, and bodily structure of man. Contrary to the naïve illusions of certain scholars, neither the use of telescopes and microscopes, nor the employment of most unusual algebraical formulae, nor even a contempt for the principle of noncontradiction will allow it to get beyond the limits of this structure. Moreover it is not desirable that it should. The object of science is the presence of Wisdom in the universe, Wisdom of which we are the brothers, the presence of Christ, expressed through matter which constitutes the world.

We reconstruct for ourselves the order of the world in an image, starting from limited, countable, and strictly defined data. We work out a system for ourselves, establishing connections and conceiving of relationships between terms that are abstract and for that reason possible for us to deal with. Thus in an image, an image of which the very existence hangs upon an act of our attention, we can contemplate the necessity which is the substance of the universe but which, as such, only manifests itself to us by the blows it deals.

We cannot contemplate without a certain love. The contemplation of this image of the order of the world constitutes a certain contact with the beauty of the world. The beauty of the world is the order of the world that is loved.

Physical work is a specific contact with the beauty of the world, and can even be, in its best moments, a contact so full that no equivalent can be found elsewhere. The artist, the scholar, the philosopher, the contemplative should really admire the world and pierce through the film of unreality that veils it and makes of it, for nearly all men at nearly every moment of their lives, a dream or stage set. They ought to do this but more often than not they cannot manage it. He who is aching in every limb, worn out by the effort of a day of work, that is to say a day when he has been subject to matter, bears the reality of the universe in his flesh like a thorn. The difficulty for him is to look and to love. If he succeeds, he loves the Real.

That is the immense privilege God has reserved for his poor. But they scarcely ever know it. No one tells them. Excessive fatigue, harassing money worries, and the lack of true culture prevent them from noticing it. A slight change in these conditions would be enough to open the door to a treasure. It is heart-rending to see how easy it would be in many cases for men to procure a treasure for their fellows and how they allow centuries to pass without taking the trouble to do so.

At the time when there was a people's civilization, of which we are today collecting the crumbs as museum pieces under the name of folklore, the people doubtless had access to the treasure. Mythology too, which is very closely related to folklore, testifies to it, if we can decipher the poetry it contains.

Carnal love in all its forms, from the highest, that is to say true marriage or platonic love, down to the worst, down to debauchery, has the beauty of the world as its object. The love we feel for the splendor of the heavens, the plains, the sea, and the mountains, for the silence of nature which is borne in upon us by thousands of tiny sounds, for the breath of the winds or the warmth of the sun, this love of which every human being has at least an inkling, is an incomplete, painful love, because it is felt for things incapable of responding, that is to say for matter. Men want to turn this same love toward a being who is like themselves and capable of answering to their love, of saying yes, of surrendering. When the feeling for beauty happens to be associated with the sight of some human being, the transference of love is made possible, at any rate in an illusory manner. But it is all the beauty of the world, it is universal beauty, for which we yearn.

This kind of transference is what all love literature expresses, from the most ancient and well-worn metaphors and comparisons to the subtle analyses of Proust.

The longing to love the beauty of the world in a human being is essentially the longing for the Incarnation. It is mistaken if it thinks it is anything else. The Incarnation alone can satisfy it. It is therefore wrong to reproach the mystics, as has been done sometimes, because they use love's language. It is theirs by right. Others only borrow it.

If carnal Love on all levels goes more or less directly toward beauty—and the exceptions are perhaps only apparent—it is because beauty in a human being enables the imagination to see in him something like an equivalent of the order of the world.

That is why sins in this realm are serious. They constitute an offense against God from the very fact that the soul is unconsciously engaged in searching for God. Moreover they all come back to one thing and that is the more or less complete determination to dispense with consent. To be completely determined to dispense with it is per-

haps the most frightful of all crimes. What can be more horrible than
not to respect the consent of a being in whom one is seeking, though
unconsciously, for an equivalent of God?

It is still a crime, though a less serious one, to be content with
consent issuing from a low or superficial region of the soul. Whether
there is physical union or not, the exchange of love is unlawful if, on
both sides, the consent does not come from that central point in the
soul where the yes can be nothing less than eternal. The obligation
of marriage which is so often regarded as a simple social convention
today, is implanted in the nature of human thought through the affinity
between carnal love and beauty. Everything that is related to beauty
should be unaffected by the passage of time. Beauty is eternity here
below.

It is not surprising that in temptation men so often have the feeling
of something absolute, which infinitely surpasses them, which they
cannot resist. The absolute is indeed there. But we are mistaken when
we think that it dwells in pleasure.

The mistake is the effect of this imaginary transference which is
the principal mechanism of human thought. Job speaks of the slave
who in death will cease to hear the voice of his master and who thinks
that this voice harms him. It is but too true. The voice does him only
too much harm. Yet he is mistaken. The voice is not harmful in itself.
If he were not a slave it would not hurt him at all. But because he is
a slave, the pain and the brutality of the blows of the whip enter his
soul by the sense of hearing, at the same time as the voice, and
penetrate to its very depths. There is no barrier by which he can
protect himself. Affliction has forged this link.

In the same way the man who thinks he is in the power of pleasure is really in the power of the absolute which he has transferred to
it. This absolute is to pleasure what the blows of the whip are to the
master's voice; but the association is not the result of affliction here; it
is the result of an original crime, the crime of idolatry. Saint Paul has
emphasized the kinship between vice and idolatry.

He who has located the absolute in pleasure cannot help being
dominated by it. Man does not struggle against the absolute. He who
knows how to locate the absolute outside pleasure possesses the perfection of temperance.

The different kinds of vice, the use of drugs, in the literal or metaphorical sense of the word, all such things constitute the search for a state where the beauty of the world will be tangible. The mistake lies precisely in the search for a special state. False mysticism is another form of this error. If the error is thrust deeply enough into the soul, man cannot but succumb to it.

In general all the tastes of men from the guiltiest to the most innocent, from the most usual to the most peculiar, are related to a combination of circumstances or to a set of people or surroundings which they imagine can give them access to the beauty of the world. The advantage of this or that group of circumstances is due to temperament, to the memories of a past life, to causes which are usually impossible to recognize.

There is only one case, which moreover is frequent, when the attraction of the pleasure of the senses does not lie in the contact it offers with beauty; it is when, on the contrary, it provides an escape from it.

The soul seeks nothing so much as contact with the beauty of the world, or at a still higher level, with God; but at the same time it flies from it. When the soul flies from anything it is always trying to get away, either from the horror of ugliness, or contact with what is truly pure. This is because all mediocrity flies from the light; and in all souls, except those which are near perfection, there is a great part which is mediocre. This part is seized with panic every time that a little pure beauty or pure goodness appears; it hides behind the flesh, it uses it as a veil. As a bellicose nation really needs to cover its aggression with some pretext or other if it is to succeed in its enterprises, the quality of the pretext being actually quite indifferent, so the mediocre part of the soul needs a slight pretext for flying from the light. The attraction of pleasure and the fear of pain supply this pretext. There again it is the absolute that dominates the soul, but as an object of repulsion and no longer as an attraction. Very often also in the search for carnal pleasure the two movements are combined; the movement of running toward pure beauty and the movement of flying far from it are indistinguishably tangled.

However it may be, in every kind of human occupation there is always some regard for the beauty of the world seen in more or less distorted or soiled images. As a consequence there is not any department of human life which is purely natural. The supernatural is secretly present throughout. Under a thousand different forms, grace and mortal sin are everywhere.

Between God and these incomplete, unconscious, often criminal searchings for beauty, the only link is the beauty of the world. Christianity will not be incarnated so long as there is not joined to it the Stoic's idea of filial piety for the city of the world, for the country of here below which is the universe. When, as the result of some misapprehension, very difficult to understand today, Christianity cut itself off from Stoicism, it condemned itself to an abstract and separate existence.

Even the very highest achievements of the search for beauty, in art or science for instance, are not truly beautiful. The only true beauty, the only beauty that is the real presence of God, is the beauty of the universe. Nothing less than the universe is beautiful.

The universe is beautiful as a beautiful work of art would be if there could be one that deserved this name. Thus it contains nothing constituting an end or a good in itself. It has in it no finality beyond universal beauty itself. The essential truth to be known concerning this universe is that it is absolutely devoid of finality. Nothing in the way of finality can be ascribed to it except through a lie or a mistake.

If we ask why such and such a word in a poem is in such and such a place and if there is an answer, either the poem is not of the highest order or else the reader has understood nothing of it. If one can rightly say that the word is where it is in order to express a particular idea, or for the sake of a grammatical connection, or for the sake of the rhyme or alliteration, or to complete the line, or to give a certain color, or even for a combination of several reasons of this kind, there has been a seeking for effect in the composition of the poem, there has not been true inspiration. In the case of a really beautiful poem the only answer is that the word is there because it is suitable that it should be. The proof of this suitability is that it is there and that the poem is beautiful. The poem is beautiful, that is to say the reader does not wish it other than it is.

It is in this way that art imitates the beauty of the world. The suitability of things, beings, and events consists only in this, that they exist and that we should not wish that they did not exist or that they had been different. Such a wish would be an impiety toward our universal country, a lack of the love of the Stoics. We are so constituted that this love is in fact possible; and it is this possibility of which the name is the beauty of the world.

The question of Beaumarchais: "Why these things rather than others?" never has any answer, because the world is devoid of finality. The absence of finality is the reign of necessity. Things have causes and not ends. Those who think to discern special designs of Providence are like professors who give themselves up to what they call the explanation of the text, at the expense of a beautiful poem.

In art, the equivalent of this reign of necessity is the resistance of matter and arbitrary rules. Rhyme imposes upon the poet a direction in his choice of words which is absolutely unrelated to the sequence of ideas. Its function in poetry is perhaps analogous to that of affliction in our lives. Affliction forces us to feel with all our souls the absence of finality.

If the soul is set in the direction of love, the more we contemplate necessity, the more closely we press its metallic cold and hardness directly to our very flesh, the nearer we approach to the beauty of the world. That is what Job experienced. It was because he was so honest in his suffering, because he would not entertain any thought that might impair its truth, that God came down to reveal the beauty of the world to him.

It is because absence of any finality or intention is the essence of the beauty of the world that Christ told us to behold the rain and the light of the sun, as they fall without discrimination upon the just and the unjust. This recalls the supreme cry of Prometheus: "The heavens, where the common orb of day revolves for all." Christ commands us to imitate this beauty. Plato also in the *Timæus* counsels us through contemplation to make ourselves like to the beauty of the world, like to the harmony of the circular movements that cause day and night, months, seasons, and years to succeed each other and return. In these revolutions also, and in their combination, the absence of intention and finality is manifest; pure beauty shines forth.

It is because it can be loved by us, it is because it is beautiful, that the universe is a country. It is our only country here below. This thought is the essence of the wisdom of the Stoics. We have a heavenly country, but in a sense it is too difficult to love, because we do not know it; above all, in a sense, it is too easy to love, because we can imagine it as we please. We run the risk of loving a fiction under this name. If the love of the fiction is strong enough it makes all virtue easy, but at the same time of little value. Let us love the country of here below. It is real; it offers resistance to love. It is this country that God has given us to love. He has willed that it should be difficult yet possible to love it.

We feel ourselves to be outsiders, uprooted, in exile here below. We are like Ulysses who had been carried away during his sleep by sailors and woke in a strange land, longing for Ithaca with a longing that rent his soul. Suddenly Athena opened his eyes and he saw that he was in Ithaca. In the same way every man who longs indefatigably for his country, who is distracted from his desire neither by Calypso nor by the Sirens, will one day suddenly find that he is there.

The imitation of the beauty of the world, that which corresponds to the absence of finality, intention, and discrimination in it, is the absence of intention in ourselves, that is to say the renunciation of our own will. To be perfectly obedient is to be perfect as our Father in heaven is perfect.

Among men, a slave does not become like his master by obeying him. On the contrary, the more he obeys the greater is the distance between them.

It is otherwise between man and God. If a reasonable creature is absolutely obedient, he becomes a perfect image of the Almighty as far as this is possible for him.

We are made in the very image of God. It is by virtue of something in us which attaches to the fact of being a person but which is not the fact itself. It is the power of renouncing our own personality. It is obedience.

Every time that a man rises to a degree of excellence, which by participation makes of him a divine being, we are aware of something impersonal and anonymous about him. His voice is enveloped in silence. This is evident in all the great works of art or thoughts, in the great deeds of saints and in their words.

It is then true in a sense that we must conceive of God as impersonal, in the sense that he is the divine model of a person who passes beyond the self by renunciation. To conceive of him as an all-powerful person, or under the name of Christ as a human person, is to exclude oneself from the true love of God. That is why we have to adore the perfection of the heavenly Father in his even diffusion of the light of the sun. The divine and absolute model of that renunciation which is obedience in us—such is the creative and ruling principle of the universe—such is the fullness of being.

It is because the renunciation of the personality makes man a reflection of God that it is so frightful to reduce men to the condition of inert matter by plunging them into affliction. When the quality of human personality is taken from them, the possibility of renouncing it is also taken away, except in the case of those who are sufficiently prepared. As God has created our independence so that we should have the possibility of renouncing it out of love, we should for the same reason wish to preserve the independence of our fellows. He who is perfectly obedient sets an infinite price upon the faculty of free choice in all men.

In the same way there is no contradiction between the love of the beauty of the world and compassion. Such love does not prevent us from suffering on our own account when we are in affliction. Neither does it prevent us from suffering because others are afflicted. It is on another plane from suffering.

The love of the beauty of the world, while it is universal, involves, as a love secondary and subordinate to itself, the love of all the truly precious things that bad fortune can destroy. The truly precious things are those forming ladders reaching toward the beauty of the world, openings onto it. He who has gone farther, to the very beauty of the world itself, does not love them any less but much more deeply than before.

Numbered among them are the pure and authentic achievements of art and science. In a much more general way they include everything that envelops human life with poetry through the various social strata. Every human being has at his roots here below a certain terrestrial poetry, a reflection of the heavenly glory, the link, of which he is more or less vaguely conscious, with his universal country. Affliction is the tearing up of these roots.

Human cities in particular, each one more or less according to its degree of perfection, surround the life of their inhabitants with poetry. They are images and reflections of the city of the world. Actually, the more they have the form of a nation, the more they claim to be countries themselves, the more distorted and soiled they are as images. But to destroy cities, either materially or morally, or to exclude human beings from a city, thrusting them down to the state of social outcasts, this is to sever every bond of poetry and love between human beings and the universe. It is to plunge them forcibly into the horror of ugliness. There can scarcely be a greater crime. We all have a share by our complicity in an almost innumerable quantity of such crimes. If only we could understand, it should wring tears of blood from us.

IMPLICIT AND EXPLICIT LOVE

Even the most narrow-minded of Catholics would not dare to affirm that compassion, gratitude, love of the beauty of the world, love of religious practices, and friendship belonged exclusively to those centuries and countries that recognized the Church. These forms of love are rarely found in their purity, but it would even be difficult to say that they were met with more frequently in those centuries and countries than in the others. To think that love in any of these forms can exist anywhere where Christ is absent is to belittle him so grievously that it amounts to an outrage. It is impious and almost sacrilegious.

These kinds of love are supernatural, and in a sense they are absurd. They are the height of folly. So long as the soul has not had direct contact with the very person of God, they cannot be supported by any knowledge based either on experience or reason. They cannot therefore rest upon any certainty, unless the word is used in a metaphorical sense to indicate the opposite of hesitation. In consequence it is better that they should not be associated with any belief. This is more honest intellectually, and it safeguards our love's purity more effectively. On this account it is more fitting. In what concerns divine things, belief is not fitting. Only certainty will do. Anything less than certainty is unworthy of God.

During the period of preparation, these indirect loves constitute an upward movement of the soul, a turning of the eyes, not without some effort, toward higher things. After God has come in person, not only to visit the soul as he does for a long time beforehand, but to possess it and to transport its center near to his very heart, it is otherwise. The chicken has cracked its shell; it is outside the egg of the world. These first loves continue; they are more intense than before, but they are different. He who has passed through this adventure has a deeper love than ever for those who suffer affliction and for those who help him in his own, for his friends, for religious practices, and for the beauty of the world. But his love in all these forms has become a movement of God himself, a ray merged in the light of God. That at least is what we may suppose.

These indirect loves are only the attitude toward beings and things here below of the soul turned toward the Good. They themselves have not any particular good as an object. There is no final good here below. Thus strictly speaking we are no longer concerned with forms of love, but with attitudes inspired by love.

In the period of preparation the soul loves in emptiness. It does not know whether anything real answers its love. It may believe that it knows, but to believe is not to know. Such a belief does not help. The soul knows for certain only that it is hungry. The important thing is that it announces its hunger by crying. A child does not stop crying if we suggest to it that perhaps there is no bread. It goes on crying just the same.

The danger is not lest the soul should doubt whether there is any bread, but lest, by a lie, it should persuade itself that it is not hungry. It can only persuade itself of this by lying, for the reality of its hunger is not a belief, it is a certainty.

We all know that there is no true good here below, that everything that appears to be good in this world is finite, limited, wears out, and once worn out, leaves necessity exposed in all its nakedness. Every human being has probably had some lucid moments in his life when he has definitely acknowledged to himself that there is no final good here below. But as soon as we have seen this truth we cover it up with lies. Many people even take pleasure in proclaiming it, seeking a morbid joy in their sadness, without ever having been able to bear facing it for a second. Men feel that there is a mortal danger in facing this truth squarely for any length of time. That is true. Such knowledge strikes more surely than a sword; it inflicts a death more frightening than that of the body. After a time it kills everything within us that constitutes our ego. In order to bear it we have to love truth more than life itself. Those who do this turn away from the fleeting things of time with all their souls, to use the expression of Plato.

They do not turn toward God. How could they do so when they are in total darkness? God himself sets their faces in the right direction. He does not, however, show himself to them for a long time. It is for them to remain motionless, without averting their eyes, listening ceaselessly, and waiting, they know not for what; deaf to entreaties and threats, unmoved by every shock, unshaken in the midst of every upheaval. If after a long period of waiting God allows them to have an indistinct intuition of his light or even reveals himself in person, it is only for an instant. Once more they have to remain still, attentive, inactive, calling out only when their desire cannot be contained.

It does not rest with the soul to believe in the reality of God if God does not reveal this reality. In trying to do so it either labels something else with the name of God, and that is idolatry, or else its belief in God remains abstract and verbal. Such a belief prevails wherever religious dogma is taken for granted, as is the case with those centuries and countries in which it never enters anyone's head to question it. The state of nonbelief is then what Saint John of the Cross calls a night. The belief is verbal and does not penetrate the soul. At a time like the present, incredulity may be equivalent to the dark night of Saint John of the Cross if the unbeliever loves God, if he is like the child who does not know whether there is bread anywhere, but who cries out because he is hungry.

When we are eating bread, and even when we have eaten it, we know that it is real. We can nevertheless raise doubts about the reality of the bread. Philosophers raise doubts about the reality of the world of the senses. Such doubts are however purely verbal; they leave the certainty intact and actually serve only to make it more obvious to a well-balanced mind. In the same way he to whom God has revealed his reality can raise doubts about this reality without any harm. They are purely verbal doubts, a form of exercise to keep his intelligence in good health. What amounts to criminal treason, even before such a revelation and much more afterward, is to question the fact that God is the only thing worthy of love. That is a turning away of our eyes, for love is the soul's looking. It means that we have stopped for an instant to wait and to listen.

Electra did not seek Orestes, she waited for him. When she was convinced that he no longer existed, and that nowhere in the whole world was there anything that could be Orestes, she did not on that account return to her former associates. She drew back from them with greater aversion than ever. She preferred the absence of Orestes to the presence of anyone else. Orestes was to have delivered her from slavery, from rags, servile work, dirt, hunger, blows, and innumerable humiliations. She no longer hoped for that. But never for an instant did she dream of employing another method which could obtain a luxurious and honored life for her—the method of reconciliation with those in power. She did not want wealth and consideration unless they came through Orestes. She did not even give a thought to such things. All she wanted was to exist no longer, since Orestes had ceased to exist.

At that moment Orestes could hold out no longer. He could not help declaring himself. He gave certain proof that he was Orestes. Electra saw him, she heard him, she touched him. There would be no more question for her now as to whether her savior was in existence.

He who has had the same adventure as Electra, he whose soul has seen, heard, and touched for itself, he will recognize God as the reality inspiring all indirect loves, the reality of which they are as it were the reflections. God is pure beauty. This is incomprehensible, for beauty, by its very essence, has to do with the senses. To speak of an imperceptible beauty must seem a misuse of language to any-one who has any sense of exactitude: and with reason. Beauty is always a miracle. But the miracle is raised to the second degree when the soul receives an impression of beauty which, while it is beyond all sense perception is no abstraction, but real and direct as the impression caused by a song at the moment it reaches our ears. Every-thing happens as though, by a miraculous favor, our very senses themselves had been made aware that silence is not the absence of sounds, but something infinitely more real than sounds, and the center of a harmony more perfect than anything which a combination of sounds can produce. Furthermore there are degrees of silence. There is a silence in the beauty of the universe which is like a noise when compared with the silence of God.

God is, moreover, our real neighbor. The term of person can only be rightly applied to God, and this is also true of the term impersonal. God is he who bends over us, afflicted as we are, and reduced to the state of being nothing but a fragment of inert and bleeding flesh. Yet at the same time he is in some sort the victim of misfortune as well, the victim who appears to us as an inanimate body, incap-able of thought, this nameless victim of whom nothing is known. The inanimate body is this created universe. The love we owe to God, this love that would be our crowning perfection if we were able to attain to it, is the divine model both of gratitude and com-passion.

God is also the perfect friend. So that there should be between him and us, bridging the infinite distance, something in the way of equal-ity, he has chosen to place an absolute quality in his creatures, the absolute liberty of consent, which leaves us free to follow or swerve from the God-ward direction he has communicated to our souls. He has also extended our possibilities of error and falsehood so as to leave us the faculty of exercising a spurious rule in imagination, not only over the universe and the human race, but also over God himself, in so far as we do not know how to use his name aright. He has given us this faculty of infinite illusion so that we should have the power to renounce it out of love.

In fact, contact with God is the true sacrament.

We can, however, be almost certain that those whose love of God has caused the disappearance of the pure loves belonging to our life here below are no true friends of God.

Our neighbor, our friends, religious ceremonies, and the beauty of the world do not fall to the level of unrealities after the soul has had direct contact with God. On the contrary, it is only then that these things become real. Previously they were half dreams. Previously they had no reality.

CONCERNING
THE OUR FATHER

*In the summer of 1941 Simone Weil lived on Gustave
Thibon's farm at Saint-Marcel d'Ardèche, about 150 miles
north of Marseilles. In the evenings she undertook to teach
him Greek, using as her text the Lord's Prayer. Soon she
had memorized it, continuously repeating it in Greek as
she worked in the vineyards during the grape harvesting.
The effects were electrifying. Hitherto, as she was to admit, she had never prayed, but now "the very first words
tear my thoughts from my body and transport it to a place
outside space," a divine silence "filling every part of this
infinity of infinity." And now, too, during this recitation,
or at other times, "Christ is present with me in person, but
his presence is infinitely more real, more moving, more
clear than on that first occasion [in 1938] when he took
possession of me." It is the presence of Christ that illuminates Simone Weil's "Concerning the Our Father," a meditation that crowns her witness with the jewel of faith.*

Πάτερ ἡμῶν ὁ ἐν τοῖς οὐρανοῖς,
"Our Father which art in Heaven."

He is our Father. There is nothing real in us which does not come
from him. We belong to him. He loves us, since he loves himself

492

and we are his. Nevertheless he is our Father who is in heaven—not elsewhere. If we think to have a Father here below it is not he, it is a false God. We cannot take a single step toward him. We do not walk vertically. We can only turn our eyes toward him. We do not have to search for him, we only have to change the direction in which we are looking. It is for him to search for us. We must be happy in the knowledge that he is infinitely beyond our reach. Thus we can be certain that the evil in us, even if it overwhelms our whole being, in no way sullies the divine purity, bliss, and perfection.

ἁγιασθήτω τὸ ὄνομά σου·
"Hallowed be thy Name."

God alone has the power to name himself. His name is unpronounceable for human lips. His name is his word. It is the Word of God. The name of any being is an intermediary between the human spirit and that being; it is the only means by which the human spirit can conceive something about a being that is absent. God is absent. He is in heaven. Man's only possibility of gaining access to him is through his name. It is the Mediator. Man has access to this name, although it also is transcendent. It shines in the beauty and order of the world and it shines in the interior light of the human soul. This name is holiness itself; there is no holiness outside it; it does not therefore have to be hallowed. In asking for its hallowing we are asking for something that exists eternally, with full and complete reality, so that we can neither increase nor diminish it, even by an infinitesimal fraction. To ask for that which exists, that which exists really, infallibly, eternally, quite independently of our prayer, that is the perfect petition. We cannot prevent ourselves from desiring; we are made of desire; but the desire that nails us down to what is imaginary, temporal, selfish, can, if we make it pass wholly into this petition, become a lever to tear us from the imaginary into the real and from time into eternity, to lift us right out of the prison of self.

Ἐλθέτω ἡ βασιλεία σου·
"Thy Kingdom Come."

This concerns something to be achieved, something not yet here.

The Kingdom of God means the complete filling of the entire soul of intelligent creatures with the Holy Spirit. The Spirit bloweth where he listeth? We can only invite him. We must not even try to invite him in a definite and special way to visit us or anyone else in particular, or even everybody in general; we must just invite him purely and simply, so that our thought of him is an invitation, a longing cry. It is as when one is in extreme thirst, ill with thirst; then one no longer thinks of the act of drinking in relation to oneself, or even of the act of drinking in a general way. One merely thinks of water, actual water itself, but the image of water is like a cry from our whole being.

γενηθήτω τὸ θέλημά σου,
"Thy will be done."

We are only absolutely, infallibly certain of the will of God concerning the past. Everything that has happened, whatever it may be, is in accordance with the will of the almighty Father. That is implied by the notion of almighty power. The future also, whatever it may contain, once it has come about, will have come about in conformity with the will of God. We can neither add to nor take from this conformity. In this clause, therefore, after an upsurging of our desire toward the possible, we are once again asking for that which is. Here, however, we are not concerned with an eternal reality such as the holiness of the Word, but with what happens in the time order. Nevertheless we are asking for the infallible and eternal conformity of everything in time with the will of God. After having, in our first petition, torn our desire away from time in order to fix it upon eternity, thereby transforming it, we return to this desire which has itself become in some measure eternal, in order to apply it once more to time. Whereupon our desire pierces through time to find eternity behind it. That is what comes about when we know how to make every accomplished fact, whatever it may be, an object of desire. We have here quite a different thing from resignation. Even the word acceptance is too weak. We have to desire that everything that has happened should have happened, and nothing else. We have to do so, not because what has happened is good in our eyes, but because God has permitted it, and because the obedience of the course of events to God is in itself an absolute good.

ὡς ἐν οὐρανῷ, καὶ ἐπὶ τῆς γῆς.

"On earth as it is in heaven."

The association of our desire with the almighty will of God should be extended to spiritual things. Our own spiritual ascents and falls, and those of the beings we love, have to do with the other world, but they are also events that take place here below, in time. On that account they are details in the immense sea of events and are tossed about with the ocean in a way conforming to the will of God. Since our failures of the past have come about, we have to desire that they should have come about. We have to extend this desire into the future, for the day when it will have become the past. It is a necessary correction of the petition that the kingdom of God should come. We have to cast aside all other desires for the sake of our desire for eternal life, but we should desire eternal life itself with renunciation. We must not even become attached to detachment. Attachment to salvation is even more dangerous than the others. We have to think of eternal life as one thinks of water when dying of thirst, and yet at the same time we have to desire that we and our loved ones should be eternally deprived of this water rather than receive it in abundance in spite of God's will, if such a thing were conceivable.

The three foregoing petitions are related to the three Persons of the Trinity, the Son, the Spirit, and the Father, and also to the three divisions of time, the present, the future, and the past. The three petitions that follow have a more direct bearing on the three divisions of time, and take them in a different order—present, past, and future.

Τὸν ἄρτον ἡμῶν τὸν ἐπιούσιον δὸς ἡμῖν σήμερον.

"Give us this day our daily bread"—the bread which is supernatural.

Christ is our bread. We can only ask to have him now. Actually he is always there at the door of our souls, wanting to enter in, though he does not force our consent. If we agree to his entry, he enters; directly we cease to want him, he is gone. We cannot bind our will to-day for tomorrow; we cannot make a pact with him that tomorrow he will be within us, even in spite of ourselves. Our consent to his presence is the same as his presence. Consent is an act; it can only be actual, that is to say in the present. We have not been given a will that can be applied to the future. Everything not effective in our will is imaginary. The effective part of the will has its effect at once; its effectiveness cannot be separated from itself. The effective part of the will is not effort, which is directed toward the future. It is consent; it is the "yes" of marriage. A "yes" pronounced within the present moment and for the present moment, but spoken as an eternal word, for it is consent to the union of Christ with the eternal part of our soul.

Bread is a necessity for us. We are beings who continually draw our energy from outside, for as we receive it we use it up in effort. If our energy is not daily renewed, we become feeble and incapable of movement. Besides actual food, in the literal sense of the word, all incentives are sources of energy for us. Money, ambition, consideration, decorations, celebrity, power, our loved ones, everything that puts into us the capacity for action is like bread. If anyone of these attachments penetrates deeply enough into us to reach the vital roots of our carnal existence, its loss may break us and even cause our death. That is called dying of love. It is like dying of hunger. All these objects of attachment go together with food, in the ordinary sense of the word, to make up the daily bread of this world. It depends entirely on circumstances whether we have it or not. We should ask nothing with regard to circumstances unless it be that they may conform to the will of God. We should not ask for earthly bread.

There is a transcendent energy whose source is in heaven, and this flows into us as soon as we wish for it. It is a real energy; it performs actions through the agency of our souls and of our bodies.

We should ask for this food. At the moment of asking, and by the very fact that we ask for it, we know that God will give it to us. We ought not to be able to bear to go without it for a single day, for when our actions only depend on earthly energies, subject to the necessity of this world, we are incapable of thinking and doing anything but evil. God saw "that the misdeeds of man were multiplied on the earth and that all the thoughts of his heart were continually bent upon evil." The necessity that drives us toward evil governs everything in us except the energy from on high at the moment when it comes into us. We cannot store it.

Καὶ ἄφες ἡμῖν τὰ ὀφειλήματα ἡμῶν, ὡς καὶ ἡμεῖς ἀφίεμεν τοῖς ὀφειλέταις ἡμῶν.
"And forgive us our debts, as we also forgive our debtors."

At the moment of saying these words we must have already remitted everything that is owing to us. This not only includes reparation for any wrongs we think we have suffered, but also gratitude for the good we think we have done, and it applies in a quite general way to all we expect from people and things, to all we consider as our due and without which we should feel ourselves to have been frustrated. All these are the rights that we think the past has given us over the future. First there is the right to a certain permanence. When we have enjoyed something for a long time, we think that it is ours and that we are entitled to expect fate to let us go on enjoying it. Then there is the right to a compensation for every effort whatever its nature, be it work, suffering, or desire. Every time that we put forth some effort and the equivalent of this effort does not come back to us in the form of some visible fruit, we have a sense of false balance and emptiness which makes us think that we have been cheated. The effort of suffering from some offense causes us to expect the punishment or apologies of the offender, the effort of doing good makes us expect the gratitude of the person we have helped, but these are only particular cases of a universal law of the soul. Every time we give anything out we have an absolute need that at least the equivalents should come into us, and because we need this we think we have a right to it. Our debtors comprise all beings and all things; they are the entire universe. We think we have claims everywhere. In every claim we think we possess there is always the idea of an imaginary claim of the past on the future. That is the claim we have to renounce.

To have forgiven our debtors is to have renounced the whole of the past in a lump. It is to accept that the future should still be virgin and intact, strictly united to the past by bonds of which we are ignorant, but quite free from the bonds our imagination thought to impose upon it. It means that we accept the possibility that this will happen, and that it may happen to us in particular; it means that we are prepared for the future to render all our past life sterile and vain.

In renouncing at one stroke all the fruits of the past without exception, we can ask of God that our past sins may not bear their miserable fruits of evil and error. So long as we cling to the past, God himself cannot stop this horrible fruiting. We cannot hold on to the past without retaining our crimes, for we are unaware of what is most essentially bad in us.

The principal claim we think we have on the universe is that our personality should continue. This claim implies all the others. The instinct of self-preservation makes us feel this continuation to be a necessity, and we believe that a necessity is a right. We are like the beggar who said to Talleyrand: "Sir, I must live," and to whom Talleyrand replied, "I do not see the necessity for that." Our personality is entirely dependent on external circumstances which have unlimited power to crush it. But we would rather die than admit this. From our point of view the equilibrium of the world is a combination of circumstances so ordered that our personality remains intact and seems to belong to us. All the circumstances of the past that have wounded our personality appear to us to be disturbances of balance which should infallibly be made up for one day or another by phenomena having a contrary effect. We live on the expectation of these compensations. The near approach of death is horrible chiefly because it forces the knowledge upon us that these compensations will never come.

To remit debts is to renounce our own personality. It means renouncing everything that goes to make up our ego, without any exception. It means knowing that in the ego there is nothing whatever, no psychological element, that external circumstances could not do away with. It means accepting that truth. It means being happy that things should be so.

The words "Thy will be done" imply this acceptance, if we say them with all our soul. That is why we can say a few moments later: "We forgive our debtors."

The forgiveness of debts is spiritual poverty, spiritual nakedness, death. If we accept death completely, we can ask God to make us live again, purified from the evil in us. For to ask him to forgive us our debts is to ask him to wipe out the evil in us. Pardon is purification. God himself has not the power to forgive the evil in us while it remains there. God will have forgiven our debts when he has brought us to the state of perfection.

Until then God forgives our debts partially in the same measure as we forgive our debtors.

Καὶ μὴ εἰσενέγκῃς ἡμᾶς εἰς πειρασμόν, ἀλλὰ ῥῦσαι ἡμᾶς ἀπὸ τοῦ πονηροῦ·
"And lead us not into temptation, but deliver us from evil."

The only temptation for man is to be abandoned to his own resources in the presence of evil. His nothingness is then proved experimentally. Although the soul has received supernatural bread at the moment when it asked for it, its joy is mixed with fear because it could only ask for it for the present. The future is still to be feared. The soul has not the right to ask for bread for the morrow, but it expresses its fear in the form of a supplication. It finishes with that. The prayer began with the word "Father," it ends with the word "evil." We must go from confidence to fear. Confidence alone can give us strength enough not to fall as a result of fear. After having contemplated the name, the kingdom, and the will of God, after having received the supernatural bread and having been purified from evil, the soul is ready for that true humility which crowns all virtues. Humility consists of knowing that in this world the whole soul, not only what we term the ego in its totality, but also the supernatural part of the soul, which is God present in it, is subject to time and to the vicissitudes of change. There must be absolute acceptance of the possibility that everything natural in us should be destroyed. But we must simultaneously accept and repudiate the possibility that the supernatural part of the soul should disappear. It must be accepted as an event that would come about only in conformity with the will of God. It must be repudiated as being something utterly horrible. We must be afraid of it, but our fear must be as it were the completion of confidence.

The six petitions correspond with each other in pairs. The bread which is transcendent is the same thing as the divine name. It is what brings about the contact of man with God. The kingdom of God is the same thing as his protection stretched over us against temptation; to protect is the function of royalty. Forgiving our debtors their debts is the same thing as the total acceptance of the will of God. The difference is that in the first three petitions the attention is fixed solely on God. In the three last, we turn our attention back to ourselves in order to compel ourselves to make these petitions a real and not an imaginary act.

In the first half of the prayer, we begin with acceptance. Then we allow ourselves a desire. Then we correct it by coming back to acceptance. In the second half, the order is changed; we finish by expressing desire. Only desire has now become negative; it is expressed as a fear; therefore it corresponds to the highest degree of humility and that is a fitting way to end.

The Our Father contains all possible petitions; we cannot conceive of any prayer not already contained in it. It is to prayer what Christ is to humanity. It is impossible to say it once through, giving the fullest possible attention to each word, without a change, infinitesimal perhaps but real, taking place in the soul.

REFERENCE
NOTES

In preparing the bibliographical references to Simone Weil's writings, I have found J. P. Little's *Simone Weil: A Bibliography* and the section entitled "Notes, Bibliography, Index" in Jacques Cabaud's *Simone Weil: A Fellowship in Love*, pp. 353–92, of invaluable assistance.

The bibliographical references to Simone Weil's writings translated into English and selected for inclusion in this volume contain only the most essential information. Details regarding the original version of these writings in French, whether in journals and/or in books, are also included in the main bibliographical citations.

Textual notes are reproduced here as they appeared in their original place of publication. For purposes of clarity and consistency I have altered slightly some of these, and, on a very few occasions, I have added new notes. Following the practice of Simone Weil's other editors and translators, I have tried to keep the number of reference notes to a minimum so as not to encumber the text or divert the reader from the primary task of giving his major attention and thought to her writings.

PREFATORY NOTE

PAGE

xv   We live . . . psychic self-improvement and personal survival. / Christopher Lasch, "The Narcissist Society," *The New York Review of Books* 23, no. 15 (September 30, 1976): 5, 8, 10–13.

INTRODUCTION

PAGE

xvii   *La mia solitudine l'atrui dolore germivo fino all morte.* / Quoted by
        Vernon Sproxton, "Pilgrim of the Absolute: An Outline of Simone
        Weil's Life," *Gateway to God,* edited by David Raper (Glasgow:
        William Collins Sons, 1974), p. 36.

xxi–   as Martin Buber bitterly complained, / "The Silent Question: On
xxii   Henri Bergson and Simone Weil," *At the Turning: Three Addresses
        on Judaism* (New York: Farrar, Straus, and Young, 1952), pp. 29–44.

xxiii   Read in the special light of Catholic theology, / See Georges Frénaud,
        O.S.B., "Simone Weil's Religious Thought in the Light of Catholic
        Theology," *Theological Studies* 14, no. 3 (September 1953): 349–76.
        This study is the most authoritative and penetrating on the subject.
        Also helpful are: Gerda Blumenthal, "Simone Weil's Way of the
        Cross," *Thought* 27, no. 105 (Summer 1952): 225–34; Borisz de Balla,
        "Simone Weil, Witness of the Absolute," *The Catholic World* 179,
        no. 1070 (May 1954): 101–9; Miklos J. Veto, "Simone Weil and
        Suffering," *Thought* 40, no. 157 (Summer 1965): 275–86.

xxv   The search of an individual Jew . . . it has been observed. / J. M.
        Cohen, "The Jewish Predicament" [A composite review of *Two
        Types of Faith* by Martin Buber, *The Pillar of Fire* by Karl Stern,
        Waiting on God by Simone Weil], *The Spectator* 187, no. 187 (Sep-
        tember 28, 1951): 402.

xxv–   her innate pessimism, her denial of and alienation from life . . . the
xxvi   Old Testament conception and affirmation of "blessing"; / See Peter
        Watkins, "Simone Weil: Antisemitism and Syncretism," *Church
        Quarterly Review* 163 (October-December 1962): 463–73.

xxvi   "Did she draw up the terrible indictment . . . in the eyes of the new
        God?" / Hans Meyerhoff, "Contra Simone Weil," *Arguments and
        Doctrines: A Reader of Jewish Thinking in the Aftermath of the
        Holocaust,* selected with introductory essays by Arthur A. Cohen
        (New York, Evanston, and London: Harper & Row, 1970), pp.
        75–76.

xxvi   "The absurdity, the absolutism . . . for all her blemishes, their ter-
        rible purity." / Leslie A. Fiedler, "Simone Weil: Prophet out of
        Israel: A Saint of the Absurd," *Commentary* 2, no. 1 (January
        1951): 46.

PAGE

xix   Iris Murdoch perceives . . . when she writes: / "Knowing the Void," *The Spectator* 198, no. 6697 (November 2, 1956): 613.

xxii   Eliot . . . in his essay "Second Thoughts About Humanism": / *Selected Essays* (New York: Harcourt, Brace, and World, 1950), p. 433.

I. A NEW SAINTLINESS

10   "Spiritual Autobiography" / *Waiting for God,* translated by Emma Craufurd, with an introduction by Leslie A. Fiedler (New York: G. P. Putnam's Sons, 1951), pp. 61–83. This letter to the Reverend Father J.-M. Perrin was written in 1942. ["Autobiographie spirituelle," *L'Attente de Dieu,* introduction et notes de J.-M. Perrin. Paris: La Colombe, 1950.]

14   That contact with affliction / No English word exactly conveys the meaning of the French *malheur.* Our word "unhappiness" is a negative term and far too weak. Affliction is the nearest equivalent but not quite satisfactory. *Malheur* has in it a sense of inevitability and doom.

15   It is called "Love." / The reference is to Simone Weil's favorite poem by George Herbert, the seventeenth-century English metaphysical poet. She also enjoyed some of Herbert's other poems: "Discipline," "Bitter Sweet," "The Cellar," "Dialogue," "Justice," "Denial," "Affliction," "Redemption." "Love" is quoted in full and used as the epigraph on p. xlx.

27   "Sketch of Contemporary Social Life" / *Oppression and Liberty,* translated by Arthur Wills and John Petrie, with an introduction by F. C. Ellert (Amherst: University of Massachusetts Press, 1973), pp. 108–24. ["Esquisse de la vie sociale contemporaine," *Oppression et Liberté.* Paris: Gallimard, 1955.] The quotations from Spinoza and Marcus Aurelius originally appeared as epigraphs to the longer study from which this section is taken, "Reflections Concerning the Causes of Liberty and Social Oppression" / "Reflexions sur les causes de la liberté et l'oppression sociale," *Oppression et Liberté.*

40   What exactly will perish / The "Conclusion" of "Reflections Concerning the Causes of Liberty and Social Oppression" begins at this point and ends on page 43.

44   "Reflections on the Right Use of School Studies with a View to the
      Love of God" / *Waiting for God*, pp. 105–16. ["Réflexions sur le
      bon usage des études scolaires en vue de l'amour de Dieu," *L'Attente
      de Dieu*.]

51   (the miraculous vessel / According to some legends the Grail was
      made of a single stone, in color like an emerald.

53   "Factory Work" / Translated by Félix Giovanelli, this essay ap-
      peared in *Politics* 3, no. 11 (December 1946), a journal edited in
      New York by Dwight Macdonald, pp. 369–75. [Réflexions sur la
      vie d'usine"; extract from "Expérience de la vie d'usine," *Economie
      et Humanisme*, Marseilles, no. 2 (juin-juillet 1942), pp. 187–204, signed
      "Emile Novis," anagram of Simone Weil. See also *La Condition
      ouvrière*. Paris: Gallimard, 1951.]

73   "Letter to Georges Bernanos" / *Seventy Letters*, translated and ar-
      ranged by Richard Rees (London, New York, Toronto: Oxford
      University Press, 1965), pp. 105–9. ["Lettre à Georges Bernanos,"
      Societé des amis de Georges Bernanos, Bulletin trimestriel, Paris, no.
      4 (juin 1950), pp. 11–14; in *Ecrits historiques et politiques*. Paris:
      Gallimard, 1960.]

74   the Spanish C.N.T. / *Confederación Nacional de Trabajadores*, the
      anarchist trade union organization.

74   and F.A.I. / *Federación Anarquista Ibérica*, the anarchist political
      party.

75   the *Ballillas* / An Italian fascist corps.

75   the 'Somaten' / The meaning of this slogan is obscure. Possibly
      "We are ready" (*Somos atentos*).

79   "What Is a Jew? A Letter to a Minister of Education" (November
      1940) / *Politics* 6, no. 1 (Winter 1949), 40. ["Lettre à M. le Ministre
      de l'Instruction Publique" (Carcopino), *Etudes matérialistes*, Cannes
      (A.-M.), no. xvii (décembre 1947), pp. 2–4.]

      An appended "Editorial Note" in *Politics* reads as follows:

          This letter was not answered. Almost two years later, however,
          on June 21, 1942, the Vichy Government amended the Statute

on Jews so that it defined as a "Jew" any one with three or more grandparents "of the Jewish religion." It added, perhaps with a sideglance at the above letter: "Non-participation in the Jewish religion is to be established by proof of adherence to one of the other religious confessions recognized by the State before the law of December 9, 1905." Thus Simone Weil's freethinking grandparents were put in their place—the Ghetto—by a Nazi-Catholic regime claiming to represent the country of Voltaire and Diderot!

82 "Letter to Déodat Roché" / *Seventy Letters*, pp. 129–31. [*Pensées sans ordre concernant l'amour de Dieu*. Paris: Gallimard, 1962. Extracts of this letter appeared in *Les Cahiers d'Etudes Cathares*, no. 2 (avril-juin 1949), pp. 4–6.]

82 the Oc number / A special number of *Les Cahiers du Sud* (1942) devoted to "The Genius of Oc and the Mediterranean Man."

86 "Letter to Joë Bousquet" / *Seventy Letters*, pp. 136–42. [Extracts from this letter, with some variations on basic text, appeared in *Les Cahiers du Sud* 26, no. 284 (1947): 567–70; in *Pensées sans ordre concernant l'amour de Dieu*.]

Joë Bousquet was permanently paralyzed as the result of a wound received in the first world war. Simone Weil had sent him her Plan for an Organization of Front-Line Nurses and he had replied with a letter of commendation, of which she hoped to make use. See pages 96–105.

94 "Letter to Maurice Schumann" / *Seventy Letters*, pp. 144–53. [*Ecrits de Londres et dernières lettres*. Paris: Gallimard, 1957.]

94 Jacques Cabaud observes, / *Simone Weil: A Fellowship in Love* (New York: Channel Press, 1964), p. 194. Cabaud's volume remains the definitive biography. See also Richard Rees, *Simone Weil: A Sketch for a Portrait* (Carbondale: Southern Illinois University Press, 1966); J.-M. Perrin and Gustave Thibon, *Simone Weil as We Knew Her*, translated by Emma Craufurd (London: Routledge and Kegan Paul, 1953).

94 listened to Chartier. / Better known in England by his nom de plume, Alain.

106   "Last Thoughts" / *Waiting for God*, pp. 88–101. This letter is addressed to Father Perrin.

II. PRELUDE TO POLITICS

126   "Analysis of Oppression" / *Oppression and Liberty*, pp. 56–83. This is a section from "Reflections Concerning the Causes of Liberty and Social Oppression." ["Analyse de l'oppression," *Oppression et liberté*.]

153   "The *Iliad*, Poem of Might" / *Intimations of Christianity Among the Ancient Greeks*, collected and translated by Elisabeth Chase Geissbuhler (Boston: Beacon Press, 1958), pp. 24–55 ["*L'Iliade* ou le poème de la force," *Les Cahiers du Sud* 19, no. 230 (décembre 1940): 561–74, and 20, no. 231 (janvier 1941): 21–34, under the pseudonym Emile Novis; *La Source grecque*. Paris: Gallimard, 1953.]

       The first English translation, by Mary McCarthy, appeared under the title, "The *Iliad*, or The Poem of Force," *Politics* 2, no. 11 (November 1945): 321–31.

154   . . . *the horses* / The editor and translator note: "Because Simone Weil's translations are as much a part of her whole view of Greek thought as her commentaries, we have attempted to render both as faithfully as possible."

184   "Uprootedness and Nationhood" / *The Need for Roots: Prelude to a Declaration of Duties Toward Mankind*, translated by Arthur Wills, with a preface by T. S. Eliot (New York: G. P. Putnam's Sons, 1953), pp. 99–184. [*L'Enracinement: Prélude à une déclaration des devoirs envers l'être humain*. Paris: Gallimard, 1949.]

184   "lengthy programmatic essay . . . toward systematic statement." / G. L. Arnold, "Simone Weil," *The Cambridge Journal* 4, no. 6 (March 1951): 323. See also Roy Pierce, "Simone Weil: Sociology, Utopia, and Faith," *Contemporary French Political Thought* (London and New York: Oxford University Press, 1966), pp. 89–121.

190   the forty kings who in a thousand years made France / Reference to the motto heading the front page of the royalist organ *Action Française*, edited by Charles Maurras and Léon Daudet, before the war.

193   *pions* / A slang term for supervisors or undermasters in secondary schools. Used in a more general sense, it implies a coarse, narrow-minded, aggressive type of person.

201   Orlando's mare / Reference to Ariosto's *Orlando Furioso*. The mare in question possessed every quality except that she happened to be dead.

203   Guignol / Figure of popular French comedy. Dates from towards the end of the eighteenth century. Originated in Lyons, like Punch in London. Occupied in directing pointed sallies, though tinged with benevolence, at humanity in general, and in verbally castigating the powers that be.

203   epithet *"policier"* / Translator's note in answer to implied query by author of book: not in English, at any rate.

211   "Right or wrong, my country." / As in text.

216   even today / Written in 1943.

217   the people of *Action Française* / Militant royalists, convinced that the salvation of France depended on the overthrow of the Republic and its replacement by a monarchy, if necessary by violence. See also note, p. 190.

220   ". . . which he suffered." / Reference: Philippians 2:6 and 8 and Hebrews 5:8.

241   J. O. C. / *Jeunesse Ouvrière Chrétienne*. Organization founded by the French Catholic clergy, chiefly concerned with exercising an influence on working-class youth from the professional and social points of view. In the latter respect, it bears a certain affinity to the Boy Scout movement.

242   *chantiers de jeunesse* / Type of instructional center created by the Vichy government with the object of giving young people on leaving school a supplementary education and practical experience in a trade.

242   *camps de compagnons* / These camps were apparently organized on a parallel basis to the *chantiers,* and were designed to replace the period of military service prohibited by the German occupants.

III. LANGUAGE AND THOUGHT

du Sud 19, no. 245 (avril 1942): 303–8, under the pseudonym Emile Novis; in *Sur la science* (Paris: Gallimard, 1965).

303   "Freedom of Opinion" / *The Need for Roots*, pp. 22–33.

305   a young fellow who pushes somebody off a train in motion. / A reference to a gratuitous act performed by Lafcadio, hero of André Gide's *Les Caves du Vatican* (*The Vatican Swindle*, later called *Lafcadio's Adventures*), who pushes somebody off a train in Italy to prove to himself that he is capable of committing any act whatever, however motiveless, unrelated to preceding events.

313   "Human Personality" / *Selected Essays, 1934–1943*, pp. 9–34. This essay appeared in *La Table Ronde* (décembre 1950), pp. 9–33, with the title "La Personnalité humaine, le juste et l'injuste"; in *Ecrits de Londres et dernières lettres*, with its real title, "La Personne et le Sacré. Collectivité–Personne–Impersonnel–Droit–Justice."

313   "Beyond Personalism." / Translated by Russell S. Young, *Cross Currents* 2, no. 3 (Spring 1952): 59–76.

313   'Your person does not interest me.' / The implications of the French *personne* cannot be conveyed completely by a single word in English. What Simone Weil meant by "person" in this context will become clearer as the essay proceeds, as also will the pejorative sense in which she uses the word "personality."

317   cradle than nurse unacted desires,' / It seems possible that Simone Weil took Blake to mean: *If you desire to murder an infant you should do so,* instead of: *If you stifle your desires, you are doing something similar to murdering an infant.* But her point does not depend on this illustration.

324   world, who set such laws among men.' / The translation is of the author's own versions of the Greek.

IV. CRITERIA OF WISDOM

350   "Decreation" / *Gravity and Grace*, translated by Arthur Wills, with an introduction by Gustave Thibon (New York: G. P. Putnam's Sons, 1952), pp. 78–86. [*La Pesanteur et la grâce*, avec une introduction par Gustave Thibon. Paris: Plon, 1947.]

V. PATHS OF MEDITATION

PAGE

412   "Contemplation of the Divine" / *The Notebooks of Simone Weil*, vol. 1, pp. 233–42. My title.

413   Violetta. / Character in Simone Weil's unfinished play, *Venise sauvée, tragédie en trois actes*. Paris: Gallimard, 1955. In this dramatic tragedy, composed partly in verse and partly in prose, Violetta represents "happy innocence."

423   "The Things of the World" / *First and Last Notebooks*, translated by Richard Rees (London, New York, Toronto: Oxford University Press, 1970), pp. 140–48. My title. [The Pre-War Notebook was first published in French in the *Cahiers*. Paris: Plon, 1970. The New York and London Notebooks were first published in French as *La Connaissance surnaturelle*. Paris: Gallimard, 1950.]

432   "The Father's Silence" / *First and Last Notebooks*, pp. 93–99. My title.

432   Jaffier. / Hero of Simone Weil's unfinished dramatic tragedy, *Venise sauvée*.

434   ἀπεθάνετε, καὶ ἡ ζωὴ ὑμῶν κέκρυπται σὺν τῷ Χριστῷ ἐν τῷ θεῷ / For ye are dead, and your life is hid with Christ in God (Colossians 3:3).

434   οὐαὶ ὑμῖν, / Woe unto you . . .

434   δειλοῖσι βροτοῖσιν. / to wretched mortals.

439   "The Love of God and Affliction" / *On Science, Necessity, and the Love of God*, pp. 170–98. The first part of this essay ("L'Amour de Dieu et le malheur"), pp. 439–53, written before May 1942, appeared in *Waiting for God*, pp. 117–36. The second part was discovered later among Simone Weil's papers and was published, with the first, in *Pensées sans ordre concernant l'amour de Dieu*.

453   Christ, which passeth knowledge.' / Epistle to the Ephesians 3:17–19.

469   "Forms of the Implicit Love of God" / *Waiting for God*, pp. 158–81 and 208–15. ["Formes de l'amour implicite de Dieu," *L'Attente de Dieu*.]

PAGE

472   were entering in ye hindered." / Luke 11:52.

492   "Concerning the Our Father" / *Waiting for God*, pp. 216–27. ["A propos du 'Pater,'" *L'Attente de Dieu*.]

495   "Give us this day our daily bread" / Genesis 6:5.

BIBLIOGRAPHY

BOOKS BY SIMONE WEIL IN ENGLISH

First and Last Notebooks. Translated by Richard Rees. London, New York, Toronto: Oxford University Press, 1970.

Gravity and Grace. Translated by Arthur Wills. With an introduction by Gustave Thibon. New York: G. P. Putnam's Sons, 1952.

Intimations of Christianity Among the Ancient Greeks. Collected and translated by Elisabeth Chase Geissbuhler. Boston: Beacon Press, 1958.

Letter to a Priest. Translated by Arthur Wills. New York: G. P. Putnam's Sons, 1954.

The Need for Roots: Prelude to a Declaration of Duties Toward Mankind. Translated by Arthur Wills. With a preface by T. S. Eliot. New York: G. P. Putnam's Sons, 1953.

The Notebooks of Simone Weil. Translated by Arthur Wills. 2 vols. New York: G. P. Putnam's Sons, 1956.

On Science, Necessity, and the Love of God. Collected, translated, and edited by Richard Rees. London, New York, Toronto: Oxford University Press, 1968.

Oppression and Liberty. Translated by Arthur Wills and John Petrie. With an introduction by F. C. Ellert. Amherst: University of Massachusetts Press, 1973.

Selected Essays, 1934–1943. Chosen and translated by Richard Rees. London, New York, Toronto: Oxford University Press, 1962.

Seventy Letters. Translated and arranged by Richard Rees. London, New York, Toronto: Oxford University Press, 1965.

Waiting for God. Translated by Emma Craufurd. With an introduction by Leslie A. Fiedler. New York: G. P. Putnam's Sons, 1951.

BOOKS AND ARTICLES ABOUT SIMONE WEIL IN ENGLISH
(SELECTIVE LIST)

ANDERSON, DAVID. *Simone Weil.* London: S.C.M. Press, 1971.

ARNOLD, G. L. "Simone Weil." *The Cambridge Journal* 4, no. 6 (March 1951): 323–38.

BALLA, BORISZ DE. "Simone Weil, Witness of the Absolute." *The Catholic World* 179, no. 1070 (May 1954): 101–9.

BLUMENTHAL, GERDA. "Simone Weil's Way of the Cross." *Thought* 27, no. 105 (Summer 1952): 225–34.

BRAMLEY, J. A. "A Pilgrim of the Absolute." *The Hibbert Journal 66,* no. 260 (Autumn 1967): 10–14.

BUBER, MARTIN. "The Silent Question: On Henri Bergson and Simone Weil." *At the Turning: Three Addresses on Judaism.* New York: Farrar, Straus, and Young, 1952.

CABAUD, JACQUES. *Simone Weil: A Fellowship in Love.* New York: Channel Press, 1964.

COHEN, J. M. "The Jewish Predicament," *The Spectator* 187, no. 187 (September 28, 1951): 402.

COHEN, ROBERT S. "Parallels and the Possibility of Influence Between Simone Weil's *Waiting for God* and Samuel Beckett's *Waiting for Godot,*" *Modern Drama* 6, no. 4 (February 1964): 425–36.

DAVY, MARIE-MAGDELEINE. *The Mysticism of Simone Weil.* Translated by Cynthia Rowland. Boston: Beacon Press, 1951.

FIEDLER, LESLIE A. "Simone Weil: Prophet Out of Israel. A Saint of the Absurd." *Commentary* 11, no. 1 (January 1951): 36–46.

FITZGERALD, DAVID. "Simone Weil: A Note on Her Life and Thought." *The Dublin Magazine* 4, no. 1 (Spring 1965): 30–49.

FRÉNAUD, GEORGES, O.S.B. "Simone Weil's Religious Thought in the Light of Catholic Theology." *Theological Studies* 14, no. 3 (September 1953): 349–76.

FRIEDMAN, MAURICE. "Simone Weil." *To Deny Our Nothingness: Contemporary Images of Man.* New York: Delacorte Press, 1967.

GODMAN, STANLEY. "Simone Weil," *The Dublin Review* 224, no. 450 (Fourth Quarter 1950): 67–81.

GREENE, GRAHAM. "Simone Weil." *Collected Essays.* London, Sydney, Toronto: Bodley Head, 1969.

HARPER, RALPH. "Simone Weil." *Human Love, Existential and Mystical*. Baltimore, Md.: Johns Hopkins University Press, 1966.

JENNINGS, ELIZABETH. "A World of Contradictions: A Study of Simone Weil." *Every Changing Shape*. Philadelphia: Dufour Editions, 1962.

KAZIN, ALFRED. "The Gift." *The Inmost Leaf: A Selection of Essays*. New York: Harcourt, Brace, 1955.

LITTLE, J. P. *Simone Weil: A Bibliography*. London: Grant and Cutler, 1973.

———. "The Symbolism of the Cross in the Writings of Simone Weil." *Religious Studies* 6, no. 2 (June 1970): 175–83.

MARCEL, GABRIEL. "Simone Weil." *The Month* 2, no. 1 (July 1949): 9–18.

MARK, JAMES. "Simone Weil: A Christian in Exile." *Prism* 94 (February 1965): 9–18.

MEYERHOFF, HANS. "Contra Simone Weil." *Arguments and Doctrines: A Reader of Jewish Thinking in the Aftermath of the Holocaust*. Selected with introductory essays by Arthur A. Cohen. New York, Evanston, and London: Harper & Row, 1970.

MURDOCH, IRIS. "Knowing the Void." *The Spectator* 197, no. 6697 (November 2, 1956): 613–14.

NICHOLL, DONALD. "Simone Weil, God's Servant." *Blackfriars* 31, no. 365 (August 1950): 364–72.

OTTENSMEYER, HILARY, O.S.B. "Simone Weil, 'Mystic' and Lover of the Poor." *The American Benedictine Review* 15, no. 4 (December 1964): 504–14.

PERRIN, J.-M., and GUSTAVE THIBON. *Simone Weil as We Knew Her*. Translated by Emma Craufurd. London: Routledge and Kegan Paul, 1953.

PÉTREMENT, SIMONE. "The Life and Thoughts of Simone Weil." Translated by Lionel Abel. *Politics* 6, no. 1 (Winter 1949): 13–19.

———. *Simone Weil: A Life*. Translated from the French by Raymond Rosenthal. New York: Pantheon Books, 1976.

PIERCE, ROY. "Simone Weil: Sociology, Utopia, and Faith." *Contemporary French Political Thought*. London and New York: Oxford University Press, 1966.

RAPER, DAVID (ed.). *Gateway to God*. Glasgow: William Collins Sons, 1974.

REES, RICHARD. *Brave Men: A Study of D. H. Lawrence and Simone Weil*. Carbondale: Southern Illinois University Press, 1959.

———. *Simone Weil: A Sketch for a Portrait*. Carbondale: Southern Illinois University Press, 1966.

———. "Simone Weil on Israel and Rome." *Modern Age* 14, no. 1 (Winter 1969–70): 94–97.

TOMLIN, E. W. F. *Simone Weil*. New Haven, Conn.: Yale University Press, 1954.

TRACY, G. M. "Simone Weil: A Mission in Charity," *Renascence* 6, no. 2 (Spring 1954): 97–105.

VETO, MIKLOS J. "Simone Weil and Suffering." *Thought* 40, no. 157 (Summer 1965): 275–86.

WATKINS, PETER. "Simone Weil: Antisemitism and Syncretism." *Church Quarterly Review* 163 (October-December 1962): 463–73.

WEST, PAUL. "Simone Weil." *The Wine of Absurdity: Essays on Literature and Consolation*. University Park and London: Pennsylvania State University Press, 1966.

INDEX